Simc?

Celebrating London's Bicentennial

1 7 9 3 - 1 9 9 3

edited by

Guy St-Denis

The editor and publisher gratefully acknowledge the enthusiastic co-operation of the London and Middlesex Historical Society in the preparation of this manuscript.

Simcoe's Choice
Celebrating London's Bicentennial
1793 - 1993

edited by
Guy St-Denis

Editorial Board

Frederick H. Armstrong
Daniel J. Brock
David R. Spencer

DUNDURN PRESS
Toronto & Oxford
1992

Editing: Doris Cowan

The publisher wishes to acknowledge the generous assistance and ongoing support of **The Canada Council, The Book Publishing Industry Development Program** of the **Department of Communications, The Ontario Arts Council,** and **The Ontario Publishing Centre** of the **Ministry of Culture and Communications.**

Care has been taken to trace the ownership of copyright material used in the text (including the illustrations). Credit for each quotation is given at the end of the selection. The author and publisher welcome any information enabling them to rectify any reference or credit in subsequent editions.

J. Kirk Howard, Publisher

Canadian Cataloguing in Publication Data
Main entry under title:
Simcoe's choice

Includes bibliographical references.
ISBN 1-55002-173-7

1. London (Ont.) – History.   2. Simcoe, John Graves, 1752–1806.   I. St-Denis, Guy, 1960–

FC3099.L65S25 1992   971.3'26   C92-095334-4
FC1059.5.L65S25 1992

Dundurn Press Limited
2181 Queen Street East
Suite 301
Toronto, Canada
M4E 1E5

Dundurn Distribution Limited
73 Lime Walk
Headington, Oxford
England
OX3 7AD

Contents

For
Ruth & James J. Talman

Introduction

Despite the rather definite pronouncement of this book's subtitle, namely that we are "*Celebrating London's Bicentennial*," London is *not* 200 years old. It was not until 1826 that Mahlon Burwell was instructed to lay out London's town plot so that the London District capital could be moved inland from Vittoria, near Long Point. Therefore, the bicentennial of London's urban beginnings will not arrive until the year 2026, another thirty-three years into our future. Of course, some of us might even feel that it would be more appropriate to commemorate the bicentennial of London in its present city status, which would delay the celebrations to 2055. In any case, having established that London is not in fact 200 years old, there remains the unresolved matter of our misleading subtitle. An explanation is in order, but first some background.

We in the London and Middlesex Historical Society knew full well that the 200th anniversary of Lieutenant-Governor John Graves Simcoe's visit was coming up in 1993. But we did not think the bicentennial of Simcoe's visit would attract any particular attention, especially since its centennial back in 1893 does not appear to have been celebrated to any significant degree. We thought that, like the July 1992 200th anniversary of the renaming of the Thames River (formerly La Tranche), the occasion would pass more or less unnoticed. Both of the big anniversary parties in the past centred around the 1826–1926 centennial of London's survey and its centennial as a city in 1955, so it seemed to us that the city's bicentennial celebrations would not occur until 2026 and 2055. Much to our surprise, however, well-meaning city officials announced that there would be a 1993 bicentennial in honour of what they thought was London's 200th "birthday." When the London 200 Committee was formed to orchestrate the year's celebrations, its organizers also no doubt honestly believed that the city's bicentennial was looming just over the horizon. But, like the equally well-meaning speakers at the unveiling of the People and the City Monument in 1991, who referred to Lieutenant-Governor Simcoe as Lord Simcoe (possibly a subliminal association with the one-time Toronto hotel of the same name), they were mistaken.

Before the Society knew what happened, it found itself caught up in bicentennial preparations some thirty years sooner than anticipated. We were rather miffed at the premature nature of the bicentennial celebration, but the city's timing is really no worse than that of Ontario's bicentennial back in 1984, which was instigated by the then Conservative government. The problem with that commemoration was that the Province of Ontario was not established in 1784, but rather at the time of Confederation, in 1867. The year 1984 was really the bicentennial of the arrival of the United Empire Loyalists. But, despite the grumblings about the timing and the ethnic exclusivity of our provincial bicentennial, it did at least provide us with an increased awareness of the rich legacy of Ontario's history.

Returning to our own bicentennial: we do not attempt to excuse or mitigate the inaccuracy of the claim that 1993 is London's 200th anniversary. As we have already noted, London dates from 1826 and is therefore *not* 200 years old. So, why is the Society going to all the trouble of publishing a book of articles in commemoration of London's bicentennial when London is only 167 years old? The main reason is that 1793 is as significant to London's history as is 1826, and it should have been celebrated in 1893 to a much greater degree than it was. If it had not been for Simcoe's 1793 visit, the bicentennial preparations now under way here in London might well be taking place in some other locale. Hypothetical though this observation might be, the point is this: Simcoe's choice of the forks of the Thames as the site of the future capital of Upper Canada was the first step in the founding of London. While it can be argued that the subsequent transfer of the district capital inland was not directly related to Simcoe's plan, his reservation of the forks certainly influenced the later decision to set the capital at London. With this line of reasoning, the London and Middlesex Historical Society commemorates 1993 not as the 200th "birthday" of London, but rather as the equally significant bicentennial of "Simcoe's Choice."

Apart from the significance of 1993, there is also another reason for the Society's participation in the upcoming bicentennial: the opportunity to provide new material on various aspects of London's history. At first, finding enough articles to fill a book this size seemed a daunting task. London, however, is fortunate to have a major university and an active historical society. Together, they supplied most of the authors. We are doubly fortunate in that much of the authors' research sources are housed in archival repositories right here in London. The most extensive local history collection is that of the Regional Collection in the D.B. Weldon Library at the University of Western Ontario. The London Room at the London Public Library is the other major source.

With all the makings of a book of essays conveniently at hand, plus the opportunity to publish new histories of London and honour Governor Simcoe at the same time, we decided to overlook the discrepancy of thirty-three years and contribute to the bicentennial. We will, however, expect the city to host a similar celebration in both 2026 and 2055 – in keeping with the tradition established in 1926 and 1955. For our part, we in the Society will pick up the slack in the meantime by continuing to preserve and promote London's history.

I would now like to acknowledge all those who played a part in helping with the realization of *Simcoe's Choice*. In addition to all the authors, a number of people contributed in a significant way to the production of this volume. My fellow members of the Society's editorial board, Frederick H. Armstrong, Daniel J. Brock, and David R. Spencer, not only served in an advisory capacity, but also contributed in numerous other substantial ways. As well, there was a special committee established for the production of this book; it consisted of Frederick H. Armstrong, Daniel J. Brock, Les Bronson, Lottie Brown, Bill Hitchins, Steven Liggett, Bill Monroe, Doris Ray, Guy St-Denis, Betty Spicer, and James J. Talman. In addition, the assistance of the numerous proofreaders proved crucial in the preparation of the articles. Without their good work, the burden of double-checking all the manuscript submissions would have proved overwhelming to me and the other committee members.

The staffs of the various institutions approached by the authors of this book were all very helpful, including those at the Regional Collection in the D. B. Weldon Library at the University of Western Ontario; the London Room in the London Public Library; the London Regional Art and Historical Museums; Ontario Hydro; the Baldwin Room in the Metropolitan Toronto Reference Library; the Royal Ontario Museum; the Archives of Ontario; and the National Archives of Canada.

More specifically, J. Kirk Howard, the president of Dundurn Press, provided us with the opportunity to publish. Without him this book would not have come to fruition. Judith Turnbull, also of Dundurn Press, was responsible for co-ordinating the project, and she has my praise for a job well done. We are indebted to Doris Cowan, our copy editor, who performed an excellent service by maintaining a high standard of accuracy and consistency throughout the text of this book. Dr. Paul Bator of the Ontario Heritage Foundation was unstinting in his advice regarding grant applications. Mr. Doug Gordon, the chairman of the Education Sub-committee of London 200, was very supportive of our endeavour and provided much encouragement. I would also like to give a special acknowledgment to Professor Frederick H. Armstrong. His committee has been very generous in its support and will sponsor the distribution of this book to every school in London. He was a willing and able source of advice and assistance at every stage of the project and I am grateful for his participation.

Above all, we in the London and Middlesex Historical Society would like to thank Ruth and James J. Talman for their ready support of research into the history of London and its region. Moreover, Dr. James Talman – as Western's chief librarian from 1947 to 1970 – deserves recognition here for his good work in building up the Regional Collection, without which this book could not have been possible.

Guy St-Denis
London, Ontario

CHAPTER ONE

LONDON POSTPONED
John Graves Simcoe and His Capital in the Wilderness

John Mombourquette

John Graves Simcoe, the first lieutenant-governor of Upper Canada, remains a controversial figure in Ontario's history some 200 years after his departure from Upper Canada. Historians have bequeathed to the modern reader two contradictory portraits of Simcoe: one image is that of a heroic visionary who sought to challenge both the wilderness and government bureaucrats; the other image is that of a pompous upper-class English gentleman whose ambition clearly exceeded his own personal capabilities.

Perhaps Simcoe's most criticized (and misunderstood) scheme was his plan to establish the capital of Upper Canada at the forks of the Thames River, on the site of the present city of London. Most Londoners are vaguely aware of the popular story of how Simcoe, then a colonel in the British army, halted at the forks on March 2, 1793, during a journey from Detroit to the Niagara frontier settlement of Newark. The story continues with Simcoe exploring the London site for a day, and then declaring before leaving that the forks, then a pristine wilderness far from any white settlement, was a perfect location for his city of "New London." This story, in its barest form, is a source of both puzzlement and amusement for the layman and the scholar alike.

Lieutenant-Governor Simcoe's plans for London, his proposed capital in the wilderness, make little sense unless they are understood within the broader context of the political and military situation that faced Upper Canada, Britain, and the United States in the 1790s. Simcoe, because of his lieutenant-governorship, was an important player in a dangerous game of power politics in the years following the American Revolution. And London, the wilderness capital that was never to be, was itself the centrepiece of Simcoe's ambitions for Upper Canada; ambitions that, had they been fulfilled, would have resulted in a very different Ontario from the one that we know today. Simcoe did not travel to the forks of the Thames on a whim; his visit in March 1793 was part of a planned and deliberate strategy.

Indeed, Simcoe's trip to the London site is only one part of the overall story. The lieutenant-governor's ambitions for London can be understood only if several questions are answered. What was the background to Simcoe's choice of London as his Upper Canadian capital? Why was the London project postponed indefinitely? How did Simcoe's personality and actions affect his career, as well as our impressions of his legacy to both London and Ontario? In order to find the answers to these questions, this paper will analyse Simcoe's plans for London within the context of his famous visit of March 2–3, 1793, and then examine how the lieutenant-governor's character and public life influenced the progress of the London project. The story that emerges shows how, for a few short years, one man's enthusiastic vision played a central part in determining the future of Upper Canada.

SIMCOE'S LONDON: WHY WAS IT IMPORTANT?

John Graves Simcoe was a man who rarely took half measures when performing his duty. An impressive, muscular figure who was nearly six feet tall, Simcoe personally explored vast tracts of Upper Canada, planning future lines of communication, settlement, and defence as he went. Needless to say, the modern reader, taking into consideration the difficulties of wilderness travel in Upper Canada in the 1790s, will understand that being a member of Simcoe's staff would have been an adventurous, if exhausting, experience.

Simcoe was determined in 1793 to make a detailed assessment of the British position on the western frontier of Upper Canada. In February, Simcoe, a staff of six army officers (including his adjutant, Major Edward B. Littlehales; Lieutenant David W. Smith, the first surveyor-general of Upper Canada; and Lieutenant Thomas Talbot, future founder of the Talbot Settlement) and a dozen or so soldiers left Newark (today's Niagara-on-the-Lake), the tiny capital of Upper Canada located at the mouth of the Niagara River. Their destination was Fort Detroit, which would remain in British hands until 1796. In order to make a thorough reconnaissance of this part of the colony, the lieutenant-governor and his men would travel mostly on foot through the dense and forbidding forest. Major Littlehales, in his journal, estimated that the particular route that they followed from Newark to Fort Detroit was some 270 miles (432 km) one way, roughly following the Grand and the Thames Rivers. The latter river's French name of "La Tranche" (meaning the "ditch" or "trench") had recently been changed by Simcoe, because, in the lieutenant-governor's mind, the name "Thames" more accurately reflected the river's future importance to Upper Canada.

There was less snowfall in February 1793 than was usual, although the weather was cold enough to form a thick layer of ice on the Thames River. Simcoe and his men had packed away their snowshoes early in the journey, as moccasins alone proved to be more suitable footwear for the relatively snowless terrain. The pace was exacting: Simcoe's party rose before dawn and marched until dark. As they proceeded to Fort Detroit, the monotony of wilderness travel was broken by a courtesy visit with Chief Joseph Brant of the Six Nations and stops at the few other aboriginal and white settlements along their route. During his four-day stay at the Mohawk village on the Grand River, Simcoe must have enjoyed Brant's hospitality, and was perhaps even a bit envious of his host's lifestyle. Simcoe's own quarters at Newark, located in a hastily converted naval supply storeroom, were austere to say the least, while Brant owned a large and gracious house. However, Simcoe, a declared abolitionist, was disturbed by the presence of Brant's black house slaves.[1] On February 9, Simcoe and his men attended an impressive Anglican service at the Mohawk Chapel. The next day the party left the Mohawk village, accompanied by a dozen warriors who acted as guides and hunters. Brant himself travelled with Simcoe for much of the remaining journey to Detroit, as well as the return trip to Newark.

The next stage of the march to Detroit was less eventful, although there was the occasional interesting occurrence. Simcoe gave food to a starving traveller, a man who (he later discovered) was wanted for theft. One of the officers,

Lieutenant Gray, left his pocketwatch at one of the encampments, but two of Brant's men insisted on making a round trip of twenty-six miles (41.6 km) in order to retrieve the missing item. The party encountered a government messenger from Detroit *en route* to Newark, and they briefly visited a Delaware village and a small but prosperous missionary station. Their nights were spent in temporary shelters constructed by the skilful Mohawk guides. A staunch monarchist and a stickler for proper form, Simcoe continued his custom of singing "God Save the King" with his staff prior to retiring for the night.

The route from Newark to Detroit was covered in just over two weeks. Only five days were spent at Fort Detroit before the lieutenant-governor hurried back to Newark. There was some urgency to this particular trip. Simcoe, the senior civil and military official in Upper Canada, was also a key figure in a tense political standoff between the British and Americans. At that time war between the two countries was a very likely proposition, and Simcoe knew that he did not have the resources for even a modest defence. There were only some 400 soldiers of Simcoe's regiment (the Queen's Rangers), along with a few other units concentrated in isolated garrisons, available to him for the protection of the 10,000 or so settlers who were scattered from Detroit to Kingston.

In the early 1790s war threatened Upper Canada on two fronts. First, Britain, in the years following the American Revolution, had maintained its occupation of what was now American territory. Nine military and trading posts in the old Northwest, which together controlled the American side of Lakes Erie and Huron, were still garrisoned by British troops (see map I). Two of these posts were Detroit and Niagara, the latter being directly across the Niagara River from

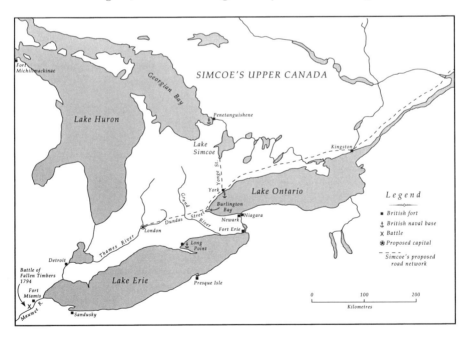

Map I

Simcoe proposed a rapid development of the western interior of Upper Canada, with a new capital city at London. However, the threat of war with the United States and Lord Dorchester's opposition prevented the fulfilment of the lieutenant-governor's ambitions.

Simcoe's capital of Newark. Although the posts were located on American territory after 1783, the British continued to hold them in response to the American federal government's failure to live up to key terms of the Treaty of Paris, the peace treaty that formally ended the Revolution. To be fair, the American federal government before 1789 found it difficult to honour this treaty. The first constitution of the United States, the Articles of Confederation, authorized only a weak central government that individual state governments could ignore at their pleasure. As a result, Congress could neither force individual states to pass laws that would protect Loyalists and their property in the United States, nor ensure that American citizens paid pre-war debts owed by them to their British creditors. The British were thus in no hurry to return the Northwestern posts, at least until the Americans lived up to their legal obligations.

The question of the Northwestern posts was not settled in 1789, when the United States adopted a new constitution that gave the federal government much stronger powers. Britain's friends in President George Washington's cabinet, led by the secretary of the treasury, Alexander Hamilton, strongly urged a prompt settlement of the Northwest border question and the re-establishment of normal relations with the British. Unfortunately, Hamilton was bitterly opposed by the popular pro-French faction under the leadership of the secretary of state, Thomas Jefferson. A few years later, in 1793, Britain began its two-decade-long struggle with revolutionary France. Many Americans were convinced that, with the British increasingly distracted by political events across the English Channel, aggressive diplomacy, backed by a veiled threat of military action, could secure for the United States its rightful territory. [2]

The second front that threatened Upper Canada was the increasingly hostile situation that existed between the Americans and the aboriginal tribes of the Northwest who lived in what are now the states of Pennsylvania, Michigan, and Ohio. Two American military expeditions had been dispatched to the Northwest in 1790 and 1791. These American armies were in turn humiliated in battle by the native alliance, and the Americans were forced to withdraw from the disputed territory. Brant, who with British backing was attempting to build a powerful inter-tribal confederacy, knew that such military successes could only be temporary victories. A negotiated settlement with the Americans, backed up by British power, was essential. The British in turn felt obligated to their former allies in the American Revolution, and they were not unaware of the advantages of an Indian buffer state in the Northwest. However, the Americans were preparing a third punitive expedition for 1794, this time under the leadership of General "Mad Anthony" Wayne, a hero of the Revolution. And Brant, despite his efforts, found it increasingly difficult to check the chiefs within his confederacy. It was entirely probable that Britain, with Upper Canada the battlefield, might be drawn into a renewed Indian-American conflict.

Yet Simcoe, himself a brave and resourceful regimental commander during the Revolution, was undaunted by the volatile international situation that he faced in 1793. Historian Donald Creighton has observed that Simcoe "found in the new frontier society of the lakes a stimulus sufficient to arouse all his ingenuous enthusiasm and tremendous energy."[3] This enthusiasm and energy was liberally expended by the forty-one-year-old lieutenant-governor in the service of King, country, and Upper Canada.

Simcoe had three options for the colony's defence against a possible American attack. First, he attempted to assist Brant and the other native leaders in their negotiations for a peaceful settlement with the United States. As Simcoe was only too well aware, a negotiated solution for the Indian-American crisis in the Northwest would be immeasurably better than all-out war. Second, Simcoe began to make whatever local defensive preparations he could (and these could only be meagre at best) in anticipation of the worst-case scenario, a bloody frontier war. Last, and most ambitiously, Simcoe began to lay the groundwork for a great strategic plan of his own design. The lieutenant-governor, basing his belief on his experience in the Revolution and the inherent convictions of his class, was firmly convinced that America's experiment with republican democracy was a failure. Britain could again dominate the North American frontier by making Upper Canada a beacon for hundreds of thousands of dissatisfied Americans in King George's former colonies. Simcoe was convinced that superior government and a robust economy would attract American settlers in such numbers to Upper Canada that they would ensure *de facto* British control over the American Northwest. Needless to say, this third strategy was a long-range plan that Simcoe realized would take several years, if not decades, to implement. It was this strategy, however, that would influence his selection of sites for new settlements and the roads that would connect them. That Simcoe's superiors might find political, economic, and military liabilities in his strategy was something not readily apparent to the industrious lieutenant-governor.

He did, however, consult prominent men on the viability of his grand plan for Upper Canada. In January of 1791, shortly after his official appointment as lieutenant-governor of Upper Canada, Simcoe had laid out his strategy in a letter to Sir Joseph Banks, the president of the Royal Society, then the world's pre-eminent scientific organization. Banks was a good candidate from whom to seek practical advice, for as well as being a wealthy patron of science he had a sound scholarly reputation. Most noteworthy, from 1768 to 1771 he had accompanied Captain James Cook on his famous voyage to Australia, which had enhanced scientific knowledge, as new botanical specimens were discovered and then catalogued by Banks.

In his letter to Banks, Simcoe stated that the military and economic key to the North American continent lay in "that Great Peninsula between the Lakes Huron, Erie, and Ontario, a spot destined by nature, sooner or later, to govern the interior world." Britain, using the peninsula as a base, could make Upper Canada, through aggressive economic policies and good government, the undisputed heartland of North America. As a result, the development of Upper Canada demanded that the administrative and economic centre be located in the interior, where it could influence events in the American Northwest. Simcoe, poring over maps in the comfort of Wolford Lodge, his home on his 5,000-acre (2,023 ha) estate in Devon, England, informed Sir Joseph Banks that he was determined

> to establish a capital in the very heart of the country, upon the River La Tranche, which is navigable for batteauxs for 150 miles – and near where the Grand River which falls into Erie, and others that communicate with Huron and Ontario, almost interlock. The capital I mean to call Georgina – and aim to settle in its vicinity Loyalists who are now in Connecticut, provided that Government approve of the system.[4]

After raising several other issues, Simcoe concluded his letter by asking Banks for his support and patronage in developing an education system for the new colony. The lieutenant-governor proposed the eventual building of a library and a college.[5] Sir Joseph's reply is not found in Simcoe's collected correspondence, but the fact that a charter for a college was not granted until 1827 indicates that Simcoe may have been alone in his enthusiasm for higher education in remote Upper Canada.

Upon his arrival in Upper Canada in June 1792, Simcoe at once began to put his plan for "Georgina" (named in honour of King George III) into motion. The Loyalist merchants of Kingston were already upset over the lieutenant-governor's prompt decision to move the capital from their town of fifty houses to the even smaller village of Newark. That village, however, was intended as merely a temporary base camp for Simcoe's exploration of the interior and the selection of a site for "Georgina," by this time renamed "New London" by Simcoe.

MARCH 2, 1793: SIMCOE ARRIVES AT THE FORKS

In September 1792, three months after Simcoe's arrival in Upper Canada, the lieutenant-governor ordered the construction of a road from Burlington Bay to the forks of the Thames River. The road was named Dundas Street, after Sir Henry Dundas, secretary of state for the Home Department, the cabinet minister responsible for the Colonial Office and a patron of Simcoe's. Dundas Street (referred to locally as the Governor's Road) was intended by Simcoe to be the route that would both direct settlement from Lake Ontario into the interior and be a vital military corridor for the British regiments. The lieutenant-governor, pressed by administrative and diplomatic concerns, could not go on a personal inspection of his wilderness capital until his trip to Fort Detroit in February 1793. On March 2, a week into his return journey to Newark from Fort Detroit, Simcoe made a planned stop at the location that he had promoted as the ideal site for the new capital of Upper Canada.

Simcoe's adjutant, Major Littlehales, records in his journal their activities on that momentous day:

> We struck the Thames at one end of a low flat island enveloped with shrubs and trees; the rapidity and strength of the current were such as to have forced a channel through the mainland, being a peninsula, and to have formed the island. We walked over a rich meadow, and at its extremity came to the forks of the river. The Governor wished to examine this situation and its environs; and we therefore remained here all the day. He judged it to be a situation eminently calculated for the metropolis of all Canada …[6]

Simcoe spent the day surveying the site, and he was impressed. London would be centrally located, with excellent lines of communication to the continental interior. There was prime agricultural land, plus fine stands of timber and a good climate for the anticipated hordes of loyal American settlers whom Simcoe had described in his letter to Banks. At London a major trading post could also be built that could give Britain greater leverage in its dealings with the aboriginals. Mrs. Elizabeth Simcoe, today noted for her diary and amateur paintings, would later make a crude map of the forks based on her husband's descriptions of the London site. This drawing indicates that Simcoe's proposed "metropolis" was planned initially to be centred between the south branch of the Thames River and what are now oxbow ponds, known locally as the Coves.

Simcoe and his party set up camp at the forks. Littlehales and Lieutenant Smith made note of a number of minor details in their respective journals.

Littlehales, for example, observed "a fine eagle on the wing," and discovered some impressive aboriginal figures drawn on the bark of trees with charcoal and vermilion. A less pleasant incident of note involved "Jack Sharp," the Newfoundland dog that was travelling with the party. Jack took a hasty bite of the carcass of that night's dinner – a large porcupine – and he "soon got his mouth filled with the barbed quills, which gave him exquisite pain."[7] Fortunately for the dog, a native patiently pulled out the quills and soothed the wounds with a special root, though Mrs. Simcoe was advised that Jack was in pain for several days thereafter.[8]

The next morning, March 3, Simcoe's party left the forks. They were glad to depart, despite the enthusiasm of the previous day. The night of March 2–3 must have been an uncomfortable experience for Simcoe and his men: Littlehales writes that it "rained incessantly the whole night; besides, the hemlock branches on which we slept were wet before they were gathered for our use."[9] According to Littlehales, Simcoe's party made an early departure from their campsite on March 3.

Simcoe's adjutant and secretary, Major Edward Baker Littlehales (1763-1825) was created a baronet in 1802 and eventually reached the rank of lieutenant-colonel. Littlehales in 1805 married the daughter of the Duke of Leinster, and ten years later, following the death of his cousin, Peter-William Baker, M.P., he inherited the Ranston House estate near Blandford, Dorsetshire. In 1817 Littlehales changed his surname to "Baker," and was henceforth known as Sir Edward B. Baker, Bt. Today Littlehales is best known for his slim journal that describes Simcoe's trek of February 4 to March 10, 1793, of which the focal point is the visit to the London site. The French nobleman Rochefoucauld-Liancourt was favourably impressed by Littlehales during his 1795 visit to Upper Canada, stating that Littlehales's "worth, politeness, prudence and judgement give this officer peculiar claims to the confidence and respect which he universally enjoys." Metropolitan Toronto Reference Library, T-16339

An idea of the varied terrain that was then found south of the forks can be seen in a description by Littlehales of Simcoe and his men as they

> ascended the height at least one hundred and twenty feet into a continuation of the pinery ... quitting that, we came to a beautiful plain with detached clumps of white oak, and open woods; then crossing a creek running into the south branch of the Thames, we entered a thick swampy wood, where we were at a loss to discover any track; but in a few minutes we were released from this dilemma by the Indians, who making a cast, soon descried our old path to Detroit. Descending a hill, and crossing a brook, we came at noon to the encampment we left on the 14th of February ...[10]

As soon as he arrived in Upper Canada, Simcoe was impatient to build his proposed capital of London. His first opportunity to visit the London site came during a famous march to Detroit in February 1793. On the return journey, Simcoe stopped at the forks on March 2, exploring the London site for the better part of the day before leaving early the following morning. The lieutenant-governor was greatly impressed by what he saw, confirming his strong belief that London would be "the metropolis of all Canada." It is impossible to know exactly what winter clothing Simcoe and his men wore during their survey of the London site (although some clues are given in Mrs. Simcoe's diary). The above illustration is an artist's conception showing Simcoe and his men, in clothing common to the period, exploring near the forks of the Thames. Paul Mombourquette, London

At this encampment, Simcoe and his men were greeted by Brant and several Mohawks, who, two days earlier, had travelled ahead of the main party and prepared a feast of deer and porcupine for the lieutenant-governor's arrival. After several more days of travel over terrain made swampy by the melting snow and persistent rainfall, the lieutenant-governor finally reached Newark on March 10; Mrs. Simcoe recorded that "He is remarkably well & not fatigued," although he came down with his old complaint – the gout – a few days later.[11] Simcoe must have considered this expedition to be a singular success: he had a site for his new capital, and his long-range plans for the colony could now begin to take shape.

LONDON POSTPONED

In April 1793, Simcoe sent a small party to the forks of the Thames to begin an initial survey of the proposed capital. As well, over the next few years land was purchased from local aboriginals in order to establish a Crown reserve on which the future city would be built. This, however, is as far as the development of London was to proceed for the next three decades. To Simcoe's disappointment, his dream of an Upper Canadian capital at the forks of the Thames River never materialized. Practical considerations, among them a scarcity of resources (money, men, and time), as well as the prompting of his superiors, forced Simcoe to significantly alter his plans. In 1796, York, the future city of Toronto, and not London, the proposed "metropolis" at the forks of the Thames, replaced Newark as the capital of Upper Canada.

Indeed, for the next thirty-three years London would be a settlement on paper only. The forks remained the pristine wilderness the lieutenant-governor and his party had left on March 3, 1793. Simcoe, his successors, and government cartographers would place "London" on official maps; but it was not until 1826 that a village began to develop. London in that year *did* become a capital, but only as the administrative and judicial seat of the London District, an enormous tract of land that included all of present-day Middlesex, Huron, Oxford, Norfolk, and Elgin Counties, along with portions of what are now Perth, Brant, and Bruce Counties. Simcoe's "metropolis of all Canada," which was intended to be the strategic centre of both Upper Canada and the continental interior, began its formal existence in 1826 as a few rough buildings clustered around a temporary frame courthouse.

Simcoe's overnight stay at the forks in 1793, unlike the later decision to build a courthouse at London, was a fairly romantic beginning for London, one that underscores (at least among Londoners) the city's early historical importance. Certainly the 1826 transfer of the courthouse is a more mundane tale. The growing population of the London District had demanded a central and convenient location for a courthouse, and Simcoe's site was considered to be a good choice in the mid-1820s for such a public work. There was the Crown reserve that had been set aside by Simcoe at the forks, as well as the potential for future travel along that portion of Dundas Street that was still not yet opened all the way to the London site; there was also the fact that land speculators had not yet bought up property in the area as some already had done in the vicinity of the rival village of Dorchester.[12]

The only real excitement connected with this second "founding" of London occurred in Vittoria, a small community within the Long Point Settlement, which served as the capital of the London District. A fire in November 1825 had destroyed the courthouse there, giving the government an excuse to construct the new building in a more suitable locale, namely London.

Joseph Brant (1743–1807), known also as Thayendanegea, was one of the most controversial native figures in Canadian history. Simcoe and Brant had frequent disagreements over the direction of British policy toward the native peoples.

*The above portrait of Brant was painted (*circa 1800*) by the multi-talented William Berczy. With encouragement from Simcoe, Berczy undertook the colonization of lands north of York with settlers from Germany and the United States.* National Gallery of Canada, Ottawa

The 200th anniversary of Simcoe's journey to the forks of the Thames occurs in 1993. As a result, Londoners are poised to celebrate the city's bicentennial with a series of special events, including a re-enactment of Simcoe's 1793 arrival, sports competitions, the RCMP Musical Ride, the book you are now reading, and other commemorative projects.[13] But this is not the first time this century that Londoners have marked an anniversary of their founding. The first was a centennial celebration held in 1926, commemorating the original settlement and building of the courthouse at the forks, and the second occasion was in 1955, observing the 100th anniversary of London's incorporation as a city. As with the 1993 Simcoe bicentennial, London's two centennial parties were marked by civic merry-making on a grand scale, suggesting that Londoners have an occasional interest in rediscovering their history, especially if a party is involved.[14]

In the case of the 1993 London bicentennial celebration, criticisms have been levelled at the historical significance of Simcoe's connection with the city. One journalist has made the wry comment that Simcoe "stopped on this site, ostensibly because he needed food, drink, and to relieve himself."[15] While well off the mark of Simcoe's primary reason for his 1793 inspection, the comment does underscore the difficulty many have in determining the exact legacy the lieutenant-governor gave to London. Certainly there is no direct physical evidence today of Simcoe's visit to London, save of course Dundas Street or the controversial downtown "people's" statue that features an abstract interpretation of Simcoe.[16] Aside from the occasional aboriginal band and area squatter, no permanent settlement was established at Simcoe's New London until Peter McGregor (the first homesteader at the forks, tavernkeeper, and prison turnkey – a veritable jack-of-all-trades) built his cabin in 1826, shortly before the temporary court house/jail was finished and ready for business.

It would be hasty, however, to conclude that John Graves Simcoe was not the founder of the city of London. Simcoe's principal legacy to London lies in his vision of a city at the forks of the Thames River. It was his intention to build his capital here; the years of planning and his visit of March 1793 attest to this fact. Unfortunately, the lieutenant-governor was in the colony for only four years, and there was simply no time or opportunity for him to begin building even a modest settlement at the forks.

Simcoe had the enormous responsibility of building from scratch the government and administrative structure of an isolated, backwoods colony. Prior to 1784 there was virtually no white settlement of any significance in what is now Ontario. The first major influx of white settlers – the United Empire Loyalists – came after the American Revolution, when the British government gave these refugees lands in what was then the western frontier of Quebec. The Constitutional Act of 1791 created a government for Upper Canada, which was then separated from the predominately French-speaking Lower Canada. Simcoe was charged with laying the administrative, defensive, and economic foundations of the newly created Upper Canada, and he went at these tasks with characteristic vigour. Although he made mistakes, he accomplished much in a remarkably short period of time. It is with some justification that one of Simcoe's biographers has claimed that "it is unlikely that any governor before Lord Durham, except Carleton in his first term at Quebec, had so much impact on a Canadian province."[17] What this successful colony-building also meant (alas for London!) was that Simcoe spread himself thin, leaving little time for the development of a capital city at the forks of the Thames.

This portrait, attributed to Johan Zoffany (1733–1810), shows a young John Graves on the eve of his departure to the American colonies in 1775. To Simcoe's right in the portrait is a large urn that has the date "1759" (the year of his father's death) engraved on it.

There is a second contemporary portrait by William Pars that has Simcoe in the same pose, but with two gentlemen friends to his right rather than the urn. Both portraits were probably commissioned by John Graves's mother. The Samuel E. Weir Collection, Queenston

The difficulty of settlers reaching the interior in large numbers guaranteed Toronto's position as the pre-eminent city in Ontario. As Simcoe discovered, water transportation is an advantage in settling a wilderness, and although London had the partially navigable Thames River, it definitely was not as accessible as Lake Ontario. Simcoe had begun a survey of that lake in May 1793, looking for a naval base that would offer protection from storms and marauding Americans. He came to the site of Fort Rouille, an abandoned French trading post that was called "Toronto" by the aboriginals. Toronto (renamed York by Simcoe) had a fine natural harbour. It was also the starting point for the northern portage route, a route that was soon followed by Simcoe's other great road, Yonge Street. Circumstances would force Simcoe's hand; he had to choose York over London for his capital in the wilderness. As a result, one additional (and ironic) legacy Simcoe bequeathed to modern London was that the city would forever be in the shadow of Toronto, the lieutenant-governor's second choice for his "metropolis of all Canada."

Thus London did not become a settlement in 1793 for several reasons: there was the unsettled international situation that existed between the United States and Britain, a difficulty that would distract Simcoe from his plans; there was also the problem of the resources needed to build a wilderness capital, and these resources were always in scant supply, especially when the threat of war loomed; as well, other settlement sites, namely Toronto, were much more promising for immediate and rapid development. But, perhaps most important, Simcoe's superiors did not share his urgency for a wilderness capital. Critically, Simcoe's immediate superior, Lord Dorchester, the governor-general of Upper and Lower Canada, believed that the London scheme was totally ill-advised.

Yet Simcoe, throughout his tenure as Upper Canada's lieutenant-governor, did carry on a bitter quarrel with Dorchester over the London site. Why did he do so, especially when his plans for London placed him in conflict with those with influence over his career? In order to examine the reasons for Simcoe's choice of London as Upper Canada's capital, his passionate promotion of the site, and its ultimate rejection by Dorchester and others, it is best to begin with an analysis of Simcoe's character and career, and the perceptions that people have had about the lieutenant-governor.

EARLY INFLUENCES ON SIMCOE'S LIFE

Simcoe's visit to the London site in March 1793 was part of a larger strategy designed to make the remote and underpopulated colony of Upper Canada the heartland of North America. Only a daring (and perhaps somewhat foolhardy) man with great confidence in his personal abilities would stake his career on so audacious a proposal. What was it about Simcoe's personal background that would enable him to focus so single-mindedly on the London project?

John Graves Simcoe was born on February 25, 1752, in Cotterstock, England. His namesakes were his father, Captain John Simcoe, R.N., and his godfather, Admiral Samuel Graves, a close friend of the captain. John Graves Simcoe was the only one of four sons to survive into adolescence. His mother, Katherine Stamford, was widowed in 1759 when her husband died of pneumonia while serving on General James Wolfe's expedition against Quebec.

Captain John Simcoe, an instructor of the future Captain James Cook (the great navigator and explorer), was an experienced and capable officer who had held several commands in the Royal Navy. From his surviving correspondence, it can be seen that Simcoe Senior held enthusiastic opinions about a wide range of military topics. One of his most forcefully advocated positions in the 1750s was the necessity of the British conquest of New France. In 1754 he wrote a detailed code of conduct for young officers that was eventually adopted by the Royal Navy in the training of its midshipmen. The common-sense advice given by Captain Simcoe in this document, which he planned to use in the education of his sons, was sound and practical, as it encouraged patriotism, devotion to duty, personal sacrifice, and constant attention to even the smallest detail in order to ensure success.[18]

Although he was only seven when Captain Simcoe died, John Graves Simcoe was strongly influenced by his father. From his father the young Simcoe gained an interest in North America, the continent that would shape his future military and administrative career, just as it had played a role in Captain Simcoe's. Certainly John Graves was very familiar with his father's written code of conduct, as it was passed on to him by his mother. In the code one can see the type of officer John Graves was to become, one who believed that success in peace and war came only through diligence and hard work.

It is probable that Simcoe romanticized his father, and perhaps exaggerated details of his career later in life. A portrait of John Graves Simcoe as young man, dressed in a junior officer's uniform on the eve of his departure to the American colonies in 1775, shows Simcoe standing next to a tombstone surmounted with an urn that has the year "1759" (the date of his father's death) engraved on it. In a contemporary obituary of John Graves Simcoe, there is a story that his father, Captain Simcoe, was made prisoner by the French during the siege of Quebec. The good captain escaped, and the detailed information that he gained while a prisoner of the French greatly assisted Wolfe in his final attack on the city. Of course, this is not possible, as Captain Simcoe died before Wolfe's force reached the capital of New France.[19] To be fair, however, Captain Simcoe (along with Cook) did play a key role in developing the navigational charts of the St. Lawrence River that were essential to Wolfe's invasion fleet. In any event, John Graves Simcoe left a permanent memorial of his father for modern Ontarians when he changed the name of Lac aux Claies to Lake Simcoe in 1793.

BUILDING A MILITARY REPUTATION: THE AMERICAN REVOLUTION

Admiral Graves took an active interest in his godson following the death of Captain Simcoe, and the widowed Mrs. Simcoe moved her small household to Devon in order to be near the admiral's estate. Young John Graves Simcoe attended Eton and then Oxford, until ill-health forced his withdrawal from university in 1769 after only a year of study. He had decided on a military career, so a tutor was hired to instruct the boy in military science and tactics. Simcoe's education gave him a passion for history, as well as an amateur's interest in poetry and prose. His efforts (and family influence) paid off in 1770 when he obtained an ensign's commission in the 35th Regiment of Foot.

Simcoe's constant ill-health was to plague him throughout the rest of his life. It has been suggested that the reason Simcoe did not choose a naval career like his father was that his family felt that he did not have the physical stamina for a seafaring life.[20] Yet a soldier's life proved to be equally arduous. In 1930, Ernest A. Cruikshank, the historian responsible for organizing Simcoe's correspondence, published a twenty-page outline of Simcoe's day-to-day activities during his four-year stay in Canada. During this period Simcoe never seems to have remained idle:

his trip to London in March 1793 was just one of his many strenuous tours through the vast wilderness stretching from Lake Ontario to Georgian Bay. He relished the discipline and comradeship of a soldier's life, a life that he knew intimately following his nearly six years of service during the American Revolutionary War. Interestingly, Simcoe's energy and enthusiasm allowed him to soldier on despite physical discomforts from several illnesses. Cruikshank records that Simcoe, while in Upper Canada, suffered from gout, various fevers, and severe migraines. Simcoe also fell victim to the occasional accident. For example, at Newark his finger was badly injured when a soldier, who was shooting at a stray dog, sprayed the lieutenant-governor and a small party with lead pellets.[21] Simcoe's constitutional stamina appears all the more remarkable when it is considered that he was seriously wounded three times during the Revolutionary War, and was invalided home before its conclusion suffering from fever and malaria.

Simcoe's military career began in earnest when his regiment was sent to Boston in June 1775, arriving shortly after the Battle of Bunker Hill. Purchasing a captaincy in the 40th Foot, he spent the next two years fighting in campaigns throughout New York and New Jersey. Simcoe was always looking for an opportunity to distinguish himself. Shortly after his arrival in the American colonies, Simcoe (with the support of Admiral Graves, who was now in command of the Royal Navy's North American Squadron) made a formal request to raise a Loyalist regiment of free blacks. This petition was soon turned down, and Simcoe had to look for other outlets for his energies. While Simcoe would soon lose the immediate patronage of his godfather (Admiral Graves was recalled in 1776 following criticism of his handling of the blockade of Boston Harbour), he would eventually find the opportunity for which he was looking. Anxious for an independent command, Simcoe was appointed a major in October 1777 and given the Queen's Rangers, a regiment whose authorized strength was 400 men, but casualties and disease often left the unit at half that number. The Queen's Rangers were distinguished both by their military reputation and their distinctive green uniforms, the latter useful camouflage for close-quarter wilderness fighting.

Simcoe immediately began a reorganization of the Queen's Rangers.[22] As was the custom of the day, Simcoe was expected to use his personal resources in this effort; but the dividends reaped were well worth any sacrifice. Major Simcoe was not a believer in traditional eighteenth-century military practice, where much of a soldier's training was on the parade square. He wanted (and got) an élite corps, well trained in the use of the bayonet and in backwoods tactics, that could strike with surprise and speed at General Washington's forces. His innovative methods earned him a well-deserved reputation as one of Britain's best regimental commanders during the Revolutionary War. In 1787 his military standing was strengthened among his peers with the publication of his wartime memoirs.[23]

The American Revolution was the formative event of Simcoe's adult life. The war confirmed or shaped many of his beliefs about the Empire and a man's place in society. Certainly Simcoe had no respect for American republicanism; this is borne out in his second literary effort, a published attack on a French work that justified France's support of the rebel cause.[24] However, while it is clear that Simcoe had no love for the American government or its leaders, it must be added that he admired the American people themselves: he recognized them as a hardy and industrious people, the obvious choice as settlers for his beloved Upper Canada. What these Americans needed was proper guidance and a sound example, which could not be provided by men like Washington.

Simcoe had his reasons for nursing private grudges against the rebel leadership. A friend, Major John Andre, had been captured by the rebels and was subsequently executed following charges that he was a spy. The rebel leaders, to Simcoe's mind, were scoundrels who did not obey the rules of war. Twenty-five members of the Queen's Rangers, all Loyalists whom Washington considered to be traitors, were shot immediately following the British surrender at Yorktown in 1781.[25] Added to these crimes against prisoners of war was the general mistreatment of Loyalists and their property in the United States during the years following the Revolution, outrages that were clearly condoned by Washington and

other rebel leaders. While he liked Americans, Simcoe could never be a friend of the United States and its republican government.

CHANGE IN FORTUNES: MARRIAGE AND SOCIAL ADVANCEMENT
Simcoe, a lieutenant-colonel at the war's end, was not present at the Yorktown surrender. Severely weakened by illness and exhaustion, he was earlier sent home by Lord Cornwallis, the British commander. In December 1781, on the invitation of his godfather, Admiral Graves, the acknowledged war hero moved to the admiral's estate in order to recuperate from his wounds. It was here that Simcoe came to the attention of the admiral's niece, Elizabeth Posthuma Gwillim. At this time he was nearly thirty, while Elizabeth was nineteen years of age.

An attractive, quiet woman with a slight speech impediment, Elizabeth never knew her parents; before she was born her father, Colonel Thomas Gwillim, died while serving with the British Army in Germany, and her thirty-eight-year-old mother passed away hours after the birth of her only child. Elizabeth was raised by her wealthy grandmother and three aunts, who incidentally named her after her mother, thus her middle name of "Posthuma." When Elizabeth was six, one of her aunts married Admiral Graves and she became "the daughter he had never had."[26] Elizabeth spent much of her youth living with the admiral and his wife. As Elizabeth was heir to a significant fortune, Graves was anxious that she marry the right man; he thus encouraged the friendship between his godson, John Graves, and his niece. By all accounts John Graves Simcoe and Elizabeth fell in love, and after a proper engagement and the customary marriage settlement, the two were wed on December 30, 1782. They would remain husband and wife until Simcoe's untimely

---

(Previous page) *The Queen's Rangers, the regiment with which John Graves Simcoe made his military reputation, had a short but illustrious history. Originally organized by Major Robert Rogers during the Seven Years War (1756–1763), "Roger's Rangers" (1st Regiment of Queen's Rangers) took part in engagements at Ticonderoga, Louisbourg, Quebec, and Montreal. The Rangers were drawn from experienced American backwoodsmen who used their knowledge of the frontier to deadly effect against the French. Following the 1763 uprising of the native tribes under Pontiac, the Rangers were disbanded.*

In 1776 Rogers recruited loyal Americans to serve in a reorganized Queen's Rangers. The Rangers soon became known as one of the most effective of the British regiments during the American Revolution. Their reputation was confirmed during the savage fighting at Brandywine Creek, Pennsylvania (September 11, 1777), where one of every three Queen's Rangers was either killed or wounded.

Simcoe (who, while serving in another regiment, was seriously wounded at Brandywine) took command of the Queen's Rangers in October 1777. Major Simcoe made a significant reorganization of the Rangers, adding artillery and cavalry to the existing eleven companies of infantry, which already included both a grenadier and a highland company. Distinctive in their green coats and black headdress, the infantrymen in the picture trained and fought under the practical leadership of Simcoe. In recognition of the Queen's Rangers' outstanding service, the regiment was given the title of "The First American Regiment" in May 1779.

Disbanded again after the Revolution, the Queen's Rangers were reactivated in December 1791 at Colonel Simcoe's request. Simcoe used the Rangers in the construction of his public works in Upper Canada, most notably Dundas and Yonge Streets. The Queen's Rangers remained on active service in Upper Canada until 1802, when they were again disbanded. The regiment's traditions are carried on today by Toronto's Queen's York Rangers (The First American Regiment). Paul Mombourqette, London

death in 1806. Elizabeth did not remarry after the passing of her husband; she stayed faithful to his memory for the remaining forty-four years of her life.

From this marriage Simcoe gained a devoted partner and great wealth. Mrs. Simcoe, although she had a very traditional view of a woman's duty to her husband, was supremely confident of her own personal abilities. She bore John Graves eleven children (eight daughters and three sons), nine of whom survived into adulthood. Simcoe's wife would travel with him to Upper Canada and remain his most trusted supporter and confidante, enduring the rigours of pioneer life in the Upper Canadian wilderness where she often lived in what can be considered very primitive conditions. For part of their stay in Upper Canada, the Simcoes' year-round living quarters was a canvas tent (modified for Upper Canadian winters!) that Simcoe had bought from the estate of Captain Cook. She was a keen observer, and her diary and paintings have given us lively portraits of life during that period. But there was pain in Upper Canada for Elizabeth Simcoe: a daughter, Katherine, died at York in 1794, some sixteen months after her birth.

Simcoe himself had not been a man of great means, but his marriage changed his fortunes. He and Elizabeth purchased the large estate at Wolford, and he became a country squire. However, what Simcoe wanted was either another military command or an important administrative post. Neither was forthcoming, so he spent the period from 1783 to 1789 managing the Wolford estate, raising a growing family, editing his war journals, and making and entertaining important friends. He also found time for a little political intrigue. A link of sorts with the new United States was formed in early 1790 when Levi Allen, one of the Allen Brothers of "Green Mountain Boys" fame during the Revolution, visited Simcoe at Wolford Lodge. The Allens, taking advantage of a confused political situation back in the United States, proposed the formation of an independent Vermont republic (with the Allens, of course, as leaders) that would be allied with Britain. Simcoe eagerly took up the Allens' cause, although the British government, quite understandably, preferred to keep the Vermonters at arm's length.[27]

In 1790 Simcoe's connections finally paid off; the government party, led by Prime Minister William Pitt, secured his election as member of Parliament for St. Mawes, Cornwall. St. Mawes was what has been called a "rotten" borough: Simcoe was responsible to only the handful of constituents who were eligible to vote. He was not much interested in politics, however, and he made only a few speeches in the House of Commons. Instead, he lobbied for any military or administrative post in which he could further distinguish himself. Here his well-regarded expertise in North American affairs and his political connections worked to his advantage again. Within a year of his election to the House, he was promoted to the rank of colonel and then appointed the first lieutenant-governor of Upper Canada. However, initially this frontier outpost may not have been enough for the ambitious Simcoe; in March 1791 he suggested that the lieutenant-governorship be combined with the new position of minister to the United States. This suggestion was quickly turned down: certainly the Americans would not have accepted the commander of the Queen's Rangers as the British representative in their country, and one wonders how a soldier who at this time had no diplomatic experience and an obvious grudge against American republicanism could have succeeded in such a position.[28] In any event, Simcoe threw himself enthusiastically into the flurry of administrative preparations that had to be made prior to his departure from England. He, Elizabeth, and their two youngest

Aside from their brief stays at Quebec City, the Simcoes' accommodations in Canada were far from luxurious. At both Newark and York the family lived for a time in a canvas tent. Their permanent home at Newark was "Navy Hall," four wooden naval supply buildings, which Simcoe himself described during their renovation as "an old hovel, that will look exactly like a carrier's ale-house."

At York, a summer home was begun by the Simcoes in 1795, and was christened "Castle Frank" in honour of their son, Francis. Castle Frank remained standing some two miles (3.2 km) upstream from the mouth of the Don River (near present-day Bloor Street) until it was destroyed by fire in 1829. Paul Mombourqette, London

children (four older daughters remained at home for their education) boarded H.M.S. *Triton* in September 1791, bound for Canada. After a very rough North Atlantic crossing, the Simcoes arrived at Quebec City in November. There he impatiently waited (although his French-speaking wife enjoyed the winter social season) until his ministers arrived in the spring and he could be officially sworn in as lieutenant-governor in June 1792. Once this was accomplished, he immediately set out for Upper Canada and his new post.

IMPRESSIONS OF SIMCOE: HISTORIANS AND CONTEMPORARIES
Even his strongest critics agree that Simcoe was a fine officer who deserved his reputation as one of Britain's best regimental commanders during the American Revolution.[29] It is at the point where Simcoe becomes the lieutenant-governor of Upper Canada that this consensus disappears. As with many other significant historical figures, the appraisal of Simcoe's career has changed over time, influenced in some cases by the political and social climate of succeeding generations. Early biographers, such as David B. Read (1890), Duncan Campbell

Scott (1905), and W. R. Riddell (1926) generally confirm Simcoe's status as the respected Father of Upper Canada and as an inspiration for the greatest province in the Dominion. Perhaps the most extravagant claim made about Simcoe's lieutenant-governorship was written by Stephen Leacock, who observed "as Napoleon made France so did Simcoe make Upper Canada."[30]

American scholars could be expected to subject Simcoe to more critical scrutiny. Samuel Flagg Bemis, for one, in his landmark 1923 study of Jay's Treaty, stresses "the prejudices and excitability of Simcoe's character," although he is careful to note the lieutenant-governor's "great services to the founding of the province of Upper Canada."[31] Canadian William Smith in 1931 followed suit with a critical appraisal of Simcoe, but states that "it is impossible to withhold admiration for the self-sacrificing energy with which he strove to translate those ideas, good and not so good, into achievements."[32]

By the Second World War, when the "high Toryism" of Simcoe and his contemporaries was generally out of academic favour, Simcoe's stature suffered a noticeable decline. Even Leacock notes in a backhanded compliment that Simcoe "had a vision that looked a hundred years ahead, and that lingered also a hundred years behind."[33] By the 1950s some university professors liked to see Simcoe merely as "a stock figure, useful, along with Sir Francis Bond Head and his brace of pistols, to enliven lectures a little."[34] In other words, Simcoe was a good example of an overzealous eccentric who worked doggedly, if somewhat misguidedly, for king and country.

Some of the criticisms of Simcoe over the past forty years have centred on such areas as his overly enthusiastic passion for Upper Canada,[35] his "amateurish" efforts at diplomacy with the aboriginals and the Americans,[36] his open confrontations with Joseph Brant over the Six Nations' lands,[37] the viability of his grand military strategy for Upper Canada,[38] and his political and social agenda, which strove to make Upper Canada more British than Britain itself.[39] Journalist Walter Stewart, writing in 1985, makes possibly the breeziest (and for some the most accurate) dismissal of Simcoe when he writes that the lieutenant-governor was "both literally and figuratively, a fathead."[40]

Interestingly, over the years at least one of Simcoe's critics has changed his opinion of the lieutenant-governor's career. S.R. Mealing in 1958 delivered a paper to the Canadian Historical Association in which he concluded that Simcoe "was an intellectual magpie" who lacked the inherent ability to bring his most cherished projects (especially London) to a successful conclusion. Twenty-five years later Mealing authored the lieutenant-governor's entry in the *Dictionary of Canadian Biography*, where he praised Simcoe for his energy and his positive contributions to Upper Canada.[41]

If historians' opinions of Simcoe are divided, how then was the lieutenant-governor seen by his contemporaries? The Simcoes regularly entertained their small circle of friends in the villages of Newark and York, and received visitors and dignitaries as they passed through the colony. Among the guests at Newark in 1795 was the Duc de la Rochefoucauld-Liancourt, a French nobleman, who, after he fled the ravages of revolutionary France, had become a traveller and diarist. Although Mrs. Simcoe cared little for the Duc's company, Rochefoucauld-Liancourt recorded a favourable impression of the Simcoes, especially the lieutenant-governor:

> In private life, Governor Simcoe is simple and straightforward; he lives
> in a miserable little wooden house formerly occupied by the

Commissioners for the navigation of the Lake. He is guarded there by four soldiers who come from the Fort in the morning and return in the evening. There he lives generously and hospitably without ostentation: his mind is facile and enlightened; he speaks well on all subjects, more willingly on his projects than on anything else ...[42]

Rochefoucauld-Liancourt's observations of Simcoe have been confirmed by others: he was a well-meaning man without pretension, zealous in the pursuit of his objectives, sympathetic to the King's loyal subjects, and always willing to grant someone an audience.[43] However, it should not be presumed that the Simcoes were "democratic" in their behaviour; both Mr. and Mrs. Simcoe were well aware of their station in society. In one revealing story, Simcoe, while at Quebec City, refused to attend the performance of a play put on by his brother officers because he believed that acting was a pastime beneath the dignity of a king's officer. And Mrs. Simcoe, "young, wealthy, demanding, and very proud of her position in the colony," played a dominant role in the dinners, balls, and outings of Newark and York's tiny social elite.[44]

While Simcoe may have been personally well-liked by many of his contemporaries, his policies continually annoyed several members of the colony's small political and business élite. Historian Jane Errington observes that the pomp and circumstance that Simcoe insisted be part of official ceremonial occasions (such as the opening of the colonial legislature) was designed to strengthen the bonds that the colonists had with the mother country, but these rituals alone could not foster an exact copy of the Britain Simcoe left behind. Simcoe's early idea to create an aristocracy in Upper Canada ("a hereditary council with some mark of nobility"[45]) eventually would be abandoned in a colony that was a "heterogenous mixture of Germans, Scots, Dutch, English, and French" among its white settlers. Prominent Loyalists such as Kingston's Richard Cartwright mocked Simcoe's grand vision for Upper Canada, especially the quixotic plan for New London. There were serious concerns among the Loyalists about Simcoe's insistence on one established church, vocal complaints about Simcoe's system of allocating land grants, and definite misgivings about his decision to begin the process of freeing black slaves in the colony.[46]

Simcoe was equally exasperated with those colonial leaders who nursed grudges over his making Newark rather than Kingston the capital and then moving it to York. As Errington shows, Simcoe was firm in his belief that both Kingston and Newark were in the long run indefensible, and that there was a "need to physically separate the colonial administration from the influence of the already existing merchant oligarchy in the two older towns."[47] The course of future settlement, the lieutenant-governor believed, had to be directed into the western interior, along the roads being slowly carved out of the wilderness by the Queen's Rangers. Yet Simcoe, even though the usefulness of his plans was certainly not apparent to many of these merchants, was determined to improve the long-term economic prosperity of Upper Canada through his grand strategy for London.

In 1943 Mattie M.I. Clark argued that Simcoe's policies during his term in office were dictated as much by economic as by military concerns. Simcoe disliked the Montreal fur monopoly, which at that time controlled the Upper Canadian fur trade, then the key economic staple in the colony. To Simcoe, the fur traders of Montreal were directly opposed to extensive settlement and new industries in Upper Canada. The lieutenant-governor's vision of Upper Canada's future, one that would have seemed absurd to many in the 1790s, was that of "a great potential market for British goods, and more important still, a granary for the world."[48] Simcoe believed this potential prosperity could only be accomplished when roads spanned the interior and a capital city was established deep in the heart of western Upper Canada.

Simcoe attempted to turn Upper Canada into a copy of English society, but his efforts at a social transformation in the colony were largely a failure: the Loyalists were Anglo-Americans, not Englishmen born and bred. As well, Simcoe was unable to mobilize enthusiasm for his economic strategy, especially when it concerned the development of London. Moving the capital from Kingston to the western interior threatened the influence of much of the established business class. The members of the local political and business élite continued to have their own agendas, and few of them included subservience to an appointed official who would be gone in a few years. Indeed, some Upper Canadians were quite happy to bid Simcoe a fond farewell when he left the colony in 1796.

SIMCOE AND DORCHESTER

The one contemporary in Canada who *really* mattered when it came down to actually implementing Simcoe's grand strategy for Upper Canada was Lord Dorchester, governor general of the two Canadas and Simcoe's immediate superior. Formerly Guy Carleton, Lord Dorchester had earlier served as the governor of Quebec from 1768 to 1778, and is most familiar to students of Canadian history as the chief supporter of the 1774 Quebec Act. Dorchester defended Quebec during the American invasions of 1775–1776 and 1777, and was commander-in-chief of the British forces at New York at the end of the Revolution. In 1791 he was appointed governor general of Upper and Lower Canada, but Dorchester departed Canada in August of that year on a leave of absence, not to return until September 1793. Simcoe, during this entire period, had virtually no official direction from his governor general on the policies that he should pursue as lieutenant-governor. As a result, he got in the habit of directly corresponding with the Colonial Office and Henry Dundas, a clear breach of bureaucratic etiquette.

Dorchester and Simcoe, to put it mildly, did not get along very well. The sixty-nine-year-old Dorchester, a secretive and aloof man, was never in the mood to take often rather pointed advice from a brash regimental commander who was twenty-eight years his junior. Even more conservative than Simcoe, Dorchester had opposed the creation of elected assemblies in the 1791 Constitutional Act, not to mention the very creation of the colony of Upper Canada. But perhaps the conflict between the two men was inevitable. Simcoe bore a grudge against Dorchester for some unflattering remarks that he made about the Queen's Rangers at the end of the Revolution, and Dorchester disliked Simcoe because his own man, Sir John Johnson, was passed over in favour of Simcoe for the appointment of lieutenant-governor of Upper Canada.[49] More significantly, the Constitutional Act itself would tie Simcoe's hands and give the strongest powers to Dorchester: most of the important military decisions affecting the colony, including the disposition of troops, would have to be deferred by Simcoe to the governor general, namely Dorchester himself.

While Dorchester was away in Britain, Simcoe had virtually a free hand in Upper Canada. He began to implement his grand strategy for Upper Canada, visiting the London site and using the Queen's Rangers to begin the construction of Dundas Street. Even though he would note in June 1793, that more pressing concerns were preventing his occupation of "New London," [50] by September he had written Dundas and argued strongly for the choice of London as capital.[51] However, Simcoe's plans for London were about to be abruptly stopped. Dorchester finally arrived at Quebec that same September and soon began to assess the Upper Canadian situation: Dorchester may not have cared much for Simcoe, but he liked the lieutenant-governor's wilderness capital of London even less.

THE POSTPONEMENT OF SIMCOE'S DREAM

In early October 1793, Dorchester sent a dispatch to Simcoe advising him to abandon any ideas about building and fortifying new settlements, which of course meant London. To make matters worse, the Queen's Rangers, the force that Simcoe had been using to build his roads and other public projects, were to be used at the governor general's pleasure. Dorchester made it very clear that the Queen's Rangers were ultimately under his command, and that in case of war with the United States, they would be used for the defence of Lower Canada.[52] The lieutenant-governor of Upper Canada, needless to say, was outraged. Immediately upon receipt of this dispatch, Simcoe (not for the last time) went over Dorchester's head and wrote directly to Dundas, heatedly arguing that the possible withdrawal of the Queen's Rangers was "immoral," as it would leave the Upper Canadians utterly defenceless in the face of a possible American attack.[53] Simcoe followed this letter by sending Dundas a detailed military assessment of why Upper Canada, and not Lower Canada, was the key to the defence of British North America.[54]

Simcoe's passionate pleas to Dundas about Dorchester were unwise in more ways than one. Unknown to Simcoe, Captain Charles Stevenson, one of Simcoe's subordinates and the bearer of his dispatches to New York and London, had, in the summer of 1793, seriously misrepresented him. For whatever reason, Stevenson had met with Dundas and other ministers, boldly requesting (without Simcoe's authorization), among other things, a promotion for Simcoe and more men and material to counter the American threat in the Northwest. Dundas, in his next dispatch, coolly reprimanded the lieutenant-governor, reminding him that caution was the order of the day, and that it was not British policy to escalate the situation in the Northwest any further. Dorchester, who was asked by Dundas to comment on Simcoe's "requests," was furious about his subordinate's apparent violation of the chain of command. Simcoe himself wrote a humbling apology to Dundas in February 1794, disavowing any knowledge of Stevenson's actions.[55]

This seemingly minor incident not only underscored the tension between Simcoe and Dorchester, but it emphasized how carefully the British government trod in its relations with the new United States. Britain did not want a war started by an indiscreet lieutenant-governor running amuck in the Upper Canadian wilderness. On Simcoe's part, he was only too well aware of the dangers that he faced over the Northwestern post controversy. On one hand, an active defensive policy was necessary, but on the other hand, too much military activity could encourage an American attack. Simcoe was unyielding in his belief that Upper Canada could not be abandoned as part of a grand defensive strategy for British North America. What Dorchester and Dundas were equally adamant about was that Simcoe would no longer have a completely free hand in Upper Canada, a situation that forced him to put the London project on hold.

In any event, Simcoe had very little time at this point to even consider the relocation of the capital to London. The issue of the Northwestern posts, the sore spot between Britain and the United States, would have to be settled at the conference table by professional diplomats. In the meantime, Simcoe, a soldier with little diplomatic experience, found himself to be a key mediator in the increasingly dangerous situation between the aboriginals and the Americans.

The native confederacy that Brant had worked so hard to forge was seriously divided. Many of the western tribes were determined to create an Indian buffer state between the United States and Upper Canada that would have seen the United States cede territory that included all of modern Ohio, Indiana, and Michigan. Brant, a shrewd leader who had met frequently with American officals (including Washington himself) at the federal capital of Philadelphia, knew that the demands of the western tribes would be unacceptable to the United States. To Brant, native unity could only be maintained if the demands of the western tribes were moderated.

In early October 1792, the western tribes held a conference at the juncture of the Glaize and Maumee Rivers, some 60 miles (96 km) southwest of Detroit. Through Alexander McKee, the deputy superintendent general of Indian affairs, Simcoe stated the British position: Britain would assist the native peoples in their negotiations with the United States; however, she would not go to war on their behalf. A very complex and delicate series of negotiations then continued, ending at a conference held at Sandusky, Ohio, in July 1793. Three American commissioners were dispatched to the conference, and they stayed with Simcoe at Navy Hall (his quarters at Newark) from May until July. Simcoe took part in some of the negotiations during this period, which were marked by Brant's desperate attempt to find a compromise position. But there was no compromise to be had: the western tribes insisted that the United States must create a final boundary along the Ohio River. By mid-August both Brant's tattered confederacy and the United States were preparing for war, with a perplexed Simcoe looking on.[56]

Simcoe has been accused of bungling these intricate negotiations,[57] but this criticism overstates his personal influence with the native peoples, especially the western tribes. As well, the Americans were clearly intent on war if the natives did not agree to their terms. Early in 1794 General Wayne began his march into the Ohio country, seeking battle with the aboriginals. In Quebec City, Dorchester was clearly alarmed by this turn of events, for it appeared to him that Wayne was intent on taking Detroit. Dorchester sprang into action and made two rash decisions. First, in order to reassure a visiting delegation of native leaders, Dorchester officially noted his disappointment in the Americans and stated that he would "not be surprised if we [i.e. Britain] are at war with them in the course of the present year." To Dorchester's chagrin, his speech was printed in full in American newspapers, adding to a growing war fever.[58] Dorchester was even angrier when he received a mild reprimand from Dundas over the incident, who urged greater prudence in the governor general's dealings with the Americans.[59]

Dorchester's second action was to order Simcoe to take an expeditionary force and re-occupy Fort Miamis, an abandoned post near present-day Toledo, Ohio. Although Simcoe was to avoid taking any action that would appear to be hostile, he had to be prepared to "resist Wayne's attack should he attempt by Force to take possession of the Country."[60] In late March of 1794, he hurried down the Thames by canoe and by April had established a small garrison at Fort Miamis, returning immediately afterwards to his headquarters at Newark.

This action by Simcoe, under Dorchester's orders, was seen as being very close to an act of war by many Americans. Simcoe himself was alarmed enough at this strong American reaction to evacuate his family to Quebec City. On August 20, the dreaded conflict between Britain and the United States almost occurred. Within earshot of Fort Miamis, Wayne, although suffering heavy losses, broke the native alliance at the Battle of Fallen Timbers. Two days later, Wayne approached the commander of Fort Miamis and demanded that the small British garrison leave the fort. The British commander refused Wayne's request. After some deliberation, Wayne withdrew from his position opposite Fort Miamis and everyone drew a sigh of relief.

Wayne's prudence was critical in more than one respect: not only did it save lives, but it unwittingly prevented the possible cessation of talks between the Americans and the British. Unknown to Dorchester, Simcoe, or Wayne, peace between the United States and Britain was in the process of being achieved around the conference table. In July an agreement (which was eventually known as Jay's Treaty) had been reached between British and American diplomats. Jay's Treaty was almost all that Hamilton and the pro-British faction in the United States wanted. Among other things, there would be a British evacuation of the Northwestern posts by June 1796; a free flow of goods between the United States and Canada; and a commitment by the United States to pay pre-Revolutionary War debts.

Jay's Treaty meant that nearly all of the outstanding political differences between the United States and Britain that were left over from the Revolution were now solved. It also meant that Simcoe's "New London" was no longer an important consideration. Simcoe saw London as a means of controlling the American interior; with Jay's Treaty such a mercantilist policy was no longer necessary or wanted. Dorchester's insistence that London was not necessary had been reinforced earlier, in March 1794, by a dispatch from Dundas that seemed to dampen much of the Colonial Office's earlier support for London. Because of the possibility of hostilities with the United States, Dundas advised Simcoe to concentrate his efforts on York over London.[61] With peace at hand, London was even less necessary. Nevertheless, Simcoe continued his vigorous arguments for the London site. In an October 1794 letter to McKee, Simcoe defiantly wrote that he was

> convinced more & more of the necessity of my getting to a central Position – the King's Ministers approve of the necessity of my Plans, no lesser men *shall* counteract them – The Rangers are compleated to four Hundred & I hope to spend next Winter in London – I invite you to partake of its hospitality for part of the Season.[62]

Simcoe's confidence was unfounded. After the signing of Jay's Treaty, the government's support for London noticeably waned. The Duke of Portland, who in July 1794 had succeeded Dundas in the Colonial Office, appears to have had very little interest in the London matter, and did not give Simcoe the support that he needed against Dorchester. To all intents and purposes, Simcoe's London proposal was indefinitely postponed, no matter what Simcoe said or did.

By now thoroughly frustrated by his battles with Dorchester and again in uncertain health, Simcoe applied for a leave of absence from Upper Canada in 1796. He turned the administration of the colony over to Peter Russell, his receiver-general, who would supervise Upper Canada for the lieutenant-governor until Simcoe's official resignation in January 1798. Russell would continue to refer public matters concerning Upper Canada to Simcoe until that date. By now promoted to the rank of major-general, Simcoe left Canada in September 1796, never to return.

A month after his return to England, the ever-restless Simcoe accepted (to Mrs. Simcoe's dismay) the governorship of the former French West Indian colony of San Domingo (now Haiti), a post made more attractive by an accompanying promotion to the rank of lieutenant-general.[63] The government of William Pitt needed experienced officers in the bitter struggle for the control of the French West Indies and the valuable sugar plantations located there. The fever-plagued island of San Domingo was widely recognized as an extremely difficult assignment; thousands of British soldiers – nearly all victims of yellow fever – had already died there. To further complicate matters, Simcoe would have to deal with an extremely violent racial war, as well as bring administrative order to a very confused local political situation. It was the kind of assignment that challenged Simcoe. Unfortunately for him, the Caribbean island of San Domingo proved to be too much. A lack of administrative and military support from Britain, plus his weakened health, forced Simcoe to quit San Domingo and his post in July 1797.

Upon his return to England, Simcoe was treated by the government as a pariah. Prime Minister Pitt was by now under intense criticism for his French West Indian policy (over 40,000 British soldiers would eventually die of fever during this particular campaign against revolutionary France), and Simcoe's early departure from San Domingo caused him serious embarrassment. Neither Pitt nor Dundas, now minister of war, wanted to have anything to do with Simcoe, and the Duke of York, the King's son and commander-in-chief of the British army, demanded that charges be laid against him for abandoning his post. Eventually friends in the government rallied around Simcoe, but promises of a peerage and the governor-generalship of Canada remained unkept. Simcoe was given a command in England, and he prepared to resume his former life as a country squire at Wolford.

Finally, the death of Pitt in January 1806 gave Simcoe the great opportunity that he had awaited all his life. Powerful friends now dominated the cabinet, and Simcoe was offered the post of governor general of India in July. Although by now in very poor health, Simcoe accepted immediately. Just as he was making his preparations for India, the government asked him to perform a critical mission in the war against France. Simcoe was made a military ambassador assigned to assess the Portuguese preparations against an expected French invasion, and he was to report back to

Guy Carleton, 1st Baron Dorchester (1724–1808), the son of an Irish landowner, was Wolfe's quartermaster-general during the siege of Quebec in 1759. Dorchester was governor general of Quebec from 1766 to 1778, and then Quebec and Canada from 1786 to 1796. By nature cautious and reserved, Dorchester was constantly irritated by Simcoe's open impatience with his policies.

National Archives of Canada, C-2833

England about events in Portugal prior to sailing for India. While *en route* to Lisbon, he was struck down by illness (probably recurrent malaria), and, near death, he was rushed home to his family. He never made it to Wolford Lodge. Lieutenant-General John Graves Simcoe, at the pinnacle of his career and in his fifty-fourth year, died at Exeter, England on October 26, 1806.

SIMCOE AND LONDON: AN ASSESSMENT

One of the difficulties that the lay reader has in assessing Simcoe's career is the rather parochial view that even distinguished historians have had of Upper Canada's first lieutenant-governor. After all, Simcoe's story is intertwined with that of early Upper Canada, and his tenure of office is a benchmark by which we judge many of that colony's eventual successes and failures. Some writers, perhaps in their efforts to personalize (and perhaps simplify) history, give Simcoe either too much or too little credit for how Upper Canada was to develop in the decades to come.

It is incorrect to judge Simcoe's actions strictly from today's perspective. Errington, for one, observes that our knowledge of Upper Canadian society in the 1790s is fragmentary at best. She further writes that "the historian must accept that early Upper Canada is a foreign world and translate its historical records accordingly."[64] It is too easy to make light of both Simcoe and his plans for "New

The Simcoe Memorial, Exeter Cathedral, England. In 1811 friends of John Graves Simcoe began the Memorial, which has a bust of Simcoe in the centre, a Queen's Ranger to the left, and a native warrior to the right. In 1812 an inscription was added to the bottom of the Memorial to honour Simcoe's son, Francis Gwillim Simcoe, who was killed in action during the siege of Badajoz, Spain, earlier that year.

John Graves Simcoe was buried at Wolford Chapel, on the site of the former Simcoe family home. In 1966 the chapel was purchased by the government of Ontario as a historic site.

Regional Collection, University of Western Ontario Library

London," the great wilderness capital that never was to be. Simcoe was a man of his times, and his times are far removed from today's experiences. A career soldier steeped in the aristocratic traditions of the late eighteenth century, Simcoe had a paternalistic view of society and the individual's place within it. American republicanism was not just something to be viewed with suspicion; it was a very real threat to the political and social order that Simcoe knew and cherished. Thus his plans for the rapid transformation of a wilderness colony into a great empire that could challenge the new United States were not merely sentimental ones. Simcoe had a vision for the salvation of British power in North America, and he worked hard to achieve it.

But the question needs to be asked: if Simcoe was such a practical soldier with so much common sense, why London? It certainly can be argued that Simcoe grossly underestimated the resources needed to achieve his dream. The establishment of London would necessarily be expensive: the back-breaking opening of Dundas Street alone would cost more in money and time than Simcoe had available to him. This lack of resources for the settlement of the western interior was doubly compounded by a volatile international situation where, until the signing of Jay's Treaty, war with the United States was a certain danger. Under such circumstances, London, to Simcoe's great disappointment, would have to be a secondary concern.

London must be seen as only part of the equation; Simcoe's wilderness capital was, in a sense, "the icing on the cake." Simcoe saw great commercial potential for Upper Canada. But this potential could only be achieved if the new colony's development were separate and distinct from that of Lower Canada. Simcoe's great legacy to Upper Canada was that he saw the colony as more than just a hinterland of the St. Lawrence Valley. His policies enabled a more rapid and efficient exploitation of the interior. For example, if Simcoe had chosen Kingston as Upper Canada's capital, as a more cautious lieutenant-governor might have done, then the opening of central and south-western Upper Canada could have been delayed by a generation or more. The opening of the interior was the reason for the two key roads of Dundas and Yonge Streets, which, although they went from nowhere to nowhere in the 1790s, became the principal routes for settlement in the following decades. Simcoe's dream would have been complete (and Ontario's subsequent history quite different) if he had been able to build London, but Dorchester and others would see that this project did not occur as he had envisioned it. His greatest ambitions unfulfilled in Upper Canada, Simcoe would move on to other challenges. Tragically, circumstances and his health continued to conspire against him throughout the remainder of his life.

It is difficult for us to appreciate this today, but without Simcoe the settlement of Upper Canada would not have proceeded in the way that it did. And if Simcoe had been given the resources and support that he needed during his tenure of office, London, and not Toronto, would probably have become the principal city of Ontario. Nevertheless, credit must be given to Simcoe for the eventual founding of London, an idea that, despite its detractors, did prove to be "eminently calculated" in the end.

ENDNOTES

1. Mary Beacock Fryer, *Elizabeth Posthuma Simcoe, 1762-1850: A Biography* [hereafter *Elizabeth Posthuma Simcoe*] (Toronto, Ontario, and Oxford, England: Dundurn Press, 1989), p. 72. For Brant's views on slavery, see: Isabel Thompson Kelsay, *Joseph Brant, 1743-1807: Man of Two Worlds* (Syracuse, New York: Syracuse University Press, 1984), pp. 279, 527, 533.

2. For a thorough analysis of the political situation that existed between the United States and Britain in the period immediately following the American Revolution, see: Charles R. Ritcheson, *Aftermath of Revolution: British Policy Toward the United States, 1783-1795* [hereafter *Aftermath of Revolution*] (Dallas, Texas: Southern Methodist University Press, 1969).

3. Donald Creighton, *The Empire of the St. Lawrence* (Toronto, Ontario: Macmillan, 1956), p. 116.

4. E.A. Cruikshank, ed., *The Correspondence of John Graves Simcoe, with Allied Documents Relating to his Administration of the Government of Upper Canada*, 5 vols. (Toronto, Ontario: Ontario Historical Society, 1923-1931) [hereafter *Correspondence of Simcoe*], vol. I, pp. 17-19.

5. *Ibid.*, pp. 18-19.

6. The description of Simcoe's journey is partly drawn from Edward Baker Littlehales's *Journal of an Exploratory Tour Partly in Sleighs, but Chiefly on Foot from Navy Hall, Niagara, to Detroit, Made in the Months of February and March, A.D. 1793, by his Excellency Lieut.-Gov. Simcoe, with Introduction and Notes by Henry Scadding, D.D.* [hereafter *Journal*] (Toronto, Ontario: Copp, Clark, 1889; reprint ed. Toronto, Ontario: Canadiana House, 1968), pp. 12-13. Lieutenant D.W. Smith also left a record of the journey that gives a slightly different slant to Littlehales's version. See: D.W. Smith, "Thames: Its Banks Transcribed and Annotated by R.M. Lewis," *Ontario History*, XLIV, no. 1 (Jan. 1952): pp. 15-22.

7. Littlehales, *Journal*, p. 13.

8. Two entries in Mrs. Simcoe's diary, dated Feb. and Mar. 10, 1793, describe the lieutenant-governor's departure and arrival at Newark, as well as giving a slightly different focus to Littlehales's and Smith's journals. See: Mary Quayle Innis, ed., *Mrs. Simcoe's Diary* [hereafter *Mrs. Simcoe's Diary*] (Toronto, Ontario: Macmillan, 1978), pp. 85, 88-89.

9. Littlehales, *Journal*, p. 13.

10. *Ibid.*, p. 13. Orlo Miller gives a brief description of the forks in Simcoe's day in relation to the present city. See: Orlo Miller, *This was London: The First Two Centuries* (Westport, Ontario: Butternut Press, 1988), pp. 3-4. In order to gain a broader appreciation of the route followed by Simcoe in the Lower Thames Valley, see: Fred Coyne Hamil: *The Valley of the Lower Thames 1640 to 1850* (Toronto, Ontario: University of Toronto Press, 1951).

11. Innis, *Mrs. Simcoe's Diary*, pp. 88-89.

12. *History of the County of Middlesex, Canada* (Toronto and London, Ontario: W.A. & C.L. Goodspeed, 1889; reprint ed., Belleville, Ontario: Mika Studio, 1972), p. 482.

13. *London Free Press*, Jan. 3, 1992, p. E2, cc. 2-4.

14. For details of both the 1926 and 1955 centennials, see: London Public Library, London Room, "London Centennial Scrapbooks 1926, 1955."

15. *London Free Press*, Mar. 17, 1992, p. B1, c.1.

16. *Globe and Mail*, (Toronto, Ontario) Metro ed., Aug. 5, 1991, p. C2, cc. 4-6.

17. S.R. Mealing, "Simcoe, John Graves" [hereafter "Simcoe"], *Dictionary of Canadian Biography* [hereafter *DCB*], V: p. 759.

18. See William Renwick Riddell, *The Life of John Graves Simcoe: First Lieutenant-Governor of the Province of Upper Canada 1792-1796* [hereafter *Life of John Graves Simcoe*] (Toronto, Ontario: McClelland & Stewart, 1926), pp. 17-37. Captain Simcoe's "Rules for Your Conduct," the memorandum to his sons, is reproduced on pp. 31-35.

19. *Gentleman's Magazine* (London, England), Dec. 1806, p. 1165. For a discussion of the story of Captain Simcoe at the siege of Quebec, see: Riddell, *Life of John Graves Simcoe*, pp. 27-29.

20. Marcus Van Steen, Governor Simcoe and His Lady [hereafter *Governor Simcoe*] (Toronto, Ontario, and London, England: Hodder and Stoughton, 1968), p. 19.

21. E.A. Cruikshank, "Lieut.-Governor Simcoe: A Chronological Record," Ontario Historical Society *Papers and Records*, XXVI (1930): pp. 16-36. For more information on the "stray dog" incident, see: Fryer, *Elizabeth Posthuma Simcoe*, pp. 105-106.

22. C.J. Ingles, *The Queen's Rangers in the Revolutionary War*, ed. H.M. Jackson ([Montreal, Quebec: Industrial Shops for the deaf] 1956), pp. 55-57. For a brief history of the Queen's Rangers, along with three coloured plates of the Queen's Rangers from Simcoe's published war journal, see: W.Y. Carman, "The Uniform of the Queen's Rangers, 1777-1783," *Journal of the Society for Army Historical Research*, LVII, no. 230 (Summer, 1979): pp. 63-70.

23. John Graves Simcoe, *A Journal of the Operations of the Queen's Rangers from the end of the Year 1777 to the Conclusion of the Late American War* (Exeter, England: Printed for the Author, [1787]). Simcoe's first extensive biography, written by David B. Read, Q.C. draws heavily on Simcoe's journal. See: David B. Read, Q.C., *The Life and Times of General John Graves Simcoe* [hereafter *Life and Times*] (Toronto, Ontario: G. Virtue, 1890), pp. 9-114.

24. John Graves Simcoe, *Remarks on the Travels of the Marquis de Chastellux in North America* (London, England: G. and T. Wilkie, 1787).
25. Van Steen, *Governor Simcoe*, p. 24.
26. Fryer, *Elizabeth Posthuma Simcoe*, pp. 9-18. See also: Edith G. Firth, "Gwillim, Elizabeth Posthuma (Simcoe)," *DCB*, pp. 361-363. Some sources place the year of Elizabeth's birth at 1766, but Fryer and Firth show it as 1762.
27. Ritcheson, *Aftermath of Revolution*, pp. 151-159.
28. *Ibid.*, p. 140.
29. For a noteworthy exception to the generally favourable treatment of Simcoe's military career, see: James Kirby Danglade, "John Graves Simcoe and the United States, 1775-1796: A Study in Anglo-American Frontier Diplomacy," (Ph.D. thesis, Ball State University, Muncie, Indiana, 1972).
30. Stephen Leacock, *Canada: The Foundations of Its Future* [hereafter *Canada*] (Montreal, Quebec: Gazette Printing Company, 1941), p. 118. See also: Duncan Campbell Scott, *John Graves Simcoe: Makers of Canada Series*, vol. 7 (Toronto, Ontario: Morang, 1905); and Riddell, *Life of John Graves Simcoe*.
31. Samuel Flagg Bemis, *Jay's Treaty: A Study in Commerce and Diplomacy* (New Haven, Connecticut and London, England: Yale University Press, 1962), p. 173.
32. William Smith, *Political Leaders of Upper Canada* (Toronto, Ontario: Thomas Nelson and Sons, 1931), p. 21.
33. Leacock, *Canada*, p. 117.
34. S.R. Mealing "The Enthusiasms of John Graves Simcoe," [hereafter "Enthusiasms"] Canadian Historical Association *Report*, 1958, p. 50. For a further study of the family and political links between Bond Head and Simcoe, see: Ged Martin, "The Simcoes and Their Friends," *Ontario History*, LXIX, no. 2 (Jun. 1977): pp. 101-112. Martin sees Simcoe as part of "a comic sub-plot" in Upper Canadian history that is finally completed with Lieutenant-Governor Bond Head's activities during the Rebellions of 1837–1838.
35. Mealing, "Enthusiasms," pp. 50-62.
36. S.F. Wise, "The Indian Diplomacy of John Graves Simcoe" [hereafter, "Indian Diplomacy"], Canadian Historical Association *Report*, 1953, pp. 36-44.
37. Charles M. Johnson, ed., *The Valley of the Six Nations: A Collection of Documents on the Indian Lands of the Grand River* (Toronto, Ontario: The Champlain Society/University of Toronto Press, 1964), pp. xlv-xlvii.
38. Malcolm MacLeod, "Fortress Ontario or Forlorn Hope? Simcoe and the Defence of Upper Canada," *Canadian Historical Review*, LIII, no. 2 (Jun. 1972): pp. 149-178.
39. Walter Stewart, *True Blue: The Loyalist Legend* (Toronto, Ontario: Collins, 1985).
40. *Ibid.*, p. 187.
41. Mealing, "Enthusiasms," p. 62; *ibid.*, "Simcoe," pp. 754-759.
42. Riddell, *Life of John Graves Simcoe*, p. 273.
43. Mealing, "Enthusiasms," pp. 54-55.
44. Innis, *Mrs. Simcoe's Diary*, pp. 1-25.
45. Cruikshank, *Correspondence of Simcoe*, vol. I, p. 18.
46. Jane Errington, *The Lion, The Eagle, and Upper Canada: A Developing Colonial Ideology* [hereafter *The Lion*] (Kingston, Ontario, and Montreal, Quebec: McGill-Queen's University Press, 1987), pp. 1-34.
47. *Ibid.*, p. 31.
48. Mattie M.I. Clark, *The Positive Side of John Graves Simcoe* (Toronto, Ontario: Forward Publishing, 1943), p. 9.
49. Cruikshank, *Correspondence of Simcoe*, vol. I, p. 10.
50. *Ibid.*, vol. V, p. 52.
51. *Ibid.*, vol. II, pp. 56-65.
52. *Ibid.*, pp. 83-84.
53. *Ibid.*, p. 122.
54. *Ibid.*, pp. 157-163.
55. Ritcheson, *Aftermath of Revolution*, pp. 243-263.
56. *Ibid.*, pp. 243-263. For a detailed survey of the 1794 border crisis, see: Carl Benn, "The Military Context of the Founding of Toronto," *Ontario History*, LXXXI, no. 4 (Dec. 1989): pp. 303-322.
57. Wise, "Indian Diplomacy," pp. 36-44.
58. Cruikshank, *Correspondence of Simcoe*, vol. II, pp. 149-150.
59. G.P. Browne, "Carleton, Guy, 1st Baron Dorchester," *DCB*, vol. V: p. 152.
60. Cruikshank, *Correspondence of Simcoe*, vol. II, p. 154.
61. *Ibid.*, pp. 184-187.
62. *Ibid.*, vol. V, p. 121.
63. For a detailed account of Simcoe's governorship of San Domingo, see: E.A. Cruikshank, "Simcoe's Mission to Saint Domingo," Ontario Historical Society *Papers and Records*, XXV (1929): pp. 78–144
64. Errington, *The Lion*, pp. 9-10.

CHAPTER TWO

THE LONDON STRATEGEM
From Concept to Consummation, 1791–1855

C.F.J. Whebell

A n undergraduate once wrote in an examination: "All the great cities in the world have this in common – at one time nobody lived there." While undeniable as a statement of fact, it was singularly unhelpful as a principle for analysis, and thus received a low mark. Nevertheless, as a truism it does serve to sharpen the complex question addressed by this article: why might a remote spot in the midst of an almost unpopulated wilderness be identified as a desirable location for a capital city, be indeed developed subsequently as a capital, though of local government, and grow so fast as to become in less than one generation only the fourth place to be incorporated as a city (1855) under the municipal laws of Upper Canada?

Answers to this very large question turn upon three more particular questions:

I. What broad objectives had John Graves Simcoe in mind when he conceived for his new province of Upper Canada a capital city in its western wilderness, in the face of obvious and massive logistical problems?

II. What was the overall context within which, thirty-five years later, it was decided to "activate" Simcoe's reserved site to be the seat of the London District, which was itself not created until well after Simcoe had left Upper Canada and the governorship?

III. Under what circumstances was London selected as the location for a large garrison of imperial troops in the aftermath of the 1837–1838 rebellions?

IV. How were the consequent very significant improvements in the land settlement and road communications in the London District related to the town's need for better internal government and financing?

In this article, I do not expect to answer all these complex questions finally and definitively. If much obvious documentation existed, it surely would have been found by now, given the activity of local and regional historians over the decades, and the answers to such questions well assimilated into the historiography of London. Instead, I argue, largely circumstantially, and from an approach that these days should probably be termed geopolitical, that for all of the questions I posed just now, the foundations for the answers lie in understanding the British views of the importance of Upper Canada for their own imperial interests. Though these clearly varied in some respects over time, it would appear that at a number of significant conjunctures, they came back to the same position: *that this territory was too important to be simply abandoned.* My argument is supported with references to original documents, a number of which may be new to some students of London's local history.

I. ORIGINS OF SIMCOE'S LONDON STRATEGEM

In discussing the first question – what, exactly, had Simcoe in mind? – it is necessary first to consider the state of play, as it were, in the 1780s in the great geopolitical arena of the trans-Appalachian interior of North America (see Map 2.1). The contest between the insurgent armies of the Continental Congress and those defending the interests of the Crown (including many units of loyal American settlers and Indians) was resolved by the partition of the cis-Mississippi territory by the Treaty of Paris. This 1783 boundary, though ambiguous in some

Map I. *The Trans-Allegheny Interior 1783–1796.*
The boundaries agreed upon at the conclusion of the American Revolution and confirmed by Jay's Treaty of 1794 left the wedge-shaped interlake peninsula now known as southwestern Ontario in British hands. London was to be the capital of the province of Upper Canada: from this point Simcoe would be well able to check American adventurism and also to manage relationships with the numerous Indian nations of the interior.

details, created *de jure* the area later to become Upper Canada: a broad peninsula thrusting like a spear point southwestwards from the main Canadian settlements on the St. Lawrence lowlands towards the much-coveted rich plains of the Illinois country and the Mississippi River.

Since 1763, the British had controlled the whole of this huge area from their tidewater base in Quebec, by means of a string of forts, termed collectively the "Barrier Forts," all of which lay on the south bank of the lakes or rivers of the Laurentian system. According to the 1783 treaty, therefore, every one of these posts fell on the United States' side of the boundary. But that infant federation was quite unable to take over these posts immediately, and the British continued to occupy them and carry on business (mainly the fur trade) as usual. Moreover, an active Indian insurgency (encouraged by the British) in the area south of Lake Erie inhibited for a time the expected flood-tide of American land settlement, which was building up pressure east of the Alleghenies.[1]

The tract of land that was to become Upper Canada was quite large enough for a colony – larger than the whole of New England, in fact – but lay within a power vacuum at that time, with no state able to project its authority unchallengeably and enforce its rule upon the residents, whether Indians or white settlers. The British were naturally apprehensive lest this political void invite further adventurism by the irrepressible American frontiersmen, who considered they had a self-evident natural right "to pass into every vacant country, and there to form their constitution."[2] To assert their own sovereignty it was therefore clearly necessary for the British to fill up the territory as soon as possible with loyal *bona fide* settlers, who could act as a local defence force, and, perhaps even more important, by means of their land titles add much legitimacy to what was otherwise a merely political claim to *res nullius* territory.[3]

Loyalists displaced from the former American colonies and some disbanded soldiers were suitable and available – indeed were even a considerable embarrassment to the British – and were deployed for the purpose beginning in 1784, following the instructions of Lord North, who had urged that the Loyalists might be settled "in such a situation as may be most likely to serve as a Barrier to the Province [Quebec] against any Incursions from the Inhabitants of other Allegiance."[4]

The British government, however, took an even larger view of the significance of the interior of North America than merely as an expedient place to dump refugees; this was exemplified by a position paper written in 1788 for the secretary of state for war and colonies:

> [From its] natural advantages of soil and climate, and the rapid progress in population and cultivation, the Western Territory [of the United States] must soon become the chief seat both of numbers and wealth, and on that account ought naturally to stand on at least an equal footing of political power and authority; but Congress have got the start, and may keep it long should the Western Territory continue, as at present, subject to Congress taxation. [Though the settlements of Loyalists and others on Lakes Erie and Ontario have good commercial potential] we are to remember that the settlers on the Western Waters must in every event be liable to a long land carriage from the Ocean; with which they have in all four ways of communicating: [across the Alleghenies] to the ports of Congress; [by the Mississippi] through the territories of Spain; [by the St. Lawrence; or through Hudson Bay].

[In these territories] people are not to sit still waiting for our pleasure, but on the contrary they will not fail to shift for themselves. If government decline to take part in their Interests, they will proceed to act independent of Government. If we do not chuse [*sic*] to go along, we must certainly be left behind. [A free-trade policy such as was tried to seduce Vermont from joining the United States might be used in the west, where] the great and interesting consideration would be its tendency to preserve a proper balance of power between them and Congress. [The British in Canada should therefore appear as] hearty and zealous patrons of Independence, a character worthy of us and in which we need not yield to any.[5]

The thrust of this extensive document, then, was to argue that the British should use their control over the St. Lawrence route to tidewater to inhibit the economic integration of the new settlements in the American interior with the established power centres on the eastern seaboard such as Boston, New York, and Baltimore, counting on the self-interest of the settlers in seeking the cheapest way to get their produce out to distant markets. In this context, a solid British position within the lower Great Lakes would be crucial; and the document, though long and rather unwieldy in rhetoric, clearly signals an appreciation of the long-term geopolitical value of what was shortly to be set aside as Upper Canada. Perhaps even more interesting is the fact that the document's location in the records, displaced so as to be in the midst of papers dated in the late 1830s, suggests that it had been brought forward out of some older file for reference when the third of the questions addressed by this article was under consideration in the Colonial Office.

At the time Lieutenant-Colonel John Graves Simcoe was nominated for appointment as lieutenant-governor of Upper Canada in 1790, therefore, actual British control still extended well beyond the agreed boundaries of 1783, and the merchants of Montreal still enjoyed the profits of trade throughout the entire Great Lakes basin and beyond. Many people doubted that the new, federally united state to the south would be able to survive its internal rebellions and insurgencies, and its massive financial problem.[6] In that same year, the resounding defeat by an Indian force of General St. Clair, governor of the Northwest Territory (the title given from 1787 to all United States national domain north of the Ohio and west of the Pennsylvania state line: that is, all that part of Quebec given up by the British diplomatic negotiators), underlined this uncertainty, and gave the British to hope that the boundaries might be renegotiated so as to give them a greater share of the lucrative interior, and most particularly, to keep the state of New York off the banks of the St. Lawrence River.[7]

Simcoe was not, therefore, presented with a firmly fixed territorial situation to which he had merely to adapt; there appeared to be considerable room for initiative as well. Advancing the settlement and military influence of British North America by a great leap forward into the wilderness was an obvious reason for designating what would today be termed "growth poles." Simcoe, by his own avowal, was fully in sympathy with the British geopolitical assessment of the interior, and at first operated on the assumption that the peace of 1783 was only a truce, which might break down at any time, on any of a host of pretexts. He wrote later that his intention in coming to Upper Canada had been "to acquaint myself with every power that it possessed of offence and defence," and, should war with the United States recur, to come forward with all my pretensions & experience & offer my services for the division of those states which I am satisfied can never be suffered to consolidate & essentially unite without the utmost damage to the Power, & what is of more consequence, the established Constitution of Gt. Britain.[8]

Shortly after the question of dividing the territory of Quebec into two colonies came before Parliament in the autumn of 1789, Simcoe (who was a member of the House of Commons at the time) wrote an appreciation of the new geopolitical

John Graves Simcoe
The first lieutenant-governor of Upper Canada was a professional soldier whose service during the American Revolution was in New Jersey, principally. In his analysis of what was needed in Upper Canada, John Graves Simcoe focused closely on the peninsula bounded by the Lakes Ontario, Erie, and Huron. He also determined the site he named "London" to be the focal point of this "minor continent."
Metropolitan Toronto Reference Library, T-18042.

situation of Canada, and some of the implications for British policy. Indeed, he referred back to an idea his own father (Captain John Simcoe, R.N.) had expressed in 1755 about the Montreal–Quebec part of the St. Lawrence: "with the assistance of a few Sluices [canals] it will become the centre of Communication between the Gulf of Mexico and Hudson's Bay, by an interior navigation." Simcoe (the son) noted two possible canal routes in this connection: from St. John's to La Prairie and "from Lake St. Clair to [Lake] Ontario," a clear indication that he was already focusing his thoughts on the southwestern peninsula.[9]

In his continuing evaluation of his anticipated responsibilities, Simcoe came to focus especially on the western portion of his new province as a key to achieving the imperial goals he identified. Some months before he left England to take up his post he had written to Henry Dundas, secretary of state

> I conceive the peninsula surrounded by the waters of the Great Lakes (a kind of lesser continent) to be the most favourable situation in nature for a British Colony. It is the Country in which Champlain, the founder of Canada, intended to have made great Establishments, but which has been since neglected except by the casual erection of a few Posts.

> The *future prospects,* This peninsular Country holds out is that proportionately as the surrounding Countries become populous, It will become the secure medium, as Holland is to Germany, of the most profitable Intercourse with all the Inhabitants between the Appalachian Mountains & the Mississippi.

> The *permanent prospect* of this Peninsula ever remaining subject to Great Britain arises also from its situation – There may be a distant period in which it may be possible that the Inhabitants on the Sea Coasts of Canada & on the River St. Lawrence shall conceive that an unrestrained Trade shall be more beneficial to them than a dependant connection with Great Britain but such can never be the Ideas of the Inhabitants of Upper Canada.[10]

Even earlier, in January of 1791, Simcoe had specified the exact focus of his territorial scheme as the region surrounding present-day London:

> For the purpose of commerce, union, and power, I propose that the site of the Colony should be in the great peninsula between the Lakes Huron, Erie, and Ontario, a spot destined by nature sooner or later to govern the interior world."[11]

In Simcoe's discourse at this time, the word "Colony" seems not to have denoted some vague and undelimited area of settlement and plantations, but to have been used consciously in the same sense as in the Roman Empire: a planned and compact community made up basically of retired, meritorious, professional soldiery, with their dependants and, of course, the apparatus of a government. Simcoe professed himself to be an admirer of the Roman style of managing an empire; the straight roads he later had opened through the forest in 1793 (including Dundas Street) had their conceptual origins in this same admiration. But in 1791 he intended to name this colony-settlement "Georgina" (rather than Londinium).[12]

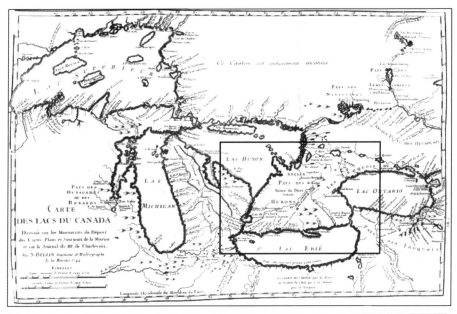

The Travels of Père Charlevoix

In 1720, under instruction from France, the Jesuit Pierre Francois X. de Charlevoix undertook a journey of inspection from Quebec to New Orleans via the Great Lakes. His report, published in 1744, includes maps by a leading cartographer, Nicolas Bellin. His map provides the earliest cartographic representation of the present Thames River, then known to the French as La Tranche. The existence of this river as depicted on Bellin's map, or on certain later maps, which borrowed from it, was to figure very centrally in John Graves Simcoe's analyses of the geopolitical situation he would have to deal with as lieutenant-governor of Upper Canada. From Histoire et description générale de la Nouvelle France

Arriving in North America late in that year, Simcoe of course brought with him the first-hand knowledge of Americans he had gained during his extensive field service fighting the American rebels,[13] and in addition he appears to have consulted whatever sources of information he could find in England. From entries in Mrs. Simcoe's diary it is clear that, in particular, an account of New France by the Jesuit Pierre Francois Xavier de Charlevoix (republished in English in 1761 and later) gave him the insights he needed to formulate his particular strategy.[14] With respect to the north-central shore of Lake Erie, Charlevoix had written:

> In every place where I landed, I was enchanted by the Beauty and Variety of a Landscape, bounded by the finest Forest in the World. Besides this, Water-Fowl swarmed everywhere: I cannot say there is such Plenty of Game in the Woods, but I know that on the South Shore there are vast herds of wild Cattle [buffalo].[15]

Accompanying the publication of Charlevoix's acount in 1744 was a map published by the French Geographer Royal, Nicolas Bellin, entitled *Carte des Lacs du Canada*. Prominently on this map, which cites Charlevoix's journal as a source, the position of the Thames River is closely approximated for the first time, without a name, but with the notation *"Riv. qu'on remonte 80 lieues sans trouver de Saults"* (a river which one can ascend for eighty leagues without encountering rapids) – a remark made in exactly those words by Charlevoix, though from hearsay, as he did not ascend the river himself. Information from this map quickly made its way into England, in a map published in 1747 by Emmanuel Bowen, and appeared in a simplified form in an English translation of Charlevoix's narrative in 1763.[16] Although it is not impossible that Simcoe could have read the French original, it seems more likely that he would have studied one of the English editions. Either way, he would have perceived, as a "tactical theorist" the utility of such a quick and unerring route to and from the Detroit area from the east.

In Quebec during the winter of 1791–1792, Simcoe sought more particular information about the waters and rivers around Toronto (then the name in use for the location), Long Point in Lake Erie, the Grand River, the La Tranche River (he renamed it the Thames in mid-1792 in his proclamation of the system of counties he delimited at that time) and the northeast side of Lake Huron (Georgian Bay). He was averse to fixing his capital as far east as Kingston, at the time the largest settlement above Montreal, since he perceived that the Detroit frontier was the most likely source of trouble.[17] He also came to believe that Montreal would be made the capital of a new province which would include the settlements along the St. Lawrence northeastwards of Kingston.

Shortly before finally leaving Quebec to take post in the territory of the newly proclaimed province, Simcoe again urged his idea of an interior capital, the site of which

> by what I can gather from the few people who have visited it will afford a safer, more certain, and, I am inclined to think by taking due advantage of the seasons, a less expensive route to Detroit than that of Niagara, and at the same time by the Grand River and other streams parallel to it, will have many communications to [Lake Erie].[18]

From Montreal, he wrote that he had found, in the surveyor's office, a map of the River La Tranche that confirmed his concepts:

I am happy to have found in the Surveyor's Office an actual Survey of the River *La Tranche*. It answers my most sanguine expectations & I have but little doubt but that its communication with the [Lakes] *Ontario & Erie* will be found to be very practicable[,] the whole forming a rout[e] which in *all* Respects may annihilate the political consequence of Niagara & Lake Erie.[19]

Simcoe made his temporary capital at Niagara-on-the-Lake during the summer of 1792, where he continued to gather intelligence about the state of affairs south and west of Lake Erie, especially the activities and intentions of various Indian nations, and the implications of these for the maintenance of British power at Detroit. And of course he sought more information about the topography of the southwestern peninsula. He had earlier in that year proclaimed the division of Upper Canada into counties as preparation for election of the first legislative assembly. Since there were so few man-made points of reference, he used natural features to describe the limits of the counties and ridings, for example: Suffolk County, occupying the central north shore of Lake Erie so glowingly described by Charlevoix, was defined as extending eastwards from the line of portage ("carrying place") between Point aux Pins (Rondeau) and the Thames to a line from the mouth of the Rivière Barbue (Catfish Creek) running north 16 degrees west to intersect the Thames and then back down the Thames to the first-mentioned carrying place.[20]

Simcoe's final choice for the site of London lay on the north or right bank of the east branch of the Thames as Simcoe then understood its course, and therefore would have lain outside the first county system, as it was proclaimed; this fact may account for the existence of plans showing a place he reserved for a townsite on the left or south bank at what is now called the Coves, which would have lain in Suffolk County. But as soon as Simcoe had made his pilgrimage along the Thames valley in 1793, and selected a site in or including the V of the forks and some of the right or north bank, he arranged for some 164 square miles north of the river to be purchased from the Indians, and this was blocked out into London Township.[21]

The first elections to Upper Canada's sixteen-seat legislature were held on the basis of Simcoe's county system in the summer of 1792. As a result Simcoe made the acquaintance of Lieutenant David William Smith (or Smyth) of the 5th Regiment (Northumberland Foot), who had been elected as the representative of the County of Essex, then encompassing the small French settlements across the river from Detroit and the Loyalists along the nearby shore of Lake Erie.[22] Simcoe was so impressed with Smith's abilities that he appointed him to fill the role of surveyor general of Upper Canada. As such, Smith became very much a part of further developing and implementing the grand design that Simcoe had adopted, and continued to further it even after Simcoe had returned to England in 1796.[23]

Another of Simcoe's close associates in these first years was his private secretary, Lieutenant Thomas Talbot, who lived *en famille* with the Simcoes and was of course privy to all the thoughts and concerns of his governor.[24] It is hardly necessary to particularize Talbot's later roles as a principal shaper of the settlement of the London District: he has been much written about. During the autumn and winter of 1792–1793, these two men must often have discussed with Simcoe his strategic plan for a "New London" as he was then calling his imagined "Colonia" in the forest.[25]

In order to induce habits of Civilization and
Obedience to just Governments and to cherish the
spirit of Loyalty to his Majesty, and attachment to
the British Nation; I remain still of my former
Opinion that the seat of Government should be
situated in the internal Part of the Colony, and by
no means be placed in a port on the Confines of
the Lakes—

It is apparent that there is no spot in Upper Canada
so central as to have a speedy and ready communication
with all parts of the Province; which may be considered
as confined between the Ottawa and French Rivers
and the Lakes; but it is equally evident that sooner or
later as population encreases, and circumstances shall
admit, it will be necessary for the purposes of public
convenience to make some further division of the
Canada's, and perhaps Montreal presents itself as
the Center of an intermediate Government ——— I beg
Sir, to state these Ideas, as in pursuance of them, they
lead to the propriety of establishing a Capital of

The Simcoe Dispatch of 1793

Simcoe's definitive recommendation to make the site he named London into the capital of the Province of Upper Canada was written on September 16, 1793, after he had personally explored both the Thames Valley trail to the Detroit frontier, and the overland route from Toronto to Georgian Bay.

Upper Canada; which may be somewhat distant from the center of the present Colony; were their no immediate motives or political Reasons that may render it ⌣⌣ expedient —

This Capital, I propose to be established at New London, as marked on the Map of The Thames —

There is also marked on the same Map, a situation at the Head of the carrying Place between Lake Ontario and the Thames called *Oxford*, as being a position likely to become a town; and another also, near the mouth of the River which has many advantages that may ⌣ make it the Capital of the lower District;.... This Place is called *Chatham*, to which, and for many miles the River is a perfect and safe Harbour; tho at its mouth there is a *Bar*, which possibly may ⌣⌣⌣ contribute as much to its defence, as it is takes off ⌣ from the conveniency of loaded Vessels entering the River —

It is to be observed that tho no accurate survey has been taken of the Country between Lake Erie and the River Thames; It is generally understood that their course

During these months, Simcoe encountered yet another and possibly even more cogent, because more immediate, reason for looking to a capital site well to the west of Lake Ontario, in addition to the larger one of projecting British power deep into the interior of North America. He had always been highly aware that a large part of his role would be in managing political relations with the Indian

David William Smith (Smyth)
David William Smith was closely associated with Simcoe as his surveyor-general, a position of critical importance to the implementation of Simcoe's strategic scheme. Smith was appointed to the executive council in 1796, the year Simcoe returned to England. He remained on the council for eight years and was the chief architect of the reconfiguration of the province's territorial units in 1800, which produced both Middlesex County and the London District. National Archives of Canada, C-116823

nations, to keep them on the side of the British and against the American states. A key group in this rather fluid situation was the politically astute confederation of the Six Nations of the Iroquois.

The Six Nations had both before and during the American Revolution occupied the territory immediately to the south of Lake Ontario, of which the Crown had guaranteed them perpetual occupancy under a treaty negotiated in 1768 at Fort Stanwix, and supported by the terms of the Quebec Act of 1774. Because of the geographical position of this extensive Six Nations tract astride major trade routes between the English ports on tidewater (via Albany and the Hudson River) and the basins of the interior Lakes and the Ohio River system, the Six Nations were able not only to benefit from the highly lucrative fur trade, much of which had to pass through territory they occupied or dominated, but were also as a consequence enabled to act as power brokers and intermediaries in the political relationships between the English of the Atlantic seaboard and the numerous but less well organized Indian nations of the deeper continental interior (see map I).

Having chosen an alliance with the Crown during the Revolution, the Six Nations found themselves on the losing side. The Crown had thus lost the power to make good on its promises of 1768 and 1774, but offered compensatory land in the large area it had managed to retain to the north of the lower Lakes. Two parcels were considered by the Iroquois confederacy: one a single township on the Bay of Quinte, amidst a fairly extensive settlement of Loyalists, the other on the Grand River, which emptied into Lake Erie west of the Niagara peninsula. Thayendanegea (Joseph Brant), their paramount leader, opted for the tract described as "six miles either side of the Grand River from its mouth to its source," and led the main part of his followers there, though a portion of the group did choose to settle at Deseronto on the Bay of Quinte.[26]

It is clear that Brant perceived the Grand River Tract as not just a place to subsist, but a geopolitical equivalent of his people's former territory: just west of the new main area of European settlement (the Lake Ontario basin) and astride the inland trade routes – the winter routes especially – between the entrepôts of both the St. Lawrence and the Hudson Valleys and the deep interior of the continent. As Simcoe explained to his superiors in 1793, his choice of London had two immediate objectives: first, to help "seperate [*sic*] and command the Indian nations." With reference to the area west of the Grand River tract he wrote:

> The circumstances of the Indian War have hitherto influenced the [Executive] Council not to encourage the peopling of a Country which, should the Six Nations become engaged, might become the War Path … [but establishing a powerful settlement to the west of the Grand River tract might] separate the Mohawks on the Grand River from the other Indian nations, and prevent what Captain Brant once intimated to me in a letter: 'the Six nations becoming a Barrier between the British and the Western Indians.'[27]

Second, Simcoe hoped to make this capital at London "the mart of all the Independent Indian Nations," and with some other settlements he designated along the line of route from Burlington Bay to Chatham, "will in a short time effectually add the influence of Command over all the Nations within British Territory."[28]

Simcoe's matured stratagem, then, had two components: to hinder the integration of the new American interior territory into their union, and to keep control over the Indian groups by a twofold policy of separate-and-rule plus commercial dependency. The extensive infrastructure he needed for this grand scheme was not to be realized in his own lifetime. He had argued that it was not only feasible but essential that the British depart from their hoary doctrine of clinging to coastal areas where influence might be best exerted and fractious colonial populations coerced by sea power. He had deprecated the site of Kingston as indefensible, especially in winter.[29] However, his own enthusiastic endorsement of the importance and defensibility of the harbour of Toronto (which he renamed York about August 1, 1793, in honour of a minor victory by the Duke of York in the war then in progress against the French) rather undermined his much-iterated case for London, and thus clearly played into the hands of the Colonial Office traditionalists who insisted that the first line of defence in Upper Canada must be gunboats. Writing in March 1794, Henry Dundas, the English secretary of state, concealed the iron of his final decision behind some velvety rhetoric

> I also agree with you [that] the place upon the River Thames which you have marked as the Scite for London, is well situated and judiciously chosen for the future Capital, but as the Defence of the Colony is the first object, if that Defence should be maritime, it follows that the settlement of York is the most important for the present [–] not as the future Capital, but as the chief place of strength and security for the Naval force of the Province – if to these [forces], the occupation of London was now to be added, it appears from your letter that they altogether would require a greater force than can be spared at this moment – and in the mean time, I see no objection in your taking any preparatory steps for that purpose [the occupying of the London site] the adoption of which do not require any immediate military force to be stationed there.[30]

In designating certain locations along the Thames as townsites (London, Woodstock, Dorchester, and Chatham), and in imposing upon the region a township survey framework keyed largely to his Roman-style road (Dundas Street) and the lower Thames River route, Simcoe and his surveyor general, David W. Smith, did at least manage to lay down the basic elements of the infrastructure necessary to reach those larger geopolitical objectives that he had identified. His general idea of an east-west trunk road was confirmed by the Executive Council of the province in 1799,[31] after Simcoe had left Upper Canada for good, although in detail the route followed by the road commissioners later appointed under this policy (hence the present local street name "Commissioners' Road") did not pass through the exact sites of either Woodstock (which Simcoe had designated Oxford) or London. Dundas Street, along which London and Oxford were sited, had included some very poorly drained and difficult woodland sections; the established road followed much better drained and easily improved alignments.

What might London have been like as a community had Simcoe's wish come to fulfilment during his own tour of duty? Perhaps the experience of Cincinnati might provide a hint or two. Fort Washington was built at that location in 1789 by the United States, for reasons closely similar to those Simcoe had in mind in selecting London, though the current relationships with most of the nearby Indian nations were definitely hostile. The village next to the fort exhibited the character of all such garrison communities since time (or at least civilization) began:

While only a little town of several hundred people and makeshift cabins surrounding Fort Washington, Cincinnati had a disproportionately large number of taverns, warehouses, and trading posts. Its population also was heterogeneous and transient, ranging from women following the army to peaceful Indians seeking to exchange furs for goods...Soldiers found amusement and relaxation in heavy drinking, gambling, and petty quarrels...the army set the character of the entire town; idleness predominated and almost all the lawyers were confirmed 'sots.'"[32]

It may seriously be doubted whether, situated so far in the van of the European advance into North America, London would have been a much more salubrious place than Cincinnati, in the 1790s at least, even allowing for the calming influence of Simcoe's intended colonial aristocracy (this never worked out) and the gentlemanly manners of the officers of the proposed garrison of imperial troops.

The creation of the London District by a statute of 1798 (effective January 1, 1800) may not have been at the direct orders of Simcoe, who had returned to England two years earlier; but it was certainly brought about as a result of great confusion in local affairs which resulted from his creation of three independently defined layers of internal divisions: townships (as survey and property-description units), counties (as land registration, legislative representation, and militia units), and districts (as judicial units with the most important powers of local government).

All County lines divide Townships, and all District lines divide Counties and Townships. The consequence is, that some Counties being in two Districts, and several Townships in two Counties and separate Districts, they are neither assessed nor enrolled [in militia units] to the great hindrance of a due organization of the Province.[33]

To tidy up this confusion, the provincial executive determined on a policy, which has been followed ever since with almost total rigour, of making all higher-level units conform to the boundaries of the townships they include. The new arrangement of districts and counties made express allowance for Simcoe's plan:

The head of the Navigation of the River Thames, and the confluence of its two principal Branches, are two of three points which I have already had the Honor to observe naturally present themselves as points of rendezvous and consequently as places for the transaction of public business, both were accordingly long ago selected by His Excellency the Lieutenant Governor for the Sites of Towns[:] to that at the former he gave the name of Oxford, – to that at the latter he gave the name of London – In forming the present Arrangement therefore, care was taken to distribute the Townships which lie near those places in such a manner as it was conceived would best promote His Excellency's intentions.[34]

At its inception the huge new London District extended from six miles (9.6 km) west of the Grand River to near present-day Bothwell, and from Lake Erie north to Lake Huron and part of Georgian Bay, but included only a handful of settlers scraping a living near Long Point, plus a very few more along the line of Dundas Street and on the lower Thames; and these comprised *all* the European residents of this large area. No one lived nearer than the Delaware Mills to the site designated "London." The choice of the same name for the new district, as well as the designation of a new "Middlesex" county within it, must almost certainly be taken as strong indications that Simcoe's strategy for the western part of his domain was being kept alive by his successors in the provincial administration, no doubt chiefly by D.W. Smith, but also perhaps by Peter Russell, Simcoe's finance expert, who took over the administration after Simcoe's departure.

It seems furthermore pretty certain that Thomas Talbot, who as private secretary from 1791 through 1794 had been in Simcoe's confidence, was himself following this strategy when he selected the central north shore of Lake Erie as the place for the grand scheme of colonization he began in 1803, and especially in his reaching inland towards the site of London, as well as eastwards and westwards parallel to the Erie shore. Talbot would certainly have known of Henry Dundas's decision to make York the *temporary* capital of the province, and would have been familiar with Simcoe's own considered assessment of the region, written a decade earlier in 1793, but consciously or unconsciously echoing Charlevoix:

> The tract of Country which lies between this river (or rather navigable Canal, as its Indian name and French translation import) and Lake Erie, is one of the finest for all agricultural purposes in North America, and far exceeds the Soil or Climate of the Atlantic States. There are few or no interjacent swamps, and a variety of useful streams empty themselves into the lake or River.[35]

II. THE LOCATION OF THE LONDON DISTRICT SEAT, 1825–1826

A quarter of a century after the London District (1800) began functioning, Simcoe's designated capital site, for so long only an idea, became a reality. The reason, or more properly the occasion, for moving the district offices to the forks of the Thames from the older settlement near Long Point, was the accidental burning of the district court house erected at Vittoria in 1816.[36] Explanations for this change also refer to political pressure by the numerous settlers who had taken up land in the interior of the peninsula, to influence exerted for his own benefit by Colonel Thomas Talbot, and to the general desire of the government to place its local institutions at a greater reach from marauding Americans than was the case during the War of 1812.[37]

All these reasons are probably valid; but are they *sufficient*, especially to explain why the executive moved on the matter with what for the age was almost indecent haste? It is certainly true that by 1825 the four townships of London, Westminster, Dunwich, and Yarmouth comprised the largest concentration of settlement in the London District (4,980 persons) exceeding the total of the whole of Norfolk County as it was then constituted (4,472 in nine townships).[38] These western residents had had to struggle along some 120 kilometres (75 miles) of bush roads to near Turkey Point in order to participate in the processes of justice; as a result they let go many issues of small debt and trespass, to mention only two kinds of common cases. Providing a location for regular courts of justice in their midst would therefore have been entirely consistent with the principle of 1798 "that none of His Majesty's subjects in this Province will be at a greater distance from the place to which the discharge of his public duties calls him than an easy day's journey."[39]

Norfolk County, the constituency that included Vittoria, had tended to be politically radical, produced many defectors during the War of 1812, and was to see more violence in the 1837 and 1838 uprisings. In the mid-1820s that riding may well have lacked favour in government circles to offset that enjoyed by the more westerly settlers of the London District, and the influence that Talbot might exercise with the executive council. And certainly increases of settlement generally, as well as in his particular domains, would have benefited Talbot financially; but his settlement scheme was already of less interest to the government than it had been, and he was shortly to have a major corporate rival, the Canada Company, in his own backyard, as it were.

Even before the war, the executive was trying to promote inland settlement in the vicinity of the Thames: Simon Z. Watson was given permission in 1810 (the same year as the road commissioners designated their line of east-west road) to lay out two concessions of Westminster Township for settlers coming from Lower Canada; and in 1811 Mahlon Burwell was instructed to "run a line for a Road through Westminster to join Colonel Talbot's Road as the ground may best suit."[40]

In 1818 London Township itself was at last opened up, no doubt as a consequence of the new roads laid out connecting it with Lake Erie and the eastern settlements; in the next few years its population rose rapidly to over 900 in 1823.[41] In the meantime, the wilderness tract to the west of London known as the Long Woods was purchased and the trail along the Thames west of Delaware began to be improved.[42]

By 1825, then, the site of London was entirely surrounded by areas undergoing settlement and serviced by tolerable roads—and most of the decisions that brought about these conditions, so necessary to the viability of any prospective town, were made by the executive council of the province, rather than through the independent operation of local interests. All these facts constitute circumstantial evidence that there was more behind the decision to start the town of London than provincial internal politics, patronage and the pork barrel. It is not merely an interesting coincidence, therefore, that just at this time, a high-level military commission was touring Upper Canada on a mission from the War Office, to assess the defence problems and capabilities of the province; and it is certain that the executive would have been briefed by the members of the commission while they were on the ground that year.

As a result of the War of 1812, the gunboat defence of the earlier period had been discredited.[43] In the immediate aftermath, a naval mission under Commodore W.F.W. Owen was sent to survey the shores of the lower lakes (one of Owen's officers, Lieutenant Henry Bayfield, continued his meticulous work in the upper lakes over the next fifteen years). One of the outcomes of the Owen survey was the realization that the mouth of Kettle Creek, though far from perfect, was the best location along the central north shore of Lake Erie for a harbour of refuge. In the later 1820s this notion was given effect by the provision of physical infrastructure and the appointment of a port collector of customs. It was named Port Stanley in 1828.[44]

Land defences were subjected to a separate review. Under the instructions of the Duke of Wellington, master-general of the ordnance, a commission of three officers led by Lieutenant-General Sir James Carmichael Smyth was dispatched to British North America early in 1825 with a remit to examine the defensive capabilities and shortcomings of British possessions from the Atlantic to Sault Ste. Marie. The documents submitted to the Duke by this commission included a précis of the military actions and outcomes in Canada from 1755 to 1814. In his comments on the last of these wars, and specifically on the ultimate failure of British arms on the Detroit frontier, Smyth wrote:

> Had the British troops had a fortress on the Thames containing a sufficient supply of provisions and ammunition to which they could have retired, the Americans would not have been able (notwith-standing [*sic*] their command of Lake Erie) to have over-run the district of the Thames. The British kept the field sufficiently long to have prevented the enemy from laying siege to any fortress during that [1813] season. The contest in the Amherstburg district would, consequently, not have been concluded in 1813; and the Americans would have been foiled in the only operation in which they were successful. These considerations, added to the beauty and fertility of the country; the loyalty and good disposition of its inhabitants; and the facilities it will, hereafter, afford for an invasion by the Thames, seem to point to the propriety of placing a respectable work, capable of serving as a point d'appui to the troops and militia of the district, upon this river.[45]

The Smyth commission appears to have had the site of Chatham more in mind than the then non-existent London, as evidenced by the following extract from the report itself:

> The object of the fortification of Amherstburg with the island of Bois Blanc being more with a view to prevent the uncontrolled communication enjoyed by the Americans between Lakes Erie & Huron than for the maintenance of His Majesty's authority in this part of Canada, which would be more effectually secured by the construction of the proposed work at Chatham.[46]

The Duke of Wellington, in transmitting the Smyth report to the secretary of state, Earl Bathurst, basically reiterated (though certainly without knowing it) Simcoe's appreciation of the importance of Canada:

> In considering this subject I entreat your Lordship to observe that it is impossible for his Majesty's government to withdraw from these dominions. Whether valuable or otherwise, which can scarcely be a question, they must be defended in war; and an attentive perusal of this Report will show what it is necessary should be done beforehand, and in time of peace, to enable his Majesty to defend these dominions at the least possible burden to the resources of the empire in time of war.[47]

Although nothing is said directly in Smyth's report about London (fortresses are proposed at Chatham and on the "Ouse" or Grand River at the site of present-day Cayuga), it took note of the possibility of joining the Thames with the Ouse (Grand) by a canal, using Hornor's and Cedar Creeks, "as they form a valley extending from Oxford [Woodstock] (i.e., nearly parallel to Dundas Street) as far as the Mohawk Village on the Ouse" – (near enough, to Brant's ford). Clearly, since the gunboat defence had been discredited, the Thames routeway as conceived by Simcoe was still perceived as a valuable military asset.

The commissioners' conclusion on this last point was that the military value of a canal would not justify the expense. But it is curious that not long after this date, an unusual concentration of retired (half-pay) British officers, including an admiral and several colonels, took up land along this very tract, in Oxford and Blandford townships especially, and tried to get such a canal built.[48]

Despite the early running of the line of Dundas Street, much of it remained unopened for some years. The main (Commissioners') road west from Lake Ontario, which followed Hornor's (or Whiteman's) Creek westwards from near Brant's ford through the Burford plains, passing south of the site of Woodstock, thence keeping to the south flank of the Thames valley through to Delaware, continued as the main thoroughfare. In the early 1820s, stagecoach communication along this line had begun, if sporadically at the outset; the uncleared site of London was at least less isolated from, if as yet hardly well connected to, the provincial power base on Lake Ontario.[49] All these reasons point to the logic of making London a point of defence organization, if not a fortress as such. But why was it expedient to make it a judicial centre into the bargain?

While the military analyses just discussed were essentially retrospective, a major transport innovation was about to effect truly revolutionary changes in the economic situation of the so-called "American north coast," and to a much lesser extent, of southwestern Upper Canada. The Erie Canal, opened in 1825 to link the east end of Lake Erie with the tidewater ports of the Hudson River and Buffalo, dramatically lowered the transport charges – for both outbound produce and inbound immigrants – to a small fraction of what they had been by roads, and became the gateway to continuous navigation throughout the Great Lakes. The riparian states from New York to Minnesota have never looked back. But, shackled by the British shipping laws and their United States equivalents, Upper Canada failed to see anything like as much relative development; in fact, many settlers who had come to Upper Canada moved on to the new lands even across the Mississippi.[50]

The Welland Canal, connecting Lakes Erie and Ontario, was begun the same year the Erie Canal was opened, though it was on a much smaller scale and could be hardly more than a palliative. Nevertheless, the creek-mouth harbours along the Erie north shore began to look commercially more attractive; as early as 1824 Thomas Talbot was promoting legislation for improvements at the mouth of Kettle Creek (Port Stanley), and the Burwells were not far behind this with respect to the mouth of Otter Creek, which unsurprisingly became known as Port Burwell.[51]

In the same year, 1825, the Canada Land and Colonization Company was under formation in London, England, to purchase the extensive reserved lands from the Crown and place *bona fide* settlers on them; in 1826 it obtained a charter to purchase all Crown reserves, plus a block of one million acres on Lake Huron in lieu of Clergy reserve lands upon which no agreement could be reached.[52] The Crown reserves, which had been available for sale or lease, but without many takers, were to be found in almost every surveyed township throughout the entire province; naturally these had been sold or granted least extensively in the less settled townships, many of which were at that time to be found west of Hamilton. And with the huge Huron Tract, which began at the northern line of London Township, it must have been obvious that a great part of the Canada Company's land sales would be in the southwestern peninsula, though not at first concentrated along the Huron shore.

The need for additional facilities of government in the peninsula, especially the courts, registries, and land offices, clearly would soon become pressing from this source alone, if the Company's undertaking to bring in tens of thousands of immigrants was to be believed (in fact, they did). But even allowing for the already quite large population near and south of London, merely dividing the large London District was not at that time feasible, since the major officials – sheriff, judge, clerk of the peace, and, if a new county were involved, registrar – depended on fees for their incomes. Therefore unless and until the "case load" could be built up to a respectable level, it would have been seen as impracticable to create a new district surrounding the Town of London, since the old-populated London District core around the Long Point settlement would not on its own have been able to supply reliable fee-income sufficient to support the public officials in an era of rising wealth and expectations.

Had the courthouse at Vittoria not burned down so very conveniently in late 1825, then, settlement and economic development in the middle belt of the London District would have gone ahead anyway, under both Talbot's scheme and that of the Canada Company, but also as a reflection of the rapid growth in the adjacent United States. The "bridge" role of the southwestern peninsula became increasingly evident as migrating families from the eastern United States creaked along the main road in their wagons from Niagara by way of Hamilton as a short cut to Michigan.[53] There would inevitably have arisen a movement centred in that middle belt of the London District to separate from the older Long Point core area – though it is not at all certain that the exact site of London would necessarily have been the *popular* choice for the location of the district offices.

Of course, the legislation brought in by the government specified the forks of the Thames as the site.[54] And Thomas Talbot was, it seems, completely in favour of that location. As chairman of the commission charged under the act with arranging for the location and construction of the new courthouse and jail, he might well have sought to reverse or modify the directive so as more to benefit his particular domain closer to Lake Erie. But he did no such thing, reporting that the commission considered that "The situation in every respect eligible for the Town, is immediately in the Fork ... the ground is high, and there are excellent springs of water." He even asked for the privilege of selecting the exact spot for the courthouse: if His Excellency the lieutenant-governor "should see fit to leave the selection of the spot for the Court House to my judgment, I will do the best I can."[55]

Talbot indeed had his way. His surveyor, Mahlon Burwell, described the spot he had selected in the following terms:

> The most eligible and beautiful scite for the necessary tract is lots nos. 21, 22, 23, & 24 on the south side of Dundas Street, and extending to the first street to the southward of it, making together four acres – and the best situation for the building is near the centre of the block – from whence there is a fine view of the River and its flats below the Forks, and of the North Branch to a great extent, and will be as fine a view of the East Branch (as far as the sudden bend you will observe in the map) as soon as the heavy timber with which the ground is covered shall be cleared away. The Bank along the Block just described is about fifty feet perpendicular height above the Surface of the River, and the width of the slope is represented on the map.[56]

One can easily imagine that it gave Talbot a good deal of satisfaction to see the implementation (the "end of the beginning" at least) of Simcoe's scheme for the organization of peninsular Upper Canada to which he had been privy a third of a century earlier, and which must have been a major part of his own considerations when he founded Port Talbot to begin his scheme of colonization in 1803. Like a great many of the provincial elite of the day he had been a professional soldier, and understood the tactical needs of defence; Burwell's description of Talbot's site

Thomas Talbot
As private secretary to Simcoe from 1791 to 1794, Talbot was thoroughly familiar with Simcoe's strategic scheme. His selection of the north-central sector of Lake Erie for his own settlement programme in 1803 is demonstrably consistent with what he had learned a decade earlier while resident in the Simcoe household. So, too, was his selection in 1826 of the place for the new courthouse of the London District, which was the same spot as that chosen by Simcoe in 1793. University of Western Ontario

for the courthouse indeed reads very much like a military appreciation of the location of a strong point, emphasizing lines of sight and of fire across and along the moat-like obstacle provided by the converging streams.

Interestingly, the eccentric member of the Legislative Assembly for Middlesex County, John Matthews, who seems ordinarily to have opposed whatever the local élite was up to, endorsed the site selection, though well after the fact, as an eminently defensible site, "as a military position, and depot for stores and ammunition." He further argued that a canal joining Lakes Erie and Huron through that locality "would not only make it the emporium of that part of the Province, but also a most important *point d'appui*, and would greatly add to its general facilities for defence." The terminology in this letter, as well as its date late in 1826, makes it very probable that Matthews had read the Carmichael Smyth report, which as a former gunner he would have understood very well.[57]

It is thus very much in the context of the strategic thinking exemplified by the military reports, the thrust of which must also have been known to Talbot as a sometime professional soldier, a legislative councillor and a local commander of militia, that the anomalous nature of the architecture of the London courthouse must be sought: an easily fortifiable "keep" on the best tactical site, facing the most probable direction of hostile approach (the front entrance was at first on the west), and with a supply route (Dundas Street) almost to the (then) back door.[58]

COUNTY COURT HOUSE, LONDON.

The London District Court House and Gaol
Unlike every other formal courthouse built in Upper Canada before or since, this structure looks like a fortress, a defensive structure, and was built in 1826 on a site which was the best available tactical position for both strategic and local defence. Perhaps the style was chosen, in part, from some antiquarian Irish impulse on the part of Thomas Talbot, chairman of the building commission. But, like Simcoe, Talbot had been a professional soldier, and would have drawn inspiration from his military background.

Overall, and allowing for the sheer difficulty of finding bullet-proof materials at the time, this must be seen as first and foremost a building of severe and timeless military utility, and only secondarily as an expression of a new age of romantic revivals. The London District Court House could hardly contrast more strongly in style with those other district (now county) court houses built in the same general period, such as that of the Ottawa District at L'Orignal (1825) and of the Prince Edward District at Picton (1832–1837); both of these neoclassical structures well exemplify Alan Gowans's concept of the "horizontality" preferred in Georgian official architecture, as symbolizing the stability and legitimacy of received authority rather than transcendent flights of Gothic fancy.[59]

III. THE GARRISON FINALLY ARRIVES, 1838

It took a tuppenny-ha'penny rebellion, forty-five years after Simcoe had formally requested a garrison for his intended capital, before a contingent of imperial troops finally arrived to take station. The vulnerability of coastal positions around the peninsula had been well demonstrated by the American raids during the War of 1812. Subsequently, armed vessels had been eliminated from the lakes under the Rush-Bagot agreement of 1818 and the British continued their reluctance to provoke the always touchy Americans by any such moves as stationing regular troops so far west.[60] The Rebellions of 1837–1838 were, however, only one aspect of a much longer-drawn-out period of tension with the United States. In fact, the idea was advanced that the extensive involvement of Americans in that crisis, and their armed aggression, constituted sufficient excuse for the stationing of troops and building of defensive works in the southwestern peninsula without risking a war on that point alone.[61]

The activities of sympathizers to the rebel-radical cause of William Lyon Mackenzie and his cohorts, which led to armed violence along the Detroit border area, continued after the main crisis. Threats from secret societies in the United States, the "Hunters' Lodges," to carry out renewed incursions against Upper Canada, were taken very seriously by the administration in Canada. London, in 1837–1838, the only established district seat west of Kingston that was not on navigable water, was not merely the best but the only choice in the southwestern peninsula for a garrison establishment. The defensive strategy chosen by the government of the day included establishing a line of posts "all along the frontier," from Lancaster (at the Lower Canada boundary) to Sandwich (the seat of the Western District, now a section of Windsor), as ordered in May 1839 by Sir John Colborne.[62]

By the early 1840s the British had 20,000 regular troops in British North America. London's place in this scheme was to house and sustain a substantial force of regular infantry, with some artillery, to be deployed against any invasion from the west or from a lakeshore, with at first a detachment and a blockhouse in Chatham, thus essentially fulfilling the prescription of the Carmichael Smyth report.

> By the arrangement we shall expose a small front to the temptation of desertion; while at the same time we should be able to bring 500 men against the Brigands or Rebels, in a few hours, or days[,] at any point they may be inclined to try their fortune.[63]

Locally raised militia units were stationed right at the trouble spots at Sandwich and Amherstburg to provide the piquets, the trip-wires, so to speak. These troops, though much inferior in battle training and discipline to the imperial units, were seen to have the advantage of acting in defence of their own homes, families, and property. As Smyth's words, quoted above, show, it was well understood that to station imperial troops right at the interface with the United States was to invite large-scale desertion and demoralization, from the exposure of the soldiers to the propaganda of popular democracy if not also to the blandishments of American crimps.

The overall geopolitical situation of the southwest peninsula remained unchanged from the British perspective: providing a forward position thrusting into the United States' northern flank and a zone of defence in depth for the heartland of British North America. But the regional context had changed dramatically in detail by 1838 from what it had been in 1793, and even notably from that of 1825 (see map II). The entire area of the old Northwest Territory had been divided into five parts: four full states plus the rapidly developing Wisconsin Territory. These riparian states in 1840 held a population of about three million, half of them in Ohio, while Upper Canada that year contained only some 450,000; Michigan had been admitted to the Union only in 1837, with a population of some 175,000, but in a great boom. Everywhere around the American shores of the lower lakes, rapid progress in settlement and in commerce had followed upon the opening of the Erie Canal, but as noted not much of this was rubbing off on Upper Canada, owing to the restrictive British trade laws. By this date, a number of other canals joining Lake Erie with the Ohio River and Lake Michigan with the Mississippi River were in place or in contemplation.

Even more significantly, the first railroads had begun operating in the United States, as well as one short line in Lower Canada. The state of Michigan passed internal improvement legislation immediately after becoming a state early in 1837, and as a result two lines of railroad had begun actual operations by the spring of 1838.[64] Steamboat traffic along and across the Detroit and St. Clair Rivers was frequent; and, indeed, one Canadian boat, the *Thames,* serviced the river after which it was named as far up as Chatham between 1833 and 1838, when it was burned at its moorings at Sandwich on the Detroit River during an armed incursion from the United States early in that year.[65]

These years saw the height of Jacksonian democracy in the United States: all adult white males had the vote, rapid expansionism was the chief value of the day, and competition for new lands was fierce at all levels from the predatory promoter down to the pushy pioneer. Aggressive rhetoric was the normal idiom of political discourse, turning for example on the issues of Mexican intransigence over Texas and revenge for the humiliating loss of the Alamo. Anti-British sentiment was very much a part of this syndrome, sustained beyond 1838 by two major unresolved boundary issues between the United States and British North America, as it then was.[66]

First, the long-standing dispute over the boundary location between Maine and Lower Canada was creating various troubles and violence in the upper Saint John and Connecticut Valleys.[67] Second, the Oregon boundary quarrel, in which the United States claimed all the Pacific coastline between the northern limit of Mexican California and the southern extremity of Russian-controlled Alaska, produced the famous bellicose slogan of the 1844 presidential election: "Fifty-four forty or fight." The eastern boundary issue was not finally settled politically until 1843, and the Oregon question not until 1846; such pretexts for inflaming popular sentiment for war greatly worried the civil and military administration of British North America. The splendid fortifications in Kingston, which served as capital of United Canada between 1841 and 1844, resulted from this period of tension.[68]

Once again the British government was required to reassess the role of Canada, and particularly Upper Canada, in imperial affairs. The Duke of Wellington no longer had the dominating influence he once held, as the government in the later 1830s was composed of reforming Whigs, who depended, for support of their legislation, on a yet more radical clutch of members of Parliament. Even before the 1837 outbreaks, voices had been raised advocating, on economic grounds, the termination of imperial interest in Canada, and these

Map II. *The Trans-Allegheny Interior, 1835–1845.*
The pattern of road and water navigation improvements in Upper Canada after 1838, and especially after the Union of the Canadas in 1841, were developed along the lines promoted by Simcoe. On this map the post routes are shown for Upper Canada and for the United States west of Pennsylvania as in the late 1830s, as well as the railroads operating in 1840, and the Erie Canal. For each state or province, and selected cities and towns, populations are shown. Numbers in parentheses indicate the growth experienced in the following decade for these units as a percentage of that poopulation.

became rather strident at the prospect of even more British money being spent to quell the revolt.[69] But the Whigs in power, though much interested in reform of all kinds – they had already effected drastic reforms in the parliamentary representation, the poor laws, and municipal government, and had brought about the abolition of slavery – were still staunch imperialists.

Charles Buller, one of the more outspoken parliamentary radicals, represented a considerable school of thought when he argued strongly in the House for the retention of colonies, in large part as a relief valve for the surplus population of Britain.[70] Buller served as secretary to Lord Durham on the famous mission to Canada in 1838, and the influential report that came out of that mission was strongly coloured by such radical ideas. The idea of shifting large numbers of surplus British population to settler colonies was very attractive to the government of the day, which was faced with a massive problem of growing poverty in industrializing Britain. "Systematic colonization" therefore became part of the general colonial policy of British governments from the late 1830s.[71]

The politician (not, for a change, a general) sent out in 1839 as governor general to effect union of the Canadas became especially enthusiastic about Upper Canada as a field for emigrant settlement. Charles Poulett Thomson made a rapid swing around the western division of his province in the summer of 1840 to whip up political support for his government, visiting most of the settled areas of the peninsula. On his return, he found that he had been created Baron Sydenham and Toronto. He voiced great optimism about both the people he met and the resources of the land:

> I am delighted to have seen this part of the country; I mean the great district, nearly as large as Ireland, placed between the three lakes – Erie, Ontario, and Huron. You can conceive nothing finer! The most magnificent soil in the world – four feet of vegetable mould – a climate certainly the best in North America – the greater part of it admirably watered. In a word, there is land enough and capabilities enough for some millions of people, and for one of the finest provinces in the world.[72]

The geopolitical significance of peninsular Ontario was of course also evaluated by those Whigs closely involved with the Canada question. Sydenham, who had been in the cabinet as president of the Board of Trade, was referring to the expected results of the major navigation improvements planned for the St. Lawrence system as well as to the massive migration he expected would be coming into peninsular Upper Canada, when he wrote that

> in two to three years we shall have a good hold on the vastly increasing western States by their interest thro' the St. Lawrence, indeed we have some now. The Eastern seaboard is certainly with us, and the South have their cotton interest as well as their slave fears, so that I really anticipate no cause for alarm of war thro' the ambition or restlessness of the people.[73]

In his anticipation of the extension of British influence through commercial routeways and infrastructure, Sydenham reprises one of the precepts of John Graves Simcoe. It is remotely possible that he knew at least the gist of the latter's dispatches of the 1790s; the undersecretary of the Colonial Office at the time,

James Stephen, who would have briefed Sydenham on his taking up the post in late summer 1839, was extremely well informed about the history of the policies of that office. Be that as it may, Sydenham's comment may safely be taken to indicate continuity in British geopolitical perceptions of central North America. Relationships with the Americans were not to be quite as calm as he so blithely expected, however, and the soldiers remained on station.

Meanwhile London-in-the-bush had developed in important ways, but its growth in numerical terms was slow at first, even though the fact that the courts for the district were held "on the Plot" as early as 1827, despite the difficulties of accommodation.[74] The Township of London holds the honour of having held the first governmental session in the new town: its annual meeting of ratepayers (called the "Town Meeting" without any urban connotation) met in the temporary courthouse on January 1, 1827, and in the following two years.[75] London's status as a district seat led inevitably to its becoming a centre for capital accumulation, even without a garrison, since the four sessions of court per year drew people and money from all over the district as jurymen, witnesses and suitors – and, of course, as consumers. At its first official mention in the district census in 1833, the town's population was 603.[76] In 1836 it was demonstrated to have 1,037 souls, and at the following year's election gained its own member of the Legislative Assembly, under a law of 1820 providing that a town which was the seat of the sessions courts would qualify as a constituency once it reached a population of 1,000.[77] In that year, out of the thousand-odd residents, there would have been a few dozen voters at best, under the electoral laws requiring specially high property qualifications for the vote. In fact, only sixty-four votes were cast.[78]

Perhaps London might have grown faster had it been possible to assemble all the officials normally present in district seats right away; though they travelled to the site for court sittings, it proved not so simple to get the functionaries to relocate their residences (and their land and business interests) to the parvenu town. John B. Askin, who as clerk of the peace was the district's chief administrative officer under the system prevailing before 1842, remained domiciled in Woodhouse Township until 1832. The district treasurer, John Harris, delayed his move until 1834, and then relocated amidst hints of official sanctions against him.[79] The sheriff, Abraham Rapelje, finding there was no law that compelled him to move his office to the district seat, reported in August 1833 that he intended to do so; meanwhile he had "a Bailiff stationed in London to attend to the necessary business of my office."[80] The district judge and the registrar of the surrogate court both refused to move before 1837, when they were absolved from doing so by the separation of Norfolk County to become the Talbot District. The judge, James Mitchell, responded to the complaints of some barristers by arguing that spending four months a year in London was a sufficient discharge for duties that paid him only £100 a year. The government was prepared to respect his seniority by appointing an associate judge for the district, providing that the latter would undertake to keep his residence in London.[81]

In 1836 there began thrice yearly Free Fairs, which the Agricultural Society of the London District (President, John B. Askin) sponsored under letters-patent of the province.[82] The grammar school, which each district was entitled to have, could only be pried out of the Norfolk area by special legislative act in 1837.[83] But one of the most significant legal institutions in a pioneer community, the land title register, resisted such centralization the longest of all. The registrarship for Middlesex County (which at first comprised only the Lake Erie townships) had been bestowed upon Mahlon Burwell under Talbot's patronage in 1809, and he stubbornly retained the registry at his home near Fingal in Southwold Township, despite strong representations from the legal profession of London, until he was forced to give it up under legislation in 1843. And then it was one of his sons, Hercules Burwell, who received the appointment.[84]

IV. THE INCORPORATIONS OF LONDON 1840–1855

By 1838, then, London had everything – or almost everything – that Simcoe would have expected of a capital, though of course at the less prestigious level of the district rather than the province. In that year its population had slipped in the aftermath of the rebellion to just under 800, but swiftly rebounded to some 1,400 in 1839, to 1,716 in 1840, and to over 2,000 in 1841.[85] Keeping peace and order in such a town was no longer a simple matter of the district magistrates' unsystematic efforts. If we can imagine what Cincinnati was like in 1789 – a frontier garrison town in the wilderness – then we can understand the kinds of pressures the authorities of London had to cope with, even allowing for a more civilized state of society, including the large population of established farmers and farm workers now surrounding the town, and the constant traffic that passed through or nearby as the settlement system continued to expand. In 1841 the rural population of Middlesex County alone (the present Middlesex and Elgin Counties, more or less) stood at well over 21,000, not including the town (2,078), a gain of some 150 percent from 1825, when the same area contained only 8,750 persons.[86]

The resident district officials and their immediate employees, plus a few professionals, merchants, mill-owners, and entrepreneurial land-proprietors, constituted together an urban élite class, which had a double vested interest in the well-being and prosperity of their community – rather like a pocket version of the famous Family Compact that ran the province earlier in the century. Those who came to take up official positions in the first place became investors and entrepreneurs as well; while the professionals, merchants and landed proprietors were awarded official positions such as postmaster, justice of the peace, coroner, militia officer, special commissioner, and collector of customs.[87] The more the region prospered, the higher would be both the profits of the capitalists and the fee-incomes of the officials. Therefore, the local conditions that secured and enhanced property values and merchants' turnover, and thereby encouraged new residents and new investment, were of vital interest to this combined group. The earlier nineteenth century had not arrived at the modern concept of "conflict of interest," which requires public officials to be personally financially disinterested in the creation of wealth in their own communities.

The three incorporations of London, effective in 1840, 1848, and 1855, can therefore be seen as progressive moves by this urban élite, to take advantage of the changing political and legislative context in the province, to establish the fullest possible municipal autonomy for their growing community and, of course, thereby to enhance the creation of wealth. Incorporated status for London in 1840 under a board of police provided some urgently needed special safeguards, for the protection of citizens and their property: such as a fire engine (with fire-prevention rules), health and sanitation regulations, a town market building and market regulations including the prevention of forestalling (price gouging), inspection of weights and measures, and the "assize of bread" (ensuring full weight), and most important, street improvement.[88] This last still had to be done in large part by the direct physical contribution (statute labour) of those inhabitants who could not or would not pay a "fine" or money commutation in lieu; this system, though anciently established, was always very awkward to administer.

The five-man Board of Police (four of them elected directly) required a property qualification of moderately high value – £40 – to be a member of the Board; the voting franchise was placed at the provincial urban norm of £5. The board had considerable freedom to make local rules and levy a tax on the property owners, and to organize and carry out local improvements within their fiscal limitations. The control of criminal behaviour, however, remained in the hands of the existing justices of the peace; presumably lawlessness and disorder were not yet such as to require a paid magistrate. Nevertheless, the presence of a Board of Police must have greatly moderated the boisterousness of the rapidly growing garrison town and political centre.

A good deal of London's growth during the 1840s was derived from the major road improvements that eased the difficulties of inland communication between London and Hamilton to the east, London and Port Stanley to the south (increasingly a gateway for migrants into the London District), and to the United States boundary points to the west. These road improvements were carried out under the oversight of the Board of Ordnance by the Board of [Public] Works, and as well as their obvious domestic and commercial role, formed part of the general improvement in the military preparedness of the province. Perhaps the greatest stimulus of all, if a somewhat indirect one for inland London, was the rebuilding of the Welland Canal, at long last bringing commercial activity on a relatively large scale to the Lake Erie shores of Upper Canada. Port Stanley was considerably upgraded as the preferred supply conduit to the garrison; in mid-decade it was assigned a resident emigrant-agent to facilitate the growing stream of new settlers into the interior of the peninsula.[89]

In the decade of the 1840s, the whole province grew under the stimulus of massive, mostly British immigration, from a total of 455,000 in 1841 to over 950,000 in 1851, a growth rate of 109 percent. London plus its two adjoining townships, an area which we might term with some diffidence "Greater London," slightly bettered that rate, at 111 percent from 8,937 in 1841; but the town of London itself, with no annexations to be reckoned in, grew from 2,078 to 7,035, or 239 percent. However, the London District as a whole (taking the area it had in 1838 for comparison, since by 1851 it had been divided into six separate counties) increased in the same decade by not less than 400 percent – this included of course the rapidly forming towns and villages in this vast area.[90]

But despite the incorporation of 1840, the town, or at least those whose interests were identified with the town, still lacked the grade of autonomy that at higher levels was being touted as "responsible government." The reason was the creation in 1842 of elective councils for each district, which indeed enjoyed that autonomy. Sydenham's District Councils Act of 1841 provided for one or two (depending on population) members to be elected from each township to a municipal council for the whole district, but it took no account whatever of the existence of such other incorporated bodies as towns or cities.[91] London Town was merely a portion of London Township for these purposes, and in addition to the rates imposed by the town Board of Police, the householders had also to meet directly imposed district tax rates – on the same basis as the freeholders and householders in the rural areas. But of course the town had no statutory representation on the district council, beyond sharing in the two members for London Township. In 1841 London Township reported more than twice the population of the town, and so might outvote the latter at the annual township meetings at which the council elections were held. Even after the town had achieved near equality in numbers with the township later in the decade, the two combined could still send only two members to a council that in 1846 comprised twenty-six members.[92]

Under these arrangements the ratepayers of London Town were really being taxed without representation: the substantial district revenues coming out of the pockets of the London ratepayers to the district treasury, which were collected by the township collector, were thereby out of the control of the town Board of Police and at the disposal of the district council, which was dominated by farmers and had a different set of priorities. In 1846, the town's expenditures exceeded its revenues by 50 percent, a result quite possibly aggravated by the serious fire of 1845; and the recovery from such a predicament was hamstrung by the rate cap of fourpence in the pound imposed under the 1840 incorporation.[93] The member of the Legislative Assembly for Essex, John Prince, supported by a petition, introduced a bill in 1847 for an escape from this trap. The preamble to the act incorporating London as a fully-fledged town put this principle into unusually pithy language:

> whereas from the increase of the population and commerce of the said Town, and other causes, it is found that the provisions of the said [1840] Act are insufficient; And whereas the several laws now in force relative to the levying and collecting of rates and assessments have in their application to the Town of London produced well founded complaints from the inhabitants of the said Town – and whereas it is expedient that the whole of the rates and assessments rated and assessed on property within the said Town should be paid and applied to the uses of the said Town, the said Town paying to the funds of the London District a certain yearly sum as the proportion which the said Town ought to bear and pay of the general expenses of the District.[94]

The pool of candidates for town mayor and councillors would have been considerably reduced by the new requirement that such candidates possess property in the value of £300 for mayor and £100 for councillor – and that the said property be entirely within the town. Real property and chattels (livestock and wheeled vehicles) were to be assessed at actual value, though the tax rates were capped at one penny in the pound for real property and threepence for chattels. Even so, this would have produced a substantial increase in tax yield for the town council to deploy according to its own priorities.

That the efforts of the town council and other leading citizens were tolerably successful is evidenced by the accelerated growth of London's population in the following seven years, from the act of incorporation in mid-summer 1847 with a population of 3,456, to the middle of 1854, when a special census was taken in London. The immediate stimulus for this latter action was an amendment to the Municipal Corporations Act of 1849, which lowered the population threshold for full city incorporation from 15,000 to 10,000, "as shown by the census."[95] The act did not specify *which* census, and so Mr. Richard Steel Talbot perambulated the streets, including the hotels, to provide a certified count of the residents of the town, and found joyfully they totalled 10,060 – the town had very nearly tripled in the seven years. And so the petition for incorporation by Order in Council was sent in by the town corporation and duly signed by the attorney general to take effect on January 1, 1855.[96]

Under the Municipal Corporations Act passed in 1849 (the Baldwin Act)[97] London had retained its town status, but now was forced back into the county council, with two representatives (its reeve and deputy reeve) out of a total of some twenty-six members, twenty-four of them of unrepentant rural outlook; moreover, the county council promised to grow rapidly as villages and towns were incorporated and so added their reeves and deputy reeves to the sectional interests within the county. By the Baldwin Act, however, a city did not form part of a municipal county, but rather what might be termed a "county-borough;" and so in 1855 London at last attained the autonomy that the town fathers had thought they had acquired in 1847.

Three external factors (apart from greed, ambition, and general "boosterism") may have contributed to London's general need to separate from Middlesex County. First, the railroad had arrived in reality after nearly two decades of hoping, scheming, and skulduggery. This epochal event was accompanied by great hopes of accelerated prosperity, and certainly some if not most of the rapid growth between 1851 and 1854 must be attributed to the railroad's construction phase. Second, the United States border was now, in part, open, under the Reciprocity Treaty signed that year. This, too was a signal of improved prospects. And why then should the city be milked for the benefit of the then-dominant rural interests of the county? Such complaints of urban corporations became epidemic during the 1850s, resulting in a new category of municipality, the "separated towns."[98] London was able to solve the same problem by taking advantage of a change in the law; other towns were too small for this option.

But there was also the fact that London's garrison, after stimulating the economy and establishing the ethos of the town for sixteen years, had been withdrawn to fight a distant imperial struggle on the shores of the Black Sea. This had already occurred before the opportunity for city incorporation arose.[99] The downturn that hit the city after that loss must have been anticipated; and it reinforced the need, aggravated by municipal overindulgence in railroad debentures, to keep all possible revenues within the community.[100] In truth, the need for a large garrison had largely evaporated with the clearing up of the Oregon question in 1846; why it was kept on so long afterwards is not at all clear – and it was certainly never a hardship posting.

What you gain on the swings, you lose on the roundabouts. The wave of railway construction moved on, as the soldiers moved out. London's population growth rate flagged in the later 1850s, being reported as 11,555 in 1861; it did not reach the usual standard of 15,000 for city incorporation until nearly 1871.[101] As the year 1855 opened, two-thirds of a century after John Graves Simcoe first started to focus on the southwestern peninsula of Upper Canada as the key to the defence and the civil organization of his province, London had finally achieved the corporate dignity of a city, under the municipal laws of the day. Simcoe would not, as a realist, be much disappointed to learn that his Georgina–New London–London never became a provincial capital, but on the other hand he would be quite unsurprised today to find a large and vibrant city on the spot that so caught his fancy during his winter ramble along the Thames two centuries ago.

CONCLUSIONS

This article has attempted to trace over a long period one of the major strands in the web of London's history, from its inception at the first major conjuncture, about 1791, to another major conjuncture, in 1854–1855. Throughout this time, the geopolitical concept identified by John Graves Simcoe between 1789 and 1793, though articulated only intermittently in subsequent decades, was never far below the surface of the stream of decisions that ultimately led to the fully-fledged city at the forks of the Thames. Even today, some aspects of his appreciation are still relevant, especially now that the continental trade he envisaged is, we suppose, about to flow more freely than ever before.

But there was never any *inherent* quality about the actual site of London that gave it a primordial destiny to be a major city, though at the same time there was also little or nothing to inhibit its becoming one. Had the 1783 peace settlement resulted in different boundaries so that there was no peninsular imperial salient thrusting into the northern flank of the United States; or had the British and Americans not maintained often bellicose postures towards each other during the next seven decades, it seems highly probable that London's modest site advantages (it lacked powerful mill sites, for example) would in the same historical processes have produced only a moderately sized market-and-mill town on the scale of, say, modern Woodstock. After all, it was not a port, not on the road to anywhere much, and not capable of being promoted to be the principal focus of a large and productive agrarian region.

As it turned out, of course, some centre of military-political power, of judicial authority, of social control, was absolutely required somewhere in the centre of the peninsular spear-point, in those days of bad communications and painfully slow response times to crises. Such a centre, however, might just as well have been at Dorchester, at Kilworth, or even at Wardsville, in broad geopolitical terms. Simcoe, placing perhaps undue emphasis on the supposed navigability of the Thames, fancied "The Forks" mainly for that reason, as well as for the aesthetic appeal of the river's bosky setting, and probably also for its health-giving properties of good soil drainage.

But that is as far as anyone's choice in personal, arbitrary, and accidental terms could have gone. Any competent field officer would have been bound to select the general location of today's Middlesex County, given the geopolitical situation he had to deal with; the actual site he chose would have been of secondary significance. It is perhaps a tribute to Simcoe's astuteness, however, that thirty years on, when the provincial executive had an opportunity to activate his selected townsite as an administrative and defensive location, they confirmed in 1826, as again in 1838, the choice he had made in 1793. This geopolitical reality was amply confirmed by the location of the first operational railroads in the early 1850s.

So that readers may judge for themselves just how prescient his forecasts were, let us allow John Graves Simcoe to have the last word in this discourse:

> I considered it proper to colonize the great Peninsula between the Lakes Ontario, Erie, and Huron – which must in the course of nature become the medium for the transport of English Manufactures to all the Settlements, whether native or foreign, that should be formed [inland of] the Mountains which separate the Waters that flow into the Atlantic from those that fall into the Mississippi, the St. Lawrence, or the Southern Ocean.[102]

ENDNOTES

Much of the research on which this article is based was done under various research grants provided by the Canada Council, the Social Science and Humanities Research Council of Canada, and the University of Western Ontario, which I hereby acknowledge. In the preparation of the article, I have benefited much from discussions, advice, and technical help from a number of persons, including Guy St-Denis, Fred Armstrong, Neville Thompson, and the efficient cartographers of the Department of Geography, Trish Chalk and Gord Shields.

1. Donald W. Meinig, *Atlantic America, 1492–1800*, vol. 1: *The Shaping of America* (New Haven, Connecticut: Yale University Press, 1986). See especially: pp. 348-370.
2. Andrew R.L. Cayton, *The Frontier Republic: Ideology and Politics in the Ohio Country, 1780-1825* [hereafter *Frontier Republic* (Kent, Ohio: Kent State University Press, 1986), p. 9.
3. The "Northwest Ordinance," was passed by the Continental Congress in July 1787 to assert the right of the United States to govern the vast tract of territory north of the Ohio and east of the Mississippi, formerly under Quebec. Its first substantive section established the nature of property rights and conveyance in the British mode as it was known in the Atlantic colonies, and thereby wiped out the French mode of real property enfiefment which had existed throughout the whole area under Quebec jurisdiction including what was to become Upper Canada. This ordinance thus posed a direct challenge to the legitimacy of British rule in the interior, given the strong preference of all English-speaking settlers in the interior for freehold land tenure. It undoubtedly helped the Loyalist settlers in their lobbying for the division of Quebec. For the Ordinance, see: Peter S. Onuf, *Statehood and Union, a History of the Northwest Ordinance* (Bloomington, Indiana: Indiana University Press, 1987). For the division of Quebec into two provinces, see: E.A. Cruikshank, "The Genesis of the Canada Act," Ontario Historical Society *Papers and Records*, XXVIII (1932), pp. 155-237.
4. National Archives of Canada [hereafter NAC], Colonial Office Series [hereafter Colonial Office] (CO 42), vol. 44, letter, North to Haldimand, Aug. 8, 1783, pp. 316-317.
5. *Ibid.* (CO 47), "Observations Political and Commercial relating to Canada," vol. 112. Endorsed "Wrote in 1788," the hand is consistent with that date, though the other volumes around it deal with the second quarter of the nineteenth century. It is entirely probable that J.G. Simcoe read this document as part of his preparation for taking up his post as lieutenant-governor of Upper Canada, and quite possible that Charles Poulett Thomson (Lord Sydenham) read it in 1839.
6. Cathy D. Matson and Peter S. Onuf, *A Union of Interests: Political and Economic Thought in Revolutionary America* (Lawrence, Kansas: University Press of Kansas, 1990), pp. 50-66.
7. E.A. Cruikshank, *The Correspondence of Lieut. Governor John Graves Simcoe*, 5 vols. (Toronto, Ontario: Ontario Historical Society, 1923-1931) [hereafter *Correspondence of Simcoe*], vol. I, p. 112.
8. Archives of Ontario [hereafter AO], Robertson-Mackenzie Papers (F 1174), Personal Letterbook of John Graves Simcoe [hereafter Simcoe Letterbook], p. 3.
9. Cruikshank, *Correspondence of Simcoe*, vol. I, pp. 7-9. Captain Simcoe's letter may be found in: Alexander Fraser, *Thirteenth Report of the Bureau of Archives for the Province of Ontario* (Toronto, Ontario: Legislative Assembly of Ontario, 1916), pp. 137-144.
10. Cruikshank, *Correspondence of Simcoe*, vol. I, pp. 27-28.
11. *Ibid.*, vol. I, pp. 17-19.
12. *Ibid.*
13 S.R. Mealing, "Simcoe, John Graves," *Dictionary of Canadian Biography*, V: pp. 754-759.
14. Mrs. Simcoe wrote in her diary on August 11, 1793: "Lt. Smith has drawn a fine map of the La Tranche River. From what has been surveyed it is proved that Charlevoix, the French explorer, describes the country with great truth. If the line from the road to the river La Tranche was laid down according to its true bearings on any map but Charlevoix's it would strike Lake Erie instead of La Tranche." See: John Ross Robertson, *The Diary of Mrs. Simcoe* [hereafter *Diary*] (Toronto, Ontario: Ontario Publishing Company, 1934), p. 184.
15. Pierre Francois Xavier de Charlevoix, *Letters to the Duchess of Lesdiguieres, giving an Account of a Voyage to Canada, etc.* (London, England: R. Goadby 1763), p. 190. It is of course possible that Simcoe had access to the original French print of 1744, but this English translation is quite faithful. The Goadby edition contains a map, somewhat simplified from that of Bowen, showing the course of the unnamed Thames/Tranche, whereas the other English editions of 1761 and 1766 do not appear to have this map. Charlevoix's work was issued over a long period in numerous editions with a variety of titles. The original was: *Histoire et description générale de la Nouvelle France, avec la Journal historique d'un voyage fait par l'ordre du Roy dans l'Amérique septentrionale*, 3 vols. (Paris, France: Nyon fils, 1744).
16. Emmanuel Bowen, *A New and Accurate Map of Louisiana, with part of Florida and Canada*, in *A New and Complete System of Geography* (London, England: Emmanuel Bowen, 1747). Bowen quite explicitly acknowledges Bellin's maps for Charlevoix's publications as his source. There seems not to have been an English copy of the best map in Charlevoix's work for Simcoe's purposes: *Carte des lacs du Canada, dressée ... [inter alia] sur le Journal de RP de Charlevoix par N. Bellin* (Paris, France, 1744). A facsimile of this map may be found in: Louis C. Karpinski, *Bibliography of the Printed Maps of Michigan* (Lansing, Michigan: Michigan Historical Commission, 1931), plate XIII, following p. 224.
17. Cruikshank, *Correspondence of Simcoe*, vol. I, pp. 51-53. See also: AO, Robertson-MacKenzie Papers (F 1174), Simcoe Letterbook, p. 21.
18. Cruikshank, *Correspondence of Simcoe*, vol. I, p. 144.
19. *Ibid.*, p. 90. The map referred to, if it is the one reproduced with this dispatch, is of the lower Thames only, near Lake St. Clair.
20. Arthur G. Doughty and Duncan A. McArthur, eds., *Documents Relating to the Constitutional History of Canada, 1759-1828*, 3 vols. (Ottawa, Ontario: King's Printer, 1914), vol. 2, p. 81.
21. NAC, Colonial Office (CO 42, B series), vol. 317, "The Simcoe Dispatch," ff. 283, 283r. The full dispatch is reproduced in: Cruikshank, *Correspondence of Simcoe*, vol. II, pp. 56-65.
22. Cruikshank, *Correspondence of Simcoe*, vol. I, pp. 182-183.
23. Simcoe appointed Smith to the executive council on Jun. 27, 1796, not long before the former left the province. Smith was therefore very intimately involved in the government of Upper Canada during the interregnum of the next four critical years. See: *ibid.*, vol. V, pp. 159-199.

24. Talbot is often mentioned in Mrs. Simcoe's diary in this period. See: Robertson, *Diary, passim.*

25. *Ibid.*, p. 155, entry for Mar. 10, 1793. On Apr. 3, Peter Russell wrote "Nothing determined on respecting the site of the new city but the Governor seems delighted with the lands about the forks of the La Tranche." See: AO, Russell Papers (F46), Russell to Alex Davison, Apr. 3, 1793.

26. A recent documentary account of this move can be found in: Donald J. Bourgeois, *The Six Nations Indian Land Claim to the Bed of the Grand River* (Toronto, Ontario: Queen's Printer for Ontario, 1986).

27. Cruikshank, *Correspondence of Simcoe*, vol. I, p. 62.

28. *Ibid.*

29. Robertson, *Diary*, p. 110. "The situation [of Kingston] is entirely flat, and incapable of being rendered defensible. Therefore, were its situation more central, it would still be unfit for the seat of government."

30. Cruikshank, *Correspondence of Simcoe*, vol. II, pp. 186-187.

31. *Ibid., The Correspondence of the Honourable Peter Russell*, 3 vols. [hereafter *Correspondence of Russell*] (Toronto, Ontario: Ontario Historical Society, 1932-1936), vol. 3, p. 46.

32. Cayton, *Frontier Republic*, p. 64.

33. NAC, Colonial Office (CO 42), vol. 322, letter, Russell to Portland, Mar. 31, 1798, ff. 127-129.

34. Cruikshank, *Correspondence of Russell*, vol. 2, pp. 239-241.

35. NAC, Colonial Office (CO 42), vol. 317, letter, Simcoe to Dundas, Sep. 20, 1793, f. 283. See also: Cruikshank, *Correspondence of Simcoe*, vol. II, p. 56.

36. NAC, Civil Secretary's Correspondence, Upper Canada Sundries [hereafter Upper Canada Sundries] (RG5 A1), Askin to Hillier, Nov. 19, 1825, pp. 39896-39902

37. For example, see: Orlo Miller, *This was London: the First Two Centuries* [hereafter *This was London*] (Westport, Ontario: Butternut Press, 1988) p. 5; Frederick H. Armstrong and Daniel J. Brock, "The Rise of London: a Study of Urban Evolution in Nineteenth-Century Southwestern Ontario" in F.H. Armstrong, H.A. Stevenson, and J.D. Wilson, eds., *Aspects of Nineteenth Century Ontario* (Toronto, Ontario: University of Toronto Press, 1974), pp. 86-89.

38. Upper Canada, House of Assembly, *Journal Appendix*, 1828, no. 10, p. 55.

39. Cruikshank, *Correspondence of Russell*, vol. 2, pp. 239-241.

40. NAC, Upper Canada Sundries, letter, Halton to Ridout, Apr. 30, 1810, pp. 4836-4837; *ibid.*, letter, Halton to Ridout, Feb. 12, 1811, pp. 5229-5230.

41. Daniel J. Brock, "Richard Talbot, the Tipperary Irish, and the formative years of London Township, 1818-1826" (M.A. thesis, University of Western Ontario, London, Ontario, 1969), chapter V.

42. For a legal description of the entire tract's outer boundaries, see: NAC, Upper Canada Sundries, Description of the Longwoods, Jan. 25, 1819, pp. 20279-20281.

43. Richard A. Preston, *The Defence of the Undefended Border: Planning for War in North America, 1867-1939* [hereafter *Undefended Border*] (Montreal, Quebec: McGill-Queen's University Press, 1977), pp. 13-14.

44. Thomas Talbot proposed legislation to improve the mouth of Kettle Creek as early as 1824. See: NAC, Upper Canada Sundries, Talbot to Hillier, Apr. 11, 1824, pp. 34903-34906. An act relative to the harbour was passed in 1827. See: Upper Canada, House of Assembly, *Journal Appendix*, 1827, no. N, "Report...relative to the formation of a harbour at the mouth of Kettle Creek..."; Upper Canada, statute (1827), 8 Geo. IV, c. 18.

45. Lt. Gen. James Carmichael Smyth, *Precis of the Wars in Canada from 1755 to the Treaty of Ghent in 1814.* (London, England: War Office Print, 1826), pp. 175-176.

46. *Idem, Report to His Grace the Duke of Wellington ... relative to His Majesty's North American Provinces* [hereafter *Report to His Grace*] (London, England: War Office Print, 1825), appendix (memoranda), p. 24.

47. Wellington, [Second] Duke, ed., *Supplementary Despatches and Memoranda of Field Marshal Arthur Duke of Wellington*, 12 vols. (London, England: John Murray, 1848-1865), vol. II, pp. 572-574.

48. Smyth, *Report to His Grace*, pp. 84-85. See also: Brian Dawe, *"Old Oxford is Wide Awake!"* ([Toronto, Ontario]: Brian Dawe, c1980), p. 46.

49. From Jul. 1828, a line of stages ran three times weekly between Niagara (now Niagara-on-the-Lake) and Sandwich (now part of Windsor), with connections from Buffalo. The trip took four days with an overnight stop at "Westminster." The owners claimed their route was "130 miles less than any other route from Buffalo to Detroit." See: *Farmers Journal and Welland Canal Intelligencer* (St. Catharines, Upper Canada), Jul. 23, 1828, p. 3, c. 5.

50. Complaints about the slowness of development abounded. Here are some comments by the commissioner of Crown lands, R.B. Sullivan, in 1838: "It has been a melancholy duty to read the petitions from the settlers in the rear parts of the Province setting forth their difficulties and praying for some comparatively trifling expenditure for their relief[;] it is a discouraging and pitiable answer to these petitions that there is no power in the local government to assist the petitioners...The consequence of this state of things is that the back country remains almost a wilderness, while those who would occupy it are driven to seek a residence in the United States, or to return impoverished and despairing to Europe..." See: C.R. Sanderson, ed., *The Arthur Papers: Being the Canadian Papers, Mainly Confidential, Private and Demi-Official of Sir George Arthur, K.C.H. Last Lieutenant-Governor of Upper Canada in the Manuscript Collection of the Toronto Public Libraries* [hereafter *Arthur Papers*] (Toronto, Ontario: Toronto Public Libraries and University of Toronto Press, 1957-1959), vol. I, pp. 150-151. Some leading reformers even went so far as to consider group immigration to Iowa. See: Gerald M. Craig, *Upper Canada: The Formative Years, 1784-1841* (Toronto, Ontario: McClelland and Stewart, 1963), p. 253.

51. In 1832 legislation was passed that incorporated a harbour company for the Otter Creek. An attempt had been made a few years earlier to have the place named Port Colborne. See: NAC, Upper Canada Sundries, letter, Foster to Mudge, Apr. 24, 1830, pp. 56154-56159.

52. Alan Wilson, *The Clergy Reserves of Upper Canada: a Canadian Mortmain* (Toronto, Ontario: University of Toronto Press, 1968), pp. 72-87.

53. Fred Landon, *Western Ontario and the American Frontier* (Toronto, Ontario: Ryerson Press, 1941), pp. 197-199.

54. Upper Canada, statute (1826), 7 Geo. IV, c. 13. This act specified that the courts were to be held at the new site as soon as accommodation was available. This arrangement was the case at the beginning of 1827, one year after the act was passed, though in temporary quarters.

55. NAC, Upper Canada Sundries, letter, Talbot to Hillier, Mar. 7, 1826, pp. 41088-41091.

56. *Ibid.*, Burwell to Hillier, Jun. 29, 1826, pp. 42041-42044.

57. *Ibid.*, Matthews to Hillier, Dec. 13, 1826, pp. 43468-43470. He signed himself "Late Capt. R. Ind. Artilly."

58. The case made by Nancy Z. Tausky and Lynne D. DiStefano regarding Colonel Talbot's "Somewhat Gothic" Courthouse, and the pre-eminence of aesthetic-romantic impulses in the decision to adopt a non-classical design, is not implausible, but is almost entirely circumstantial. So too, is the "defensive site" hypothesis presented here. Both could of course be simultaneously correct. See: Nancy Z. Tausky and Lynne D. DiStefano, *Victorian Architecture in London and Southwestern Ontario: Symbols of Aspiration* (Toronto, Ontario: University of Toronto Press, 1986), pp. 3-55.

59. Alan Gowans, *Building Canada*, revised ed. (Toronto, Ontario: Oxford University Press, 1966), pp. 43-44, 77.

60. This point was made by Simcoe, who was quite opposed to fortifying Amherstburg. In the 1830s the economic cutbacks of the British Whig government produced the same result, until the 1837 and 1838 rebellions. See: Richard A. Preston, *Undefended Border*, pp 15-17.

61. *Ibid.*, pp. 13-14. Sir George Arthur later recommended in 1841 that London be one of the fortified places. See: Sanderson, *Arthur Papers*, vol. 3, p. 414.

62. Albert B. Corey, *The Crisis of 1830-1842 in Canadian-American Relations* (New York, New York: Russell & Russell, 1970), pp. 113-129, 781.

63. Sanderson, *Arthur Papers*, vol. I, pp. 119.

64. Albro Martin, *Railroads Triumphant* (New Haven, Connecticut: Yale University Press, 1991): pp. 12-17. See also: Willis F. Dunbar, *Michigan: a History of the Wolverine State*, revised by George S. May (Grand Rapids, Michigan: Eerdmans Publishing, 1980), pp. 266-273.

65. The burning of the *Thames* by brigands is recounted in many places. For the fullest account, see: NAC, Provincial Secretary, Canada West, Correspondence Files, 1821-1867 [hereafter Provincial Secretary West] (RG5 C1), vol. 14, no. 1717. The docket is headed by a petition for inhabitants of Chatham, December 5, 1838. This steamer had stimulated the growth of Chatham in eight years from six houses to 110, and 600 souls; it had also generated much growth in that part of Kent County.

66. Norman L. Nicholson, *The Boundaries of the Canadian Confederation* (Toronto, Ontario: Macmillan-Carleton Library, 1979), pp. 27-56.

67. W.F. Ganong, "A Monograph on the Evolution of the Boundaries of New Brunswick," *Proceedings and Transactions of the Royal Society of Canada*, second series, VII, sec. II (1901), pp. 139-449.

68. The Martello towers, in particular, were built at the time of the Oregon controversy.

69. Joseph Hume, MP for Westminster, had long espoused the idea (promoted earlier by Jeremy Bentham) of liberating all colonies, and also strenuously promoted economy in government. Even Edward Ellice, MP for Coventry and also a large investor in Canada, thought at one stage that Upper Canada should be let go.

70. *Hansard's Parliamentary Debates*, third series (London, England: Thomas Curson Hansard, 1839), vol. 49, Jul. 11, 1839, cc. 179-186.

71. This policy was founded upon a scheme proposed by Gibbon Wakefield, and was endorsed by a parliamentary committee in April 1840. See: NAC, Colonial Office (CO 885/1), Confidential Print, Canada, miscellaneous, no. 1B. It was recommended to Sydenham in Aug. 1840. See: *ibid.* (CO 42), letter, Russell to [Sydenham], Aug. 31, 1840, vol. 310, ff. 119-121.

72. George Poulett Scrope, *A Memoir of the Life of the Right Honourable Charles, Lord Sydenham, G.C.* (London, England: John Murray, 1843), pp. 199-200.

73. NAC, Papers of Lord John Russell (MG24 A28), letter, Sydenham to Russell, Apr. 12, 1841.

74. NAC, Upper Canada Sundries, letter, Talbot to Hillier, Apr. 24, 1827, pp. 41419-41426. Orlo Miller implies that the Quarter Sessions took place on Jan. 9 of that year. See: Miller, *This was London*, p. 19.

75. University of Western Ontario, the D.B. Weldon Library, Regional Collection [hereafter Regional Collection], London Township, Council Minutes, 1819-1850, Jan. 1, 1827, p. 11.

76. Upper Canada Legislative Assembly, *Journal Appendix*, 1833, "Population Returns," p. 144.

77. NAC, Upper Canada Sundries, letter, Jameson to Joseph, Jun. 13, 1836, pp. 91339-91340. This letter constitutes the fiat for the writ of election.

78. Upper Canada, statute (1820), 60 Geo. III, c. 2. While the general franchise was a household annual value of £2, in towns the vote required property worth £5. In London's act of incorporation in 1840, it was provided that any town lot would be rated at £5, as would any part of a lot with a house on it – in other words, a household franchise. The 1836 election results (on a probably smaller electorate) are cited in: Frederick H. Armstrong, *The Forest City, an Illustrated History of London, Ontario* [hereafter *Forest City*] (Northridge, California: Windsor Publications, 1986), p. 46.

79. This information was inferred from the locations shown on the reports that the clerks and sheriffs had to send in annually, which are printed in the *Journal Appendices*. See also: Regional Collection, Harris Papers, letter, Askin to Harris, May 4, 1834.

80. NAC, Upper Canada Sundries, letter, Rapelje to Rowan, Aug. 2, 1833, pp. 72524-72526.

81. *Ibid.*, petition of John Tenbroek and others, Nov. 3, 1834, and response of Mitchell, Dec. 22, 1834, pp.

79998-80003; *ibid.*, letter, Mitchell to Rowan, Jul. 7, 1835, pp. 84802-84805.

82. *Ibid.*, letter, Askin to Rowan, Sep. 4, 1835, pp. 85958-85961; *ibid.*, Askin to Joseph, Feb. 5, 1836, pp. 88330-88332. Though the order in council had been issued in 1835, the necessary letters patent were held up awaiting a fee payment of £7.10.0, which Askin and the others were not expecting. He asked for an exemption.

83. Upper Canada, House of Assembly, *Journal*, Feb. 11, 1837, p. 446. The petition, led by Benjamin Cronyn, was approved on Feb. 11 by the education committee chaired by Mahlon Burwell. Petitions had been sent in on this topic in 1831 and 1832–1833 to no avail. It was hardly worth the effort, as only one month later Norfolk County was set apart as its own district, the Talbot District.

84. NAC, Provincial Secretary West, vol. 12, petition of the London barristers and others, Jul. 12, 1838, no. 1501. Also, see: *ibid.*, letter, Burwell to Macaulay, Aug. 18, 1838, no. 1538. In this letter, Burwell alleges that the proposal was intended to get even with him for constraining the financial initiatives of the magistracy.

85. Upper Canada, House of Assembly, *Journal Appendix*, 1839, "Population and Assessment Returns," p. 447; *ibid.*, 1840, "Population Returns," p. 151; Canada, Legislative Assembly, *Journal Appendix*, 1841, no. T, "Population of the District of London"; *ibid.*, 1842, no. M, "Population of the District of London."

86. *Ibid.*

87. Armstrong, *Forest City*, pp 31-62.

88. The use of the term "Board of Police" is very much in the meaning of "Board of Trustees." "Police" in this context denotes a rather abstract concept, loosely comprehending public safety and good order – indeed "peace, order and good government" – at the community level. The board was representative because it was elected, but did not act as magistracy in any judicial functions except under their own by-laws. The first boards of police in Upper Canada in 1817 and later comprised the existing magistrates. Elected boards of police began with Brockville in 1832. See: Frederick H. Armstrong, *Handbook of Upper Canadian Chronology*, revised ed. (Toronto, Ontario: Dundurn Press, 1985), pp. 199-216. London's act was passed in 1840. See: Upper Canada, statute (1840), 3 Vic., c. 31. The "Assize of Bread" is prescribed for police towns in: *ibid.* (1825), 6 Geo. IV, c. 6.

89. There was a mutual reinforcement between the rate of migration and public works improvement as under the policy established by the British government in 1840. See: note 73. In addition, local roads were extended and improved under new taxation laws, which raised much more money to supplement local units' own statute labour resources.

90. Canada, Legislative Assembly, *Journal Appendix*, 1842, no. M, "Population of the District of London"; *Census of the Canadas, 1851-2*, 2 vols. (Quebec, Quebec: Lovell and Lamoureux, 1855), vol. I, pp. 5-35.

91. C.F.J. Whebell, "The Upper Canada District Councils Act and British Colonial Policy," *Journal of Imperial and Commonwealth History*, XVII (1989): pp. 185-209.

92. Regional Collection, London District Council, minutes, 1842-1849.

93. NAC, Colonial Office (CO 47), *Blue Book for 1846*, vol. 161, p. [24]. London's tax revenue was £642.7.2; its expenditure was £953.6.1.

94. Canada, statute (1847), 10 & 11 Vic., c. 48.

95. *Ibid.* (1853), 16 Vic., c. 181, sec. 19. It is arguable that this provision was inserted for the benefit of the Town of Bytown, to help it in its quest to become, as the City of Ottawa, the permanent capital of Canada. The *de facto* premier, Francis Hincks, had financial interests in the Ottawa Valley. See: C.F.J. Whebell, "Why Pembroke? The Politics of Selecting a County Capital in the Mid-Nineteenth Century," *Ontario History*, XXVIII, no. 2 (Jun. 1986): p. 133. Bytown got its timing wrong, however, and still needed an act of the legislature to gain city status on Jan. 1 1855, so as to avoid a year's statutory delay. Legislation was passed on Dec. 18, 1854, to make Ottawa the *fifth* city incorporated in Ontario. See: Canada, statute (1854), 18 Vic., c. 23.

96. NAC, Census of the Town of London (RG5, C1), vol. 417, no 1000. The census was taken July 9, 1854; the petition from the Town Council was drawn up on Aug. 18, and both were received by the provincial secretary on Aug. 24. Various office procedures ensued, with approval being given by the governor general on Sep. 15. The recommendation for proclamation was added by John Ross on the 17th and the proclamation issued on the 21st. Interestingly, there was a change of government during this period, on Sep. 10–11, when the Hincks-Morin administration gave way to the Macdonald-Tache government.

97. Canada, statute (1849), 12 Vic., c. 81. This act created the general structure of the local government system for Upper Canada and Ontario, and standardized for many decades the forms of village, town, and city governments.

98. A number of towns disconnected themselves from their county governments in the later 1850s. See: Canada, statute (1858), 22 Vic., c. 99. Some were in fact county seats.

99. Orlo Miller, "The Fat Years and the Lean: London (Canada) in Boom and Depression, 1851-61," *Ontario History*, LIII, no. 2 (Jun. 1961): pp. 73-80.

100. Armstrong, *Forest City*, pp. 87-88. This reference includes George J. Goodhue's account of the financial difficulties, given in 1861.

101. Growth resumed as a result of the United States' Civil War, and the relative openness of American markets to Canadian produce under the Reciprocity Treaty of 1854. Reciprocity ended in 1866, but London's growth rate remained much higher than the province overall for the rest of the century.

102. NAC, Upper Canada Sundries, letter, Simcoe to Duke of Portland, Dec. 30, 1799, pp. 382-388.

CHAPTER THREE

REBELLION DAYS IN AND ABOUT LONDON

Colin Read

Sunday, December 10, 1837, dawned dark and drear over the little town at the fork of the Thames. The long, slate grey sky, heavy with menace, did nothing to warm the hearts and homes of those below. It shed a cold, dispiriting drizzle. As "meeting" time approached, many residents slipped out of their homes, glanced unhappily skywards, then hurried off to church. Today of all days, shivering with cold and damp, parishioners would welcome a hellfire-and-brimstone sermon!

Unusually, the residents of Eldon House, high on the bank of the Thames just beyond the town's limits, stayed home. Inside, they had the stove blazing high, not only to banish December's chill, but, more important, to melt lead for one of London's *grandes dames* and her young children, who were casting bullets! As Amelia Harris herself later confessed, "I was rather abashed," when Margaret, the wife of the Church of England rector Benjamin Cronyn, "came in & caught me at it." If Amelia feared a scolding from a scandalized Margaret, she need not have worried. Mrs. Cronyn promptly produced a pair of bullet moulds which "she had just borrowed & was going home to employ her self in the same way!" No, Margaret understood perfectly. Amelia and her offspring were merely taking sensible precautions. After all, she had heard "several times" that her husband John, treasurer of the London District, "was to be shot & our house burned." As for Mrs. Cronyn, she "was notified that her house would be Burned as it was church property but she need not be alarmed as her [*sic*] & the children would be allowed to walk out." Amelia thought that "very civil."[1]

As early as September 1836, the Reverend William Proudfoot of the United Secession Presbyterian Church had confided to his diary that "the society of the village [London] is now very little to be desired. The influence of political strife has eradicated everything amiable that was in it."[2] Now, in December 1837, in decided contrast to the weather, political passions had become so heated that some women feared for the safety of their little ones, their husbands, and themselves. What had gone so very wrong?

The situation in London was a miniature of that elsewhere in the province. Residents had been increasingly cast into two opposing camps, espousing different views and cherishing different visions of society. The Province of Upper Canada had been created in 1791 as the British answer to the emergence of republicanism and democracy in North America. The colony had a "balanced" government, one that blended the elements of King, Lords, and Commons. The King was represented by an appointed lieutenant-governor who selected the "Lords" by appointing the legislative and executive councillors. The latter acted much like modern cabinet ministers, setting policy and administering government departments. The former helped create legislation, both by initiating it and by sitting in judgement on that coming up from the "Commons," the elected house of assembly. Though the assembly was to be a partner in a tripartite system of government, many of its advocates correctly came to feel that it was a very minor partner indeed. Even if its legislation survived the scrutiny of the

This portrait of Amelia Harris (1798–1882) by James B. Wandesforde, captures her in mid-life. The daughter of Loyalists Samuel and Sarah Ryerse of Norfolk County, she married John Harris in 1815, moving with him to the district capital of London in 1834. Here she and John raised three sons and seven daughters. After her husband's death she became a diarist, for twenty-five years recording with keen eye events in London and her household.

legislative council, it might be reserved for the consideration of the British government by the lieutenant-governor! To many, the governmental structure lacked the very balance that was supposed to make it an attractive alternative to democratic republicanism. Indeed, the perception grew that the "Lords," along with their relatives, friends and associates, formed a tight clique, a "family compact," that was able to "surround the Lieutenant-Governor, and mould him,

Born in Devon, John Harris (1782–1850) joined the Royal Navy, rising to the rank of master. He was helping chart the waters of Lake Erie about Port Ryerse when he met his wife-to-be. A whirlwind courtship ended in marriage. He took his young bride to Kingston, where he worked with the hydrographic survey. John retired on half pay in 1817, and the couple settled in Norfolk County, where John a few years later began his long career as district treasurer. He was treasurer the rest of his life. This portrait by Wandesforde of John Harris, like that of Harris's wife, Amelia, dates from the early 1850s.

like wax to their will."[3] According to this criticism, they not only directed affairs at the provincial capital, York (renamed Toronto in 1834), but also insinuated themselves and their representatives in the apparatus of local government throughout the province.

The province was divided into local administrative districts – eleven of them in 1837. The London District was one. Its settled parts consisted of the modern counties of Norfolk, Oxford, Elgin, Middlesex and thin slices of Perth and Huron. London, like all of the other districts, had officials of note. One was Amelia Harris's husband, John, the district treasurer. To some, in both his office and his person, he represented much that was wrong. An appointed official, he oversaw district finances (ever a difficult job) and he was well paid, receiving a portion of the land taxes assessed in the district. To this he added several fees.[4] Little wonder, critics thought, that he and Amelia could afford a beautiful residence overlooking the Thames, and could pride themselves on the generous hospitality they extended to those of their circle. Little wonder, too, that taxes and fees weighed heavily on the ordinary folk of the London District! The higher the taxes and the heavier the fees, the more money for John and Amelia, and the grander their parties!

Nor, in envious eyes, was John Harris the only appointee so favoured. Another was John B. Askin, clerk of the peace of the London District and its chief administrative officer. Like other district clerks, he had a myriad of duties – everything from drawing up jury lists and compiling population returns to composing writs for the sale of lands in arrears of taxes. Like other clerks, he levied fees at every turn.[5] And like Harris, he lived well, enjoying the luxury of a

This pen-and-ink sketch of Eldon House is inscribed by Sarah Harris: "Eldon House as it was when I married in 1846." Unfortunately, the artist is unknown. As for Sarah, having caught the "scarlet fever," she married a British army officer, Captain Robert Alexander George Dalzell, the fourth son of the Earl of Carnwath. By 1847 the couple was back in England with Dalzell's regiment. Eldon House, which had been built in 1834, continued to be the social centre of London's smart set. The descendants of John and Amelia Harris made a gift of it to the city of London in 1960. Regional Collection, University of Western Ontario Library

large estate in Westminster, overlooking the south branch of the Thames at the present juncture of Askin Avenue and Wortley Road.

A Devon man, John Harris had taken to the sea, rising to the rank of master in the Royal Navy before retiring on half-pay in Upper Canada where he became treasurer of the London District in 1821. Askin's origins were very different. He had been born into a prominent fur trading family at Detroit in 1788 when the fort, though anticipating transfer, was still in British hands. Treasurer Harris was English-born in a British colony, and he had come in early, at a time when capable, educated, loyal men were in relatively short supply. By the 1830s other Britishers of undoubted loyalty and talents were showing up in the colony, but often they found the job hunt far less satisfactory than had John Harris. There were too many "qualified" applicants for too few positions. Askin had been in the province from the first and had had ample opportunity to prove his loyalty during the War of 1812, when he had participated in the capture of Fort Michilimackinac in the first summer of hostilities.[6] Here he was fortunate, for those who had not demonstrated their loyalty in convincing fashion could not hope for office. This applied particularly to American settlers, of whom Askin *might* have been considered a representative.

The disadvantages facing immigrants from the south became manifest in the celebrated Alien Controversy. At war's end Upper Canadian officials, doubtful of the loyalty of the Americans already in the colony, tried to cut off further American immigration by denying citizenship to settlers from the republic. A bitter controversy ensued, which was not resolved until 1828 when legislation decreed that Americans *already in the province* could, after meeting stringent residence requirements, take the oath of citizenship, thereby becoming eligible to secure full legal title to their property and gain the right to vote in assembly elections.

Issues involving the Church of England, which was tied directly to the mother country and regarded by some as alien to the North American continent, often produced division also. At Upper Canada's creation, official thinking had it that the infant colony needed an "established" church, to provide vital social cement along with true religion and sound learning. Without such an establishment the residents would be hurled into the moral vacuum of revolutionary America or France. Hence, the "official" church, the Church of England, enjoyed from the outset various privileges – the exclusive right to marry, the proceeds from the clergy reserves (which comprised one-seventh of all the surveyed lands of the province), and rectories for its clergy, to name the most obvious. Of course, these privileges invited attack. A few concessions were made, but never enough to satisfy critics. These were apoplectic when, in 1836, the outgoing lieutenant-governor, Sir John Colborne, decreed the creation of fifty-seven new Anglican rectories, all to be supported from the clergy reserve revenues. Only forty-four were actually established, but Benjamin Cronyn received two, one at Arva, the other in London. This – plus his never hesitant support of the government – helps explain why in 1837 some hotheads thought to burn his house.

Religious issues shaded off into secular ones. Among the complaints against the clergy reserves was that they impeded settlement, since the authorities were believed to be holding them back in their unimproved state until the farms around them were developed. However true or untrue, it was undeniably the case that profligate land policies had conspired to vest privileged interests, whether the Church of England or large land speculators (such as the celebrated Thomas Talbot of the Erie shore), with vast tracts of land. In London such leaders as Cronyn, with his rectories, and John Harris or John Askin, with their large private holdings, were clear reminders of this fact. Close to London, the small population of Dorchester Township, just 752 in 1836[7], where speculators sat on large chunks of land, underlined the retarding effects of widespread speculation.

A host of other issues were debated loudly in the alehouses and on the hustings – the poor state of the roads, the lack of money for public education, the privileges accorded private concerns such as the Canada Company, the Welland Canal Company, or the Bank of Upper Canada. Over and over the Reform refrain came down to the complaint that "them what has, gets." Privilege needed curbing! Ordinary folk deserved a much bigger share of the pie! Such sentiments gained added force as Andrew Jackson won the presidency of the United States in the election of 1828 and inaugurated the era of the "common man" there. In symbolism too pointed to be overlooked, he invited all and sundry to his inauguration party. People in homespun made merry in the White House! Then there were the various revolutions and rebellions of 1830, which convulsed much of Europe. They too underlined the fact that new political winds were blowing. Even Britain, one of the leading counter-revolutionary states, was affected, with the government granting a significant widening of the parliamentary franchise in the Great Reform Bill of 1832.

In Upper Canada, reformers clamoured to be heard; increasingly, they organized themselves into a party. By the early 1830s their leaders were men such as Marshall Spring Bidwell of Bath, east of Belleville, and Dr. William Warren Baldwin and his son Robert of Toronto. They inclined ever more towards responsible government – letting the leaders of the majority party in the assembly select the executive councillors, the cabinet of the day, who would thus be "responsible" to the assembly.[8] Not every Reformer was so bent. The tempestuous William Lyon Mackenzie, the little Scot who had come to Canada in 1820 and embarked on a stormy newspaper career – his fiery temperament suggested by the flaming red wig he wore – flirted with the notion of reponsible government now and then before ultimately settling on the simplicities of elective government as practised in the United States. Let the people decide! It was an effective cry. But not quite as effective as some historians believe.

That there were grievances in Upper Canada is undeniable. That many of them were well founded is equally so. That most of the residents of Upper Canada could be persuaded by the existence of such grievances to espouse the cause of fundamental political reforms, whether responsible government or the wholesale adoption of the elective principle, is far less certain. The best gauges of public opinion are the elections to the assembly. These swung in pendulum fashion back and forth, putting alternately the Tories in power (1828, 1832), then the Reformers (1830, 1834). The results point to a nearly even division of opinion in the province. After winning and losing power twice in eight years, both sides were anxious to capture the ninth, the "swing" contest, that of 1836.

In that year, the British government sent out Sir Francis Bond Head as lieutenant-governor. Despatched to propitiate the Reformers and bring peace to the troubled political scene, he was a political neophyte, and a vainglorious one at that. He started well by inviting Robert Baldwin and his Reform colleague Dr. John Rolph of Norfolk into the executive council. He faltered badly when he dismissed them and their co-councillors for demanding the establishment of reponsible government. First, a confrontation with the assembly ensued, then a general election. Head did not hesitate to put himself at the head of the Tory forces, relying on super-patriotic appeals and dark hints of imminent invasion to carry the day. *"Let them come if they dare!"* he challenged the unnamed enemy.[9]

The elections were strung out over several days. Voting was *viva voce*, by voice, not the secret ballot. Elections could be turbulent, as this one proved. London, which constituted a provincial riding for the first time, saw its share of skulduggery. A deported Reform partisan, Elijah Woodman, later recalled that those linchpins of local government and justice, the magistrates

> ceased to do their duty and a general riot ensued every day that the polls were open. I attended the election on Saturday, the last day, which is as fresh in my memory as yesterday. A procession [was] headed by a negro with a national standard, waving it, and at the same time shouting an offer of five pounds for any Liberal [Reform] heads. This procession turned out to be an Orange mob who commenced beating a number of Liberals who were taken up for dead. Two hours before the polls closed Member [Thomas] Parke had to be rescued by a guard and marched to a place of safety and Member [Elias] Moore had to make his escape out of town for home. The Liberal poll was secured by two clerks who made their escape into the jail for protection and were locked up.[10]

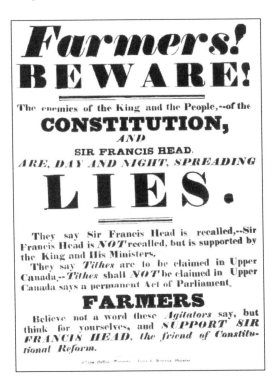

The language of this broadside illustrates the heated nature of the political debate of the day. Its message, that Sir Francis Bond Head had the support of the British government and that the residents of the province were not going to be forced to pay tithe to the Church of England, indicates the sort of rumours that were sweeping the province. While reformers sought by means foul as well as fair to undercut Tory support, their opponents repaid them amply, using a host of "dirty tricks" of their own. Metropolitan Toronto Reference Library, MTL836 F1

Evidently the ministrations of the Orange Order, noted for its perfervid loyalty, were effective. Only thirty-eight of London's 1,090 residents raised their voices in vote. Thirty-one named Tory John Burwell of Southwold (now in Elgin County); just seven called for Reformer John Scatcherd of London. In the surrounding countryside, where property served to enfranchise more, and vote tallies were substantially larger, local Reformers were triumphant, with the rescued Parke and the escaped Moore both triumphant in the double-member constituency of Middlesex. Reformers Charles Duncombe and Robert Alway headed the polls in Oxford. Two more – John Rolph and David Duncombe – captured Norfolk. Aside from London, only Huron County in the London District returned a Tory – albeit one of a decidedly independent bent.[11]

While London fell solidly into an already well-established urban pattern by voting Tory, the surrounding countryside, noted for the American origins of much of its population, bucked a decided provincial trend by going Reform. In the new house there were to be just sixteen Reformers – six from the London District alone – facing no fewer than forty-four Tories. Many discouraged Reformers, oversimplifying, were convinced that corrupt practices explained all. Matters were more complicated than that – for one thing, the recent wave of British immigrants, in part swayed by Head's appeal, had gone Tory, as had various religious leaders, also caught up in the loyalty cry.[12]

The election was so upsetting to some reformers that they unsuccessfully protested the results to Great Britain. Others, notably Bidwell and Robert Baldwin, became discouraged and forsook the shabby world of politics, leaving leadership of the Reform grouping to the radical Mackenzie,who had started a new journal, the *Constitution*, on a significant date, *July 4*, 1836. His type was set in acid. "Our government is one of the meanest which it is possible to conceive," he wrote. "Individuals are lifted up high in society in these colonies, whom our farmers, if aware of their real character, would not permit to associate even with the dogs of their flocks."[13] In the west the *Liberal*, published in St. Thomas on and off since 1832, joined in. By the summer of 1836 it was under the editorship of John Talbot. Despite his generally more moderate tone, Talbot could produce some ringing denunciations. When the *London Gazette* appeared in 1836, Talbot hailed it as a "vile, rascally, Orange Tory paper, under the management of a pack of officials, without one single ray of genius or talent."[14] *Gazette* editors Thomas and Benjamin Hodgkinson replied in kind. No "more libellous and blackguard paper" than the *Liberal* existed. Talbot, its editor, was barren of any "principle connected with truth, decency, or order," displaying "a vindictiveness of feeling always to be found in the absence of virtue."[15]

There was no middle road for these papers! And that was unfortunate. Papers were passed around at taverns or read aloud for the benefit of the many who could not read. While we should not assume that everyone hung avidly on every word, we, who have access to so many means of communication and sources of information, would find their influence astounding. In the era of the rebellion they were for most the main link with the wider world. In the crisis of the rebellions they brought little logic and reason to bear – prejudice and misinformation were their mainstays. This was doubly unfortunate, since Upper Canadians faced a series of crises and painful adjustments. They needed reliable, trustworthy information.

Besides the many heated issues in the political arena, Upper Canadians had to deal with the large numbers of immigrants from Britain flooding into the province. From 1829 to 1837 no fewer than 260,387 landed at the port of Quebec alone. Two-thirds of these moved on to Upper Canada,[16] a province which itself had just 396,719 people in 1837. In the long term, immigrants meant prosperity through growth and development, but in the short term they meant competition for jobs and land, and sometimes worse. In 1832, in common with much of the world, Upper Canada was ravaged by a cholera epidemic. Immigrants introduced the frightful disease, which would have inevitably arrived on trading ships in any case. As increasing numbers of poor and penniless newcomers landed, some reformers suspected that Bond Head, who had been assistant poor law

Mahlon Burwell (1783–1846) lived most of his life on the Lake Erie shore. Yet he had substantial London connections. A land surveyor, he laid out much of southwestern Ontario, including the south part of London Township. As a militia colonel who served with distinction in the War of 1812, a large property owner, an ardent defender of the Church of England, and a confidante of Colonel Thomas Talbot, politics beckoned Burwell. When he became London's first member of the Legislative Assemby in 1836, he was a parliamentary veteran, having been first elected to the House in 1812. A multiple officeholder, he was firmly on the government side. (Artist unknown.) Huron College, University of Western Ontario

commissioner in Kent County, England, intended to import paupers wholesale, thus "unjustly and wickedly" laying "the foundation of a system which must result in taxation, pestilence and famine."[17] Mackenzie and other Reform editors dutifully reported such suspicions.

All this came at a time when "famine" seemed ever more likely as the province descended into economic depression. First, crop yields in 1836 were short, then an international contraction produced a shortage of both credit and cash. Responding in 1837, the provincial government allowed the chartered banks, the major ones in the province, to suspend payments in cash. This meant that a depositor, such as merchant Charles Latimer of London, was unable to withdraw his money in coin, the one generally acceptable medium of currency, from the local branch of the Bank of Upper Canada.[18] No matter that his creditors might be pressing him and he might be ruined! In fine, nature and man combined to produce real hardship. Settlers whose crops failed often lacked the money to supply the deficiency. The *Liberal* reported "unprecedented severity and distress" in Middlesex County, where many of the poorer classes "are reduced to starvation."[19] Mackenzie, not to be outdone, reported that settlers in the rear of the London District and elsewhere "are glad to gnaw the bark off the trees."[20] Exaggerated as such reports were, they did little to calm political passions.

In any case, Mackenzie had no interest in tranquillity. His watchword was "Agitation! agitation! agitation!"[21] He called for the creation of political unions in the province to further the process of demanding reform. These, he noted, might "be easily transferred ... to military purposes."[22] In response, Reformers did create unions, perhaps a score or more.[23] Most were formed in the hinterland north of Toronto and in the London District – not always without incident. Occasionally the Reformers attending conducted "turkey shoots," much to the annoyance of local Tories, who saw these as training for armed rebellion. On occasion, donnybrooks ensued, notably in Bayham Township, southeast of London. As for London's Reformers, they were part of the throng of 1,000 and more who swarmed onto a farm field in Westminster on October 6, 1837, to decry things as they were and demand change. Worried Tories replied with a smaller meeting in London a few weeks later, asking the lieutenant-governor to take measures to assure the maintenance of law and order. He made comforting noises.[24] In fact, oblivious to the problems of Upper Canada, he had already compromised the safety of the province by sending all of the British regulars in it to Lower Canada (Quebec), where the situation was even more strained. There, a deadly mix of political and economic discontents, overlaid by French-English tensions, combined to produce an ever more combustible situation.

In one sense Head's decison to send the troops was not so foolish. Despite appearances, Reformers at the time were not planning rebellion. Their aim, after all, was "agitation," not armed revolt. But as the situation in Lower Canada deteriorated and the upper province was denuded of troops, Mackenzie, prompted in part by Head's action, began to counsel more radical action. In late October he spoke to a small group of Reformers about the possibility of revolt. Prodded, they agreed to send an emissary to Lower Canada to get in touch with the radicals there to discuss possibilities. Though little was to come of this action, Mackenzie began claiming close contact with his Lower Canadian brethren in an attempt to persuade his colleagues about Toronto to take up arms.[25] On November 16 he published a draft constitution for the province that borrowed heavily from American examples.[26] The outbreak of fighting in Lower Canada a week later helped him persuade many that capture of Toronto and the overthrow of the government was merely a matter of marching. December 7 was to be the day of liberation.

No sooner had these plans been set than they became unravelled. Mackenzie's co-conspirator in the capital, John Rolph of Norfolk, believing the government about to arrest the plotters, precipitately moved the date of rebellion forward to Monday, December 4. "Little Mac," as Mackenzie was known, on hearing this, rushed madly about, trying unsuccessfully to stay the change. On the fourth, men began mustering north of Toronto anyway. Faced with a *fait accompli,* Mackenzie decided to push ahead. But instead of acting decisively, he dithered, giving the authorities in Toronto time to collect their wits ... and volunteers. A final, pathetic scene saw a force of several thousand loyalists scatter the far fewer rebels on Thursday, December 7. Mackenzie rode off to safety, following Rolph, who had fled even before the fighting started. Hundreds of their followers were not so lucky.

It is mute testimony to the state of communications in that age that, just as Mackenzie and his men wrongly believed the rebels in Lower Canada to have been successful, so first reports of the affair at Toronto typically had "Little Mac" successful. These emboldened Charles Duncombe and fellow radicals in the Brantford area to begin mustering men to march to Toronto to support their supposedly triumphant colleagues. This second revolutionary movement swept up men from Brantford to St. Thomas, south of London. About 500 gathered southwest of the city on the Grand.[27]

At that other riverine centre, London, to the west, thirty reformers met on the night of Friday, December 8, in the bar at Flannagan's Tavern. They considered what action, if any, to take in response to the confused reports emanating from Toronto. A participant, Edward Allen Talbot, sometime inventor, author, newspaper editor, and brother to John of the *Liberal,* later told authorities, defensively, that after considerable discussion those present, worried lest the local Tories attack them in retaliation for Mackenzie's outrage, accepted a resolution he had drafted. It read:

> The Undersigned Reformers of the town of London do solemnly pledge ourselves that in event of any attack being made upon the lives liberty or property of any reformer in this Town we will to the utmost of our power aid each other in any Constitutional way in repelling any such attack[.]

Should one occur, they were to "assemble in the neighbourhood of the Scotch Church [Proudfoot's St. Andrew's] on a signal being given, which signal was to be the firing of two Guns and the blowing of a Bugle."[28]

John Harris, aware of the meeting, importuned Sheriff James Hamilton to arrest those present. In the words of a scornful Mrs. Harris, Hamilton's response was "Oh no we must re main [*sic*] quiet, we must not irritate them ... had I been a man & clothed with any authority," she blustered, "they should have all been lodged in the cells to keep them out of harms way." On Saturday night firm news came of Mackenzie's defeat. Hamilton "said dont Hurrah[,] do not Hurrah, it will excite them [the local radicals] but I am happy to say," Amelia wrote, "it was not in his power to suppress the true British feeling." She also noted that merchant James Latimer, one of the participants at Flannagan's, was "weighing out Powder to the Radicals." Her husband John and his young friend, lawyer John Wilson, finally persuaded a very reluctant sheriff to agree to its seizure. A scornful Amelia felt that Hamilton "will never be able to recover the confidence of the Towns people." [29]

The rumour mill continued working overtime. On Monday the 11th, John Askin, the district clerk, received word that London was to be attacked that night. This seemed to be confirmed in a confused account he later received of the decisions taken at Flannagan's. He wrote that

> the signal intended to be used by the attacking party for assembling ... was the firing [of] two Guns and to be immediately followed by the blowing of a Bugle, and their place of rendezvous the Scotch Church; this notice enabled me to rouse all the inhabitants that could be relied upon who instantly repaired to the Court House with all the Arms and Ammunition within their reach, in all about 200 strong; who soon put that building in a state of defence, capable of resistance for a period. I am fully satisfied now, that the Zeal displayed by the Loyalist[s] on that night frustrated such plans as might have been in progress of maturity by the Rebels.[30]

Askin had also received instructions from the province's attorney general to arrest John Talbot of the *Liberal* and to seize his correspondence. He set off the next day for St. Thomas, only to find that Talbot had flown two days previously. The next morning he received word from the east of the mustering of the Duncombe rebels. A major in the militia, he immediately volunteered his services to Colonel John Bostwick of Port Stanley, the commander of the local militia regiment. With Bostwick's, he quickly raised a force of approximately 200 volunteers who joined hundreds of others in putting the Duncombe rebels to flight.[31]

Just as Askin received word of the mustering of the Duncombe rebels in St. Thomas on the morning of the thirteenth, so the residents of London learned of their rising that same day. In response, the militia in and about London were summoned and marched down to St. Thomas by Sheriff James Hamilton, who was now acting in his capacity as a militia colonel. London was not to be left unprotected, however. Hoping to be of help in quelling rebellion, John Longworth, the superintendent of the Canada Company, led a force of 200 into London from the Goderich area on Thursday, December 14. Volunteers also mustered in Adelaide for London.[32] No wonder that Henry John Jones, travelling to London from Sarnia, recorded on the same day, after reaching the fork of the Thames, that

> long before our arrival at London we learnt that there was nothing like danger there, [having] arrived, [we found] it was as far to the East as ever. Symptoms of the military mania now however began to be apparent, the loyal citizens were keeping guard and drinking grog with much perseverance, heroes might be seen walking around in Buffalo robes and armed with sundry weapons[,] raggamuffins were in much demand for volunteers and were proportionably drunk and impertinent ...

He also heard "various reports of battles fought or to be fought at or about Oakland (10 m[iles]. west of Brantford) between the rebels under Duncombe and the loyalists under Askin, Bostwick &c."[33]

On Sunday the 17th, the Reverend William Proudfoot recorded with profound disgust that he had "preached in London from Heb. 1. 6-14 to about 49 persons. – The whole town taken up with catching the radicals so that no body had time to attend meeting for the worship of God. Such a scene I never witnessed." The next day, on his way home to his farm two miles north of the village he "was examined by a military picket, and got a *passport* for London!!"[34] The magistrates were active on another front, authorizing the seizure of weapons from those deemed less than loyal.[35]

The magistrates, like their counterparts elsewhere in the province, doubted the allegiance of many. Indeed, if Henry Jones was correct, they had good reason. Besides commenting acidly on the mock heroics of the volunteers he met in London on December 14, he also recorded that on his way into London from the west he had

> met numbers of young men with light packs making their way west. They were all radicals but took good care to keep their opinions to themselves. Every bar room was full of politicians the greater part of whom, if not radically inclined, showed no great attachment to the other side – I heard from no single individual any thing like a warm expression of loyalty.

Indeed, as Jones's comments suggest and as the recent past demonstrated, the radicals were well represented in and about London. Just as those in the district capital had met to decide what to do, so had those in both Dorchester and Delaware Townships. They got together, after the failure of the Duncombe revolt became common knowledge, evidently to take measures to assure their mutual safety. Less innocent were the actions of Robert Davis in Nissouri to the east of London, and of Alexander Roberts in Mosa to the west. They counselled armed resistance, indeed revolt.[36] However overzealous London officials may have been, it is not surprising, given all of this, that they felt obliged to take precautions. And indeed their village *was* soon awash with rebels.

Colonel Allan Napier MacNab had led the descent of loyalist forces from Brantford, southwest to Oakland Township, the site of Duncombe's encampment. As at Toronto, so in the west – the leaders escaped. But many of the rank and file did not. MacNab came to London to complete the job of pacification. He, or those trailing him, brought along a number of prisoners they deemed "notorious."[37] On December 22, thirty-eight more were cast into the London jail; these had been taken by Askin and his men.[38] In fact, the cells beneath the new court house were very soon desperately overcrowded. Within weeks ninety-three men implicated in the Duncombe rising were imprisoned, as were a further sixty-one (forty-eight of whom were from London and environs), accused of a variety of other misdeeds.[39] Not all could be crammed into the jail; some were jammed into makeshift quarters.

A board of magistrates sat to examine the prisoners. It began its deliberations on December 21, dealing with everyone from determined rebels to innocent victims. On the one hand, it questioned young Charles Lawrence, an English-born labourer from Yarmouth Township who resolutely flew his rebel colours, declaring that he

> is still a Reformer and does not regret going to Oakland [;] says that if the party had been attacked he would have fired and

> fought – He would have done any thing his Commander had told him – If Dr. Duncombe had told him with others to go to take Simcoe [and] if they had been resisted in any way he would have fired – "[40]

On the other, it had to consider the accusations against two proselytizing Mormons of sowing "seditious doctrine,"[41] as well as the case of Gaius Woolly of Dorchester. He had been taken up on passing through London "to Port Sarnia to get work to support his family."[42] Though the board sent Lawrence back to the cells, where he remained until released the following June, it sensibly freed the two Mormons and Woolly. In fact, the magistrates, aware of overcrowding, inadequate facilities, and the flimsy nature of some cases, were anxious to reduce the number of prisoners, freeing some outright, and admitting ninety-five others to bail. Still, the numbers incarcerated were sufficiently high to produce a "continual bableing [*sic*]," resembling "the shouts and peals of a thundering Bedlam,"[43] or so thought a continuing prisoner, John Grieve, a young Scottish farmer and a parishioner of William Proudfoot who had been active at the Westminster meeting in October. Proudfoot thought him "the best man" in his congregation and felt he had been imprisoned "not for any fault, but simply because being a man of great weight of character, it was needful to weaken his influence."[44]

Grieve was accused, among other things, of recruiting men for Duncombe's army.[45] The magistrates decided that the information against him did not prove treason, unless the Westminster meeting of the fall had been treasonous, but it did show his use of seditious language.[46] The grand jury, which began its deliberations on April 9, did not agree. His was one of the first cases it considered. It failed to indict him. He walked out of the London jail on April 10, a free man. Tragically, he was also a very sick one. Leaving a young family behind, he soon succumbed to "jail fever,"[47] becoming the second victim of the cold and damp of the London jail. The first was twenty-year-old Joseph Moore of Yarmouth, a nephew of Elias Moore who had won election to the assembly in 1836 as a member for Middlesex. Committed as a Duncombe rebel, Joseph had been released on bail in January, only to die soon after,[48] likely from the same ailment as Grieve.

John Moore, Joseph's father, was one of the eighty-one men indicted by the grand jury at London. At the time a number were out on bail; some promptly fled. Others petitioned for pardon under a provincial statute holding out the prospect of clemency for prisoners who threw themselves on the mercy of the lieutenant-governor.[49] By the time the London trials began, those at Toronto and Hamilton were already over. Samuel Lount and William Matthews, the two most notable Mackenzie rebels captured, had been hanged. A further fourteen were under sentence of death – not a happy note for John Moore and the eighteen others scheduled for trial in London. Actually, only fifteen made it to court, with cases being dropped by the Crown against four, at the last minute. John Moore and seven others were tried for involvement in the Duncombe revolt. Six, including John, were found guilty. John bid fair to join son Joseph in sacrificing his life for the rebel cause.[50]

The seven defendants from the London area fared much better. Three – Charles Latimer of London, the merchant who could not get at his money in the Bank of Upper Canada, William Hale of London Township and William Putnam of Delaware (previously of Dorchester) – were tried for their part in the December 8 meeting at Flannagan's Tavern. All three were acquitted, the jury

PROCLAMATION.

REWARD.

By Command of His Excellency the Lieutenant Governor.

A REWARD is hereby offered, of

Five Hundred Pounds,

To any one who will apprehend and deliver up to Justice,

CHARLES DUNCOMBE;

And a Reward of *Two Hundred and Fifty Pounds* to any one who will apprehend and deliver up to Justice, ELIAKIM MALCOLM; or FINLAY MALCOLM; or ROBERT ALWAY; and a Reward of *One Hundred Pounds,* to any one who will apprehend and deliver up to Justice, ——— ANDERSON, (said to be a Captain in the Rebel Forces); or JOSHUA DOAN.

All the above persons are known to have been traitorously in arms against their Sovereign; and to entitle the party apprehending either of them to the Reward, he must be delivered to the Civil Power, at Hamilton, Niagara, London, or Toronto.

GOD SAVE THE QUEEN.

16th December, 1837.

The government offered large rewards for the apprehension of the rebel leaders. Finlay Malcolm and Robert Alway were the only ones named in this proclamation to be captured immediately after the revolt. Alway, a member of the provincial parliament for Oxford, had played an equivocal role in the proceedings. He was jailed but the Crown did not proceed with the case against him. Malcolm, an admitted rebel, appealed for clemency under a provincial statute and was ordered transported overseas for fourteen years. He was freed in England in 1839. Finlay's brother, Eliakim Malcolm, and Charles Duncombe, David Anderson, and Joshua Doan had all been active in the rebellion. They escaped to participate in the "patriot" cause. Doing so cost Anderson and Doan their lives. Anderson died from wounds suffered in January 1838. Doan was executed at London for his part in the Windsor raid of December 1838.

thus signalling its doubt that the London reformers had indeed been plotting rebellion.

The last four placed in the dock were all involved in the so-called "Delaware conspiracy." When the Delaware Reformers had met on December 15 in the wake of the twin rebellions, they had decided to ask the Munceys and Delawares of the local reserve not to participate in any attack on them.[51] Suspicious magistrates believed that the Reformers had intended to enlist the natives in the rebel cause. The jury was not entirely persuaded, setting free three defendants – Gideon Tiffany and the brothers John and Moore Stephens. It convicted the fourth – merchant Alvaro Ladd. The verdict surprised Justice Henry Sherwood, since Ladd had been convicted on evidence that had secured the acquittal of his three co-accused. Sherwood reserved Ladd's case for further consideration.[52] The prisoner's situation aroused considerable attention. An anonymous, undated government memorandum noted that the Vermont-born Ladd was "of good private character" and "considerable influence," but that he was "a very dangerous

Philip Bainbrigge produced this water colour of the Moravian Indian village on the Thames, near present-day Thamesville, in 1838. As the "Delaware Conspiracy" of December 1837 and its repercussions illustrate, the settlers of Upper Canada, both Reform and Tory, feared unduly that the native people of the province posed a threat to their safety. Neither those at Moraviantown nor those at Delaware became involved in the rebellion, though the Six Nations peoples near Brantford were active on the side of the government.

National Archives of Canada, C-011829

character, in fact one of the most active and influential in his neighbourhood."
He had done, the author concluded, "much mischief." The merchant, however,
was quite ill and had a large family, as well as the backing of many locals who
signed a petition on his behalf.[53] His original death sentence was eventually
commuted to imprisonment for life in one of Britain's overseas penal colonies.
Then in late August of 1838 he, along with a number of others, was freed on bail,
since the government now had a whole new range of prisoners at its disposal. It
could make a better example of them.[54] These were the "patriots," American
raiders and their Canadian confederates.

Immediately after the failure of the Upper Canadian risings, border raids
began, as escaped rebels such as William Lyon Mackenzie and Charles Duncombe
joined with American sympathizers to try to revolutionize the province from
without. From the Niagara frontier to the Detroit River, to Pelee Island in Lake
Erie, to the Thousand Islands in the St. Lawrence, to the Short Hills area below
St. Catharines, they launched attacks. Each was a failure, with government troops

*The most celebrated of the "patriot raids" was the first. In mid-December 1837 Mackenzie
and his supporters seized Navy Island (item D in this bird's eye view) and for several weeks
defied the forces massed against them on the Canadian side. Late that month several boatloads
of Upper Canadians rowed across the river to Fort Schlosser (not shown) on the other side of
the river and cut out the Caroline, which had been ferrying supplies to the patriots. She
grounded above the falls, caught fire, and broke up. Though Mackenzie and company were
soon obliged to withdraw from Navy Island, the memory of the Caroline "outrage" burned
brightly in many a patriot breast for many a year.*

typically capturing some of the aspiring "liberators." It was the captives from the Short Hills raid who unwittingly provided Ladd with his release. The hanging of one and the scheduled executions of nineteen others (which, mercifully, never occurred), were thought by the authorities to promise example enough.

Aside from Ladd's liberation, the raids had other impacts on the London District. For one thing, they took Colonel James Hamilton and men from his regiment off to the Detroit frontier for several weeks in December and January of 1837–1838. For another, they brought a regular British garrison to London, with men of the 32nd Regiment arriving first, followed by some from the 83rd. By May there were some 300 regulars in town, with more expected.[55] The soldiers brought with them hard cash, and security – of a kind. One young resident later recalled:

> There were many complaints of the recklessness and lawlessness of the young officers; no doubt they thought they were out in the woods, and did not take into account the rights of property ... There was one company they called the "flying artillery." It would come rushing down the main street at any hour, and everything had to get out of its way; and it was only just out for a drill, or to exercise the horses.[56]

There were social compensations for some. Young Sarah Harris wrote from New Brunswick, where she and her father were staying with friends, to her mother, Amelia:

> I am sure the Scarlet Fever will be raging in great style with *so* many officers[.] Pray have any of the ladies of London got it? Mr. Hudson is teasing me about them. He says I will not be home a minute before I have it. I think I can stand fire.[57]

When danger threatened, the enthusiasm for the soldiers extended beyond the young ladies of the town and encompassed the rank and file as well as the officers.

In common with other Upper Canadian communities London was inundated periodically by rumours of intended patriot invasions. These reached a crescendo in the early summer of 1838 at the approach of a significant day, July 4, American Independence Day. Men of the local militia were summoned, along with the regulars, to guard the bridges and public buildings. Families began to pack up and leave.[58] Additional troops were rushed in from afar. The men of the 34th, approaching London on the third, heard the astounding rumour "that a party of insurgents had brought a fort a mile long from the States and located it on the Canadian territory." They reached London about midnight to find it peaceful, but heavily guarded, with native warriors camped on the outskirts.[59]

Not much happened. On July 1, seventy-two suspected "patriots" from about Chatham had been brought to the London jail. Most were soon released. On the fourth, new rumours of an attack, this one to be launched from Port Stanley, terrified many. Again nothing happened.[60] The men of the 34th marched off farther west, where they were needed more,[61] leaving some to chortle at the gullibility of London's citizens. "I was highly amused," wrote Jane Steers, a Chatham resident, to Amelia Harris, "at the panic" the raiders' "threatened approach struck into the hearts of the brave Londoners who had been studying military tactics for such a length of time under the gallant Col. Askin."[62]

However laughable the immediate situation, there was a nasty edge of hard reality behind all the rumours and all the panic. The autumn brought further proof of that – first, a bloody battle at Prescott involving hundreds in which fifteen militiamen died, then a grisly episode at Windsor. There, some 150 raiders slipped across the river from the American shore on the night of December 4, and surprised the local militia, killing or wounding several who tried to flee a burning barracks. They murdered surgeon John James Hume, who had hurried to the scene, then mutilated his body. A pitched battle ensued between defenders rushed to the scene and the raiders. Twenty-five of the latter died in that battle. Five others, taken captive, were promptly executed on the orders of the officer commanding, Colonel John Prince. "A Prince by nature as he is by name," rhapsodized one Tory.[63]

The Windsor raid had decided London overtones. One of the raiders killed during the fighting was William Putnam of Delaware, freed by a London jury the previous spring. On returning home after his trial, he had found his farm buildings burnt by "a political incendiary."[64] This evidently pushed him over the "patriot" edge. Early that summer, in an obscure affair he shot and killed a militia captain in Dawn, a township near the St. Clair River.[65] This, and his earlier successful career as a militia officer, apparently endeared him to the "patriots," for he had been elevated to the rank of "general" in their service, and was one of the leaders of the Windsor expedition.

Among those Putnam led were Elijah Woodman and James Aitchison of London and Cornelius Cunningham of Beachville, near Woodstock. The latter, an unemployed wagon maker, had gone off to Michigan the previous year looking for work to support his family and had fallen in with the "patriots."[66] Woodman, like Cunningham American-born, was a former lumber dealer who had lost his business on Otter Creek near Tillsonburg at the onset of the current depression. He had moved his large family to London, where he witnessed the election abuses of 1836 and ran afoul of the Tories during the treason trials of 1838 before fleeing to Michigan for safety. There he was tricked into joining Putnam's band, or so he claimed.[67] As for Aitchison, Justice Henry Sherwood, the judge at the previous treason trials in London, who was to play a leading role in the forthcoming ones, noted that the young Scot had lived in London the past few years and had been involved in the management of a distillery. "Lately he has been very much dissipated," Sherwood observed.[68] Of more significance was the fact that he was the nephew of the Reverend William Proudfoot.

Proudfoot, "suspected and blamed as a Radical,"[69] had seen his London congregation rent by the suspicion.[70] Already fearful that he would be seized and his papers ransacked,[71] he could not have welcomed the renewed scrutiny that his relative's arrest invited. Nevertheless, he bravely petitioned the lieutenant-governor, Sir George Arthur, on his nephew's behalf. Arthur, who had been appointed in Head's place the previous winter, was a former governor of the penal colony of Van Diemen's Land (Tasmania). Since assuming his Canadian office, he had found himself faced with one crisis after another. He was not well disposed towards the rebels and radicals who had caused so much trouble. He put Proudfoot among their number.

The prisoners were brought to London for trial, to a less impassioned atmosphere than that which reigned in Windsor.[72] The lieutenant-governor came down to keep a weather eye out. He interviewed Proudfoot, telling him that Aitchison must hang. Then, in Proudfoot's words, "he charged me with being myself a disaffected person," saying "that I preached against the continuance of the connection of Canada with Britain," adding that some of Proudfoot's congregation had deserted because of it. When Proudfoot protested, Arthur replied that it was of no use. The government had papers on him.[73]

Arthur's views boded ill for Aitchison. So too did the trial format. The rebels of the previous spring had been tried before a civil court, but legislation passed in January 1838 allowed the government to try captured "patriots" before either a civil court or a court martial. Justice might be more perfunctory in the latter. The government chose to place the captured Windsor raiders before a military court, as it had already done with the Prescott captives. Things had gone hard for them. Forty-four prisoners from Windsor were brought before the panel of militia officers trying them. None had the benefit of counsel.[74] All but one were found guilty. Six were condemned to death, including Cornelius Cunningham, and two former Duncombe rebels, Daniel Bedford of Norwich Township and Joshua G. Doan of Sparta, southeast of St. Thomas. Among the remainder was Amos Perley of Burford, near Brantford, a kinsman of Charles Strange Perley, who sat on the

The symbolism of the patriot insignia here is obvious, with the Canadian maple leaf (even then!) and the American eagle and British lion. Over 1838 the patriot organization evolved, becoming more complex and arcane, invoking secret oaths and employing the grand titles and desperate language so beloved of North Americans. Likely, "General" Putnam, killed at Windsor, received just such a commission as shown here. This one is signed by Henry S. Handy, "Commander in Chief," and E. J. Roberts, "Adjutant General," of the "North-Western Army on Patriot Service in Upper Canada."

Metropolitan Toronto Reference Library

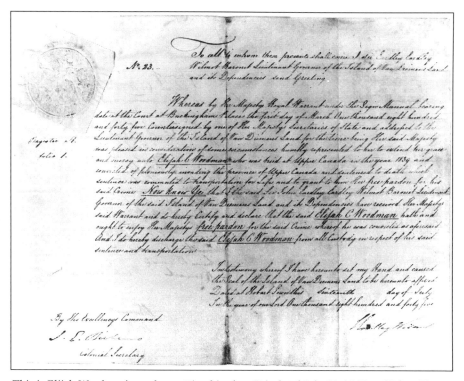

This is Elijah Woodman's pardon, setting him free. It is dated July 16, 1845, at Hobart Town, Van Diemen's Land (Tasmania) and signed by the lieutenant-governor of the colony.

Regional Collection, University of Western Ontario Library

panel condemning him to death! Arthur notwithstanding, Aitchison escaped the noose.

At the end of the treason trials in London the previous spring, six men had been sentenced to hang. They were subsequently freed on bail. The Windsor six were not so lucky. All were assigned dates with the hangman. American Hiram Lynn climbed the scaffold on January 7. Daniel Bedford, aged twenty-eight, followed four days later. Sheriff Hamilton released his body and he was buried in the Quaker cemetery in Norwich, in a ceremony attended by his wife and young child. Arthur, in London, was upset, both at Hamilton for surrendering the remains and at the 200 to 300 family and friends who turned out for the burial.[75]

A second American, Albert Clark, met his Maker on January 14. Then thirty-two-year-old Cornelius Cunningham faced the gallows on February 4. "Highly agitated," as the *London Gazette,* described him, he "could not stand erect – his head leaning upon his breast; but the drop soon ... relieved him from all earthly cares, after a struggle of a few moments."[76] His friends bamboozled Sheriff Hamilton and made off with his body, too. This, thought the sheriff, was "a matter of small amount."[77] On February 6, Joshua Doan – who had implored his young wife to "think as little of my unhappy fate as you can"[78] – and Amos Perley breathed their last. Doan was twenty-eight, Perley about the same. Both sprang "into eternity, without a struggle." Hamilton released their bodies as well. They were interred in the Quaker burying grounds in Sparta.[79] The two executed Americans, Clark and Lynn, were buried without ceremony in the jail yard.

This sketch of Woodman (artist unknown) was made in January 1844. He probably had not changed much when pardoned a year and a half later. He was then described as being five feet, four and a half inches tall, of dark complexion, with black hair and whiskers, brown eyebrows, hazel eyes, a small nose and mouth, and having a broad chin and long head and face. He was afflicted with poor eyesight. Regional Collection, University of Western Ontario Library

Despite the fact that most of the remaining prisoners were racked with illness from sleeping on the cold jail floor without beds or blankets,[80] they could count themselves fortunate. At least they were alive, and destined to remain so for the foreseeable future. Twenty-one were eventually deported back to the United States. Sixteen more were sent off to the penal colony of Van Diemen's Land (Tasmania). One of these was Elijah Woodman. Another was James Aitchison, Proudfoot's nephew. A third was John Burwell Tyrell of Bayham, who, like Aitchison, had a well-known relative – Mahlon Burwell, his uncle, London's Tory member of the assembly. The rebellion, like all civil wars, fractured many a family. Perhaps because of his family connection, however, Tyrell was the first to be released, in 1844. He returned home and resumed farming.[81] Woodman recorded in 1847 that Aitchison, now pardoned, had slipped across to Australia. "I do not think he will ever reach America," he added.[82] If Woodman had only known, he could have penned the same line about himself. Though he had received his pardon in 1845, he did not take ship for two years. Ill on embarkation, he died on the way home.[83] Clearly, the Windsor raid had many victims.

The trials of 1839 over, life in London and vicinity began to assume a semblance of normality, especially since the harsh sentences meted out did help end the "patriot" threat. Still, economic hardship continued to hound many, particularly in the countryside. The previous June a "gentleman" who had come directly from Port Burwell told the *Cleveland Herald* that in the London District prospects

> are wretched in the extreme. Discontent, fear, and anxiety prevail among the inhabitants generally, and the smothered workings of rebellion have paralyzed enterprise and ambition among the farmers and laboring classes. Business is abandoned, and towns that two years since were flourishing, now present deserted streets, and shut stores and mechanics' shops. Property has fallen to a mere nominal price, and the best families among the reformers are leaving the province daily.[84]

Things were not this bad in London, a centre aided greatly by garrison expenditures.[85] But there, too, some were persuaded by their political opinions to pack up and go. In May of 1838 Jane O'Brien, sister-in-law of the imprisoned Alvaro Ladd of Delaware, correctly predicted that he would quit the country as soon as he was freed. She noted that "great dissatisfaction and excitement prevails in the Country and many are daily leaving."[86] Another persuaded by "dissatisfaction and excitement" to flee was Edward Allen Talbot, who had drafted the reform resolution passed at Flannagan's in December 1837. He took his family off to the United States. Dogged by illness and misfortune, he soon died a pauper in Lockport, New York.[87]

Merchant Charles Latimer was a third who left. He did so after being freed by the jury in the spring of 1838. Writing back to William Proudfoot from Indiana, he tried to get him to lead a colony of London and area reformers to the head of Lake Michigan to settle.[88] Proudfoot demurred, living to see a brighter day, happily reporting in August 1839 that under the protection of Lord Durham, whose landmark report had recommended the establishment of responsible government in the Canadas, the Reformers were up and doing. Just as important, his London congregation "is recovering not only what it lost in the reign of terror, but even more."[89] As for Latimer, he became active with the "patriots" – at least as a speaker.[90] Trained in the law, he had bided his time in Upper Canada, waiting to meet the residency requirements of the bar.[91] He resumed his legal studies in Chicago, then began a practice in Potosi, Wisconsin. Fondness of the bottle proved his undoing, however. In 1844, in his cups, he picked a fight with the wrong man and was gunned down.[92] The tentacles of the rebellion reached far and wide – from Toronto and London, to the penal colonies in Australia, to Potosi – and in a far less happy way than a Mackenzie or a Duncombe ever contemplated when they raised the standard of revolt.

Today, the humorous aspects of rebellion days in London come readily to mind – Mrs. Harris's consternation at being caught casting bullets by the rector's wife! (and on a Sunday!) her daughter's easy confidence that she would be immune to "scarlet fever," the confusion caused by the mad flight of the "flying artillery" through London's streets, and, not least, the panic of "the brave Londoners … studying military tactics … under the gallant Col. Askin" at the prospect of danger. Hearts, too, can be warmed by the many assurances, then and since, that whatever happened had happened for the best. Even the dour Proudfoot found his pulse quickening in the summer of 1839 on reflecting that Reform would soon be triumphant, as the Tories had discredited themselves by their excesses.[93] Most writers since have composed an aria from this note, arguing that the rebellion set in train a process that produced, inevitably, responsible government. Perhaps the rebellion did hurry up the reform process, but if so the process was still slow, for responsible government, as we understand it, was not achieved until 1848. The logic of claiming that a failed rebellion was necessary to its much delayed arrival seems a little strained.

And so might it have seemed to those who felt obliged to sell off their farms, pack up their families and flee the province in the wake of the rebellion, or to lie awake at night wondering if the "patriot" hordes would fall upon them on the morrow. So too might that logic have been challenged by a William Putnam as he lay face down in the mud, his life oozing through the bullet wound in the back of his head, by a John Grieve coughing his last breath into a blood-spattered handkerchief, or by a Cornelius Cunningham jerking, violently at first, then ever less so, at rope's end.

ENDNOTES

1   University of Western Ontario, the D.B. Weldon Library, Regional Collection [hereafter Regional Collection], Harris Papers, letter, Amelia Harris to Becher, London, Dec. 14, 1837. This record is excerpted in: Colin Read and Ronald J. Stagg, eds., *The Rebellion of 1837 in Upper Canada* [hereafter *Rebellion of 1837*] (Ottawa, Ontario: Carleton University Press for the Champlain Society, 1985), vol. XII of the Ontario Series, pp. 321-323.

2   Fred Landon, "London and Its Vicinity 1837-38" [hereafter "London and Its Vicinity"], Ontario Historical Society *Papers and Records*, XIV (1927): p. 414. Landon's article is an excellent, pioneering piece.

3   William L. Mackenzie, *Sketches of Canada and the United States* (London, England: Effingham Wilson, 1833), p. 409.

4   J.H. Aitchison, "Development of Local Government in Upper Canada, 1783-1850" (Ph.D thesis, University of Toronto, Toronto, Ontario, 1963), vol. I, pp. 113-120.

5   *Ibid.*, pp. 102-111.

6   On Harris, see: Frederick H. Armstrong, *The Forest City: An Illustrated History of London, Canada* (Northridge, California: Windsor Publications, 1986), p. 82; on Askin, see: J.J. Talman, "Askin, John Baptist," *Dictionary of Canadian Biography* [hereafter *DCB*], IX: pp. 8-9. Talman notes that Askin's mother may have been a native but that this proved no handicap in his career.

7   For the 1836 census figures for the London District, see: Upper Canada, House of Assembly, *Journal Appendix*, 1837-38, Population Returns, p. 251.

8   The term responsible government had several competing definitions; the one used here was the one formulated by the Baldwins which became ascendant.

9   *Correspondent and Advocate* (Toronto, Upper Canada), Jun. 8, 1836, p. 3, c. 3.

10 Landon, "London and Its Vicinity," p. 414.

11 National Archives of Canada [hereafter NAC], Colonial Office Series (CO 42), "Extracts from the Poll-Books ... ," vol. 440, ff. 96-97. Some secondary sources have given the vote in London as *37* votes for Burwell and *27* for Scatcherd.

12 For a more extended discussion on the election of 1836, see: Colin Read, *The Rising in Western Upper Canada, 1837-8: The Duncombe Revolt and After* [hereafter *Rising in Western Upper Canada*] (Toronto, Ontario: University of Toronto Press, c1982), pp. 58-62.

13 *Constitution* (Toronto, Upper Canada), Jun. 28, 1837, p. 3, c. 4.

14 NAC, Civil Secretary's Correspondence, Upper Canada Sundries [hereafter Upper Canada Sundries] (RG5 A1), letter, Burwell to Joseph, Apr. 18, 1838, p. 106554.

15 *London Gazette*, Oct. 28, 1837, p. 3, c. 1.

16 NAC, Durham Papers (MG24 A27, series 2), "Evidence for the Durham Report," vol. 49, pp. 212-214.

17 *Constitution*, Aug. 2, 1837, p. 2, c. 2.

18 Archives of Ontario [hereafter AO], Mackenzie-Lindsey Papers (F37), Mackenzie section (series A-1-1), letter, Latimer to Mackenzie, Dec. 16, 1838.

19 *St. Catharines Journal*, Jul. 20, 1837, p. 2, c. 4.

20   *Constitution,* Jul. 12, 1837, p. 3, c. 2.

21   *Ibid.,* Sep. 13, 1837, p. 2, c. 4.

22   *Ibid.,* Jul. 19, 1837, p. 3, c. 4.

23   Mackenzie was later to claim that some 150-200 were formed. See: *Mackenzie's Gazette* (New York, New York), May 12, 1838, p. 3, c. 1.

24   For a detailed discussion of the political union movement, see: Read, *Rising in Western Upper Canada,* pp. 66-81; Read and Stagg, *Rebellion of 1837,* pp. xxx-xxxv.

25   On developments in Oct. and Nov., see: Read and Stagg, *Rebellion of 1837,* pp. xxxvi-xxxviii.

26   *Constitution,* Nov. 15, 1837, p. 1, c. 1.

27   For the events of the Toronto and western risings, see: Read and Stagg, *Rebellion of 1837,* pp. xxxviii-lxvi.

28   NAC, Records of the London District Magistrates [hereafter London District Magistrates] (RG5, B36), vol. II, related papers, deposition, Edward Allen Talbot, Jan. 8, 1838. Talbot went on to say that he had destroyed the resolution, but was sorry he had done so, since it "was intended to speak for itself."

29   Regional Collection, Harris Papers, letter, Amelia Harris to Becher, Dec. 14, 1837. Amelia Harris's strictures notwithstanding, Hamilton kept his job as sheriff until his death in 1858.

30   C.R. Sanderson, ed., *The Arthur Papers: Being the Canadian Papers, Mainly Confidential, Private and Demi-Official of Sir George Arthur, K.C.H. Last Lieutenant-Governor of Upper Canada in the Manuscript Collection of the Toronto Public Libraries,* 3 vols. [hereafter *Arthur Papers*] (Toronto, Ontario: Toronto Public Libraries and University of Toronto Press, 1957–1959), vol. I, pp. 35-36.

31   *Ibid.,* pp. 35-36. Here Askin suggested he had 260 men. Other sources put the force at about 100 less. As indicated, in St. Thomas he had found John Talbot gone. Talbot fled to Michigan, never to return. He had not been plotting rebellion, and he subsequently disapproved of the continuing attempts to revolutionize the province by attacking it from the United States.

32   Regional Collection, Harris Papers, letter, Amelia Harris to Becher, Dec. 14, 1837.

33   Sarnia Public Library and Art Gallery, Henry Jones Diary.

34   Regional Collection, Proudfoot Papers, Proudfoot Diary, p. 28.

35   NAC, Upper Canada Sundries, letter Laurason and Ball to Parkinson, Dec., 1837, p. 99237.

36   See: Read, *Rising in Western Upper Canada,* p. 105. Both Roberts and Davis escaped to the United States. Davis later died in an attempted invasion of the province.

37   *Patriot* (Toronto, Upper Canada), Dec. 22, 1837, p. 2, cc. 4-5.

38   Sanderson, *Arthur Papers,* vol. I, pp. 35-36.

39   Read, *Rising in Western Upper Canada,* pp. 108-109, 111-113.

40   NAC, London District Magistrates, vol. I, minutes, Jan. 26, 1838, p. 119.

41   *Ibid.,* vol. II, related papers, deposition, John George Bridges, Jan. 2, 1838; *ibid.,* deposition, Robert Mackey, Jan. 2, 1838.

42   *Ibid.,* vol. I, minutes, Jan. 6, 1838, p. 55.

43   H. Orlo Miller, ed., "The Letters of Rebels and Loyalists," *Canadian Science Digest,* 1 (Jan. 1938): pp. 72-73.

44   Regional Collection, Proudfoot Papers, letter, Proudfoot to Peddie, Aug. 1839.

45   See the evidence of Grieve *et al.* NAC, London District Magistrates, vol. I, minutes, Jan. 19, 1838, pp. 93-97.

46   *Ibid.,* vol. II, related papers, "List of prisoners as per Commr Book," notation beside Grieve's name.

47   Regional Collection, Proudfoot Papers, letter, Proudfoot to Peddie, Aug. 1839.

48   *Mackenzie's Gazette,* Jun. 2, 1838, p. 30, c. 3.

49   For the details, see: Read, *Rising in Western Upper Canada,* pp. 128-129.

50   For the details of these trials, see: *ibid.,* pp. 130-131.

51   NAC, London District Magistrates, vol. II, related papers, deposition, Alvaro Ladd, Dec. 27, 1837.

52   NAC, Upper Canada Sundries, letter, Sherwood to Joseph, May 16, 1838, p. 106820.

53   *Ibid.,* notes, "London Prisoners tried and convicted," n. d., pp. 106677-106678.

54   AO, Upper Canada State Papers (RG1, E3), Report of the Executive Council, Aug. 30, 1838, vol. 64, pp. 90-92.

55   Regional Collection, Dennis O'Brien Papers, letter, Jane O'Brien to Crichton, May 3, 1838.

56   Harriet Priddis, "Reminiscences of Mrs Gilbert Porte," London and Middlesex Historical Society *Transactions,* IV (1913): p. 69.

57   Professor Robin Harris, Harris Papers, letter, Sarah Harris and Owen to Amelia Harris, Mar. 15, 1838. Ironically, Sarah later married a British officer.

58   Regional Collection, Elijah C. Woodman Papers, Woodman Diary, pp. 12-13.

59   Metropolitan Toronto Reference Library, Baldwin Room [hereafter Baldwin Room], Diary of a Soldier in the [34th] Regiment, p. 3.

60   Regional Collection, Elijah C. Woodman Papers, Woodman Diary, p. 13.

61   Baldwin Room, Diary of a Soldier in the [34th] Regiment, p.3.

62   Professor Robin Harris, Harris Papers, letter, Steers to Amelia Harris, Aug. 1, 1838. Askin had been promoted to colonel in February, 1838.

63   NAC, Wallbridge Family Papers (MG24, 124), letter, Wallbridge to Howard, Dec. 31, 1838.

64   *Mackenzie's Gazette,* Jan. 5, 1839, p. 26, c. 4.

65   *Western Herald* (Sandwich, Upper Canada), Jul. 17, 1838, p. 173, c. 3.

66   NAC, Militia General Court Martial Proceedings (RG5, B37), Cunningham's Address.

67   Regional Collection, Elijah C. Woodman Papers, Woodman Diary. Fred Landon has recreated
        Woodman's story in full in *An Exile from Canada to Van Diemen's Land: Being the Story of Elijah Woodman
        Transported Overseas for Participation in the Upper Canada Troubles of 1837-38* [hereafter *An Exile*] (Toronto,
        Ontario: Longmans, Green, 1960).
68   NAC, Upper Canada Sundries, letter, Sherwood to Arthur, Jan. 18, 1839, pp. 117852-117854.   For a
        detailed, fascinating look at Aitchison and his misfortunes, see: Barbara C. Muirison, "Riches to Rags to
        Rebellion: The Case of James Aitchison, Sometime Resident of Scotland, Upper Canada and Van
        Diemen's Land," *British Journal of Canadian Studies*, 4, no. 2 (1989): pp. 257-275.
69   AO, Rev. William Proudfoot Papers (F974), letter, Taylor to Proudfoot, May 30, 1838.
70   Knox College (Toronto, Ontario), Proudfoot Papers, petition of members of the Presbyterian
        Congregation of London, Jun. 11, 1838.
71   Regional Collection, Proudfoot Papers, diary, p. 305.
72   NAC, Upper Canada Sundries, letter, Sherwood to Arthur, Dec. 28, 1838, p. 116920.
73   Regional Collection, Proudfoot Papers, diary, pp. 322-323.
74   *Ibid.*, p. 319. The prisoners were not allowed individual counsel. Henry Sherwood, in his role as "judge
        advocate" of the court, was to safeguard their interests by objecting to leading questions and by pointing
        out that they need not answer criminating questions. He put their questions to the witnesses. But as
        "judge advocate" he also played the part of public prosecutor.
75   Sanderson, *Arthur Papers*, vol. II, p. 20.
76   *St. Catharines Journal*, Feb. 14, 1839, p. 2, c. 4. The execution was doubtless public, since that was the
        custom at the time. The *Gazette* reporter was probably one of a throng who witnessed it.
77   NAC, Upper Canada Sundries, letter, Hamilton to MacAulay, Feb. 6, 1839, p. 128600.
78   Edwin C. Guillet, *The Lives and Times of the Patriots ...* (Toronto, Ontario: T. Nelson & Sons, 1938), p. 287.
        Fanny soon married Joshua's brother, Joel.
79   *St. Catharines Journal*, Feb. 14, 1839, p. 2, c. 4.
80   NAC, Upper Canada Sundries, letter, Moore to Hamilton, Jan. 24, 1839, p. 118210. This situation seems
        less attributable to malignity on Hamilton's part than to a chronic lack of funds.
81   Landon, *An Exile*, p. 177.
82   *Ibid.*, p. 256. Barbara Muirison was unable to track Aitchison after he crossed Bass Strait to Australia.
83   *Ibid.*, pp. 230, 257, 262.
84   *Mackenzie's Gazette*, Jun. 30, 1838, p. 59, c. 3.
85   Regional Collection, London and Middlesex Historical Society Papers, letter, Dyoel to Blin, Dec. 17, 1839.
86   *Ibid.*, Dennis O'Brien Papers, letter, Jane O'Brien to Isabella Crichton, May 31, 1838. On leaving prison,
        Ladd took his family to Michigan, but, importuned by his wife and relatives, returned to Delaware, where
        he died in 1842.
87   Daniel J. Brock, "Talbot, Edward Allen," *DCB*, VIII: pp. 842-844.
88   Knox College (Toronto, Ontario), Proudfoot Papers, letter, Latimer to Proudfoot, Sep. 1, 1838.
89   Regional Collection, Proudfoot Papers, letter, Proudfoot to Peddie, Aug., 1839.
90   NAC, Colborne Papers (MG24, A40), letter, Latimer to O'Beirne, Nov. 22, 1838, p. 5695.
91   Leslie R. Gray, ed., "The Letters of John Talbot," *Ontario History*, XLIV, no. 4 (Oct. 1952): pp. 142-143,
        editor's note.
92   *St. Catharines Journal*, Apr. 5, 1844, p. 2, c. 4. I am grateful to Daniel J. Brock for alerting me to this source.
93   Regional Collection, Proudfoot Papers, letter, Proudfoot to Peddie, Aug. 1839.

CHAPTER FOUR

EARLY VIEWS OF LONDON
Dartnell and His Contemporaries

Honor de Pencier

George Russell Dartnell was posted to Canada from 1835 to 1844 with the medical department of the British Army (Illus. 1). From May of 1840 to June 1843, he was stationed in the garrison at London with the First, or Royal Regiment, as its regimental surgeon.[1] During his three years in London he experienced professional success and enjoyed a pleasant social life, living on York Street with his family, and taking various excursions with a wide circle of friends. The respected surgeon also spent a good deal of his leisure time sketching views in graphite and watercolour, of which the surviving works now form a remarkable collection. Far more enduring than his medical contribution, his art legacy gives us a rich visual record of the town in its pioneer stage. Among his sixteen London views, four reflect the military presence, and the rest are views of the town, the Thames, and its bridges – except for three artistic studies of trees and stumps. Also worthy of mention are thirty-three works illustrating places in London's hinterland, including sixteen sketches of Port Talbot – the home of Colonel Talbot, the settlement leader of the London District.

This study will concentrate on Dartnell during his London years through the best of his sketches from that time and place. Where relevant, some connections between Dartnell's works and those by other contemporary British military artists in London will be noted as well. Such an examination will throw light on one of the most accomplished of London's pioneer artists whose work and life there have remained relatively unknown before now. At the same time, a better understanding of the military contribution to London's early artistic community emerges.

THE ARTIST'S BACKGROUND

Born of Huguenot (French Protestant) descent in Limerick, Ireland, in 1799 or 1800, Dartnell subsequently studied medicine in Cork from 1814 to 1819. Immediately after graduation, he joined the British Army's medical department. From 1821 to 1835, apart from a few short periods in the United Kingdom, he was posted to the Mediterranean, Ceylon (Sri Lanka), and India.[2] Since his training was in the field of medicine, he was not formally taught topographical drawing and sketching as were many of his fellow officers. He may have become interested in the art of drawing as a student in the intellectual and artistic community of Cork; however, the earliest works in his scrapbook are views taken in January, 1821, of Chatham, England, the site of his first military posting. These efforts, tentative and pale, suggest the hand of a learner; they lack a sense of perspective, but reveal good drawing skills and an early interest in light and shadow. Over the next fourteen years Dartnell, a keen observer and traveller, developed his artistic talent. In his small practice sketchbook dating from 1824 to 1835, he wrote notes attributed to well-known English watercolourists on instructions for painting, indicating an academic interest in improving his technique. By the time he reached Canada in 1835, his style was that of a competent, and often inspired, amateur artist, sensitively aware of the aesthetic taste of the day.

Little is known of Dartnell's wife, Anna Maria Bennett, during their Canadian years. One child, the fifth and a girl, Georgina Mary, was born on November 14, 1841, at London, and was baptized by the Reverend Benjamin Cronyn at St. Paul's on January 2, 1842.[3] Years later, probably about 1866, Georgina returned to Canada when she married Lieutenant-Colonel Frederick Wells of Davenport, Toronto. It was through her descendants that Dartnell's sketchbook, entitled "Worthless Scraps from Many Lands," in which he had pasted most of his sketches from abroad, was preserved and eventually brought to light.

Illus. 1.
(All dimensions are given in millimetres.)
George Russell Dartnell (1799/1800–1878), c. 1845.
Watercolour on ivory, 61 x 49 (sight), by Adolphus H.A. Wing (fl. 1848), London, England.

This portrait was probably taken about 1845 after Dartnell's return to England from Canada, on the occasion of his army promotion to staff surgeon, first class. That same year Dartnell published an illustrated book about the wreck of the Royal's transport, the Premier, *in the St. Lawrence River in 1843.* Private collection

THE ART OF SKETCHING

Fortunately for historians of Britain's colonial period, sketching views of memorable scenes was a popular leisure pastime for the British traveller, just as today's tourist uses the camera to record pictures for future reminiscing. Although subjective and personal glimpses of a certain place at a certain time, these *aide-memoire* exercises have often resulted in a legacy of importance far beyond their original purpose. In London, for example, the watercolours and drawings created by the military artists represent the major visual documentation of the 1840s, well ahead of the arrival of professional artists and the widespread use of photography.

The popular practice of sketching, from which London benefited to such a large degree, had its origin in Britain of the early eighteenth century. After years of touring the Continent, and seeing and collecting the landscape paintings of European masters, some of the British aristocracy and intellectuals became interested in their own countryside. The beauties of nature and the search for pleasing views inspired discussion and interpretation among writers, poets, and architects, as well as artists and the upper classes.[4] Influencing these aesthetic trends were two well-known landscape painters, Alexander Cozens (1717–1786) and Paul Sandby (1730–1809). As teachers, they had a direct or indirect impact on many of the officers who joined British garrisons abroad, for Cozens was active at Eton from 1763 to 1786,[5] and Sandby taught topographical painting at the Royal Military Academy at Woolwich from 1768 to 1796.[6]

Illus. 2.
Army manoeuvres near London, c. 1841.
Watercolour over graphite, 147 x 226, by George R. Dartnell

The garrison's regiments often marched out with artillery from London for countryside manoeuvres. These colourful exercises provided entertainment for the local farmers who sometimes left their work and went off for the day to enjoy the spectacle. Private collection

The materials most often used for sketching were graphite, pen and ink, watercolours, and paper. All were portable and fast-drying, and therefore most suitable for military purposes. The fact that these items were also easily available helped to advance the popularity of sketching as a social pastime for well-to-do amateurs of all ages, whether working indoors or in nature. Books on views and sketching also greatly influenced artists and critics alike. Among the most famous works were those by William Gilpin (1724–1804). Describing his tours in Britain and using his own landscape sketches for illustrations, he discussed "picturesque" beauty in nature and in art. His ideas of the elements desirable in an aesthetically pleasing picture became standard theories on the subject.[7] Certainly Dartnell and his fellow artists would have been familiar with them.

Following the success of Gilpin's travel books, and of new printmaking techniques for reproducing watercolour sketches as illustrations in books or as single sheets, publishers sought similar material from the British abroad. Canadian garrison life and country excursions, including descriptions of London in 1842 and 1843, were subjects discussed in a two-volume publication, *L'Acadie*, by Sir James Alexander (1803–1885), of the 14th Regiment, and illustrated by his wife, Lady Eveline-Marie Michell (*c.* 1818–1906).[8] Sir Daniel Lysons (1816-1898) of the Royals, also an artist, wrote a spirited account of his youthful adventures, *Early Reminiscences*, in which his short stay in London plays a part.[9] The early history of the city, as seen through British eyes, is enriched by both of these books.

Illus. 3.
Band field at London, June, 1841.
Watercolour over graphite, 182 x 261, by George R. Dartnell.

Victoria Park in London was once within the garrison's military reserve. The band field, part of the infantry drill and parade grounds south of the Barracks, is pictured here before it was totally cleared of stumps. This view might have been taken from Clarence Street.

Private collection

POSTED TO LONDON

As a result of the Rebellions of 1837 and 1838 in the Canadas, and the ever-present fear of war with the United States, the village of London was chosen by the British as the site of its major western garrison.[10] Its inland position made it not only less vulnerable to surprise attacks, but also considerably more isolated. As a result, the influence on London's economic and physical growth of an additional 1,000 military personnel to the civilian population of 2,000 was immense, and has been well documented elsewhere. The garrison's constant requirements of food, clothing, animal forage, general goods and support services greatly stimulated the local economy, as did the building of extensive barracks and even more housing for some of the officers with families who could afford to rent premises away from military property.

London was a popular and healthy posting in the 1840s for British officers.[11] Unlike India and Burma, the country was not constantly devastated by wars, nor did the army lose large numbers to tropical and other diseases, as it did in the Far East and the West Indies. With few military responsibilities and even fewer outside distractions in the small and insular community, the officers organized public and private events such as sporting displays, regimental band concerts, mess dinners and balls at the garrison, and indulged in theatrical evenings, hunt club meets, shooting excursions, and sleigh club outings. These activities provided varying degrees of entertainment for the local townspeople, depending on whether they

Illus. 4.

The Royals' Barracks at London, May, 1843.

Pen and brown ink with grey wash over graphite, 164 x 240, by George R. Dartnell.

Dartnell's view of the "Framed Barracks," built 1840–1841, was sketched from the north end of the military property, according to the artist, "from the Creek near the Old Saw Mill." The men's quarters seen here consisted of thirty-six rooms, each able to accommodate twenty men. To the right is the barracks hospital under Dartnell's supervision.

were of the appropriate social class to join in the events, or were only able to watch from the sidelines.[12]

The Royal Regiment marched into London on May 15 and 16, 1840, to take up duty for three years. With the 83rd and later the 14th Regiment, they replaced the 73rd and the 85th Regiments.[13] The thirty-nine-year-old Dartnell described the Royals' two-week trip from Montreal via Bytown (Ottawa) and Kingston by various water routes as exceedingly cold, crowded, and uncomfortable. But when the regiment reached Hamilton the weather was warm for their overland march and the final six days on foot to London were pleasant. The countryside they passed through, for Dartnell, was "rich and varied in scenery, undulating in beautiful hill and dale, well cleared and in many parts highly cultivated." His first impressions of London were also viewed in an artistic light:

> London is a large struggling town containing already upwards of 2000 inhabitants, the streets well laid out but the buildings all of wood, Even the gaol and courthouse which are in one, is of the same inflammable material tho' plastered to represent stone. This building occupies the centre of a fine open space called the square on the high ground above the river & at a distance has rather an imposing effect notwithstanding the sorry taste of the

Illus. 5.
View on the Thames at London, September, 1842.
Watercolour over graphite, with scraping, 234 x 320, by George R. Dartnell.

This picturesque view of London faces north towards the Court House. Easily London's most popular view, it was repeated by many visiting and local artists. Dartnell's other version of this scene (Illus. 6) is undated, but this one is probably his first on-the-spot attempt with its fresh, immediate atmosphere. Private collection

Architects & its unhappy position in the centre instead of on one side of the square ...[14]

The description of the Royals' march is the only known document written by Dartnell while in London, and so it is only through his sketches and the various references to him in letters and travel accounts by others that we learn about him and his art during this period.

DARTNELL AND HIS ART

Dartnell appears to have been well liked, judging by the many excursions he made with his new regimental and London friends. For example, on September 9, 1840, he travelled to Port Talbot, the home of Colonel Thomas Talbot. He was accompanied by Major George Bell of the Royals and Talbot's nephew, Julius Airey. The chatty Airey described their trip in a letter to his good friend Mrs. Amelia Harris, whom he had recently visited at Eldon House,

> ... Our drive from London was pleasant enough, as Dr. Dartnell is a clever man—and Major Bell, a very amusing one in his quiet, dry, way—We had, too, a luncheon at St. Thomas which was rather fun ...[15]

Illus. 6.
View on the Thames at London, c. 1842.
Watercolour heightened with white over graphite, 274 x 432, by George R. Dartnell.

The inscription on this carefully finished, luminous watercolour states that it was taken from the bank of the Thames near Mr.Wilson's house, looking north. Note the addition of the raft in the river, a detail used by other artists for this same view.

National Archives of Canada, C-13306

The same letter continues with the only known reference to Dartnell's chess ability, although his descendants do have an ivory chess set believed to have been brought back by him from India. Julius Airey suggests to Mrs. Harris,

> ... Do try your hand against Dr. Dartnell, who is held up as a *scarecrow* and give him one thorough defeat, so as to prove your preeminence over all your foes. I should be very glad to hear of your beating him!

From this exhortation we can assume that Dartnell had been introduced to the Harris family, the centre of London's social life, soon after his arrival. Another mention of their friendship is found in a letter from Lieutenant Daniel Lysons, to Amelia, one of the Harris daughters, a year after the Royals' departure from London. Lysons and Dartnell were travelling back to England together, and as a postscript in Lysons's letter, Dartnell sends his love to the Harris family.[16]

Judging from the dates on his sketches, Dartnell visited Colonel Talbot often, no doubt exchanging stories about Ireland, India, and other mutual interests. On

Illus. 7.
Gaol and Court House at London, c. 1843.
Watercolour over graphite, 157 x 242, by George R. Dartnell.

This rare, close-up illustration of the Court House and its surrounds is one of the most important records of early London. To the left of the Court House is Dennis O'Brien's three-storey brick building rented to the military for barracks. On the far left is the Mechanics' Institute opened in 1843, before its pillars were added in 1844. The Robinson Hall Hotel is to the right, on the corner of Dundas and Ridout Streets, where the disastrous fire of 1845 broke out, destroying all the buildings to the right of it and many more.

London Regional Art and Historical Museums, 48.A.61

Illus. 8.
Entrance to the West End of London, c. 1841.
Watercolour over graphite, 157 x 242, by George R. Dartnell.

As the western approach to London was via the Westminster Bridge to York Street, this must be a scene just west of the Thames. A signpost indicates that the second building on the left is an inn. Note the abominable condition of the road.

London Regional Art and Historical Museums, Art Fund, 48.A.60

June 25, 1841, he was at Port Talbot in the company of two officers of the Royal Regiment, the Honourable Charles Plunkett and Captain Trevor Davenport, both of the Royals.[17] In September of that year, Talbot wrote to the wife of another nephew, Colonel Richard Airey (1803–1881), in Toronto, and mentions Dartnell's sketching:

> ... Dr. Dartnell of the Royals has been here all last week and took 10 beautiful views of Port Talbot wh.[ich] he has taken to London to finish for me.[18]

Later that year, when the Aireys were back in England, Talbot wrote again, this time to Richard Airey, and indicated how much he liked Dartnell's work:

> ... I have not had many visitors, The officers come sometimes from London & St. Thomas, Dr. Dartnell, of the Royls. has been 3 times for a few days each time, to take views of Port Talbot, he has taken 15 and I expect him here soon with them finished. They are quite beautiful, & if I went to Engd. I should like much to have them engraved but suppose that would cost a great deal, pray inquire the expense of such work, they are coloured, & let me know... [19]

Four of Dartnell's known sketches depict the presence in the London area of the Royal Regiment. The earliest is titled "Ball Practice" and is dated July 31, 1840.[20] The work is not very visually satisfying, as the soldiers are so enveloped in gunsmoke that no details can be seen. A similar but undated outing was recorded more successfully, however, showing manoeuvres near London (Illus. 2). These drills were a part of military life, and a dangerous one at that. According to the barrack master's instructions for such exercises, "No Battery should Exercise without having a Surgeon in attendance ..."[21] Presumably, however, Dartnell's medical skills were rarely needed since he made a practice of taking along his sketching tools. Military exercises in the country became popular social occasions for the local citizens, as we learn from the diary of William Elliott.[22] The moment he saw a party of soldiers heading down the road near his property, he gave his farm help the day off and arranged to go and watch the proceedings with his family.

The good spirits and behaviour of the Royals, led by Colonel George Augustus Wetherall, who was a universally liked leader of both men and officers,[23] ensured their popularity among most of the Londoners. Wetherall put his men to work levelling the ground around the barracks, but also had them help the local authorities with the much-needed clearing of stumps and debris from the village roads. The area now known as Victoria Park had not yet been totally cleared when Dartnell made his sketch in 1841 of what he called "The Bandfield" (Illus. 3). It is difficult to determine from which angle the artist has taken this view, but those huge stumps very much in evidence in the sketch of the field eventually formed an effective fence around the space.[24]

Illus. 9.
York Street, London, C.W, c. 1842.
Watercolour with gouache over graphite, 262 x 398, by John Herbert Caddy (1801–1887).

The west entrance to London is pictured here, as the muddy road in the foreground winds down the bank to the Westminster Bridge and on up the east side via York Street.

Similar clearing was obviously necessary around the newly built "Framed Barracks" (so called to distinguish it from the already existing log and brick barracks buildings) just east of the bandfield, which was apparently occupied by the Royals in the winter of 1840–1841.[25] As regimental surgeon, Dartnell was responsible for planning appropriate health facilities for the barracks, as well as the organization of its new hospital building. It measured 89 feet by 39 1/2 (27 m by 12), and was capable of housing fifty-six patients.[26] Dartnell did an excellent job, as the following extract from Major General Armstrong's half-yearly inspection orders of 1842 for the Royals indicates:

> … but the Major General's praise is especially due to the state of the Regimental Hospl. & the judicious arrangements of Surgeon Dartnell.[27]

The first known view of the barracks appears in a watercolour sketch, dated May 1842, by Henry Francis Ainslie (1803–1879), of the 83rd Regiment.[28] Hundreds of small stumps remain dotted over the grounds, although the dirt road seems cleared. Ainslie's fresh, naive style makes the barracks look pristinely new. He also sketched an encampment of the Royals showing about forty white tents amidst stumps and dark trees.[29] Both are excellent military records. When Dartnell made his sketch of the Royals' barracks in May of the following year, his view was more picturesque (Illus. 4). It is not clear if the stumps near the buildings had been removed by this date, as most of the grounds are hidden by a

Illus. 10.
York Street, London, June 26, 1841.
Watercolour over graphite, 235 x 335 (sight), by George R. Dartnell.

Dartnell's sketch of his street is taken from the east, and shows the typical wooden houses of the period, haphazardly placed on their lots next to the roadway and surrounded by tree stumps. Dartnell's house may be the last one in view on the south side of the street next to the river. Colonel Wetherall's was apparently opposite on the north side. Private collection

dramatic, dark foreground, heavy with rough, broken tree trunks. This artistic treatment was designed to set off the main subject of the picture, the barracks, and it succeeds.

Although this barracks was London's largest building during Dartnell's time, the Court House was more important: it represented London's dominance over the surrounding counties of the London District as their judicial and administrative centre. The view looking north up the river towards the imposing white mortar Court House – built between 1827 and 1830[30] and said to resemble components in Malahide Castle, the ancestral home of Colonel Talbot – is easily the most popular London scene sketched by the early artists. Sir William Eyre (1805–1859) used it as the subject of a vignette on his map in 1839,[31] and Sir Henry James Warre (1819–1898), who referred to the Court House as the "Gaol at London," made it the centre of his rough pencil sketch of 1840.[32] In September 1842, Dartnell drew and painted a similar view. It is a warmly toned, well-finished watercolour composition, but it also has the freshness of an on-the-spot sketch (Illus. 5). Taken from quite high on the bank of the river opposite the village to the southwest, which was known as Askin's Hill, the scene focuses on the white Court House under a bright sky, framed by the dark foliage of scattered trees on either side. A grouping of two figures on the near bank adds both a sense of scale and intimacy, and two white cows standing languidly in the distant river lend a pastoral quality to the view. When Dartnell reworked this same scene, at an unknown date, into a larger, more dramatic composition, he included the same

Illus. 11.
House at London, c. 1843.
Watercolour over graphite, 123 x 180, by George R. Dartnell.

This house was situated on the south side of York Street near Westminster Bridge, which can be seen on the right. Dartnell apparently gave the sketch to Lieutenant Lysons, who inscribed it "Our House," suggesting that Lysons stayed with the Dartnells during his brief sojourn at London. National Archives of Canada, C-13301

lazy cows, and increased the number of figures in the foreground group to three (Illus. 6). This impressive view further differs from the earlier one with the addition in the near river of a rectangular log raft, manned by two men, each with a long pole.

At least two other important artists in the 1840s, Colonel Richard Airey and Captain John Herbert Caddy (1801–1887), also produced sketches of this popular river and Court House scene. Only one of these views by Airey[33] is known, but Caddy did at least two. One is an unfinished pencil sketch, which he states is from "Wortley Road Hill" (or Askin's Hill),[34] and the other a recently discovered finished watercolour of the same composition, but omitting the foreground river bank seen in his pencil drawing.[35] The fact that Airey and Caddy both show a raft in the river, not unlike Dartnell's, suggests that one of them had seen his larger work, although these rafts were a common sight. It was not unusual for amateur artists to copy successful features of their friends' paintings. Although Airey seems to have sketched with Dartnell once in 1840 at Port Talbot, Airey was back in England by the end of 1841, and he did not return to Canada West until 1847.[36] Caddy, however, arrived in London in 1842 to take up his posting with the Royal Artillery, and would soon have met Dartnell in a military or social context.[37]

There is no evidence to prove Caddy and Dartnell sketched together, but as keen artists they probably examined each other's work at some point during their year together in London. Caddy might, on such an occasion, have seen Dartnell's view with the river raft, and remembered the detail for his own rendering of the

Illus. 12.
Bridge over the Thames near London, 1841.
Watercolour heightened with white over graphite, 143 x 218 (sight), by George R. Dartnell.

The south entrance to London over the Thames was at the end of Wellington Street via "Clark's Bridge." Since this view resembles James Hamilton's mid-nineteenth century painting identifying that bridge, it is probably Clark's. If so, one of the small buildings on the right bears the grand title of Westminster Abbey Hotel. Private collection

subject. In any case, Caddy's views appear to relate more to Airey's than to Dartnell's, and it is likely that the former two were sketching companions, or that one copied the other's work after Airey's return to London; neither work is dated. Although Airey and Caddy also sketched from the southwest river bank, using

Illus. 13.

Stump Study, London, May 18, 1843.

Pen and brown ink with grey-brown wash over graphite, 259 x 182, by George R. Dartnell.

Wherever he went, Dartnell was interested in sketching trees. Broken stumps were considered a useful feature in certain compositions, and Dartnell was obviously practising his draughtsmanship with the many examples at London, just before his regiment left town.

Private collection

Illus. 14.
Finish of the Party to the Falls, January, 1843.
Pen and ink, 98 x 156, by Sir James Alexander (1803–1885).

Alexander's sketches are preserved in a small sketchbook and enhance his tales of life in Canada. Dartnell joined the Alexander party on this sleigh trip to Niagara Falls and Toronto to break the boredom of the long winter.

National Archives of Canada, C-98771

trees to frame their compositions, their views are taken from a more distant point than Dartnell's, and both place the Court House to the left side of their compositions, and not in the centre, as he did. Both Airey and Caddy have a careful, linear style, and depict more town buildings than Dartnell does. Most important, the presence in their skylines of the newly constructed St. Paul's Church dates their works after 1846.[38] A comparison of Caddy's finished watercolour with the well-known Scobie and Balfour lithograph of this same scene, published by Thomas Craig of London, C.[anada] W.[est] between 1846 and 1850, helps to confirm Caddy as the source of the print.[39]

Perhaps the most significant documentary view of the Court House and its immediate surroundings is that painted by Dartnell in 1843 (Illus. 7) This work and four other paintings by Dartnell were discovered in London, England, by an art dealer, and the London Public Library Board purchased them in 1948, at which time it was noted that the library's collection had no other pictures done by a resident of this city prior to the 1870s.[40]

This rare close-up view of the Court House has been executed in a light, airy, and confident style. A large flag flutters above the crenellated towers, shown from the river side. Below, a few figures saunter over the rough, rocky ground, and two lean against one of the piles of heavy timbers lying about. To the left of the Court

House is Dennis O'Brien's three-storey red brick building, the only other brick edifice at that time besides the Court House. It was rented to the military for barracks after 1838.[41] Next to it, small and white on a corner of the Court House square, stands the newly built Mechanics' Institute, a forerunner of the modern London Public Library. An important learning and gathering place, the Institute had rooms for day and night school, for drawing and sculpture classes, and for music, as well as a hall for lectures, balls, or meetings such as those of the Temperance Society.[42] To the right of the Court House is a group of buildings that includes the Robinson Hall Hotel, on the corner of Dundas and Ridout Streets, the market, and other commercial enterprises, all of which were lost in the fire of 1845.

In the same group of Dartnell sketches purchased in England in 1948 there was also an undated watercolour titled "Entrance to the West End of London" (Illus. 8). The journalist who first described this work remarked that the dark forest background was notable for the number of fir trees in it, not shown in other early paintings of the area.[43] Since the settlers felled most of Canada's old forests for housing, agricultural, and fuel needs, this kind of sketch is a useful record of our former timber resources. A signpost in front of the second building from the left indicates that it was an inn, and the dirt road cries out for the improvements that were then in the planning stages. Colonel Casimir Gzowski, a Polish aristocrat

Illus. 15.
London, Canada West, 1842.
Watercolour over graphite, 241 x 362, by Peter Valentine Wood (act. 1810–1855).

In his only known watercolour, of which there are two versions, Captain Wood reminds us that while excursions by sleigh provided winter entertainment for carefree garrison officers, others were concerned with bringing home game for dinner, or chopping trees for fuel and shelter. Wood's handwritten notes accompanying this sketch point out the Court House on the left and the Barracks on the right. In the centre, he later wrote, "Wooden Church since burnt & likewise the Town ..." His inscription continues "The Bayonet Tree!" and then "A plank-Road was since Constructed – and subsequently, the Rent Road ..."

London Regional Art and Historical Museums, gift of the Women's Canadian Club of London, 87.A.68

Illus. 16.
Thames River at London in winter, c. 1843.
Watercolour over graphite, 137 x 223, by George R. Dartnell.

This sketch was taken from Westminster Bridge, looking north beyond the Court House on the right towards the flats near the river. The building at the base of the slope on the right is probably John Jennings's distillery, built in 1836.

National Archives of Canada, C-13304

who had fled into exile to the United States, was hired as superintendent of roads and waterways in the London District, and in 1842 was working on the plank road that was designed to speed up communications and deliveries on the well-travelled route between London and Port Stanley.[44]

A traveller coming to London on the famous London and Port Stanley Road would have seen, as his first view of the town, the scene portrayed by Caddy in his watercolour of York Street (Illus. 9). Given a date of 1842, and incorrectly identified as "looking west," the view illustrates clearly the old York Street or Westminster Bridge from the western bank, and across the river can be seen various buildings on either side of the street as it winds up the hill. The Court House is in the background dominating the skyline. The detailed foreground reveals a dirt road, flanked by trees, plants, and bushes, turning down the western bank of the Thames to the bridge. This carefully executed work displays Caddy's keen interest in nature and his ability to make a topographical view into a pleasing picturesque composition.

Dartnell's view of York Street, on the other hand, is completely different in style and is taken from the opposite direction, looking west (Illus. 10). Inscribed by the artist, "The street we live in – York Street – London," and dated June 26, 1841, it is a loose, rough sketch portraying a straggling bunch of very humble buildings on either side of a muddy, treeless road. The foreground shows the east end of muddy York Street, flanked by dark, dead trees and stumps, and unrelieved by the lush, green foliage that softens Caddy's view. Beyond the disappearing road can be seen a glimpse of background forest on the western riverbank from which Caddy sketched. The two farthest houses in sight in Dartnell's composition, if they are closest to the river, would be Dartnell's own white house on the left, or south, side and Colonel Wetherall's on the right, if present research is correct.[45] Despite a dull composition, Dartnell's treatment of his York Street view, uplifted by a luminous sky, remains livelier and more personal than Caddy's.

That same sensitivity is evident in Dartnell's small, expressive sketch of the house we believe he lived in on York Street (Illus. 11). According to the tax records, there was a two-storey frame building on lot 26 on the south side of York Street, just east of the river, and another one-storey house next to it on the same lot.[46] The larger house had three fireplaces, two horses, and one milch cow, which were notations made for assessment purposes. In 1844, it was owned by the lawyer Henry C.R. Becher, a friend of Dartnell's. Since this watercolour sketch has come from Lieutenant Daniel Lysons's scrapbook, where he has identified it as "Our House," and notes it was painted by "G.R. Dartnell," it is possible that the bachelor Lysons lived with the Dartnells for his short stay in London. They were friends, and Dartnell likely gave Lysons this view of the house as a present.[47]

Many of Dartnell's trips out of London to enjoy the countryside would have taken him over Clark's Bridge, situated at the then south end of Wellington Street. A view by Dartnell, titled "Bridge over the Thames near London" (Illus. 12) probably represents this bridge, as it is similar to the one painted and identified as a little later by the well-known London artist, James Hamilton (1810–1896).[48] Dartnell's rendering of the thick, gloomy forest, surrounding a roughly cleared area with buildings, is enlivened by a man canoeing in rapids caused by a short waterfall under the bridge. If this is Clark's Bridge, one of the humble structures on the south shore bears the grand name, "Westminster Bridge Hotel."[49]

The details of two highly successful excursions enjoyed by Dartnell and friends have been described in published accounts. The first, a report of a trip taken by Becher, Gzowski, Dartnell, and two others from London to St. Mary's in the fall of 1842, was written by Henry C.R. Becher for the *Albion*, a New York newspaper.[50] As part of his article, the writer recounted three rambling stories told by Dartnell for the group's entertainment about his adventures with elephants in Ceylon. Dartnell's musical talents also showed up on that trip. Gzowski begged him to whistle a tune to mesmerize a grouse the two had seen in the woods, to give Gzowski time to run back to camp for his gun. Both whistler and hunter were rewarded in their efforts with an improved dinner. Another vignette involved the group's decision to return to London in a quickly constructed boat, as the road to St. Mary's was so bad. The leaky craft was bailed out by Dartnell with his hat. Not surprisingly, only one sketch by Dartnell survives from this trip, but we are told that the group admired others, especially one with a particular maple stump in front of the door of the "St. Mary's Hotel." Perhaps this praise inspired Dartnell to do more log and stump studies, as three such subjects are part of his London collection (Illus. 13).

Another excursion was made by sleigh in the winter of 1843 by Sir James and Lady Alexander, Captain and Mrs. Davenport, Lieutenant Paton, and Dartnell to Niagara and Toronto and is described by Alexander in *L'Acadie*.[51] Dartnell again regales the party, this time with stories about his adventures as a medical student in Cork, and as an army doctor in India. He also sketched the falls, and one scene shows the group visiting at their peril in the wintry weather,[52] but it is Alexander's delightful pen-and-ink drawings from his small sketchbook that provide a glimpse of the spirited and humorous side of this winter break (Illus. 14).

A sleighing excursion in the outskirts of London in winter is the subject of an original and informative watercolour by Captain Peter Valentine Wood (active 1810–1855), the paymaster of the 14th Regiment (Illus. 15). His composition, titled "A Sleigh Scene in Canada West," is lively in style and subject, though pale in colour. The barracks and other London buildings make up the background, and two groups in sleighs are depicted flying out of town on a snowy track. They pass three men, two of whom are swinging axes at a very large tree. In the foreground two hunters return home. Wood painted two versions of his successful scene with only minor variations between them. The artist was probably asked to copy his first work for a friend, as the view illustrated here is signed "P.V. Wood," and the other "P.V.W."[53] Although Wood must have lived in London with his regiment from 1842 to 1843,[54] little is known about him, and no other paintings by him have been found.

Dartnell also painted a memorable London winter scene which he gave to Lysons (Illus. 16). Although it lacks the action of Wood's subject, Dartnell's crisp view of the Thames and the flats beyond, taken from the Westminster (now York

Illus. 17.
Grand Military Steeple Chase, at London, Canada West, 9th May, 1843.
Aquatint and etching with watercolour, 377 x 515, engraved by J. Harris after a sketch by Lady Alexander (c. 1818–1906). Published by R. Ackermann, London, 1845.

The much-advertised military steeplechase finally took place in early May on the flats of the Thames below the Court House. Lieutenant Lysons, friend of the Alexanders, is seen in the lead, although he was disqualified as the winner due to a weight advantage. The white house, sketched by Dartnell (Illus. 11), can be seen on the far right.

Royal Ontario Museum, Sigmund Samuel Collection, 949.150.10

Street) Bridge, shows a couple strolling on the frozen river. Executed in an easy, yet highly finished style, the painting brilliantly renders the light of snow and sky; its luminous quality has been achieved by the use of a thin mix of pale watercolour washes on the background, so that the paper's own reflective whiteness shines through.

The same river flats depicted in Dartnell's winter view were also the site of a famous military steeplechase, which took place on May 9, 1843, shortly before the Royals left London. This event, recorded in a sketch by Lady Alexander, was reproduced in a now-famous engraving published by Ackermann of London, England (Illus. 17).[55] In the background, the Court House is visible high up on the riverbank. The white house, on the far right, is the same one portrayed by Dartnell in the small sketch which he gave to Lysons. As Lysons was also a good friend of the Alexanders', he is depicted winning the steeplechase in Lady Alexander's view (although he was later disqualified due to a weight advantage), and the house is probably included for his benefit. Despite the fact that Lysons is mentioned often in the Harris papers on the subject of sketching, apparently only one of his London works has survived. It is a delightful pen-and-ink drawing affectionately inscribed, "Go it Chass[e]," of a young pig-tailed Charlotte Harris racing on horseback against Lady Alexander.[56]

In April and May 1843, the Royals' impending departure was the occasion for comment and advertisements in the newspapers. Front pages quote formal goodbyes and mutual admiration speeches, and the advertisement sections contain numerous notices of houses for rent and auctions of various officers' household goods, carriages, horses, and cows.[57] Even Dartnell was publicly thanked by a grateful patient who sent in the following for Saturday, May 6, 1843:

> TO THE EDITOR OF THE LONDON HERALD.
> Sir,—
> Hearing that the Royal Regiment is about leaving London, I take this opportunity through the columns of your paper, to testify publicly my gratitude to Dr. DARTNELL for his kind attention to me, being under Providence, the means of restoring me to health from a dangerous disease, with which I have been afflicted for many years. His experience, as a professional gentleman, and his generous conduct towards the many individuals who have been under his care, during his long stay at this place, has rendered his going away a source of deep regret to all, particularly, to Yours, &c.

> London, May 3rd, 1843.   John Sharp.[58]

CONCLUSION

By June the Royals had marched away to Toronto, and were replaced by the 23rd Regiment; three months later the 14th took their leave.[59] The departure of these two famous regiments marked the end of a valuable period of artistic and cultural contribution to London's heritage by the British military. Some of their watercolour sketches survive as the only images of the town before the great fire of 1845. New regiments followed, and with them a few artists including Captain Edmund G. Hallewell (1803–1881) and Captain Charles H.A. Lutjens (1829–1915), both of whom were painting towards the end of the decade, as were

Caddy and Airey. Also worth noting is the existence of a charming oil painting, unsigned, of Captain, the Honourable Robert A.G. Dalzell of the 81st Regiment in his fancy sleigh, accompanied by three of the Harris sisters. They are depicted in front of the Harris home, Eldon House, in 1846, with the Thames, Blackfriars Bridge, and fenced fields in the background.[60]

On leaving Canada in November 1843, the Royal Regiment was shipwrecked in the St. Lawrence River during a storm, but no lives were lost. Dartnell, who wrote an illustrated book about this experience,[61] returned to England in the early spring of 1844, to continue his successful medical career. In 1854 he was appointed deputy inspector-general of hospitals for the army,[62] and had the honour of escorting Queen Victoria around the Fort Pitt Hospital at Chatham, of which he was in charge,[63] when Her Majesty wanted to visit soldiers wounded in the Crimean War. Dartnell continued to paint as a hobby, and exhibited watercolours between 1867 and 1873 at the Royal Birmingham Society of Artists.[64]

In 1861, Major Bell, later Colonel Sir George Bell, returned to London to revisit the scene of his pleasant posting with the Royals. He stayed in the Tecumseh House, and took a walk by gaslight into the city, but "could not recognise a house or a street in the little village where I was stationed for two years, when the stumps of the forest trees were still fast in the short wide streets ... The Railway Station here in London I find stands in my garden ... A village stands on our old steeplechase ground, a Bank and the General Post Office, fine buildings, occupy the place where my cow used to feed ... "[65] With these and other inevitable changes in the town, the sketches of London by Dartnell and his contemporaries remain as a vibrant visual legacy of a past that has vanished completely now. Without their pictures, we would have little idea of the appearance of early London.

ENDNOTES

Author's Note: I am indebted to many people for help with this article, and wish to thank them all, particularly Mary Allodi, Royal Ontario Museum; Jim Burant, National Archives of Canada; James Campbell, the Weir Foundation; Barry Fair, London Regional Art and Historical Museums; Val Girvan, Guildford, England; and Alan Watson, Metropolitan Toronto Reference Library.

1. Great Britain Public Record Office, War Office [hereafter PRO/WO], 25/3900.
2. *Ibid*, 76/238, 25/3900, 25/3907.
3. Huron College, Anglican Diocesan Archives, St. Paul's Cathedral, London, baptisms, vol. 1, Georgina Mary Dartnell, Jan. 2, 1842. I am grateful to Charles Addington for this information.
4. Christopher Hussey, *The Picturesque: Studies in a Point of View* [hereafter *Picturesque*] (London, England: Frank Case, 1967), p. 12.
5. Kim Sloan, *Alexander and John Robert Cozens: The Poetry of Landscape,* exhibition catalogue, Art Gallery of Ontario (New Haven, Connecticut: Yale University Press, 1986), p. 40.
6. Huon Mallalieu, *Understanding Watercolours* (Suffolk, England: Antique Collectors' Club, 1985), p. 48.
7. Hussey, *Picturesque*, pp. 11-124.
8. Sir James E. Alexander, *L'Acadie; or Seven Years Explorations in British America* [hereafter *L'Acadie*], 2 vols. (London, England: Henry Colburn, 1849).
9. Sir Daniel Lysons, *Early Reminiscences* [hereafter *Reminiscences*] (London, England: John Murray, 1896).
10. James L. Henderson, "A Study of the British Garrison in London, Canada West 1838-1869" [hereafter "Garrison"] (M.A. thesis, University of Windsor, Windsor, Ontario, 1967), pp. 3-4.
11. Alexander, *L'Acadie*, vol. 1, pp. 139-140, 142.
12. *Ibid.*, pp. 140, 142, 181-184, 237-238; Henderson, "Garrison", pp. 12-15; Lysons, *Reminiscences*, pp. 157, 161-163.
13. Henderson, "Garrison," p. 9.

14. George R. Dartnell, "Leaves from an Officer's Diary, 1836-1840," Women's Canadian Historical Society of Toronto, *Transaction*, no. 4 (1903): pp. 14-15. Dartnell was wrong about the Court House, which is actually brick under the mortar.

15. University of Western Ontario, the D.B. Weldon Library, Regional Collection [hereafter Regional Collection], Harris Papers, Airey to Harris, Sep. 11, 1840.

16. *Ibid*, Lysons to Amelia Harris, Feb. 13, 1844.

17. Dartnell drew two sketches of these officers, along with Colonel Talbot, standing on the cliff overlooking Lake Erie. See: Honor de Pencier, *Posted to Canada: The Watercolours of George Russell Dartnell, 1835-1844* [hereafter *Dartnell*] (Toronto, Ontario: Dundurn Press, 1987), pp. 62-63, 105.

18. Hereford and Worcester Record Officer, Garnons Collections, (G/1V/A) [hereafter Hereford and Worcester], Richard Airey Papers (Courtesy Sir John Cotterel, Bart.), Talbot to Mrs. Richard Airey, Sep. 13, 1841; Jim Burant and Judith Saunders, *The Garrison Years: London, Canada West 1793-1853*, exhibition catalogue, (London, Ontario: London Regional Art Gallery, 1983), p. 15. James Burant found these important Dartnell references.

19. Hereford and Worcester, Richard Airey Papers, Talbot to Richard Airey, Dec. 3, 1841. No such engravings are known.

20. Private Collection. See: de Pencier, *Dartnell*, pp. 61, 104.

21. Regional Collection, Thompson Wilson Papers, military notebook, "Surgeon," p. [87].

22. Metropolitan Toronto Reference Library, Baldwin Room, Judge William Elliott Diary, Jul. 6, 1841.

23. Alexander, *L'Acadie*, vol. 1, p. 138.

24. Fred Landon, "British Regiments in London," *Western Ontario Historical Notes*, XIII, no. 3 (Sep. 1955): p. 6; *London Free Press*, Jun. 20, 1959, p. 25, c. 7.

25. National Archives of Canada, British Military and Naval Records, Ordnance Records (RG8, series II), Reports and Returns, London, vol. 49, p. 9.

26. Edwin Seaborn, *The March of Medicine in Western Ontario* (Toronto, Ontario: Ryerson, 1944), p. 147.

27. PRO/WO, 25/3907, D. 52. Maj. Gen. Sir Richard Armstrong was commander of the forces in Canada West.

28. Collection: National Archives of Canada.

29. Collection: National Archives of Canada.

30. Nancy Z. Tausky and Lynne D. DiStefano, *Victorian Architecture in London and Southwestern Ontario* (Toronto, Ontario: University of Toronto Press, 1986), p. 31.

31. University of Western Ontario.

32. National Archives of Canada.

33. University of Western Ontario.

34. London Regional Art and Historical Museum.

35. Private collection. I am grateful to Barry Fair of the London Regional Art and Historical Museums for drawing my attention to this important London watercolour.

36. Alan G. Brunger, "Talbot, Thomas," *Dictionary of Canadian Biography*, VIII: p. 860.

37. Frances K. Smith, *John Herbert Caddy 1801-1887* [hereafter *Caddy*], exhibition catalogue, (Kingston, Ontario: Agnes Etherington Art Centre, 1986), p. 35.

38. Orlo Miller,, *This Was London: The First Two Centuries* (Westport, Ontario: Butternut Press, 1988), p. 57. See also: Nancy Geddes Poole, *The Art of London 1830-980*, [hereafter *Art of London*], (London, Ontario: Blackpool Press, 1984), pp. 7, 8.

39. Frances Smith, *Caddy*, p. 37.

40. *London Evening Free Press*, Oct. 8, 1948, p. 21, c.4. Guy St-Denis kindly directed me to this information.

41. Archie Bremner, *Illustrated London, Ontario, Canada* (London, Ontario, London Printing & Lithographing, 1897), p. 49.

42. *London Free Press*, Apr. 15, 1961, p. 24, c. 1.

43. *Ibid.*, Oct. 8, 1948, p. 21, c. 4.

44. Hereford and Worcester, Richard Airey Papers, Talbot to R. Airey, Apr. 14, 1842; *ibid.*, Jan. 8, 1843; Alexander, *L'Acadie*, vol. 1, pp. 140-141.

45. *London Free Press*, Jun. 20, 1959, p. 25, c. 7.

46. The late Madaline Roddick of London kindly sent me this information from the London Collector's List of 1844. See: Regional Collection, London Town, collectors list, 1844, p. 4, lot 26, York St. south.

47. Wilson, Bruce G. *et al.*, "George Russell Dartnell (1798-1878)," and "Daniel Lysons (1816-1898)." *Archives Canada Microfiches*, 10 (1977): pp. 21-28.

48. Hamilton, although not a member of the military, deserves a mention here. He was a serious amateur painter who executed many excellent views of London after he arrived in 1844 to manage its branch of the Bank of Upper Canada. He worked in oil and watercolour, and often chose unexpected angles creating original compositions of familiar subjects.

49. J. Ross Robertson, *Landmarks of Canada, A Guide to the J. Ross Robertson Historical Collection*, (Toronto, Ontario: 1917), p. 233, no. 1450. The information is from a key on a watercolour copy of a James Hamilton painting, made for the above collection.
50. *Albion* (New York, New York), Jan. 7, 1843, p. 4, c. 1. In his diary, Becher incorrectly referred to the date of this trip as Oct., 1843. See: de Pencier, *Dartnell*, pp. 16, 67-71, 94.
51. Alexander, *L'Acadie*, vol. 1, pp. 184-236.
52. de Pencier, *Dartnell*, pp. 71-73, 107.
53. National Archives of Canada.
54. Henderson, "Garrison," p. 11.
55. The print entitled, "Grand Military Steeple Chase at London Canada West, 9th May, 1843," is engraved by J. Harris, London, England, and published by Ackermann, 1845.
56. Regional Collection, Harris Papers, Charlotte Harris Diary, Oct. 22, 1848 to Nov. 30, 1849. See also: Poole, *Art in London*, p. 7.
57. *London Herald*, Mar. 25, 1843, p. 3, c. 5; *ibid.*, Feb. 25, 1843, p. 3, c. 5; *London Inquirer*, Feb. 24, 1843, p. 2. c. 7; *ibid.*, Mar. 3, 1843, p. 3, c. 4.
58. *London Herald*, May 6, 1843, p. 2, c. 4.
59. Henderson, "Garrison," p. 11.
60. The Weir Foundation, Queenston. See also: Poole, *Art of London*, p. 2. Poole identifies the artist of this painting as the young John Fitz John Harris (1830-1861).
61. Dartnell, George Russell, *A Brief Narrative of the Shipwreck of the Transport "Premier..."* (London, England: Jeremiah How, 1845).
62. William Johnston, *A List of Commissioned Medical Officers of the Army, 1727-1898*, (Aberdeen, Scotland: University Press, 1925), reprint ed. (London, England: Wellcome, 1968), no. 4031.
63. *Illustrated London News* (London, England), Mar. 10, 1855, pp. 236-238.
64. de Pencier, *Dartnell*, pp. 90-91.
65. Major-General Sir George Bell, *Soldier's Glory* (London, England: G. Bell and Sons, 1956), pp. 317-318.

CHAPTER FIVE

"HALF OF LONDON IN RUIN!"

London's Great Fires of 1844 and 1845

Daniel J. Brock

OVERVIEW

In both 1844 and 1845 London was swept by fires, which though devastating in their immediate impact also proved beneficial to the town's future development. Before the conflagrations, the town was made up of a motley collection of frame buildings – many of which abutted one another. Most had been hastily constructed during the building boom of London's pioneer stage, between 1826 and about 1845. The arrival of the British garrison in 1838 brought about a new stage in the town's development, one of a new, ready market to generate commercial activity and free labour for public improvements. Yet the frame buildings of London did not generally reflect this new era of prosperity. Within a few years, however, redevelopment as a consequence of two major fires would transform the architecture of London from a village of wood to a town of brick.

LONDON'S PIONEER STAGE

A study of land sales in the town to 1846 indicates that the most valuable lots were on the corners of Dundas and Ridout Streets. The reason for this intersection being the focal point of the town is fairly straightforward. Dundas and Ridout had become the principal thoroughfares, primarily because they led to the Court House square. This intersection was further augmented by the construction of the Westminster (1826) and Blackfriars (1831) Bridges[1] (linking York and Stanley Streets and Ridout and Blackfriars Streets respectively). Also important to the development of the square were the fords in the Thames at the foot of both Dundas and King Streets, and its location at the end of Dundas Street (then known as the terminus of the Governor's Road) and the Hamilton Road – both important thoroughfares in their day. By 1844 the Court House square was not only the site of the combined Court House and Jail, but also the Market House, the London District Grammar School, the Mechanics' Hall (the forerunner of today's London Public Library), and the partially completed new jail.[2] The commercial potential of the area had long been realized by hotel keepers, merchants, and tradesmen, and their establishments came to be concentrated at Dundas and Ridout.

Contrary to popular tradition, London was not a settlement of log dwellings during its pioneer stage of growth and development. Frame buildings of one and a half storeys were by far the most typical dwellings constructed. As early as November 1827, a little more than a year after the survey of its town plot, London was described as having twenty to thirty buildings; about half of these were frame.

By late August of 1831, it was precisely noted that the town consisted of ninety-six houses either built or under construction; twenty-two were two-storey frame buildings, fifty-nine were one-and-a-half storey frame buildings, and only fifteen were squared or other types of log houses one storey in height.[3]

London's central core could be fairly accurately described as bounded by King Street on the south, Talbot Street on the east, Carling (then known as North Street), and Fullarton Streets on the north, and Ridout Street on the west.[4] It comprised some sixteen acres (6.5 ha) in all. The main businesses were located along Dundas from Dennis O'Brien's brick block, west of Ridout, to Talbot Street, particularly on the north side, which afforded more shelter from the north winds and captured the fleeting warmth of the sun's rays, low on the southern horizon, during the cold winter months. Many of the merchants within the area lived over or behind their stores as was typical in contemporary urban centres. But there were some private dwellings within or on the perimeter of the business core: O'Brien, for example, had a detached residence on the centre lot between Ridout and Talbot on the south side of Dundas Street. The site is now part of a large parking lot to the rear of the former Talbot Inn.

Brick or stone buildings were few and far between during this early period. London's first brick structure was of course the original portion of the old Court House, today's Middlesex County Building, constructed between the years 1827 and 1829. Although often mistaken for a stone structure, it was built using local bricks, and finished with stucco lined to look like stone blocks. The second brick building was the London branch of the Bank of Upper Canada, the first bank to establish an agency in the town. Built, again using local brick,[5] during 1835 and 1836, it still survives as a branch of the Canadian Imperial Bank of Commerce in the Ridout Street (Labatt) Restoration Complex. Between 1836 and 1837, Dennis O'Brien, the town's first merchant, constructed London's earliest brick business block using a pink-coloured brick. Until destroyed by fire in 1850, it stood on the north side of Dundas Street, just in front of the present site of the London Regional Art and Historical Museums building. Cyrus Sumner, the town constable in 1842, built London's first brick dwelling between 1838 and 1839 on the north side of Dundas Street, some two-fifths of the way between Waterloo and Colborne Streets.[6] The house of the Anglican pastor, the Rev. Benjamin Cronyn, apparently built between 1840 and 1841, was the first and probably the only stone residence in the town by the mid-1840s. This cut fieldstone structure, built within the block bounded by Dundas, William, Queen's, and Adelaide, was razed in 1968 and replaced by today's London Housing Authority's Senior Citizen Apartments.[7]

By 1842 London contained 276 frame houses under two storeys in height, 108 frame houses of two or more storeys, four brick or stone houses, and only one log dwelling – this being of less than two storeys. It is probable, however, that other log cabins and shanties existed within the town limits, particularly in what was called the New Survey – that area which comprised the extension of the town's limits north to Huron Street and east to Adelaide Street. Log dwellings, if not squared on at least two sides, were not taxed and therefore would not be counted on assessment returns. In addition, the town possessed twenty-one merchants' shops and a grist mill.[8]

PRELUDES TO THE 1844 AND 1845 FIRES

In this pioneer era of frame buildings, fires were an all too common occurrence. Rarely did a newspaper appear in the province without giving the account of at least one fire somewhere within Upper Canada, North America, or Europe. For the most part, individuals were more intrigued than disturbed by these fiery visitations, unless they struck rather too close to home. More often than not these fires could be attributed to carelessness, such as live coals being dumped out with the ashes, faulty stove pipes, or sparks igniting wooden shavings. Probably a year had not passed since the beginning of settlement in London without at least one building having been consumed by flames. The earliest documented fire within the town, however, was that of a blacksmith shop belonging to the Messrs. Dickinson, on November 10, 1832. The loss of both the shop and equipment was estimated to have been £100 ($500).[9]

The most destructive fire in London prior to 1844 occurred on February 13, 1839. This fire broke out, supposedly from the stove pipe which passed through the upper story of Douglas, Warren, and Company's general store on the south side of Dundas Street between Ridout and Talbot, immediately west of O'Brien's residence. In all, four business buildings, only two of which were insured, were destroyed by the blaze and several smaller structures were pulled down to prevent the flames from spreading. As would become standard procedure, the garrison stationed in London served a two-fold purpose during such emergencies. As well as attempting to control and quell the blaze, the 32nd Regiment helped to procure and restore property stolen and mislaid during the confusion of fire fighting.[10] After the fire, ten of the town's leading businessmen held a public meeting "for the purpose of considering whether it be expedient to establish in the said District [of London] a Fire Insurance Company, on the principal of Mutual Insurance."[11] This ultimately led to the formation of the Mutual Fire Insurance Company of the London District.[12]

A few months after the fire, notice was given that an application would be made to have the provincial government "incorporate and define the limits of the town of London."[13] The Act of Incorporation, passed February 10, 1840, established the town limits and provided for a "board of police" consisting of five men, which in turn selected one of its members as "President," to "have the power of enacting such Laws and Regulations for the internal government of the said Town as to them shall seem meet [proper]; and shall have the power of appointing all such Officers as shall be required for the due execution of the Laws to be by them enacted ... "[14] In effect, the town had about the same limited powers as unincorporated police villages today, and its Board of Police passed the usual by-laws, then typical throughout North American urban centres, for the prevention and fighting of fires. They included regulations in the mid-1840s for the construction and use of chimneys, and the location of stovepipes, but no mention of hearths, stoves, or the handling of ashes. There were fire wardens, the captains of each of the two fire companies, as well as the town warden and inspector, who were authorized to enter buildings and order all violations of the fire prevention by-laws rectified, "subject to a fine of not more than 30s[hillings] in the discretion of the Board [of Police]."[15] But such by-laws, and the officers appointed to enforce them, did not go far enough to prevent conflagrations.

While the establishment of a volunteer fire company in London probably dates from 1840, the earliest known record of its existence, as well as that of a fire engine, occurs with the fire company's success in extinguishing the October 1841 fire which started in one of the chimneys of O'Brien's brick business block.[16] The following March saw the publication of the twenty-five by-laws governing the London Volunteer Fire Company. By-law four in part stated: "That it shall be the duty of the Captain or officer commanding the Engine Company to see that the

Engine and all its appurtenances are kept in good order."[17] By September 1841, London apparently had public tanks in place from which the fire engine could draw its water and citizens could fill their buckets.[18] Two years later, in November 1843, two tanks were ordered constructed – one to be placed in the vicinity of Fullarton and Ridout Streets and the other at the corner of Richmond and Horton Streets.[19]

The town had one engine and the military garrison at least two on the evening of February 16, 1844, when Edmond Austin's large three-storey frame carpenter's shop and residence, on the south side of York Street, some two lots west of Ridout, was destroyed by fire. The town's firemen and engine were on the scene in less than ten minutes after the alarm was sounded, followed by the military and its engines.[20] It was soon obvious, however, that efforts aimed at putting out the flames were useless and both firemen and London residents directed their efforts toward preventing any further spread of the fire. It was later observed that the nearest tank was in a poor state of repair and was therefore almost useless, while "every well in the vicinity was completely emptied. [V]ery fortunately there was but little wind, otherwise there is no saying what destruction of property would have ensued."[21] This was a prophetic warning of what was destined to befall London within the next fourteen months.

On Ash Wednesday, five days after the fire on York Street, St. Paul's Anglican Church was consumed by flames.[22] Both fires had been accidental, but could have been avoided had greater care been exercised. Whereas the York Street fire was caused by the snuff of a candle dropping among the shavings in the workshop, the St. Paul's fire was believed to have originated from a spark from one of the stoves falling through a knot hole in the floor and onto shavings that had been left behind after construction.[23]

THE DUNDAS STREET FIRE OF 1844

The destruction of St. Paul's and the fire of February 1839, were surpassed in the early morning hours of October 8, 1844, when flames broke out in the back kitchen of the store and dwelling occupied by the dry goods firm of McKeand, Bell and Company. This building stood on the north side of Dundas Street, between Ridout and Talbot, just west of where the walkway between the Provincial Court and Bell Canada Building is today. The blaze soon grew out of control, igniting structures on its east and west sides and destroying everything in its path. On the east, it was finally stopped by the road allowance of Talbot Street and on the north by Carling Street. To the west, on the northeast corner of Dundas and Ridout, it was curbed by the three-storey brick structure owned by the merchant John Jennings, which was built about 1840. This building was, nevertheless, greatly damaged.[24] It is believed that this structure was the only obstacle that stood between the blazing inferno and the wooden buildings on the northwest corner of the intersection. But the fire was only redirected north, not stopped. It ultimately destroyed all but two buildings on the block bounded by Dundas, Talbot, Queen's, and Ridout, on which now stand the Provincial Court and Bell Canada Buildings.

While the fire raged, its victims had attempted to save some of their possessions by placing them in the centre and on the south side of Dundas Street. Regrettably, this action frustrated the object of curbing the blaze, as the flames were carried to the wooden structures on the south side of Dundas and proceeded west from Talbot, the site of the former Talbot Inn (then William Balkwill's Hope Hotel), until halted by the gap east of Dennis O'Brien's residence. This breach, as well as the already mentioned brick structure on the northeast corner of Dundas and Ridout, now part of the site of the Provincial Court Building, saved the west half of the block south of Dundas. When the fire was over, at least thirty principal structures, as well as numerous outbuildings, were completely destroyed; these housed thirty businesses (a number of which also served as dwellings), at least five or six private residences, and the old, vacant Mansion House Hotel, which had been built by Abraham Carroll in 1827. The fire covered nearly three acres (1.2 ha) of land; it was estimated that £15,000 worth of wooden buildings and their contents were destroyed. Less than half of these premises were insured. Again, the joint efforts of the fire companies, the military, and the inhabitants had, together with a fortunate lack of wind, succeeded in preventing the flames from spreading, despite a deficient and poorly accessible water supply. A picket of fifty soldiers from the barracks also turned out to protect private property.[25]

The October 8, 1844, fire began in the back kitchen of the store and dwelling occupied by the dry goods firm of McKeand, Bell & Company. This site would be just west of where the walkway between the Provincial Court and Bell Canada Buildings is today, on the north side of Dundas Street, between Ridout and Talbot. Photo by Stephen Harding, London

John Jennings's three-storey brick building was one of several buildings which formerly occupied the present site of the Provincial Court Building. Jennings's building turned the fire of 1844 northward and thereby stopped it from burning the buildings on the west side of Ridout Street. Unfortunately, the building was later destroyed in the fire of 1845. Photo by Stephen Harding

The southwest corner of Dundas and Talbot Streets, the present site of the Talbot Inn, where William Balkwill's Hope Hotel stood. This structure was destroyed in the fire of 1844; the Talbot Inn awaits redevelopment. Photo by Stephen Harding

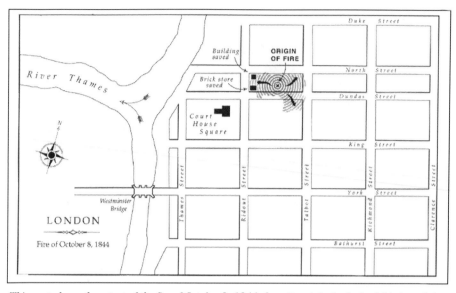

This map shows the extent of the fire of October 8, 1844, from its origin in the back kitchen of the firm of McKeand, Bell & Company on the north side of Dundas Street, between Ridout and Talbot. From *Plan of the Town of London, C.W.,* by Thomas Craig, 1846

Of the firms or business premises destroyed, the owners of two are known to have declared bankruptcy. But at least twenty-two were back in business by the time of the April 1845 fire. Probably as many as six rebuilt – or in one instance, restored – their premises on their former sites. At least three found temporary lodgings for their businesses before relocating to permanent quarters. A minimum of thirteen re-established themselves along Dundas (between Ridout and Richmond), five along Ridout (between Fullarton and York), and two along King (between Ridout and Talbot). Obviously, the fire had not caused a drastic dislocation within the core area.[26]

Trying to make the best of a bad situation, the town's newspaper, the *London Inquirer,* observed that:

> Dundas-street being the main street of our town, [formerly] presented certainly rather a motley group of buildings irregularly got up, and of wood, which rendered it probable an event of the above description would sooner or later take place. Now that it has occurred, although unfortunately at so great a loss, we hope it may be the means of causing greater vigilance and better taste, in the future formation [of] the street, and that a line of substantial brick buildings will be substituted.[27]

The growing threat of fire was noted in the following editorial which appeared in the Kingston *Chronicle & Gazette,* following its account of London's Dundas Street fire of 1844.

We have, on more than one occasion, urged upon our authorities, and we have recommended it to all others, to adopt more stringent regulations, in towns, by a systematic inspection and registration of all chimney places, hearth stones, stoves and stove pipes, ash houses, &c. &c., nor can we conceive why they are not resorted to, – such a measure would prevent three-fourths of the fires which take place, – or is it not done, because, forsooth, to have such an Inspector would be an encroachment upon our boasted independence, by which we claim a right to do as we please with our own, notwithstanding by the abuse of it we run no small risk of being burnt in our beds– and reduced to poverty, ruin and destitution, by some careless, reckless neighbour, who probably has nothing to lose.[28]

The town of London appears to have taken this advice to heart. In February of 1845 the consolidated by-laws were issued and stipulated that "it shall be the duty of every inhabitant of said Town [of London], to notify to the Town warden or one of the members of the Corporation, of their intention to put up stoves or pipes other than where a stove and pipes have heretofore been fixed, in order that the same may be inspected and reported to the Board ..." As for the placement of pipes,

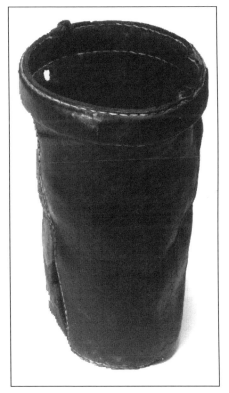

A town by-law required all households to maintain a leather fire bucket with the initials of its owner on it. In the event of a fire, it was mandatory for every man to take his place with his "cowhide dipper" in the bucket brigade. London Regional Art and Historical Museums

no stove pipe shall be carried through the roof or side of any
building; and ... all stove pipes passing through any
floors,ceiling, or partitions, shall be so secured as to have no
wood or combustible substance within four inches [10 cm] of
such stove pipe; and ... the manner of securing such stove pipes
shall also be subject to the approval of the Town warden and
Inspector, or either of the Fire wardens or their Assistants.

With regard to the fighting of future fires, the by-laws required that:

every person residing in said Town shall find and provide a good
and sufficient ladder or ladders to be appended to the houses
they shall respectively inhabit, and to be of sufficient length to
reach the roof ... [E]ach and every tenant or occupant of a
dwelling shall provide himself with a good substantial leather
bucket, containing not less than two and a half gallons [11.5
litres], having the initials of the owner's name thereon, which
bucket shall be kept in some conspicuous place near the
entrance of such dwelling [and] each Merchants Shop, Public
Inn, or Grocery, shall, in like manner be provided with two of
such buckets ... [29]

On the outbreak of a fire the alarm would be sounded, and every man with his
"cowhide dipper" was expected to take his place in the bucket brigade. For the
most part, however, the efforts of the brigade would be concentrated on
containing fires rather than quelling them.[30]

THE GREAT FIRE OF 1845
Despite the warnings of the calamitous fire of October 1844, and the precautions
taken to ensure against a similar disaster, London was again visited by a major fire.
The conflagration which broke out shortly after noon on April 13, 1845, was many
times worse than that of six months previous. It was the day before the opening of
the spring assizes – the high court hearings of criminal and civil cases within the
London District – which were to be presided over by Chief Justice Sir John
Beverley Robinson.[31] The fire ignited in the stable to the rear of the Robinson
Hall Hotel on the southeast corner of Dundas and Ridout Streets,[32] immediately
south of the present Provincial Court Building and east of the Middlesex County
Building. April 13 was also a Sunday, and the congregation of St. Paul's, pending
the completion of its new building, was worshipping in the Mechanics' Hall on
the Court House square.[33] It was during the service on this particular Sunday that
the cry of "Fire!" was heard over the reading of the psalms of the day. On the
sounding of the alarm the people nearest to the door began to rush out along the
rather narrow staircase of the only exit. Through the presence of mind of the Rev.
Benjamin Cronyn, who kept on reading, and the chief justice, who responded "in
clear, deliberate tones, until the entire congregation had quietly withdrawn ...
doubtless a panic, and probably serious accident, was averted."[34] Robinson then
barely had time to secure his belongings from the Robinson Hall, at some risk to
himself.[35]

Marcus Gunn, a Scotsman and newcomer to London, was not quite so
fortunate. He, his wife, and one of his sons by a former marriage were listening to
"a luminous Sermon" preached by the Rev. A.G. Lawrie, at the Universalist

It was on the southeast corner of Dundas and Ridout Streets that the Robinson Hall Hotel stood. The fire of April 8, 1845, started in the stables of this hotel and burned in a southeasterly direction, jumping the east branch of the Thames River and burning itself out in Westminster Township. The holocaust also destroyed businesses on the north side of Dundas Street and the old vacant market house on the Court House square. Photo by Stephen Harding, London

Church on the north side of King Street just east of Wellington, when the alarm was given. Having arrived from Nova Scotia the previous November, Gunn had left his heaviest trunk and a green box for safekeeping with the hotel keeper at the Robinson Hall while he looked for permanent quarters in the town. The trunk was retrieved, but the box "which I used for the keeping of my daily Journals from the 1st May 1822 ... was burnt or lost ... "[36] Moreover, his "private boarding accommodation in the respectable House of a Miss Timson,"[37] which he had secured only the day before, was lost to the flames.

A detailed eyewitness account of events, from a third individual who also risked his life in the retrieval of his belongings at the Robinson Hall Hotel, has been reproduced as an appendix to this article.

Meanwhile, the glorified "garden sprinkler," or fire engine, purchased in 1844 by George Jervis Goodhue, the town's wealthiest citizen, "after a minute's work" in fighting the conflagration "was abandoned, and disappeared in a general ruin."[38] The flames soon spread to the north side of Dundas and destroyed six businesses, all of which had been rebuilt since October 1844 – except the brick structure that had checked the last fire. Fortunately, the buildings north along Ridout Street from this brick structure had not yet been rebuilt, and apparently there was a gap farther east along Dundas, which prevented the fire again extending to Talbot Street. At the same time, the combination of "a stiff gale from the N.W. by N." and the close proximity of the wooden structures, with "every thing as dry as tinder," united to create a raging blaze of "indescribable fury to leeward."[39]

The flames destroyed everything in their path along the south side of Dundas Street, up to and including O'Brien's residence, which had been saved on two former occasions; a gap here prevented the fire from spreading eastward to the area beginning to be built up after the fire of the previous October. By the time the inferno reached south to York Street, it had engulfed the entire width of the block between Ridout and Talbot. As it approached Bathurst Street, it jumped Talbot to the east and burned structures to the extent of two lots. Owing to the position of the buildings on the south side of Bathurst, only one residence – that of James B. Strathy on lot 19 – the second lot east of Ridout – was spared as the flames swept down the east side of Ridout to the river's edge. While the flames apparently never extended as far east as Richmond Street, they were carried across the east branch of the Thames and cut a swath of destruction into suburban Westminster Township. The transplanted fire burned into the woods far

After the "Great Fire," James Shanly, then master and deputy registrar in chancery for Middlesex County, found this copy of the 1784 issue of The Lady's Magazine *"thrown out of some house in Richmond St. London. U.C. at old [John] 'Waterloo' Smyth's where I lodge, just north of York St. on the evening of the great fire of 13th April 1845." Smyth, who had fought under Wellington at Waterloo, boarded "respectable single gentlemen" at his home on the west side of Richmond Street, about where Ichabods is now. Presumably the volume had been tossed from a window of a building considered to be in the path of the blaze.* Special Collections, University of Western Ontario Library

beyond the residence of James Hamilton, sheriff of the London District, where it destroyed two barns.[40] This would place the extent of the fire at somewhere south of today's Grand Avenue – a quarter of a mile (0.4 km) below the east branch of the Thames.

In all, nearly 30 acres (12.1 ha) of property, consisting of more than 110 structures used as dwellings, business premises, or workshops, were destroyed in

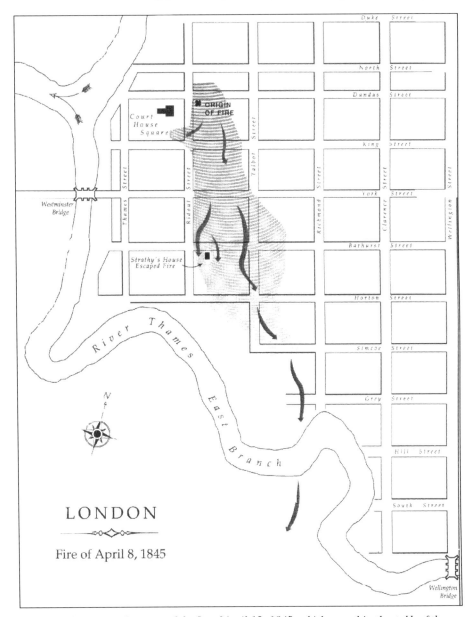

The map above traces the course of the fire of April 13, 1845, which started in the stable of the Robinson Hall Hotel, on the southeast corner of Ridout and Dundas Streets.

From *Plan of the Town of London, C.W.*, by Thomas Craig, 1846 the conflagration. If such outbuildings as stables, barns, and sheds are included, however, this figure might well be doubled. Also, there was the destruction of the buildings' contents. The greatest individual loss was believed to have been incurred by David O. Marsh's and Ellis W. Hyman's tannery works (see appendix). None of their loss of some £5,000 to £6,000 was covered by insurance.[41]

The total monetary loss in this "Great Fire of London" was variously estimated at from $200,000 to $500,000,[42] and, while difficult to assess, possibly represented at least 20 percent of London's property wealth, if the value of the land itself be excluded.[43] The amount of the destruction covered by insurance, through such companies as the British American, Gore District Mutual, Aetna, and Montreal, was thought to have been only about $60,000. This limited amount was said to have been "owing to the aversion the Insurance Offices entertained to run the risk of insuring in London, since the occurrence of the previous fire"[44] of October 1844.

Within ten days of the Great Fire, however, it was pointed out in the *Monarch,* a newspaper published in nearby Woodstock, that "distressing as the burning of London is to the contemplative mind, it is nothing compared with the awful destruction occasioned by the same ungovernable element in the city of *Pittsburgh* on the 11 inst."[45] There, twenty square blocks containing 1,000 buildings were destroyed, and the value of real estate and personal property lost was estimated to have been in excess of four million dollars. Nonetheless, the fire in London was the most devastating in the entire province to that date. Along with the Pittsburgh fire, it was reported in virtually every newspaper in the province of Canada, under such headings as: "DREADFUL FIRE IN LONDON, C.W.," and "HALF OF LONDON IN RUIN!"[46]

Fortunately, there was no loss of life in either the 1844 or 1845 fires in London. Yet, according to an item published in the *Times,* months after the 1845 fire:

> A singular incident is connected with the late fire, which has not yet been made public. Mr. Taylor, the Lieutenant of the Hook and Ladder Compony [*sic*], on hearing that a man was in one of the sheds, rushed in, in company with one of the firemen named Macintosh. They perceived a man standing in the corner with a Bible in his hand, awaiting the progress of the flames. We forbear publishing his name, as he is the son-in-law of a most respectable tradesman. It appears that he had run past the firemen into the house, and a moment later he must have perished, for the roof fell in.[47]

The local journal, the *Times,* encouraged those residents who had not suffered from the fire to assist their less fortunate fellow townspeople with donations of clothing and money, as well as giving them preference in employment and other dealings.

> It is to be hoped and cannot be doubted, that such of the inhabitants as have not suffered loss through this severe visitation will show their thankfulness for their exemption by liberally assisting the poorer class of sufferers who are left without the ordinary necessaries of life or the present means of obtaining them; to this class, donations of clothing and

provisions, and the payment in advance of a quarter or half
year's rent, would be very acceptable proofs of sympathy ... [48]

While some of those burned out found temporary shelter in the homes of
their more fortunate neighbours, as had the Gunn family,most took refuge in the
then new market buildings to the southeast of the burned out area.[49]

A committee was formed in the town on April 29 to determine the names of
the victims and the extent of their losses, in order to lessen the distress of the
most destitute through a fund raising campaign. By May 2 the committee had a
circular letter prepared for distribution to the leading cities and towns of Canada
and the adjoining States. Those who were property owners or who had a little
capital, were, according to the nineteenth-century concept of self-reliance,
expected to shun charitable assistance, despite the fact that the committee
believed them to be the major portion of the sufferers. Relief was to be granted
only to those in complete want, in other words, "large families utterly destitute of
every necessary and comfort of life and whose daily earnings can only now supply
them with food ..."[50]

Notwithstanding examples of internal dissension within the town, which
could only hurt efforts to seek relief elsewhere, funds were collected from such
centres as Hamilton, Toronto, Cobourg, Buffalo, and Montreal. At least $1,847.53
is recorded as having been sent from outside London for the relief of its victims.
Montreal alone contributed a minimum of £264.7.6 and the governor, Sir Charles
Metcalfe, donated £100. No accounts of the actual amount collected by the
committee, the distribution of the funds, or the nature and number of cases to
which it was applied is known; the committee kept silent in this regard in the face
of repeated inquiries, one as late as May 1846, by the *Times*. London's calamity was
soon to pale, however, when two catastrophic fires in Quebec City, occurring on
May 28 and June 28, 1845, consumed some 3,000 houses, left 20,000 people
homeless, and killed several others. This certainly would have had the effect of
stemming the stream of funds sent to London and diverting them to that
unfortunate city in the east.[51]

THE IMPACT OF THE FIRES

Despite the two major fires of 1844 and 1845, and numerous other fires within the
business area, no substantial changes were made immediately in the town's by-laws
governing fires and their prevention. By early 1846, however, the two fire
companies – the Engine, and the Hook and Ladder – could make their own by-
laws subject to the approval of the Board of Police.[52] The by-laws of 1847, as they
related to fires and their prevention, were identical to those of 1846.[53] No
consolidation of the town's by-laws for the years 1848 and 1849, such as exist for
the years 1845 through 1847, has surfaced. The consolidated by-laws for 1850
provide the first regulations governing stoves, hearths, and gunpowder. It was not
until June 10, 1850, however, that a by-law was passed prohibiting the construction
of wooden buildings within the town's commercial centre.

> ... it shall not be lawful for any person or persons to erect, build,
> or remove any wooden building whatever upon the land...
> contained with the following limits, that is to say, commencing on
> the north side of Dundas Street, on the west side of the Western
> Hotel [O'Brien's brick block], from thence north to the south

side of North Street [later Carling Street]; from thence, easterly, along the south side of North Street to the corner of North [now Queen's Avenue] and Clarence Streets, from thence southerly along the west side of Clarence Street, to the corner of Clarence and King Streets, from thence westerly along the north side of King Street, to the corner of King and Ridout Streets, from thence northerly along the east side of Ridout Street to the corner of Ridout and Dundas Streets and from thence, westerly, along Dundas Street, to the west side of the said Western Hotel ... [54]

In the interim the business area, including wooden buildings, had expanded from O'Brien's brick block as far east as Clarence Street.

In order to assess the immediate effect of the fires on London, a detailed study was made of the town for an eighteen-month period between the outbreak of the Dundas Street Fire of October 1844, and the first anniversary of the Great Fire of April 1845. It was observed that the fires did little to alter the relative prosperity of either the working classes or the capitalists. In the case of labourers and tradesmen, there was no lack of employment in the town as work continued on the unfinished buildings which had escaped the fire of 1844, and the task of rebuilding the area burned out by the Great Fire soon began. A minute examination of the land records for properties fronting Dundas Street between Ridout and Talbot – the most valuable commercial block in the town – indicates that there was a rise in mortgages from 30 percent in October 1844 to 55 percent in April 1846. This jump does not represent mortgages for the sake of rebuilding, but rather the sale of land in the burned-out area to individuals who, although unable to purchase what amounted to fire sale properties outright, at least had sufficient capital to cover the cost of reconstructing the businesses formerly located on them. In short, the town's business interests did not suffer an irreversible setback.

Nor did the percentage of frontage along this block, owned by interests outside London, alter dramatically during the eighteen-month period. On the eve of the October 1844 fire, non-residents held 19 percent of the frontage; in April 1846 they retained 16 percent. In this latter year 10 percent was held by a group of Hamilton merchants, who had purchased the entire lot which previously had been the site of O'Brien's residence. It was then the largest parcel of land in London held by private ownership. Earlier, in October of 1844, George J.Goodhue, also the town's first president, had owned 20 percent of the frontage on Dundas Street. Eighteen months later he reduced his holdings to less than 8 percent, while having increased his share of first mortgages along this block from 26 percent to 30 percent and second mortgages from 2 percent to 12 percent. Apparently, the investment of one's capital in mortgages at 6 percent interest was more profitable than owning and leasing out property in London during the mid-1840s. As Goodhue was the town's most important financier, the study of this block (despite its limitations) at least indicates that men of financial stature were tending to concentrate more on making profits through mortgages than through land speculation itself, and reveals that the town was in a transitional stage of evolution from a newly opened to a well established community.[55] The great fires may have accelerated this tendency, but they can hardly be said to have initiated it.

The fires did, however, substantially transform the appearance of the town's commercial centre. The irregularly constructed wooden buildings which stood along Dundas and Ridout Streets prior to the fires were replaced by substantial new brick structures. The principal business block in the town remained Dundas Street between Ridout and Talbot, which, in the early autumn of 1845, was described as consisting of

> two rows of three story [*sic*] Warehouses...which nothing in Upper Canada can surpass; they are all built of brick – chiefly light colored – and the shops are fitted up in the most elegant style. Wide showy fronts, with plate glass windows extended along the range, and the interiors are supplied with all the modern improvements which experience and good taste have suggested.[56]

CONCLUSION

Traditionally, it has been held that the eastward extension of the business area along Dundas Street and the ultimate relocation of its main intersection to Dundas and Richmond were directly attributable to the major fires of 1844 and 1845. A detailed examination of the business district for the years 1844-1846, however, reveals that the central area was already expanding eastward, and, while the fires did expedite this trend, they certainly do not account for it.

In 1843, the London or Brough's Bridge was completed, permitting traffic to travel from the north down Richmond Street to Dundas Street;[57] at the same time the importance of the route over Blackfriars Bridge and along Ridout Street

This engraving of Hope, Birrell, & Company's Great Western House illustrates the structures built on the north side of Dundas Street, near the intersection with Ridout Street, after the fire of 1845. The "spacious premises" occupied "a prominent position in this street ... and surpasses anything we have seen in Canada above Montreal."

declined proportionately. Then, in January 1845, three months before the Great Fire, the site of the market was transferred from the Court House square to the block bounded by Wellington, Bathurst, Waterloo, and York Streets, now occupied by a parking lot and the Canadian National Railway tracks. That October, another market (Covent Garden) was opened for the convenience of the central and western parts of the town in the block bounded by Dundas, Talbot, King, and Richmond Streets.[58] And it was the location of these two markets, augmented as they were by the older arterial routes eastward along York and Dundas Streets, the more recent thoroughfare southward along Wellington Street over Clark's Bridge (1840),[59] and particularly that northward along the present Richmond Street, which largely accounts for the gradual movement of the core area eastward along Dundas Street – not to mention the expansion associated with London's growth and development. It was the resulting evolution of London's road network which led to the replacement of Dundas and Ridout by Dundas and Richmond as the town's main intersection.

There were other effects which resulted from the fires of 1844 and 1845 – such as the naming of the brick business blocks for the first time. "Victoria," "Prospect," and, appropriately enough, "Phoenix" came to grace the new buildings. The first attempt to assign numbers to buildings, at least those on the north side of Dundas east from Ridout, also followed the fire.[60] When all is said and done, however, it was the dramatic transformation in the architectural appearance of the business core which was the most pronounced consequence of the great fires of 1844 and 1845.

APPENDIX

This unsigned letter to the editor, which appeared in the Toronto Herald, *and was reprinted in the* Cobourg Star, *April 23, 1845, is believed to have been written by someone who had accompanied the presiding judge, Chief Justice Sir John Beverley Robinson, to London for the spring assizes which were to open the day following the fire.*

London, April 13th, 1845.
Twelve o'clock noon.

Dear Sir: While I am now writing, a most awful conflagration is going on. At least one-fourth of the Town southeast of *Robinson Hall Hotel* is already consumed, and still the raging flame proceeds with unchecked fury, to consume everything within its range. The fire commenced in the back part of the Robinson Hall Hotel, and the alarm was given just as the ministers were concluding the Church of England ritual with prayer. A high wind, almost a hurricane, was blowing at the time; the word "fire!" was heard; the whole audience were appalled, and immediately rushed out, each to his own destination. I proceeded immediately opposite the Robinson Hall Hotel, where I stopped; and had barely time to take my trunk from the room, when the flames burst through the window; an instant later, and I should have had my trunck and every thing in it consumed. The Chief Justice [Sir John Beverley Robinson] was also stopping at the same hotel, and was at Church when the alarm was given. He has, I believe, saved everything, with a few trifling exceptions. He, with others, and myself, found security for our property in the Court House. The wind was in a south-easterly direction; and in less than ten minutes from the time the alarm was sounded, no less than two fires were observable, distant at least two hundred rods [over 1 km] from where the original fire commenced. It was actually appalling. I can give you no conception of the scene. A perfect gale is at this moment blowing, and the fire is quite unabated; everything south-east of the Robinson Hall is either consumed or being consumed. The large three story brick store in possession of Mr. John Grey [*sic*] [merchant, in the building owned by John Jennings on the north side of Dundas Street], is also consumed, with three other houses adjoining [on the east]. They were the only buildings north of the hotel that were burned. The scene beggars description. Men, women, and children all in confusion – some crying and sinking down in utter despair, mourning their loss; others exerting every nerve to save their property or neighbor's. The Chief Justice remarked, that it was the most awful sight he had beheld for a number of years. I am now writing from the office of John Wilson [the lawyer], who has had four buildings already consumed. I will let you know when it is got under, if it should be without the total destructon of the town.

At least two-thirds of the town is already destroyed, it has proceeded more than the breadth of a square in a diagonal direction. It is useless to attempt giving you a description of the scene, and I labor under the disadvantage of being unacquainted with the place, having arrived here last night for the first time, at half-past 1 o'clock.

No lives have been lost so far as I can learn. The fire has extended to the river. Mr. Gourley, a young man and nephew, I understand of R.F. [Robert Fleming] Gourley [*sic*], Esq., saved the life of a child at the imminent risk of his own. Mr. [John Hamilton Laidly?] Askin, son of Col. [John Baptist] Askin, also performed a similar act, but with still greater danger. Such disinterested acts of noble heroism deserve to be recorded. Both Mr. Gourley and Mr. Askin suffered severely from the flames, their faces having been nearly blistered.

Half-past Two o'clock.

I have just returned from an excursion I made down to the foot of Ridout-street, and along the brow of the hill extending alongside of the River Thames, to the breadth of two squares, East of Ridout street, every building on the East side of Ridout street, from the brick store of Mr. Gray's, to the water's edge, has been consumed excepting Mr. [James B.] Strathey's [*sic*] house, which was the last but one, on Ridout street, while the one below was entirely consumed. A most singular circumstance is the fire having gone round in a circular direction[;] this was caused by out buildings being connnected with each other. The house where the family of Col. [Joseph Brant] Clench lives, was burning when I came away, and the Hon. Mr. [George Jervis] Goodhue's house is already burned. Mr. [John] Balkwell's brewery, which is still further south of Col. Clench's house was in imminent danger when I returned. They were making great exertions to save it, but I fear it will go. The fire extended from Robinson Hall to York street, one square in breadth, still taking every house on the east side of Ridout street. From Ridout street it proceeded in a diagonal direction, taking two squares in breadth. To the south-east of Balkwell's brewery the fire has extended some distance, and although the houses in that quarter are very scattered, yet nothing can impede the progress of the devouring element. Even the stumps and logs in the field through which the river Thames runs are all on fire.

The dwelling house and extensive Tannery of S. [Simeon] Morrell [*sic*], Esq., the late reform candidate for this town, are consumed, and while I was passing, at least 100 cords of hemlock bark was in flames, sending forth the most intense heat. Col. [John] Prince [of Sandwich] assisted Mr. Morrell [*sic*] to save his property with a most praiseworthy energy. The gale still continues undiminished; no two elements can effect such destruction as fire and wind. Patrols of soldiers guarding the property of the unfortunate inhabitants, are stationed in every quarter. I am informed that at least 150 families will be rendered houseless by this fearful calamity. I hope the loss and destruction of property, and the ruin attendant upon it, will not be so great as is anticipated. I must close this most imperfect description of the worst calamity I ever beheld.

Half-past 4 o'clock.

The fire has done its work, every house within its range is consumed, and it has gone far beyond the Sheriff's [James Hamilton's] house into the woods, where two barns belonging to farmers have been burned. The loss is estimated variously, some say £50,000, others less; but it must be very great. The principal losers that I have heard named are Messr. [Ellis Walton] Hyndman [*sic*] and [David O.] Marsh, Tanners, £5 or 6000, no insurance; [James] Mathieson and [John] Michie, Grocers, £5000, no insurance I believe. Messrs. [Marcus] Holmes and Co., Coach Factors, £2000, no insurance.– These gentlemen are most unfortunate, have had a severe loss by fire, only a fortnight since in Hamilton. Dr. [Hiram Davis] Lee lost his house and his furniture, while he in utter ignorance of the loss he was sustaining, was rendering assistance to his neighbours. His loss is about £1500, no insurance. Messrs. Legear and Taylor, Stage proprietors, have lost £650 in Bank Bills, which they had just drawn on account of their mail contract. A great many others have sustained very severe losses whose names I cannot obtain. This calamity will very materially impede the progress of London.[61]

ENDNOTES

Author's note: This account is based on a talk given before the London and Middlesex Historical Society, on January 19, 1972; an essay submitted, on March 28, 1972, in J.M.S. Careless's Old Ontario graduate course at the University of Toronto; and a paper presented to the Canadian Historical Association, in London,on May 30, 1978.

1   University of Western Ontario, the D.B. Weldon Library, Regional Collection [hereafter Regional Collection], London District, Clerk of the Peace, Road Records.
2   [James B. Brown], *Views of Canada and the Colonists* (Edinburgh, Scotland: A. and C. Black, 1844), pp. 102-104; Regional Collection, London District/Middlesex County, Municipal Council, Clerk, letterbook, 1842-1853.
3   Clarence T. Campbell, *Pioneer Days in London* (London, Ontario: Job Printing, 1921), p. 35; *Gore Gazette* (Ancaster, Upper Canada), Nov. 24, 1827, p. 154, c. 3; *Western Mercury* (Hamilton, Upper Canada), Sep. 8, 1831, p. 1, cc. 5-6.
4   For the model used to define London's business district, see: Martyn J. Bowden, "Downtown Through Time: Delimitation, Expansion, and Internal Growth," *Economic Geography*, XLVII, no. 2 (Apr. 1971): pp. 121-135.
5   The colour, for the most part, tended to be a butter yellow.
6   Daniel J. Brock, "A Brief Sketch of the Early History of London's Court House and Jail," London Public Library and Art Museum *Occasional Paper*, XXII (1976): pp. 32-33; Ontario Land Registry Office, London, mortgage, Lawrason and Goodhue to Bank of Upper Canada, Jun. 25, 1835, no. 2604; *ibid.*, bargain and sale, Ewart to Bank of Upper Canada, Jun. 11, 1835, no. 2701; *ibid.*, release of mortgage, Bank of Upper Canada to Lawrason and Goodhue, May 3, 1836, no. 2999; *History of the County of Middlesex, Canada* [hereafter *History of Middlesex*] (Toronto and London, Ontario: W.A. & C.L. Goodspeed, 1889; reprint ed., Belleville, Ontario: Mika Studio, 1972), pp. 219, 573, 839; *London Gazette*, Apr. 14, 1838, p. 4, c. 6; Freeman Talbot, "The Fathers of London Township," London and Middlesex Historical Society *Transactions*, VII (1916): pp. 11, 13; NAC, Canada West, Nominal Census Returns (RG31), London Town, 1842, no. [408]; Regional Collection, London Township, Collector's List, 1844, lot 7, Dundas St. East.
7   NAC, Upper Canada, Land Petitions (RG1, L3), Cronyn to Davidson, Oct. 3, 1842, C1, pt. III (1842), no. 105; Madaline Roddick, "The Story of 'The Pines' 1846-1892, later named 'Woodfield' 1892-1968," London Public Library and Art Museum *Occasional Paper*, XVIII (1974): pp. 12-15.

8   Canada, Legislative Assembly, *Journal Appendix,* 1843, vol. II, DD, no. 11; NAC, Canada West, Nominal Census Returns (RG31), London Town, 1842.

9   *Liberal* (St. Thomas, Upper Canada), Nov. 15, 1832, p. 3 c. 6. In the province of Canada at that time five shillings currency equalled four shillings English sterling or one American dollar. Throughout this work, monetary figures are given in either provincial or American currency.

10 *Upper Canada Times* (London, Upper Canada), Mar. 5, 1836, p. 3, c. 3; *ibid.,* p. 4. c. 3; *St. Catharines Journal,* Feb. 28, 1839, p. 2, c. 3.

11 *London Gazette,* Mar. 2, 1839, p. 3, c. 3.

12 Unfortunately, it is not until Mar. of 1842 that mention of the company is first found in one of the few surviving issues of a London newspaper of the period. See: *Canada Inquirer* (London, Canada West), Mar. 11, 1842, p. 3, c. 4.

13 *Upper Canada Gazette* (Toronto, Upper Canada), Aug. 15, 1839, p. 142, c. 3.

14 Upper Canada, statute (1840), 3 Vic., c. 31

15 *London Inquirer,* Feb. 28, 1845, p. 2. cc. 1-2.

16 " ... the Engine was turned out and on the spot in great alacrity. We could not but admire the agility and expertness of the Firemen, for notwithstanding the height of the building and the difficulty and danger of taking up the hose and bringing the pipe to bear, it was done most effectively and very speedily extinguished the flame and drenched the building." See: *Canada Inquirer,* Oct. 20, 1841, p. 2, cc. 5-6.

17 *Ibid.,* Mar. 11, 1842, p. 3, cc. 5-6.

18 *Ibid.,* Sep. 29, 1842, p. 3, cc. 5-6.

19 *History of Middlesex,* pp. 261, 273.

20 Descriptions of these fire engines have not surfaced; but the town's engine, believed purchased in 1844, was described decades later as "simply a garden sprinkler" and "a little tub." See: *History of Middlesex,* p. 259.

21 *Chronicle & Gazette* (Kingston, Canada West), Mar. 2, 1844, p. 1, c. 4.

22 The £800 insurance it carried was far short of the actual loss and cost of replacement. See: *Toronto Patriot,* Feb. 27, 1844, p. 3, c. 2.

23 *Ibid.*

24 This 30' x 30 ' (9 m x 9 m) building can be seen in George Russell Dartnell's *circa* 1843 watercolour, at the intersection of Dundas and Ridout Streets. The frame structure, known as the "Yellow House" and facing Ridout immediately north of Jennings's building, existed as early as Jul. 1836. The three-storey commercial building, 26' (8 m) in width and immediately east of Jennings's, was opened in November of 1840. See: Frederick H. Armstrong, *The Forest City: An Illustrated History of London, Canada* (Northridge, California: Windsor Publications, 1986), p. 91; *London Gazette,* Jul. 27, 1836, p. 3, c. 4; *ibid.,* Nov. 7, 1840, p. 2, c. 4; *ibid.,* p. 3, c. 2; *Canada Inquirer,* Dec. 8, 1840, p. 1, c. 2; Ontario, Land Registry Office, London, bargain and sale, Freeman to Jennings, Apr. 30, 1839, no. 4218.

25 *St. Thomas Standard,* Oct. 10, 1844, p. 2, cc. 3-4; *ibid,* Oct. 17, 1844, p. 2, c. 5; *British Colonist* (Toronto, Canada West), Oct. 15, 1844, p. 3, cc. 1-2; *Chronicle & Gazette,* Oct. 12, 1844, p. 3, c. 1.

26 These findings were based, for the most part, on an examination of the advertisements in the surviving issues of the *London Inquirer* for 1844-1845 and the *Times* for the early portion of 1845.

27 *British Colonist,* Oct. 15, 1844, p. 3, c. 1.

28 *Chronicle & Gazette,* Oct. 16, 1844, p. 2, c. 4.

29 *London Inquirer,* Feb. 28, 1845, p. 2, c. 1-2.

30 *History of Middlesex,* pp. 258, 260-61; Clarence T. Campbell, "The Village of London," London and Middlesex Historical Society *Transactions,* IX (1918): pp. 16-18.

31 Despite the fire, the spring assizes opened on Monday, Apr. 14, as scheduled. See: *Times,* Apr. 25, 1845, p. 3, c. 1.

32 The hotel was originally the two-storey frame house the architect John Ewart had built on this site to house his workers during the construction of the Court House in 1827-1829. With the completion of the Court House, it is believed that Ewart's property was leased as an inn by Peter McGregor. By Jul. 1831 it was known as the King's Arms Hotel, and in August of 1833 it was renamed the Robinson Hotel in honour of Chief Justice Robinson who had lodged there while on circuit. By June, 1836 it had become known as the Robinson Hall Hotel. See: "King's Arms Hotel, London's Principal Centre for Accommodation and Transportation Depot, 1833," *Dan Brock's Historical Almanack of London* (Spring, 1975): p. 34.

33 The Mechanics' Hall, on the Court House square, was in use by early Feb., 1843. See: William W. Judd, ed., "Minutes of the London Mechanics' Institute," London Public Library and Art Museum *Occasional Paper,* XXIII (1976): p. 9.

34 Verschoyle Cronyn, "The First Bishop of Huron" [hereafter "First Bishop of Huron"], London and Middlesex Historical Society *Transactions,* III (1911): p. 62.

35 *Cobourg Star,* Apr. 23, 1845, p. 2, c. 1; *British Colonist,* Apr. 18, 1845, p. 2, c. 4; Cronyn "First Bishop of Huron," p. 62.

36 A fragment of the reconstructed journal of Marcus Gunn covering the years 1835 to 1846 inclusive still survives. See: Regional Collection, Marcus Gunn Papers, journal, 1835–1846 [hereafter journal], p. 152.

37 *Ibid.,* p. 151. See also: *ibid,* p. 152.

38 *History of Middlesex,* p. 259.

39 *British Colonist,* Apr. 18, 1845, p. 2, c. 4.

40   *Ibid.*, p. 2, c. 4; *ibid.*, Apr. 22, 1845, p. 3, c. 2; *Cobourg Star,* Apr. 23, 1845, p. 2, c. 1; *Times,* Apr. 25, 1845, p. 3, c. 1.

41   *British Colonist,* Apr. 18, 1845, p. 2, c. 4; *ibid.*, Apr. 22, 1845, p. 3, c. 2; *Cobourg Star,* Apr. 23, 1845, p. 2, c. 1; *Times,* Apr. 25, 1845, p. 3, c. 1.

42   *Cobourg Star,* Apr. 23, 1845, p. 2, c. 1; *Church* (Cobourg, Canada West), Aug. 15, 1845, p. 22, c. 6.

43   An examination of the Collector's List of 1844 for the Town of London (London Township), which was compiled prior to the October, 1844 fire, reveals that the amount of valuation of the property assessed, corresponding to the burned out area of Apr., 1845, was £6,092 as compared to £30,291 for the entire town. See: Regional Collection, London Township, Collector's List.

44   *British Colonist,* Apr. 18, 1845, p. 2, c. 5. Obtaining adequate insurance in a frame frontier town, however, was a perennial problem, even without a fire to frighten the underwriters.

45   *Monarch* (Woodstock, Canada West), Apr. 22, 1845, p. 2, c. 5.

46   *British Colonist,* Apr. 18, 1845, p. 2, c. 4; *Cobourg Star,* Apr. 23, 1845, p. 2, c. 1.

47   *Western Globe* (London, Canada West), Oct. 23, 1845, p. 8, c. 1.

48   *British Colonist,* Apr. 18, 1845, p. 2, c. 4.

49   Regional Collection, Marcus Gunn Papers, journal, pp. 152-153; *British Colonist,* Apr. 22, 1845, p. 3, c. 2; *Times,* May 23, 1845, p. 2, cc. 6-7; *London Fire Brigade History* (London, Ontario: Edmund J. Carty, 1928), p. [4]. These market buildings were located on the block bounded by Wellington, Bathurst, Waterloo, and York.

50   *Times,* May 2, 1845, p. 3, c. 3.

51   *St. Thomas Standard,* May 15, 1845, p. 3, c. 3; *Times,* May 16, 1845–May 8, 1846; *British Colonist,* May 13, 1845, p. 2, c. 7; *ibid.*, May 20, 1845, p. 2, c. 7; *ibid.*, p. 3, c. 1; *ibid.*, Jun. 6, 1845, p. 2, cc. 2-3, 5; *ibid.*, Jun. 13, p. 2, c. 3; *ibid.*, Jul. 8, 1845, p. 2, cc. 4-6; *Church,* May 25, 1845, p. 184, cc. 1-2; *ibid.*, p. 185, c. 3; *Monarch,* Jun. 10, 1845, p. 3, cc. 1-2.

52   *London Times,* Feb. 20, 1846, p. 2, c. 7.

53   *Ibid.*, Feb. 26, 1847, p. 3, cc. 2-3.

54   *Railton's Directory for the City of London, C. W.* 1856[–]1857 (London, Canada West: Geo. Railton, 1856), pp. 41-42. A further by-law, relating to the matter of wooden buildings, was passed on Nov. 19, 1855. See: *ibid.*, pp. 48-50

55   A study of land records for London and its hinterland supports this theory of pioneer development. When an area is opened for settlement, a significant amount of land gravitates into the hands of speculators who tend to sell off at a good profit as the community becomes more compactly settled. They then redirect their activities toward transactions in mortgages.

56   *St. Catharines Journal,* Oct. 30, 1845, p. 1, c. 5.

57   *London Inquirer,* Aug. 5, 1842, p. 3, c. 4; *ibid.*, Oct. 28, 1842, p. 4, c. 3; Ludwik Kos-Rabcewicz-Zublowski and William Edward Greening, *Sir Casimir Stanislaus Gzowski: A Biography* (Toronto, Ontario: Burns and MacEachern, 1959), pp. 34-35.

58   Frederick H. Armstrong and Daniel J. Brock, "The Rise of London: A Study of Urban Evolution in Nineteenth-Century Southwestern Ontario," in F.H. Armstrong, H.A. Stevenson, and J. D. Wilson, eds., *Aspects of Nineteenth-Century Ontario: Essays Presented to James J. Talman* (Toronto, Ontario: University of Toronto Press, 1974), pp. 89, 97, n. 27.

59   *London Gazette,* Nov. 7, 1840, p. 3, c. 1.

60   *Times,* Oct. 24, 1845, p. 3, cc. 3-4; *Western Globe,* Oct. 22-23; *ibid.*, Nov. 20, 1845, p. 7, cc. 5-6; *ibid.*, p. 8, cc. 4-6.

61   *Cobourg Star,* Apr. 23, 1845, p. 2, cc. 1-2.

CHAPTER SIX

MEMORIALS IN PAPER AND STONE

Records of the Robert Flint Family

Nancy Zwart Tausky

Robert Flint emigrated from England, with his wife and four children, in the early 1830s. He was one of thousands who left an economically depressed Britain during that period to undertake the arduous search for a more rewarding life in the New World. Except for those who achieved exceptional wealth or prominence, few among this mass of hopeful settlers are now known as names and personalities: the lives filled with heart-rending failures and soul-stirring triumphs have been reduced to lists of statistics, or enveloped in various generalizations about the North American pioneer. The Flint family forms a remarkable exception to this rule of anonymity. Robert Flint settled down in Westminster Township, Upper Canada, to a life as a farmer and local builder; he never achieved political office or even status as a local community leader, but he is well remembered because of two different kinds of unintended bequests. The first is a fascinating collection of letters, most of them written by Robert's wife and sons, and preserved by descendants. Second are some of the buildings Robert erected. Though relatively humble, they are distinctive because of their cobblestone construction, and the houses in which he and his son Pirney lived have become public landmarks because they were incorporated in London's scenic Springbank Park. This study surveys both types of memorials, those in paper and those in stone. The buildings offer a striking example of the way in which immigrants remodelled old-world traditions to fit the needs and resources of a new country. The letters provide valuable insights into the virtues and trials of a pioneer family. While they tend to deflate the idyll of family togetherness among the first settlers, they give life to the ideas of courage and adventurousness in the face of many and varied hardships, of both a psychological and physical nature.

THE LETTERS

The set of letters on which this article is based is an amalgamation of three different collections, owned respectively by Fred A. Andrewes and John F. Millerson of London, Ontario; Lloyd Blinn, also from London; and Douglas Older of St. Thomas, Ontario – all descended from various branches of the Robert Flint family. The earliest document is the will composed by Robert's father in 1824 in which, surprisingly, he leaves his estate to Hannah Flint, Robert's wife; there are several letters from J. Gordon of Saxlingham, Norfolk, England, a friend and apparently a relative of Hannah's who looked after property Robert owned in Hempnall, Norfolk; and there are about sixty letters written by various members of the family and their friends between 1840 and 1891. Together they portray a drama that has roots in both literature and life: the letters relate the facts of the characters' experiences, but they are coloured by the personalities of the writers, by ideas about the self-images they want to project, and by the potentialities and limitations of each author's facility in writing. With the exception of J. Gordon, none of the writers shows a full command of proper spelling and punctuation, but these weaknesses are balanced by the sometimes elegant handwriting and the command of syntax in the letters. The authors of these letters tend to write the way they talk, as do many persons who speak more than they write, or, in more eloquent passages, they echo the Biblical diction and syntax with which members of the Flint family were thoroughly familiar. Throughout this article, I have normalized the spelling and punctuation of the letters, not to make the writers seem more articulate than they were, but to avoid letting mechanical irregularities block a reader's appreciation of the effective rhythms of language that one finds in the letters, or the dignity of the lives they reveal.

Robert Flint had possessed various financial resources in England. It is clear from Gordon's letters that Robert Flint was a builder as well as a landlord. Speaking of the recently deceased "Old Thomas Sillett," Gordon notes as an aside, "I think you built his house at Carlton."[1] Another comment, on one of the rental properties, is more definite if less complimentary:

> I was greatly alarmed a little while ago by finding that the houses going into the street had a narrow escape from being burnt down, for the roof of the backhouse where Thirling did live caught fire from your having laid the end of a piece of wood into the chimney flue, but being at the noon hour it was soon put out and no great damage done.[2]

A sign of the difficult economic climate is the fact that Gordon finds it almost impossible to collect the rents from some of Flint's tenants:

> King the basket maker gives me great trouble. I only got the rent for 1843 by serving him with a notice to quit and threatening to seize his goods. I shall be obliged to give him the same sauce again. Thirling is transported for stealing old iron, his wife and children paupers upon the parish; the woman behaved fairly, came and told me it was impossible for her to go on with the house, and brought me one pound fifteen shillings, which from enquiry I believe to be all they could make up.[3]

One can speculate that it may have been the depressed condition of the market in real estate that led Robert to undertake a career as a fisherman, with his own fishing smack,[4] in the seaside town of Lowestoft in Suffolk.[5]

When well into middle age, approaching fifty, Robert Flint embarked on the more radical move to North America, a move that was to require many more fresh starts and some turnings from dead-end paths. His son Pirney provided a dramatic account, for a biography in Goodspeed's *History of the County of Middlesex,* of the family's abortive attempt to settle in New York State:

In 1834, Mr. Flint immigrated to America and landed in New York. He left his family in that city while he went to Pottsville to earn some money, having been robbed before leaving England. [When Robert failed to return as soon as expected,] Mrs. Flint became anxious, made inquiries, and heard that he had died of cholera. She then returned to England. In the meantime, three days after Mrs. Flint had started back to England, Mr. Flint returned to New York and found his family gone. He then went to Canada, settled in Byron, and later sent to England for his family, they coming on in 1836.[6]

Though Pirney is presumably following family tradition as to the general plot of this melodrama, his dates are called into question by a passenger list for the ship *Ontario* that shows Hannah, Robert's wife, disembarking in New York with their two youngest children on April 17, 1833.[7] It is certain, however, that in 1836 Robert bought a small parcel of land in Westminster (later Hall's Mills, then Byron), at the eastern end of what is now Hall's Mills Road, possibly intended as the site of the family home while Robert established himself in the "business" mentioned in Goodspeed's *History*.[8] In 1838, after the business failed to prosper, Robert purchased sixty-one acres (24.6 ha) just east of the village, along the Thames River,[9] where he turned to an apparently new career in farming, and also carried on in his former occupation as a builder. Among the buildings he erected was a cobblestone homestead for his own reunited family.

The family remained united for only a relatively brief period. By the time Robert was settled into his new home, in 1838, he was approximately fifty-four, his wife Hannah forty-eight, and his children twenty-two (Robert G.), twenty (George), seventeen (Mary), and thirteen (Pirney).[10] Robert G.[11] was living in New Carlisle, Indiana, by January 1840.[12] Pirney joined him, in Valparaiso, Indiana, in 1844,[13] and both sons moved to California, Robert to ranch and Pirney to mine gold, in 1850.[14] A letter written by Hannah to her sons in 1854 reveals the senior Flints' sorrow at their sons' long absence: "Your Father gives his kind love to you both. ... He often says 'I am afraid I shall not live to see my boys come home ... '" Pirney did return home in 1855,[15] four years before his father's death, and he eventually took over Robert's farm. Pirney married Ann Elson around 1857,[16] and they lived with their family of eight children in a cobblestone house Robert built a few hundred feet from his own. Robert G. remained in California; he never saw his father again, but a visit made prior to 1866[17] may have allowed him to see his mother before she died, in 1865. Subsequent trips strengthened what appear to have been strong ties to his parents' adopted home, despite his self-imposed distance from it. In the late 1860s, Robert G. married Eliza Elson, a sister of Pirney's wife, and after Eliza's death in 1877[18] he sent their five children back to the Byron-London area to be raised by various relatives; one daughter, Bessie, went to live with Robert G.'s sister, Mary, and another with his brother Pirney.[19] It was during an 1881 visit to his distant family that Robert G. found himself on board the river steamer *Victoria* when it capsized and sank with the loss of over 180 lives.[20] Robert survived; he died four years later in California, and at the wish of his relatives, his body was transported from California to Westminster, so that he could be buried with his wife and parents in the Brick Street Cemetery.[21] Around 1846, Mary wed William Blinn, a miller with whom she led a somewhat transient life – according to the account in Goodspeed's *History of Middlesex,* Blinn "was engaged in milling at different places in the county for seventeen years," six in Byron – until he bought a farm near Byron in 1858.[22] The Blinns had three children, though their only daughter died young.[23] George died in 1849.[24]

The rich collection of family letters that still exists is directly related to the travels of its various members, and they give depth to the personae in what otherwise might seem a relatively commonplace drama. The only character who remains undeveloped is George. The few allusions to him are curiously equivocal, designed, it might seem, to create suspense, to suggest a dark mystery that would evolve into an unexpected denouement. Robert's reaction, on hearing of George's death, mixes nostalgia with a guarded and reluctant hint that, like other tragic heroes, George was partially responsible for his downfall:

> I was surprised and pained at the death of George, poor brother. I remember so well of our going to school together and playing and working together as if it had been but a few days since and now he is going as it were in the prime of life. Some times my pride was hurt to see him follow the course he did but he was more to be pitied than blamed. It was his misfortune as well as error and who shall judge but the divine author of all life.[25]

It is possible, though not certain, that Hannah's later comparison between George and Pirney alludes to similar maladies. She thinks Pirney is drinking too much: "he is killing himself as fast as he can. ... I can't help fretting. He is still my child and I should like to see him do well. Poor George was nothing to compare to him and he suffered a deal but he is out of a world of trouble and he had good principles. I hope he is happy."[26] Since the plot of this drama is formed by life as well as art, however, the mystery is never explicitly solved, and George remains a sad and shadowy figure.

Predictably, the letters are most comprehensive in relation to the life and personality of Robert G.: most of the letters preserved locally were those he sent home during his long life away, and a philosophical and literary tendency in his character makes his writing particularly revealing. His earliest surviving letter, sent to his sister from New Carlisle, Indiana,[27] shows him growing wheat and performing "small jobs," while also delighting in seeing himself as an insatiable socializer and a proponent of somewhat daring opinions. "I have done nothing this winter but frolic," he boasts. "We have had a cotillion school once a week for three months. I have now finished the last waltz for this year. This is the finest place for frolics that ever I was in. There has been about forty parties in four months, including the school's, and I have not missed one of them." He judges marriage "a mere matter of moonshine ... to satisfy the prejudice of a world that we must bow to," and defends newfound sympathies with American democracy: "You [Mary] may be a Tory but you will never be an aristocrat."

Robert appears to be strongly influenced by his highly articulate seventeen-year-old roommate, Schuyler Colfax, who gives a third-person description of himself in an accompanying letter: "He is rather politically inclined for so young a subject, but does not believe in Kings or Queens. He sleeps with Mr. R.G. Flint and walks around with him – they both go to bed together and both rise at the same time; [Schuyler is] rather reserved and bashful in female company, waggishly inclined, and [one who] attended the Dancing School and Debating Club in company with your son. ... He has had, long since, an introduction to all the members of your family and knows them all, as if he had seen them for years."[28] Schuyler Colfax's political inclinations were to dictate his career: he sat in the United States House of Representatives between 1855 and 1869, acting as speaker during his last six years there, and in 1869 he was elected vice-president of the United States, under President Ulysses S. Grant.[29]

A letter written by Pirney in 1844[30] shows Robert G. in a very different milieu. Robert G. has now established a brick-making business, with which Pirney is greatly impressed: there are two kilns, each of which has apparently burned 80,000 bricks since Pirney's arrival; Robert G. has a partner "very quick at making brick," who can mould 1,500 bricks in an hour; with four hands, they can produce 30,000 a week. Robert G. is also working as a mason, and it is a sign of his general prosperity that he and Pirney are planning to build a house, on the hill above the brickyard, that will use "60 or 50 … 1000 [presumably 60,000 or 50,000] brick." The house, measuring "24 by 34 by 13 feet," (7.2 x 10.3 x 3.9 m) is nearing completion when Robert G. writes home in October 1845.[31]

The author of the 1845 letter no longer presents himself as the arch sophisticate of 1840, but his writing still reflects a self-consciousness about literary style and a search for colourful means of expression (e.g., "God temper[s] the wind to the shorn lamb," or, speaking of a friend, "with such a morose mamma who would mar the fortunes of an Angel, what could be expected"). His respect for education is evident in his ambition for Pirney: "I wish Pirney to remain [in Valparaiso] and go to school this winter for it is the last chance for it; in another year he will be too old to study." Robert G. seems caught, at this stage, between various contradictory yearnings – between an inclination towards hard work and business advancement on the one hand and the more leisurely pursuit of the arts and the world of ideas on the other, and also between his affections, urging him to return home, and his adventurousness, urging him to make his own independent successes.

The latter conflict was brought to a head in 1849, when Pirney determined to join the rush for gold in California, and Robert G. also felt the lure of the far west. A letter to his parents, dated November 26, 1849, justifies his initial decision against the move: "I have been sometime making up my mind . . . not to go to California. I could not reconcile myself to the Idea of leaving you for in the course of human events I could not expect ever to see you again." But the decision was so tentative that he postponed mailing the letter for a month: "You should have rec'd this some time since," he admits in a postscript dated December 29, 1849, "but I was still wavering about going to California and I now think I may safely send this news without fear of contradiction. … I at this time think of visiting you this winter and … I look forward to it with the eagerness of a school boy."[32] Robert G.'s uncertainty won out over his eagerness, however, for the next existing letter from Robert G. to his parents, dated November 12, 1850, comes from Sacramento, California. Pirney is "in the mines digging," and Robert has taken to trading in cattle and horses, having driven eight horses and twenty cows all the way from the United States, and purchased more in California.

When Robert G.'s prophecy about never seeing his parents again proved true as far as his father was concerned, he was penitent and eager to make some form of restitution: "I regret very much that I have put coming home until it is too late … I regret having lost the opportunity of seeing and conversing with father once more, … and if God give me health, I will be there this winter."[33] But it was in fact several years before Robert G. returned to Westminster. Long apologies for his continued absence comprise standard parts of his letters, but he clearly feels constrained by the immediate demands of his own new world:

> We are all more or less creatures of circumstances and when we
> once put our hand to the plough it is almost impossible to give it
> up or turn back (July 16, 1859).[34]

> Things and times are getting to be more settled in California
> than they were so that I can leave my affairs with some showing
> of finding them as I leave them, but one does not like to stop in
> the race and lose by it and the difficulty is in keeping what you
> have, rather than in making more (September 16, 1860).[35]

> I live on hopes of making the trip home this year. I am growing
> desperate on the subject and am determined to venture the first
> chance. . . . I have thought of it so long and so much that it is
> seldom out of my mind, and could I leave here with any degree
> of certainty of finding things on my return as I leave them, I
> would come home tomorrow, but this unfortunate war keeps
> things in such confusion that each and every one has to be at his
> post. . . .(March 1, 1861).[36]

Imprisoning though it might sometimes seem, the new world he created for himself in California was a vast one, embracing a broad geographical area and and a spectrum of experience ranging from high adventure to acute hardship. His description of his trip out to California sounds straight out of a good western, with "Indians ... stealing fourteen head of oxen and horse," and a confrontation that he won with the help of a Canadian friend, Fred Dillon from Muncey, and "ten Delaware Indians who came through from the States this summer," whose chief "took six scalps."[37] Heroism could take other forms, as in the long treks involved in transporting animals to and from market, or surviving a fall from a horse in the middle of a stampede,[38] or simply enduring the hard and sometimes unrewarding work. The early letters from California emphasize the difficulties of Robert G.'s life: " ... the weather has been such that I cannot leave the cattle. Grass do[es] not grow and the cattle ramble very much. A few old cows have perished by old age and poverty too – bad companions. And I am admonished by the same, which I stave off as well as I can" (January 20, 1855);[39] "I already see daylight through the mist of times which will enable me to see you all soon and get to rest a short time from this eternal struggle, struggle" (June 24, 1862).[40] But it gradually becomes evident that Robert is making a success of his ranch, and is engaged in raising livestock on a large scale: he complains in 1872 that his "cattle are scattered over a country a hundred miles in diameter, and later speaks of his "seventy-five hundred lambs and sheep."[41] In 1875 he estimates a crop of "fifteen or eighteen hundred calves."[42]

Robert G.'s comments on the domestic side of his life are mainly concerned with his house, especially the adobe house he built in 1867 and 1868.[43] Robert had obviously been trained in his father's trade as a builder/mason; a drystone stock-watering place he erected on part of his ranch was apparently quite famous.[44] But one suspects that he found the 1868 house worthy of report because it was being prepared for a bride. Robert married Eliza Elson on July 8, 1869,[45] after which she and her sister Lizzie joined Robert in his new home. In a letter dated July 17, 1870, Robert makes futile efforts to hide his pride in his wife and their first child behind a veil of heavy sarcasm:

Robert G. and Eliza Elson Flint. Fred A. Andrewes

> Eliza is ... very modest and give[s] me less trouble than most
> women give their husbands but that dear baby must be put into
> short clothes and go to town and be ... photographed ... in the
> busiest time. ... The truth is there was no one on the Ranch to
> admire that baby so go we must ... where there was somebody to
> see the baby. The Tavern Keeper's wife thought there never was
> such a baby. Just think of that and four days stopping cost thirty
> dollars. ... There is to be no more children or I am to be a poor
> Man.[46]

There were in fact four more children, and Robert G. seems to have been a very
happy man until his wife's death in 1877 made his home the scene of
unbearably painful memories. Writing to his nephew Robert, he bluntly
confides, " ... I am recovering very slowly from the blow I received in the death
of your aunt. At home I cannot stay, the children reminding me continually of
my loss. I feel better away from home with the outside world, who knowing
nothing of my loss, do not remind [me] of it."[47] After his children moved to
Canada,[48] Robert G. again devoted himself to ranching, until he himself died,
in 1885, as the result of internal injuries produced when he was caught under a
barrage of lumber falling from a wagon.[49] His obituary rightly described him as
a very wealthy man: when his will was probated his property was valued at
$650,000.[50] He left his largest ranch, the San Juan Ranch in the county of San
Luis Obispo, to his elder son, Robert; a smaller ranch, on the Naciniento River,
to his other son, George; and his money divided among his three daughters.[51]
Even after his son Robert had dissipated some of his inheritance through
mismanagement and gambling, the San Juan Ranch contained 58,175 acres
(23,543 ha) when it was sold in 1898.[52]

One finds less evidence in the letters concerning Pirney's character and
interests, and what evidence there is proves somewhat contradictory. He obviously

Letter from Pirney Flint to his parents, sent from California in 1852. Douglas Older

possessed qualities that caused people to admire and trust him. One of Pirney's California friends, William G. Jones, writes to Byron in 1856 when spending a reprieve from mining in caring for Robert G.'s stock and raising hogs on his own. Jones is bitter about the money he has lost on a claim, owing to poor partners and bad management, but the mines have not completely lost their lustre. He includes an assessment of the various mining activities near their old haunt, Vulcano, concluding with a heartfelt invitation: "Pirney, if you ever come back to this country I should like to take another mining tour with you though I don't think I would undertake it with any one else."[53] In a much later letter written by Pirney's sister Mary, Pirney stands as the one trustworthy figure in a world that then seems to Mary to be composed of unreliable in-laws: " ... Pirney is a very good man, ... [he] will speak the truth. You can depend upon his word."[54] A glimpse of Pirney's strong sense of integrity emerges from one of his own early letters from California. In a matter-of-fact way he presents a litany of misfortunes – he was ill, he was robbed, and the lack of water made mining impossible – with an account of his consequent financial troubles. But more passion enters his writing when he discusses his obligations: "... I have not paid my doctor's bill which is two hundred dollars and board which is one hundred and they behaved very kind when I had no money and I am sure that you would not advise me to leave until I had paid them both principal and interest and that I shall you may be sure of."[55]

Pirney appears industrious and hard-working and he shares his brother's thirst for adventure, but where Robert G. takes satisfaction in seeing his hard work pay off in gradual increments to his wealth and land-holdings, Pirney is attracted by the vision of a sudden windfall or dramatic discovery. It was Pirney's idea to respond to the lure of California riches, and his interest was in mining rather than ranching. He eventually settled for a more mundane sort of life taking over his father's farm. But his interest in the buried treasures of the earth was still alive in 1864 when, with a group of other investors from Westminster and London, he applied to incorporate "The Sulphur Spring Petroleum Company of Byron," with a declared purpose of "Boring for opening and using Petroleum, Salt or other Mineral Springs" on broken front, lot 44, in Westminster, just west of the village of Byron.[56] The Sulphur Spring Petroleum Company was short-lived, though sulphur springs did exist in the area.[57] It is perhaps ironic, though, that Pirney's local fame is owing to the pure water springs in the vicinity of his farm, which supplied London's early public water system.

The impatience that lay beneath Pirney's willingness to invest in the single lucky chance found more direct outlets in various forms of reckless, angry, and sometimes melodramatic actions. His previously doting mother claims to be heartbroken, in 1856, over Pirney's behaviour after his return from California:

> [Pirney] is never sober when he has money, ... he keeps the lowest company, brings them often home. He won't bear to be spoken to. I would sooner live in a cave in the earth than live the life I do. ... When Pirney came home, I gave him all his money, both principal and interest. What he brought home made it near nine hundred dollars, and it is all gone and more too. I have never had a dollar of his money, neither do I want it, but we might better of had it than the taverns, and so far he seems as if he could not make away fast enough. ... He drinks to madness. I cannot live here much longer.[58]

Hannah must soon have seen improvements in her son, for by 1860 he had taken over his father's farm, he was married, and he had one child.[59] But in 1864 Robert G. still greets news of Pirney's third child with the enigmatic hope that another daughter "will help to steady him" and with a meditation about how dissolute California can be for young people, whose values were not fully formed before they arrived.[60] Pirney was apparently not altogether steady yet in 1868, when he was fined "$10. and costs" on a charge of "furious driving," as reported by a completely unsympathetic local newspaper: "He ran his waggon against a buggy smashing the hinder wheel of the latter, and throwing its occupants into the road. This accident seemed to be the result of sheer carelessness."[61] By 1885 Pirney had raised a large family, suffered the trauma of his wife's death, and proven a successful farmer, but he retained enough of the old rebellious spirit to fight a proposed road through his property, in an incident that, as reported by the *London Free Press,* reads like a plot from a story of the Wild West. A road allowance had been laid out along the base line through lots belonging to Pirney and his neighbour J. Cassidy, but the road had never been realized. When an effort was made to use the allowance, Flint and Cassidy "ordered the intruders off. ... After some loud talk and threatening, some of Messrs. Cassady and Flint's party said

Pirney Flint. Lloyd Blinn

they would shoot if the others did not get out. On this threat, they did get." In this case, though, the law was on Pirney's side, and the attempt to use the road deemed illegal because the road was not recognized by a Westminster by-law.[62]

Despite his enduring rebelliousness, Pirney proved a competent farmer and a devoted husband and father. He took over his own father's sixty-one acres (24.6 ha) in 1858; in 1867 he had four cows, twenty sheep, five hogs, and five horses.[63] Letters from Robert G. make it clear that Pirney is growing crops as well; Robert G. takes a special interest in Pirney's orchard, constantly asking for more reports on its progress and productivity.[64] In 1870, Pirney added sixteen and a half acres (6.2 ha) to his holdings; the following year an additional fifty (20 ha) ; and, by 1873, twenty-four acres (10 ha) more, bringing his total acreage to 151.5 (16.3 ha).[65]

He married Ann Elson sometime in the late 1850s; Ann bore eight children,[66] and her death in 1874, two weeks after the birth of the youngest, seems profoundly to have affected Pirney's health and outlook. Robert G. sympathizes in a letter written in 1876: "I received yours of Oct. 22 and I was concerned to think you viewed your health and situation as you did. To be sure, we are both getting advanced in years, and are not as young as we were thirty years ago. And our families are young to be left alone without a head to direct them."[67] Where Robert G. was later to rely on relatives for the upbringing of his children, however, Pirney seems to have parted only with the baby, Edna, who, like three of Robert G's children, was raised by Ann's sister and her husband, Samuel Gibson.[68] And, only three years later, after the death of Eliza Elson Flint, Robert G.'s baby was sent to Pirney's household.[69] Pirney was one of the subscribers who opted, in 1889, to have his biography published in Goodspeed's *History of the County of Middlesex,* and the image he chose to have presented there presumably indicated the way he wanted himself to appear, even if the image reflected only part of the real person: "Mr. Flint takes an active interest in all laudable enterprises, and has been school trustee for a number of years. He is a Reformer in politics, and a man of liberal views on all subjects of importance. He is a member of the Masonic fraternity, and an honorable, upright citizen."[70] Interestingly, William Blinn's biography in the *History* ends in almost the same way, as if there had been some family collaboration about the endings of the write-ups, despite some contradictory details in earlier parts.[71]

While a couple of early letters to Mary from Robert G. and Pirney show their affection for their sister, and while many later letters contain allusions to the Blinns, Mary would remain a rather grey figure in the correspondence were it not that the one existing letter composed by Mary herself is a very informative one.[72] This letter, written to Robert G. in 1866, is provoked by a crisis within the Blinn household: Mary's in-laws want William to return to the milling business, in partnership with his brother Hiram; Mary is determined that he should stay on the farm. In fact, Mary has considerable control over the decision in that the sale of the farm requires her signature, a fact implying that the farm was purchased in part at least with Flint money. What is bothering her is less the threat of change than the constant pressure from her in-laws, and the tension she describes reveals much about her own views and values.

Her main arguments against the mill enterprise have to do with Hiram's ugly temper and his intemperate spending: "... he married into a poor Irish family and his wife must have a piano and keeps lots of company, keeps a girl, and has four of her sisters there to keep up [as] ladies." And, indeed, it is the ladies, and especially Mrs. Blinn Sr., who come in for the most direct attacks. "I must tell you what kind of education my husband had before he was married. The old woman [his mother] was brought up in the same way. She would have bad girls into her home to keep her boys good-natured and cover the fact from the world and have some of her nieces which were no better than bad girls to play with her. When I first got married, the old woman sent William's cousin[?] with us and she would get on the bed where she lay before me and because I would not have such creatures the old W[oman threatened to] cut my head off." She has tried to spy on Mary by hiring the sister of Mary's maid; she makes faces about Pirney when standing right behind his back; and she can turn William any way she wants, for "she is cunning as [a] fox and as revengeful as Satan." In Mary's view, Pirney also suffers, in having a wife with no respect for the truth.

The very intensity of Mary's own hostility makes her claims dubious as objective evidence. Undoubtedly the strength of her feelings owes something, not only to the immediate pressures, but also to the fact that her emotions have been pent up for some time. It seems that Mary has always felt tortured by the differences with her in-laws, but, at least since her mother's death, has had no local confidante: "You see what a lot of grief I have wrote but I have no one but you for I cannot tell Pirney anything and I do not wish to hurt any one with my affairs." Moreover, one detects in Mary's complaints a conflict of manners that may make possible a misunderstanding of morals: it is evident that the Blinns are a very lively group, without some of the Mary's inhibitions. What does emerge with more certainty than the picture of Mary's relatives-by-marriage is the picture of Mary herself. The portrayal is of a long-suffering woman, clinging firmly to the strong ethical code with which she was raised – a code that defines status in terms of honesty, thrift, and a rigorous definition of decency, rather than in terms of pianos and maids.

Hannah's letters prove that Mary's staunch uprightness was learned at her mother's knee. There are only three letters from Hannah in the collection, and only brief business letters from Robert; but Hannah's letters are comprehensive and, like Mary's, revealing, so that they show a great deal about both Hannah herself and her husband. There is a shrewd, practical side to Hannah's nature (she advises Pirney to send his money home, for example, where she has invested it with Mr. George Gunn at 6 percent interest),[73] and she seems well educated for her times and circumstances: J. Gordon, in Saxlingham, observes that she "writes and fills up a letter as few women can do."[74] A pronounced didactic strain in the three letters reflects Hannah's strong religious and ethical convictions, and her concern for the spiritual welfare of her distant sons. "I pray to God day and night," she writes Pirney in 1851, "to protect and preserve you from every evil. I know you are surrounded with many dangers and among all sorts of people but my dear Boy put your trust on God, trust not to man, and remember His mercies to you when you were sick in a strange land."[75] Her well-defined concept of a straight and narrow path leads her to be very critical of those who diverge from its courses, and to expect visible rewards for those who stay within its bounds. The case of a Scots miller makes a good exemplum: "[Customers] say they got more flour from their wheat than they ever had before so ... if a man is honest in his dealings he is sure to get along."[76]

Such a complacent attitude can easily be shattered, however, if life's punishments and rewards do not seem to be meted out fairly, and Hannah is obviously frustrated and embittered over her own sufferings – at her sons' long absences and infrequent letters, at Pirney's dissolute behaviour on his return from California, and at the hard work she and Robert have to endure even when aged and sometimes ill: "I have worked like a slave in my younger days, now I am old and worn out I am still forced to work."[77] While attempting to earn the paradise to come, she comes to regard the world of her past as a paradise on earth, contrasting her happiness in England with her sorrows in Canada, and, implicitly, her father[78] with her husband:

> Robert pray come home as soon as you can, you have lived so long away that you forget your home. Often do I recall to mind your childhood when you would paddle in the sea. Rob't, there's where I spent the happiest days of my life. Oh Rob't could you have known your grandfather Pirney, you would have been proud of him, he never had a blemish on his character and faithfully served his king and country and I trust his god and died in peace with all men. I hope I shall meet him in another and better world."[79]

The portrait of Robert Sr. in Hannah's letters is a very appealing one, sometimes because of the very qualities that irritate his wife. He is a determined worker, although "he will always be lame,"[80] and despite Hannah's wish to create an easier life for both of them: "[Mary and William Blinn] have bought the Sutherland farm, have a very honest man and his wife on it working on shares, the same people I wished your father to get four years ago. He missed a good chance as he has many a time."[81] Robert is still engaged in putting up buildings even when he is "too aged" to look after Pirney's horses.[82] Where Hannah is eager to criticize, Robert is uncomplaining. Hannah describes in detail the troubles he encounters when erecting the "English Church" [now St. Anne's Anglican Church]: "John Sims and Lackey [?] [and] your Father they were four months putting up the walls. It is not finish'd for the want of funds. If there is a show come along. . . or any other foolishness, they [other parishioners] can find money & go by waggon-loads … , but to God that gives them all [they] can spare nothing. … Old Eakins would not let them have stone although he has so many that he could not cultivate his land." Nevertheless, "your Father worked faithfull 4 months, and I never heard him grumble."[83] An even more striking example of Robert's tolerance and generosity is his attitude towards Pirney. While Hannah is wishing to die because of the shame she perceives Pirney is bringing on her and himself, Robert, to Hannah's disgust, "is building [Pirney] a very good stone house on the end of our lot next to Lackey's" and "he has given him an acre of land."[84] Hannah expects Pirney to sell the house and drink the proceeds, but instead the house was to become the centre of Pirney's farm and family.

THE BUILDINGS

It is impossible to estimate the extent of Robert Flint's work as a builder. The letters contain several allusions to his work as a mason (Robert G. wants Pirney to train in his father's "trade."[85] Hannah mentions buildings on which he is engaged, or praises the "good stone stabling he has put under the barn"[86]), but they specifically identify only three buildings: the "English Church" that was later named St. Anne's, a "stone cottage for Charles Hall … on old Mr. Eakin's place"[87] (since demolished), and the "good stone house" that Robert is building for Pirney in 1856. One can also assume that Robert built the house on his property in which he and Hannah lived. Beyond these four structures certainly erected by Robert Flint, there are five others that can be attributed to him with some definiteness because of structural or stylistic similarities with the documented buildings: the former saddle and harness shop (now, in part, the Wagging Tail Pet Grooming Salon at 1289 Commissioners' Road West) on the main street of Byron; an inn and blacksmith shop (since demolished) that formerly also stood on the main street, on the southwest corner of Boler Road and Commissioners' Road; the large extension to Pirney's 1856 house; and, two somewhat more tentative attributions, the cottage in Kilworth that was constructed *circa* 1858 as a store and residence for William Comfort,[88] and a cottage just east of Kilworth, on property that once belonged to Timothy Kilbourne.[89] The six of these eight structures that are still standing (considering Pirney's house and extension as one building) have a number of characteristics in common that provide a firm if not unbreakable link with Flint's name, though they probably form only a small part of his entire building history in the area.

The most obvious common characteristic is that they are all built of stone, with cobblestones used to face at least the front of each building. Cobblestones are easy to find in the area, where the river Thames cuts through a glacial moraine composed of a remarkable variety of rock types,[90] and local legend has it that cobblestones were therefore a popular building material around what is now Byron. Evidence in the 1861 census of Canada indicates otherwise, however. It is true that there was a cluster of stone houses in section 3 of Westminster Township, which included the Byron area: in all five sections of Westminster Township taken together there were only fourteen stone houses, and eight of these were in section 3. Nevertheless, stone houses formed a negligible percentage of the total house stock: forty-nine houses in section 3 were built of logs, a hundred were frame, and forty-five were brick. The fact that at least five of the eight stone buildings – the two Flint houses, the inn, the leather shop, and the cottage for Charles Hall – can be attributed to Robert Flint suggests that, instead of following local practice, he was introducing a personal method of building. A partial explanation undoubtedly lies in the building traditions of Norfolk, where Flint had learned his trade.

Robert Flint's cobblestone work on the cottage he built for himself. The cottage now serves as a gift shop in Springbank Park.

Photo by Stephen Harding

Flint's name in fact links him with his craft. In regions like Norfolk, where, as archaeologist David Dymond explains, "every field contains innumerable stones of flint," flint was traditionally the most widely used building material; "indeed," he argues, "flint ... is the only widespread building stone to be found in East Anglia."[91] Robert Flint's surname may well reflect a trade, in building with flint, that extends back through generations of his ancestors.

Flint is a very hard, opaque rock, with colours ranging from black to greyish white and various shades of brown; formed by sea-sponges, it has been embedded for aeons in the chalk found around England's southern and eastern coastal regions. It is sometimes

Wishing Well stone quoins on the Robert Flint cottage. Photo by Stephen Harding

found in large veins, which are mined, but the flint that lies everywhere on the ground in Norfolk consists of small nodules or cobbles encrusted with a layer of chalk. If unbroken, they would resemble misshapen greyish-white eggs, but flint is brittle, and one usually finds at least some of the flint exposed. The combination of hardness and brittleness makes flint difficult to use. Because the pieces are irregular, they must be held in place by a strong lime mortar, and because they cannot therefore be used to construct corners or edges flint buildings have pronounced stone or brick quoins. The cobble-shaped flints became especially popular during the early nineteenth century, when flints of approximately the same size were halved, and laid in courses with the circular faces of the flint showing and the rounded cobbles embedded in the mortar. [92]

Robert Flint used cobblestones in the same way one would work with flint, except that the stones did not need cutting in order to be decorative. The cobblestones are set in a thick mortar, and on his façades, at least, he seems generally to have attempted to lay cobblestones of similar sizes in even courses. Where he has used randomly shaped fieldstone for the backs and sides of buildings, he has applied essentially the same process of relying on the mortar to hold the stone in place, though here he has not concerned himself with regular coursing. And even where large pieces of granite were obviously available, he has chosen to shape the corners and edges of his buildings with quoins of a contrasting material, turning a technical necessity into a decorative advantage, as builders in flint had traditionally done.

The stone Flint most frequently used for quoins and for door and window surrounds is the material known locally as "Wishing Well stone," because it is reputed to come from an area in Kilworth, west of Byron, where there were springs owned earlier this century by the Wishing Well soft drink company.[93] The stone is calcium carbonate, consisting of the accumulated deposits of the emerging spring water.[94] Light and porous, it is a curious choice for the members of a building designed to give it strength. To someone working in pioneer Westminster, however, the ease with which the stone could be cut was an undoubted advantage. And its light tan colour (now greyed) would have made Wishing Well stone a striking complement to the many-coloured cobblestones. On St. Anne's Church, Pirney's cottage, and the Kilbourne cottage, Flint used brick for the quoins, and, on the former two buildings, he covered the brick with stucco, again following a common English practice.

Judging from the houses still standing, Flint was also accustomed to providing a system of joists on which the floor boards of the ground floor could be laid. His own house, Pirney's house, the leather shop, the Comfort house, and the Kilbourne cottage all have basements or a crawl space under the house. Above each, joists consisting of logs, either roughly squared or, more commonly with only the top flattened, rest directly on the foundations and, in some cases, a centre wall. Sometimes the joists are mortised to rest more firmly on the foundation. In the Comfort house they rest on beams which, in turn, are inserted into the foundation wall. Though some aspects of the workmanship are rather crude (e.g., bark is frequently left on the tree trunks, and the joints loosely fitted), the system is a good deal more sophisticated than the practice, found in other pioneer homes in the area, of laying a floor directly on the soil or on a bed of boulders.[95]

A final characteristic typical of Flint's buildings is that they show a degree of self-consciousness about style – in the laying of the cobblestones, the positioning of the quoins, the proportions of the buildings, and the introduction of stylish motifs. Flint seems unwilling to sacrifice style to practicality, however, in that buildings rarely possess an exact symmetry, even where the underlying design would seem to demand it. Both aspects of his approach to style – the self-consciousness and the pragmatism – are perhaps most evident in relation to the house he built for his own family.

There is no reason to doubt that Robert built the earliest cobblestone house on his property soon after purchasing the land in 1838.[96] It approximates the form that came to be known as the Ontario Cottage: one story high, it has a hipped roof and a three-bay façade with a centre door – all characteristics typical of Georgian and Regency houses in England. An unusual detail is the rounded top of the door, a simple interpretation of the Adamesque style popular in Regency England, with its round or elliptical fanlights over the doors. Because the Wishing Well stone has weathered and a thorough renovation has resulted in some changes in the masonry, it is hard to be certain just how this stone was originally placed. A photograph taken before the renovations[97] suggests that at the corners the stone was laid so as to form a roughly alternating pattern of long and short stones on each side, in the traditional manner of quoins. The door and window surrounds are more unusual, however, in that the stones formed a border of nearly uniform width around the openings, with pronounced extensions, or ears, at the level of the window sashes. The cobblestones of the façade (which

The Robert Flint cottage as it appeared earlier this century, prior to renovation.
Regional Collection, University of Western Ontario Library. Photo by Alfred S. Garrett

initially faced Commissioners' Road) were laid in tight and relatively even courses; one can clearly distinguish the original part of the present wall by the greater density of the cobbles. The cottage measures approximately 21 by 33 feet (6.3 x 10 m), nearly the classical two-thirds ratio, and the height of the walls is approximately one-third the breadth of the building. That the windows are not quite symmetrical when seen from the outside may have been the result of an attempt to achieve symmetry inside. If there was a wall extending from front to back just west of the door (a logical arrangement supposing there to have been more than one room), the front windows would be placed exactly in the middle of the resulting rooms.

A remarkable painting (recently in the possession of Fred A. Andrewes) gives a glimpse of the cottage's interior, which reveals aspirations towards architectural stylishness as well. The painting, a copy by one-time Central High School art teacher S.K. Davidson of an original by Westminster neighbour Cyrenius Hall,[98] shows Robert and Hannah Flint sitting next to their hearth. Though it bestows a strong sense of character on both the persons and the setting, the painting is in some ways quite naive: the figurines on the mantel, for example, look considerably longer than the heads of the people, when in reality they were less than six inches high,[99] and the panels on the linen press are out of perspective with other lines in the composition. The proportionately oversized scale of the mantelpiece may be a similar distortion. Nevertheless, it is clear that, even though the fireplace is designed for cooking, with its spit and hooks, the mantelpiece is adorned with fluted pilasters, supporting a nicely articulated frieze.

The building on the main street that traded over the years in several different forms of leatherwork must have been nearly contemporary with Flint's own house. It was there in 1840, housing Lanson Harrington, trunk and saddle maker, and in 1846 it was occupied by William Martin, who dealt in shoes and harnesses.[100]

What was initially a one-storey stone cottage has been significantly altered. Probably around the period between 1865 and 1875, another half-storey was added; it featured gable ends and a small gable centred over the front door, and it was initially faced with stucco. The stucco was later covered with sheets of stamped metal. More recently, the entire façade was faced with a composition stone material, and larger plate glass windows and individual shop entrances were installed. Nevertheless, one can see characteristics of Flint's work in the basement

The Robert Flint cottage today. The dense cobblestone work near the electric meter comprises the original part of the wall. Photo by Stephen Harding

Copy, by S.K. Davidson, of a painting by Cyrenius Hall showing Robert and Hannah Flint in their home. Fred A. Andrewes

and around the sides and back of the building. The visible ground-storey walls are of rubblestone, with the stones set in liberally applied mortar, and at both the corners and around the windows one finds regularly spaced quoins of Wishing Well stone. Moreover, in a partial view of the uncovered façade seen at the edge of an old photograph of the Methodist Church (since demolished), one can just discern courses of small cobblestones. Assuming the cottage to have been relatively symmetrical, one can extrapolate from the photograph an image of a one-storey, five-bay cottage, with a narrow centre door.

The inn-turned-blacksmith-shop is the largest of the buildings attributed to Flint. The only picture of the inn and blacksmith shop, said to date from 1909,[101] shows the building when it had been defaced by a wagon shed, a shop entrance wide enough to accommodate wagons, and several blocked-in windows. That the

The now demolished Methodist Church (circa 1910), with the one-time trunk and saddle shop seen at the right. May Bridge

The inn and blacksmith shop, circa 1909. London Public Library, Byron Branch

wagon door is a later addition can be deduced from the wooden lintel (other openings are headed by stone voussoirs) and the obvious repairs to the wall above where it has sagged from inadequate support. Nevertheless, on the more westerly portions of the façade one can see cobblestones of small and medium sizes, set in relatively even rows, and windows and corners outlined with large quoins of what appears to be Wishing Well stone. With six bays and the upper windows directly aligned with those below, the building must have been extremely handsome when, in the village's early history, it operated as an inn. It was apparently still functioning as a hotel in 1884, under the management of William Hood, but by that time Wallace Meriam seems also to have opened his blacksmith shop on the premises. The structure was demolished in 1917.

St. Anne's Church has also undergone many changes. Hannah wrote to Pirney in May 1854 that "Your Father built a very pretty English church last Summer in this place. It's built with Gothic windows and a Porch, but it stands in a wrong site close to the schoolhouse ... only the walls are up, and windows and doors this spring."[102] The church was built on land deeded in 1853 by Thomas McMillan to the Anglican Church Society of the Diocese of Toronto, so work on the church seems to have begun immediately. Despite the enthusiasm of community leaders such as the Hall family and the diligent building efforts of Flint and his colleagues, the Anglican community seems to have been slow in lending substantial support to the church. The building was completed after a fashion in 1855,[103] and used for occasional services by both the Anglicans and other denominations, but the fact that the roof and floor were badly in need of repair by 1874 suggests poor maintenance and perhaps a "finishing" job that was meant to be only temporary in the first place; it is evident from Hannah's letter that in 1854 both labour and money for the church were in short supply. The building committee's 1877 list of necessary repairs is nevertheless surprisingly extensive: "We found it necessary to secure the foundation and roof in order to make the building safe. The roof had to be shingled and the floor had to be entirely new together with three dwarf walls to support the same, also a new chimney and a partition across one end of the church to form a new chancel and

St. Anne's Church, circa 1900. St. Anne's Anglican Church

vestry; also a new window sash and glass and new front door, plastering the ceiling and partitions as well as painting all the new work, amounting in all to $247.23."[104] The building was finally consecrated as an Anglican church on January 28, 1878.[105]

The roof and ceiling had to be replaced again in 1912, after a strong wind on Good Friday completely removed the roof from the building and set it on the ground in front of the drive shed.[106] By 1937, the congregation felt the need for more room, with the result that a small parish hall was added on the west side of the church, and the main body of the church extended with the addition of a fourth bay and a new porch at the front.

While all of the alterations seem to have been remarkably faithful to the original concept of the church, one result of the numerous changes is that there is relatively little of Flint's workmanship still to be seen. All four sides of the building were faced with cobblestones, and one can see from what remains of the rear wall and the back parts of the side walls that Flint's stonework is denser that that of the addition, and that he made some effort to lay similar stones at regular intervals. Photographs of the original façade[107] seem to show the use of somewhat smaller stones, but the courses appear to be relatively uneven. Interestingly, the only original corner, the southeast, is made of stucco-covered brick rather than Wishing Well stone.

The two buildings near Kilworth are less certain attributions than the others, partly because of their distance (though Flint did acquire the Wishing Well stone from the Kilworth area), and partly because certain features of the buildings deviate from what appears to be Flint's customary practice. The cottage east of Kilworth cannot be dated with any precision. It sits on property owned by Timothy Kilbourn already in 1844 and later passed to his heirs. As it exists now, the cottage contains portions built in at least three different periods: though the main block is faced with cobblestones and whitewashing has obscured some differences between sections, the craftsmanship reveals the work of two very different masons, presumably working at different times; a later back wing is faced with stucco and decorative half-timbering. It is difficult to discern the chronology of the building of the main block. The east side is much more crudely constructed than the west: the cobblestones are more irregular; the mortar is thicker; and the floor boards sit

The Kilbourn cottage. Photo by Nancy Tausky

directly on a bed of unevenly-matched boulders. It is in the more refined workmanship of the west end that one sees signs of Flint's hand. The stones are laid with a degree of evenness and denseness typical of his other buildings; those on the façade are smaller; the window and door surrounds, like the corners, are formed of bricks laid in a pattern that simulates quoins; and a shallow foundation allows for the usual system of log joists, here over a crawl space. It is clear that the cottage once served as a double house, reputedly for two Kilbourn brothers,[108] and the evidence seems to indicate that a smaller cottage, probably encompassing the west part of the present structure, was at some point enlarged to accommodate two families. But the precise shape of the earliest structure and certainty about the identity of its builder are now secrets of the past.

In contrast to that of the Kilbourn cottage, the stonework of the Comfort house is considerably more elaborate than in any of the other documented buildings. The cottage resembles Flint's own house in its hipped roof, its proportions, and its use of Wishing Well stone quoins, but the Comfort cottage has two front doors, one to the house and one that originally led to a shop, and, though there is a regular alternation of windows and doors, they are irregularly spaced. The house has walls of cut fieldstone at the back and sides, with a cobblestone façade. What distinguishes this house from Flint's other buildings is that the stonework is so regular. The quoins are more evenly spaced than usual, the fieldstone is laid in nearly level courses, and the cobblestones are so similar in size and spacing that it has been possible to lay them in a herringbone pattern.

The building that the Comfort cottage most resembles is the addition to Pirney's cottage, but that is surrounded by many mysteries, in relation to both date and builder. It is clear that the cottage once occupied by Pirney, which stands a few hundred feet southeast of his parents' house, was built in two stages. Probably the good stone house constructed by Robert in 1856 comprised what is now a back wing, approximately equal in size to Robert's own house. Three corners of this structure can still be seen, all quoined with Wishing Well stone, but

The Comfort house and shop. Photo by Stephen Harding

Side view of Pirney Flint's cottage, as altered into "Verbena Villa." The older, 1856 cottage forms the projecting wing at the back. Photo by Stephen Harding

Front view of Pirney Flint's cottage. Photo by Stephen Harding

the walls have been so thoroughly disrupted that it is difficult to discern how the stone was originally laid, or even whether there was a cobblestone façade. At some later point an extension was added that approximately quadrupled the size of the house, and the façade of this addition strongly resembles that of the Comfort house in the blatantly off-centre position of the door and in the fineness of the workmanship. There is the same dramatic contrast between coarse fieldstone side walls and an intricate cobblestone façade. The quoins are of stucco-covered brick, like those of St. Anne's.

Family legend has it that the cottage was built as a wedding present for Pirney's bride, but Hannah's letter (quoted above) proves that the original cottage was built before Pirney was considering marriage. It is probable that the addition was constructed soon after the original was finished, and that it was built by way of preparing for Pirney's marriage, but there are some telling arguments that make such an early date necessarily tentative. One is, quite simply, that the cottage would have been extremely large by local standards in 1858, and another, more significant, is that there is no disproportionate rise in the tax records, such as one would expect had such a sizeable addition been made, until 1875.[109] It is not impossible that Pirney erected the addition in 1875. The letters show that he had obtained some knowledge of building from his father: he worked as a plasterer as a young man, he helped with Robert G.'s brickyard in Indiana, and a letter from California describes a log house he built there.[110] The letters say nothing about any work he did in relation to building after he returned home, but the records of St. Anne's Church show that he was hired to do masonry and plaster work as part of the 1877 renovations.[111] Moreover, the dimensions of the windows are consistent with the later date.

But there are counterarguments to the later date as well. It is difficult to imagine a family of ten living in the smaller house through all the years prior to 1875, and it seems unlikely that Pirney would have added an extension in the year after his wife died and his youngest child was sent to Mary. Moreover, while Pirney may have done occasional work as a mason, there is no evidence that he worked in his father's style.

It appears most likely, then, that the extension to the cottage followed hard on its first building, and that Pirney and his father set the precedent, later followed by Robert G., of building a large new house to welcome a bride. Robert died in 1859, and the strong resemblances between the addition to Pirney's house and the Comfort cottage suggest that, in his last houses, Robert was working towards an higher level of craftsmanship than he had been interested in achieving before.

Robert Flint's work as a builder undoubtedly encompassed many more buildings than the cobblestone structures recognized here. Quite conceivably the frame house at 249 Hall's Mills Road was his, since it stands on land he owned prior to 1838.[112] He is not improbably responsible for other stone buildings, such as the stone cottage that once stood just across the river on the grounds of "Hazeldon," the summer estate of the Little family, and probably predates the estate; Kilworth United Church; or even the fine Peter McKellar house in Lobo's fifth concession. The single available photograph of the cottage at Hazeldon shows little detail, but one is able to see a building with proportions similar to those of Robert Flint's own house, and with large contrasting quoins and voussoirs.[113] Though the Kilworth Church (*circa* 1850)[114] features no cobblestones, the fieldstones are laid in courses of liberally applied mortar in a manner strongly reminiscent of Flint's habitual technique, and both the corners and the original square window surrounds were composed of great slabs of Wishing Well stone. The same stone is used to form the quoins, voussoirs, and window surrounds of the McKellar house (pre-1861),[115] though in style and workmanship this building is considerably more sophisticated than any of the other structures discussed. It is a two-storey Georgian-style house, with five bays, and a garden front that closely imitates the street front. The fieldstone of the walls is very evenly laid, with so little mortar that in places the work almost resembles dry stone wall construction. But the practice exemplified here of filling in gaps between the larger stones with tiny slivers of stone can be discerned in a less compact form in the Kilworth Church and the Comfort cottage. The ground-floor joists of the McKellar house consist of 2-by-10-foot (0.6 x 3 m) boards instead of the more typical logs, but the way in which they are mortised into a centre rough-hewn beam is a more refined version of the method employed at the Comfort cottage.

The full extent of Robert's building cannot be ascertained. What is certain, however, is that he erected a group of highly distinctive cobblestone structures in Upper Canada, and that they represent his adaptation of the building tradition he had known in his former homeland.

The two cottages inhabited by the Flints became public buildings after Pirney's death in 1891, when his land along the Thames was purchased by the city of London for use by London Waterworks.[116] In 1878 land farther east along the river had been purchased in order to provide London with a public water supply using the abundant springs along the south bank of the Thames.[117] As demand increased, the waterworks spread west, until it reached the village of Byron.[118] Most farmhouses on the newly purchased properties were demolished to make way for more cultivation, or, later, for the parkland that grew up around the waterworks. That the Flint houses were kept attests to their solidity, and also, one suspects, to their attractiveness within the landscape.

The Kilworth Methodist Church, now the Kilworth United Church. Photo by Nancy Tausky

Whatever the original merits of the cottages, however, the city engineer's department set out to suit the houses for their new park setting by making them even more picturesque. Pirney's cottage was transformed into "Verbena Villa" as a home for the second pumping engineer.[119] In the *Annual Report* of the Board of Water Commissioners, city engineer John M. Moore described the cottage as very

The Peter McKellar house. Photo by Nancy Tausky

The Robert Flint cottage as a stop on the London Street Railway.

Regional Collection, University of Western Ontario Library

much out of repair,[120] and the thoroughness of the city's overhaul is evident from the fact that virtually all of the interior woodwork was replaced. There were significant exterior alterations as well: an extraordinarily wide wooden frieze was introduced at the cornice, and an eclectic porch, with Italianate posts and drops and a stick-style gable ornament, came to adorn the front of the cottage-turned-villa.[121]

In 1896 the London Street Railway extended a line to the park, and Robert's cottage became the new station at the western end of the line.[122] To provide a covered shelter, and also to introduce a fittingly rustic look, the commission added a veranda with rough-hewn posts and braces that extended along the new front of the cottage (initially the rear) and wrapped around the sides

With their varicoloured stones, quoins that have disintegrated to an appearance like cotton candy, the rustic veranda of the streetcar station and the picture-postcard porch of Verbena Villa, both buildings are still ornamental additions to Springbank Park. Pirney's cottage is at present used by the Garden Club of London; Robert's recently renovated[123] cottage is used as a gift shop. Above the modern fireplace now in Robert's cottage hangs a reproduction of the painting of Hannah and Robert in the room as it used to look: they are surrounded by the collected paraphernalia of a lifetime (the china figurines from England, the painted rocks thought by descendants to be from California), and a number of objects representing both present comfort (the family pets, the open hearth) and gentility (the formal clothes, the books and needlework). They have the air of people proud and content with their accomplishments, and it is most fitting that their portrait should still look out over the domain they created in their adopted world.

Postscript: Fred A. Andrewes, a grandson of Robert G. Flint, died just as this article was reaching completion. It was Fred and his wife, Eva (also deceased), who first made me acquainted with the family's collection of letters, and Fred was always generous, not only in loaning his letters, photographs, the painting or Robert and Hannah by their cottage hearth, and numerous other artifacts, but also in sharing with me many memories about his family's history. This article would not have been written without Fred's help and encouragement; I would like to think that this discussion of memorials to his ancestors will also serve as a memorial to him.

ENDNOTES

Author's Note: I am most grateful to Fred Andrewes, Lloyd Blinn, John Millerson, and Douglas Older for allowing me to read the letters in their collections, and, perhaps an even greater act of charity, for allowing me to write about them. Fred Andrewes and Lloyd Blinn also deserve special credit for providing photographs, for showing me family artifacts, and for answering innumerable questions about their early family histories. I would also like to acknowledge the assistance of the Glen Curnoe of the London Room in the London Public Library, and of Herbert S. Craig, for his willingness to share his research into the history of the Kilworth area. His technical analysis of the structure of the Comfort cottage was of particular benefit to me.

1   Douglas Older, family papers [hereafter Older Papers], will, Robert Flint, Hempnall, Norfolk, England, Apr. 4. 1824; Lloyd Blinn, family papers [hereafter Blinn Papers], letter. Gordon to Robert Flint, May 1, 1845.
2   Fred A. Andrewes and John F. Millerson, family papers [hereafter Andrewes and Millerson Papers], letter, Gordon to Robert Flint, Aug. 3, 1845.

3   Andrewes and Millerson Papers, letter, Gordon to Robert Flint, Christmas Day, 1844.
4   *History of the County of Middlesex, Canada* [hereafter *History of Middlesex*] (Toronto and London. Ontario: W.A. & C.L. Goodspeed, 1889); reprint ed., Belleville, Ontario: Mika Studio, 1972), p. 817.
5   Fred A. Andrewes, interview. The Flints' second son was christened George Beaufort Flint on Apr. 20, 1818 in the Anglican church in Lowestoft.
6   *History of Middlesex*, p. 816.
7   National Archives of the United States of America, Passenger List of Vessels Arriving at New York, 1820-1897 (micro copy 237, no. 48), *Ontario*, Apr.17, 1833, no. 177.
8   *History of Middlesex*, p. 816.
9   Ontario Land Registry Office, London, bargain and sale, McMillan to Robert Flint, Apr. 12, 1836, no. 2978; *ibid.* bargain and sale, Robert Flint to Hall, Sep. 18, 1838, no. 3943; *ibid.*, bargain and sale, Hall to Robert Flint, Sep. 10, 1838, no. 3942.
10   This information comes from the family tombstones in the Brick Street Cemetery, London, Ontario.
11   Throughout this paper, I have referred to the son of Robert and Hannah Flint as "Robert G.," as a means of distinguishing him in print from his father. In the letters he is simply called "Robert."
12   Andrewes and Millerson Papers, letter, Robert G. to Mary Flint, Mar. 14, 1840.
13   Older Papers, letter, Pirney and Robert G. to Robert and Hannah Flint, Aug.1844.
14   Andrewes and Millerson Papers, letter, Robert G. to Robert and Hannah Flint, Nov. 12, 1850; Older Papers, letter, Pirney Flint to Stephen Drago, May 15, 1854.
15   *History of Middlesex*, p. 817.
16   *Ibid.*
17   Andrewes and Millerson Papers, letter, Mary to Robert G. Flint, Sep. 6, 1866.
18   Fred A. Andrewes, interview; Lloyd Blinn, interview; and the family tombstone in the Brick Street Cemetery, London, Ontario.
19   Fred A. Andrewes, interview; Older Papers, obituary of Robert G. Flint, Mar. 1885.
20   Older Papers, obituary of Robert G. Flint, Mar. 1885.
21   Older Papers, letter, Robert G. Flint to Pirney Flint, Nov. 17, 1885; family tombstone, Brick Street Cemetery, London, Ontario. The Robert G. Flint noted here was a son of Pirney Flint, and therefore a nephew of the Robert G. Flint discussed in the text.
22   *History of Middlesex*, p. 737.
23   Fred A. Andrewes, interview.
24   Family tombstone, Brick Street Cemetery, London, Ontario.
25   Older Papers, letter, Robert G.Flint to Robert and Hannah Flint, Nov. 26, 1849.
26   Andrewes and Millerson Papers, letter, Hannah Flint to Robert G. Flint, Aug. 20, 1856.
27   *Ibid*, Robert G. Flint to Mary Flint, Mar. 14, 1840.
28   *Ibid.*, Colfax to Hannah Flint, an addendum to the letter from Robert G. Flint to Mary Flint, Mar. 14, 1840.
29   "Schuyler Colfax," *New Columbia Encyclopedia*, p. 569. Schuyler's involvement in one of the financial scandals of Grant's administration brought his political career to an end.
30   Older Papers, letter, Pirney and Robert G. Flint to Hannah and Robert Flint, Aug. 1844.
31   Andrewes and Millerson Papers, letter, Robert G. Flint to Hannah and Robert Flint, Oct. 4, 1845.
32   Older Papers, letter, Robert G. Flint to Hannah and Robert Flint, Nov. 26, 1849, cont'd Dec. 19, 1849.
33   Andrewes and Millerson Papers, letter, Robert G. Flint to Hannah Flint, Jul. 16, 1859.
34   *Ibid.*
35   *Ibid.*, Sep. 16, 1860.
36   Andrewes and Millerson Papers, letter, Robert G. Flint to Hannah Flint, Mar. 1, 1861.
37   *Ibid.*, Robert G. Flint to Robert and Hannah Flint, Nov. 12, 1850.
38   Blinn Papers, letter, Robert G. Flint to Hannah Flint, Dec. 6, 1863.
39   Older Papers, letter, Robert G. Flint to Pirney Flint, Jan. 20, 1855.
40   *Ibid.*, Jun. 24, 1862.
41   Blinn Papers, letter, Robert G. Flint to Willie Blinn, Mar. 15, 1872; *ibid.*, Robert G. Flint to Robert (Blinn?), Aug. 13, 1872. The Robert Flint here was Pirney Flint's son and a nephew to Robert G. Flint.
42   Andrewes and Millerson Papers, letter, Robert G. Flint to a nephew, Mar. 30, 1875.
43   *Ibid.*, Robert. G. Flint to Willie Blinn, Jun. 10, 1868; Blinn Papers, letter, Robert G. Flint to a nephew, Jul. 23, 1868; *ibid.*, Jul. 21, 1868.
44   Andrewes/Blinn Papers, MS., Don C. McMillan, "San Juan Ranch History" [hereafter "San Juan Ranch History"], 1975, p. 4.
45   *London Free Press*, Jul. 14, 1869, p. 3, c. 3.
46   Blinn Papers, letter, Robert G. Flint to a nephew, Jul. 17, 1870.
47   Ibid., Robert G. Flint to Robert Blinn, Oct. 23, 1877.
48   The three eldest children, Hannah Mary (b. 1870), Robert (b. 1872), and George (b. 1873) went to live with Samuel Gibson, who was married to a sister of Ann and Eliza Elson. Elizabeth (Bessie, b. 1875) was raised by Mary (Flint) Blinn, and Eliza (Lyle; b. 1877) by Pirney Flint. Fred A. Andrewes, interview; Older Papers, obituary of Robert G. Flint, Mar., 1885.
49   McMillan, "San Juan Ranch History," p. 5; Older Papers, obituary of Robert G. Flint, Mar. 1885.
50   Older Papers, obituary of Robert G. Flint, Mar. 1885. Although this obituary is said to be from a London, Ontario, newspaper, it claims to be based on an article in the *San Luis Obispo Chronicle*.

51 Fred Andrewes, interview; Older Papers, obituary of Robert G. Flint, Mar. 1885; McMillan, "San Juan Ranch History," p. 5.
52 McMillan, "San Juan Ranch History," p. 4.
53 Older Papers, letter, Jones to Pirney Flint, Sep. 1, 1856.
54 Andrewes and Millerson Papers, letter, Mary (Flint) Blinn to Robert G. Flint, Sep. 6, 1866.
55 Older Papers, letter, Pirney Flint to Robert and Hannah Flint, Jan. 17, 1852.
56 University of Western Ontario, the D.B. Weldon Library, Regional Collection [hereafter Regional Collection], Miscellaneous Papers of Middlesex County Courts (1860-1872), articles of agreement, Colville with Pirney Flint and others, Dec. 11, 1865.
57 A sulphur water drinking fountain still operates in front of the pumphouse in Springbank Park.
58 Andrewes and Millerson Papers, letter, Hannah Flint to Robert G. Flint, Aug. 20, 1856.
59 Regional Collection, Westminster Township, assessment roll, 1858, p. 12. Pirney Flint is listed as the owner of 61 acres (24.6 ha) in the northeast part of Westminster lot 43, broken front con. B, in the Westminster assessment roll for 1858. This property had previously been listed in his father's name. Pirney's daughter Charlotte was born on Dec. 25, 1860. See: note 66.
60 Blinn Papers, letter, Robert G. Flint to Hannah Flint, Aug. 8, 1864.
61 *London Free Press*, Dec. 14, 1868, p. 3, c 3.
62 *Ibid.*, Nov. 14, 1885, p. 2, c. 4.
63 Regional Collection, Westminster Township, assessment roll, 1867, no. 378.
64 For example, see: Blinn Papers, letter, Robert G. Flint to a nephew, Robert Blinn, Jul. 23, 1868.
65 Regional Collection, Westminster Township, assessment roll, 1870, no. 396; *ibid.*, 1871, no. 749; *ibid.*, 1873, no. 783.
66 The birthdates of the children are as follows: Charlotte, Dec. 25, 1860; Robert George, Feb. 28, 1862; Mary B., Apr. 7, 1864; Eliza B., Dec. 15, 1865; Annie, Nov. 8, 1867; Peter, Apr. 3, 1870; Fanny, Jun. 27, 1872; and Edna, Jun. 13, 1874. These dates are inscribed in a family Bible, now in the possession of Lloyd Blinn, London, Ontario.
67 Older Papers, letter, Robert G. Flint to Pirney Flint, Nov. 13, 1876.
68 Fred A. Andrewes, interview.
69 Older Papers, obituary of Robert G. Flint, Mar., 1885; Fred A. Andrewes, interview.
70 *History of Middlesex*, p. 817.
71 *Ibid.*, p. 737.
72 Andrewes and Millerson Papers, letter, Mary (Flint) Blinn to Robert G. Flint, Sep. 6, 1866.
73 Older Papers, letter, Hannah Flint to Pirney Flint, May 30, 1854.
74 Andrewes and Millerson Papers, letter, Gordon to Robert Flint, May, 1845.
75 Older Papers, letter, Hannah Flint to Pirney Flint, Oct. 20, 1851.
76 *Ibid.*, May 30, 1854.
77 Andrewes and Millerson Papers, letter, Hannah Flint to Robert Flint, Aug. 20, 1856.
78 Pirney Flint's biography describes Hannah's father, "Patrick Pirney, a Scotchman," as follows: "He was a soldier, and had served in America, and had charge of a fort in England in the French wars." See: *History of Middlesex*, p. 816.
79 Andrewes and Millerson Papers, letter, Hannah Flint to Robert G. Flint, Aug. 20, 1856.
80 Older Papers, letter, Hannah Flint to Pirney Flint, Oct. 20, 1851.
81 Andrewes and Millerson Papers, letter, Hannah Flint to Robert G. Flint, Aug. 20, 1856.
82 Older Papers, letter, Hannah Flint to Pirney Flint, May 30, 1854.
83 *Ibid.*
84 Andrewes and Millerson Papers, letter, Hannah Flint to Robert G. Flint, Aug. 20, 1856.
85 *Ibid.*, Robert G. Flint to Hannah and Robert Flint, Oct. 4, 1845.
86 Older Papers, letter, Hannah Flint to Pirney Flint, May 30, 1854.
87 *Ibid.*
88 Herbert S. Craig, copy of letter to Rooks, reeve of Delaware Township, Sep. 4, 1988.
89 Regional Collection, Delaware Township, assessment roll, 1844, p. T1.
90 Prof. C. Gordon Winder, Department of Geology, University of Western Ontario; Guy St-Denis, *Byron, Pioneer Days in Westminster Township*, ed. Frederick H. Armstrong (Lambeth, Ontario: Crinklaw Press, 1985), pp. 1-2.
91 David Dymond, *The Norfolk Landscape* [hereafter *Norfolk Landscape*] (London, England: Hodder and Stoughton, 1985), pp. 25-26; Alex Clifton-Taylor, *The Pattern of English Building [hereafter English Building]* (London, England: Faber and Faber, 1972), p. 195. Clifton-Taylor observes that "In Suffolk and Norfolk, flint architecture can be seen at its most ambitious and best; and part of the Norfolk coast is as famous as the Sussex seaboard around Brighton for its beach-pebbles and cobbles."
92 For example, see: Dymond, *Norfolk Landscape*, pp. 25-26; Clifton-Taylor, *English Building*, pp. 192-209; Alec Clifton-Taylor and A.S. Ireson, *English Stone Building* (London, England: Victor Gollancz, 1983), pp. 51-56.
93 Regional Collection, MS., Mae Woodhall Doan and Leo V. Harris, "Kilworth, A Look Back."
94 Prof. C. Gordon Winder, interview.
95 For example, the Lee house on Hall's Mills Rd., or the Kilbourne house farther west on Commissioners' Rd.
96 Ontario Land Registry Office, London, bargain and sale, Hall to Robert Flint, Sep. 10, 1838, no. 3942
97 Regional Collection, Alfred S. Garrett Collection.
98 Fred A. Andrewes, interview.

99   The figurine closest to Robert is in the possession of Lloyd Blinn, as is his mother's rocking chair.
100   William H. Smith, *Smith's Canadian Gazeteer* (Toronto, Canada West: H.& W. Roswell, 1846), p. 218.
101   Information about the various uses of this building and about the dates of its various tenants and its demolition are garnered from two sources: dates recorded on the photograph of the building contributed to the Byron Branch of the London Public Library by Byron historian Roy Kerr, and a set of notes attributed to "Miss McLean," once "a teacher in the Byron School." A copy of the notes is owned by Guy St-Denis. Miss McLean claims that William Hood started to operate the inn *circa* 1854, and that he was succeeded by James Reynolds.
102   Older Papers, letter, Hannah Flint to Pirney Flint, May 15, 1854.
103   Grace Bainard, *The Story of St. Anne's* [hereafter *St. Anne's*] (London, Ontario: St. Anne's Anglican Church, 1978), p. 7.
104   Bainard, *St. Anne's*, p. 9.
105   *Daily Advertiser* (London, Ontario), Jan. 28, 1878, p. 1, c. 5.
106   Bainard, *St. Anne's*, p. 16.
107   In the collection of St. Anne's Anglican Church, there are three photographs, all copies of an earlier original, showing the church with only three bays. One of these, dating from *circa* 1900, is reproduced in this article; another shows a side view of the church, with the shed in the background; the third is a photocopy of a newspaper photograph, apparently dating from the 1930s.
108   Robert and Connie Holmes, present residents in the cottage, interview; Edward Normile, owner of neighbouring property, interview.
109   Regional Collection, Westminster Township, assessment rolls, 1856-1857 (for Robert Flint); *ibid.*, 1858-1892 (for Pirney Flint).
110   Older Papers, letter, Pirney Flint to Robert and Hannah Flint, Jan. 17, 1852.
111   Bainard, *St. Anne's*, p. 10.
112   Ontario Land Registry Office, London, bargain and sale, McMillan to Robert Flint, Apr. 12, 1836, no. 1978; *ibid.*, Robert Flint to Hall, Sep. 18, 1838, no. 3943
113   Regional Collection, Photograph Collection.
114   Delaware Township Office, bargain and sale, Woodhull to the Trustees of the Methodist Episcopal Church of Canada, Dec. 13, 1850.
115   The house is indicated, on lot 3, con. 5 of Lobo Township, in the 1861 census. It sat on 100 acres owned and farmed by Peter McKellar. Peter McKellar purchased the property in 1826, though it seems improbable that the house was erected before the deed was registered ten years later. See: Ontario Land Registry Office, London, bargain and sale, Nov. 25, 1826, no. 3047. This instrument was registered on Jul. 5, 1836.
116   London Public Library, London Room [hereafter London Room], bargain and sale (copy), Peter Flint and Robert W. Blinn (executors of the estate of Pirney Flint) to the City of London and Mary B. Flint, Annie Flint, and Peter Flint, Oct. 10, 1891. The engineer's reports in the *Annual Reports* of the Board of Water Commissioners (held in the London Room) show that negotiations over the 25 acres (10 ha) Flint owned north of Commissioners' Road were in fact prolonged. The *Annual Report* for 1886 records that the City of London paid Pirney Flint $216.00 for permission to channel water through his property in underground pipes. The engineer recommended buying Pirney's 25 acres in the *Annual Report* for 1889 , but he complains in the *Annual Report* for 1890 that "the disparity between the costs as determined by the owners (including Pirney Flint) and our valuators was so great as to render arbitration absolutely necessary." Though the sale was completed after Pirney's death, he had agreed before his death to a sale price of $4,387.66 (see bargain and sale instrument described above). It is undoubtedly as a result of the city's interest in the property that it was not assessed for tax purposes after 1887 See: London, Ontario, Board of Water Commissioners [hereafter Water Commissioners], *Annual Report of the Board of Water Commissioners* [herafter *Annual Report*], VIII (1886): p. 15; *ibid.*, XI (1889): p. 12; *ibid.*, XII (1890): p. 6. Also, see entries for Pirney Flint in: Regional Collection, Westminster Township, assessment rolls, 1888-1891.
117   E.V. Buchanan, *London's Water Supply: A History* (London, Ontario: London Public Utilities Commission, 1968), pp. 1-26.; Nancy Z. Tausky and Lynne D. DiStefano, *Victorian Architecture in London and Southwestern Ontario* (Toronto, Ontario: University of Toronto Press, 1986), pp. 197-200; Water Commissioners, *Annual Report*, I (1879).
118   Water Commissioners, *Annual Report*, XI (1889): p. 12; XII (1890): p. 6; *ibid.*, XIII, (1891): p. 9. The engineer (Thomas H. Tracy) recommended in 1889 that "all springs from the Waterworks to Byron be acquired"; in 1891, the engineer (then John M. Moore) reported, "The Commissioners are now in possession of all the lands purchased for the correction and protection of the springs." The Griffiths property in Byron later needed to be renegotiated. See: *ibid.*, XVII (1895).
119   *Ibid.*, XVIII (1896): p. 13.
120   *Ibid.*
121   An architectural drawing showing the east elevation of the cottage as it existed prior to the renovations of 1896 is in the Murphy Moore Collection in the Regional Collection. Neither the porch, which still stands, nor the wooden cornice is shown; instead, stone voussoirs above the windows are very clearly depicted.
122   London Room, agreement, the Water Commissioners of the City of London with the Corporation of the City of London, and the London Street Railway Company, May 21, 1896.
123   The renovation and restoration work was carried out by Patrick Coles, Architect.

CHAPTER SEVEN

"WHISKEY IN A TIN CUP!"

James Reaney

One place I am never tired of visiting is a country called the Past. Many despise a person for this obsession – as that person should be, it is implied, interested more profitably in the Now and Present – or even the Future. In southwestern Ontario, the most quoted "expert" with these notions is, or was, Henry Ford with his famous "History is bunk" statement. He also said, when defending the social upheavals caused by his Model Ts, "To hell with your cities!" His ideas were to prove deeply destructive of tradition; as we in London, what with the Talbot streetscape and Western Hotel recently obliterated, know to our cost. Therefore, in the face of this powerful and popular opposition, I state my love of the past and my agreement with Madaline Roddick when she said that she expected Heaven to be like an historical research library.

It was the Alice McFarlane paper on the Donnellys, given at a London and Middlesex Historical Society meeting in 1946, that first gave me the feeling that there could be a play written about the Donnellys. And the five years I spent researching them in the Regional Collection at Western were some of the happiest of my life – partly because of the powerful thrill you get in a rich archival trove of time conquered, of the past coming alive again. Give me an old newspaper or a Chancery Court document (Carroll *versus* Delahaye is a favourite of mine at the Regional Collection) and I feel as if I could obliterate the years and years between this day, today, and say a certain summer day in 1881. Then, in James Carroll's native township, Stephen, Huron County, this alleged murderer of the Donnellys, obsessed with his father's land, began to say terrifying things to (the Delahaye) uncles he saw as having "grabbed" away his inheritance. He was also fond of sending anonymous notes beginning "I wouldn't like to be the man who ... ."

A great many of my journeys to the past have been such paper ones – taken through the files that Orlo Miller so wisely rescued from the Goderich and London courthouses in the thirties. But there is also another way of reaching the past, and that is by interviewing some older person who remembers someone or something in the past as if it were just yesterday. We are surrounded, particularly in senior citizens' homes, by living archives, and it is my contact with these magic carpets to the past that I should now like to emphasize.

Naturally, since I have spent so much time on Donnelly research in order to get the feeling and ambience right for a dramatic trilogy, the majority of my interview flights into the past have been to Lucan or Biddulph or Glencoe in the nineteenth century. However, in the case of *King Whistle* the interviewing had as its redemptive goal Stratford in 1933 – the year of a famous general strike that changed the town's nickname: no longer the "Classic City," it became "Red Town," or even "Little Russia."

In the High Court of Justice

Chancery Division

Writ issued the 20th day of February AD 1882

In the matter of the estate of Roger Carroll deceased

Between

Ellen Carroll, Catharine Carroll, William Carroll, James McCarroll and Margaret Carroll and Michael Carroll the two last being infants under the age of twenty one years by James McCarroll their next friend

Plaintiffs

and

John Delahay and Bartholomew Carroll

Defendants

Statement of Claim

1. Roger Carroll in his lifetime of the village of London West (then Petersville) in the County of Middlesex duly made his last will dated the 16th day of February AD 1873 whereby he appointed the Defendants executors thereof

2. At the time of his death the said Roger Carroll was the owner in fee simple of the following lands that is to say Lot number 5 on Centre Street in the village of Petersville now London West part of Lot number 3 in the 8th concession of the Township of Stephen in the County of Huron containing 50 acres more or less and part of Lots number 3 and 4 in the 9th concession of said Township of Stephen containing 66⅔ acres more or less and also personal property consisting of money in bank promissory notes due him and household effects

3. The testator at the time of his death left him surviving the Plaintiffs and one Edward Carroll his children by his first wife and Catharine his widow and Nora and Martha the children of said testator by said Catharine who was his second wife

4. The said Edward Carroll departed this life on or about the 5th day of December AD 1881

5. The testator departed this life in February AD 1873 and on the 5th day of March 1873 the Defendants duly proved said will and probate thereof was granted to them

"Give me an old newspaper or a Chancery Court document (Carroll versus Delahaye is a favourite of mine at the Regional Collection) and I feel as if I could obliterate the years ..." Reproduced in part, the Statement of Claim from **Carroll v. Delahaye** represents the scope of archival treasures available to all those interested in pursuing primary sources of local history. Regional Collection, University of Western Ontario Library

"I saw real live Communists in Stratford ..." In September of 1933 much of Stratford's factory work force went on general strike for higher wages. Violence erupted with the arrival of strike-breakers and before long troops were brought in to keep order. A deadlock between the workers and the employees resulted, with charges from the latter that the strike was Communist inspired. The standoff came to an end in early November when a settlement was reached setting the work week at 44 hours, a recognition of the Workers' Unity League, and an open shop. But Stratford, formerly the Classic City, was long afterward known as "Red Town" and even "Little Russia." Stratford-Perth Archives

Main Street, Glencoe, in about 1908. It was "the village in the extreme southwestern end of Middlesex County where the surviving Donnellys settled after 1880." Jenny Donnelly married James Currie, whose family hailed from near Glencoe.
Regional Collection, University of Western Ontario Library.

Archival work with old papers can be a loner's occupation; working as I was for my high school's centennial, I had the pleasure of helping young people under eighteen come into contact with a great many people over the age of eighty – a new experience for them and a healthy one for both sides of the interview, and also for the idea of a seamless community. As well, I have conducted interviews in order to find out more about unusual professions; for example, that of being a ferrywoman in the twenties on the Sydenham River in Sombra Township, or of being a roustabout for Maple City Midways – in the latter case, the individual interviewed was a young woman, far younger than I am myself, who had been brought up operating machinery in a gravel pit since the age of twelve.

Having a friend, a boyhood friend and cousin in James Anderson (late of the Stratford-Perth Archives) has certainly helped train me in the pastime of archaeology. We often have conversations about the old families in our neighbourhood: the Little Lakes and Brocksden, just outside Stratford in, respectively, the townships of South and North Easthope. The remarkable thing has been the way, after years and years of patiently chipping away at certain memories – you quite suddenly go beyond the gathered "facts" and – "with a wild surmise" – suddenly see the *why* of some hitherto obscure land arrangement or mysterious piece of human behaviour.

When I first came to London, I remember reading in the *Free Press* that a woman who was aged 104 could remember riding in the Donnelly stagecoach. If at the time I had known what my interests were to be in the late sixties and early seventies, I would have made immediate contact. But Orlo Miller's book had not been published yet, and besides, I was then very shy of interviewing people about the past, unless they were close relatives. What changed all this came in 1971 when a colleague teaching Canadian literature and culture (Professor Tom

Tausky) had a student (Marjorie McCracken) whose father-in-law (I believe) had, as a small boy, known Bob Donnelly. This was in Glencoe, the village in the extreme southwestern end of Middlesex County where the surviving Donnellys settled after 1880. From her interview came the following exchange.

Father-in-Law: Well, I only knew Bob Donnelly, but I was just a youngster, just a kid. I don't remember really. But he is theonly one that I knew to say I would recognize him today if he walked in – I think maybe I would. But there was also Bill Donnelly – they kept hotel in Appin. I remember seeing him a time or two.

Mrs. McCracken: Could you describe either one of those people?

Father-in-Law: Oh...

Mrs. McCracken: I mean height approximately, or weight?

Father-in-Law: Bob Donnelly would – he'd probably be six feet and 180 pounds as I remember.

Mrs. McCracken: Oh, that is big. That big?

Father-in-Law: Yes, he was...a bigger man than I am, but he wasn't getting a pudgy-pot-bellied – or anything. He was just a real chunk of man, you might say. And Bill Donnelly, if I remember rightly, wasn't as tall. He wasn't as tall as Bob.

Mrs. McCracken: Were they dark or – or redheaded or fair or what?

Father-in-Law: Gosh. They were just men.

Once an interview starts, it might be found to inter-connect with other interviews. In the above the house Jane Jennie Currie (*née* Donnelly, lived in for quite a while came up.

Father-in-Law: And then there was the man that tore down the Currie house. Well, the Currie home was there when the folks bought the place and they lived in that from the time they bought it. I think they bought it in 1881 or thereabouts – I think that's when the folks were married anyway – and about 1890-1892 our folks built the new house, the brick house that...I was raised in.

This recollection is supported by a picture from the McCracken family album in which the new brick house is shown and behind, sort of leaning over, is the wooden house the Curries once lived in.

Now, I have another interview in which we get inside the house long before the McCrackens bought it and eventually tore it down. To make this visit, I am going to switch to expanded excerpts from my diary, which I have kept since the age of twelve. I do this partly to show the reader the importance of having some sort of interview on a daily basis with...yourself.

FRIDAY 21 January 1972

A big day for talking. My lady in West Nissouri, Mrs. Doris Strawhorn, phoned to say she had remembered the name of the Donnellys' hired boy – John Casey. He said the Donnellys were very kind to animals and treated them as pets. It was very hard to get him to talk about the Donnellys.

A Mrs. C. Leach is a granddaughter of juror David Bailey. He sympathized with the Donnellys but a conviction would mean hanging all of Biddulph. The Baileys were from Armagh. He was reluctant to talk about the case.

Then Paul drove me to Mrs. Ida Langford's house at 83 Wortley Rd. Her younger sister is Ethel McCracken. They were born in Glencoe (Ida in 1882). Their father was Isaac McCracken, who had a blacksmith & wagon shop. Ida contended that the Donnellys wouldn't contribute to the local Catholic Church. Her uncle was Joe Beatson who (lived on the Granton Line). He was disgusted with the Vigilance Committee, who all died with their boots on...violent deaths. The only trouble he had with the Donnellys was when the Vigilantes or someone let their horses into his wheatfield. He put them in his barn, because he was afraid they would founder. In the morning he took them to the Donnellys who were glad to see them. All friends of the Donnellys were afraid to speak up in their behalf, as arsons kept occurring in Biddulph after 1880. Ida & Ethel are *cousins* of Marjorie McCracken's father-in-law.

Ethel remembers Jennie Currie. She was on the Newbury side road. She was a big woman. Ethel visited her with her

For a number of years Will Donnelly owned this hotel in Appin, several miles to the east of Glencoe; the establishment was referred to as the St. Nicholas. This picture post-card view dates from about 1910. The Donnelly Album

mother. They found her dancing to music on a gramophone with four chairs set out. She was practising a reel. She said she didn't "think anyone would catch me at this!" She was a very happy and very hospitable woman. She had no children.

Bob Donnelly lived in Glencoe. William kept a hotel in Appin. His son Jack was tall, handsome & curly-headed. Bessie Walker...taught Jack. He worked in London here at the CPR hotel. Irene Hayter, a hairdresser in Grand Bend, has kept in touch with the Donnelly girls. Mrs. Ida Langford has Irene Hayter do her hair in Grand Bend. William Donnelly's hotel was opposite Simpson's shoe shop in Appin. ...

And this leads me to another research situation of a somewhat different variety. Two years ago I went, on a school chum's invitation, to speak on my work with the Donnellys to the Glencoe and District Historical Society. What a vibrant group of informed and eager visitors to the Past! They were deniers of Henry Ford's stupid maxim – to a man, to a woman, to a child. After I was through, a gentleman not much older than myself asked me if I knew that Bob Donnelly had run a hotel and tavern in Bothwell. No, I had not known that. Well, the Ekrid Poet – Peter McArthur – took the then famous Maritime poet, Bliss Carman (said to be responsible for Ezra Pound leaving the U.S.A.), to visit the tavern. This visit was in the '90s and the Donnelly family were then famous for having lost five of their members to a murdering mob one dark night early in February, 1880. When they

Jenny (Donnelly) Currie "was a very happy and very hospitable woman. Once, in her more mature years, she was surprised by visitors who "found her dancing to music on a gramophone with four chairs set out. She was practising a reel." The Donnelly Album

entered the tavern, Robert Donnelly, six feet, 180 pounds, stood behind his bar and said, after being introduced:

> *Donnelly:* What'll it be?

> *Carman:* I'd like a sherry, please.

> *Donnelly:* Don't serve that. It's whiskey in a tin cup (pouring some into a tin cup) or nothing at all!

How unexpectedly the past comes beating up against your ears. Around us lies an equally lively world filled with people unblighted by couch-potatoism, eager to make contact with other people, to tell us their story, change our lives – however slightly – with their Donnelly talk or, failing that, their Maple City Midway talk, or their "I was a ferrywoman" talk, or "I saw real live Communists in Stratford" talk. And these talks encourage us to change the present, however slightly. And does it ever need to be changed! – swamped by the mechanical and the banal as it has become. For my part, I would like to liven up London, Ontario, with a new bar called Whiskey in a Tin Cup, with huge photos of the Donnelly boys pasted to the walls. I would also have a Mrs. Donnelly Tea Room across the hall. Would this not be better than the Forum, what with the Irish fiddlers I would have playing continually? Any takers? Less light-heartedly, we have a choice between two worlds. The one that Henry Ford's technology hands us is filled with individuals shut away from each other in cars on the "free" way, or on easy chairs in front of the Cyclops eye of television. Essentially, we have no past, no present, no future. The other world I have attempted to show you discovers traditions for the present and the future in community with the stories of our fellow human beings and their ancestors. That community I hereby recommend.

CHAPTER EIGHT

OBSCENITY IN VICTORIAN LONDON

The Lotto Davene Poster Trial

Frederick H. Armstrong

Most city histories tend to repeat well-known tales discovered, or invented, by early chroniclers or aged settlers. Yet, while such approaches to the past can create very interesting history, they inevitably form selective, possibly censored accounts, which fail to reveal many aspects of the real character of the city. This is particularly true for those obscure incidents of urban life which the old-timers and early chroniclers, to say nothing of their modern descendants, would be happy to forget. For the researcher attempting to fill in the gaps caused by this selectivity, forgotten incidents which greatly expand our knowledge of a city's activities and character can often be found by going through the usually neglected, and often voluminous, routine records of the municipal government and of the criminal courts.

Even a cursory perusal of these records confirms that much of our history relating to public morality in the last century has been almost completely neglected. The Victorian moral outlook has come to be regarded with considerable disdain in recent decades; but it was an extremely important factor in ordering the society of the time. To understand how it affected the city, we need to investigate specific cases.

One example that says much about how Victorian morality directed life in London, and provides a case study of how these routine records can be used to expand our knowledge, is an early 1886 obscenity trial over the display of an advertising poster for a visiting trapeze artiste named Lotto Davene. The incident would be forgotten today were it not for the fact that a copy of the poster survives, along with a large part of the related Middlesex County police magistrate's court documentation, in the custody of the Regional Collection at the University of Western Ontario's D. B. Weldon Library.

The Davene trial raises several interesting questions. London, rightly or wrongly, has earned the reputation of being a stuffy, conservative city; but one wonders, whatever the city may have been renowned for in recent decades, whether in the past it was really any more moral, or more dull, than most of its contemporary North American urban centres both large and small. The fact that the Lotto Davene case was ever brought to trial not only demonstrates something of the outlook that helped give London its stuffy reputation; but also indirectly it provides considerable evidence that, for the average citizen, late Victorian London was probably not such a dull place after all.

The story began to unfold the day before Christmas 1885, when Frank Kirchmer,[1] who was described as a bill poster, went to the customs house to pick up the advertising posters for one of the coming entertainments of the holiday season, the week-long appearance of W. M. Davene's "Allied Attractions." This troupe was to perform at the People's Theatre at 231 Dundas Street, an operation that flourished briefly in the mid-1880s under the management of a lessee named Thomas Firness. It does not appear to have had the cachet of the Grand Theatre, London's premier vaudeville house.

Davene presented what was basically a variety show which ended with a trapeze performance by himself and his daughter, Lotto. Hardly surprisingly, the lithographed New York posters featured that lady in her performing costume. A rather formidable, decidedly robust damsel – as one would expect from her occupation – with a very masculine face, by our standards she was more than adequately covered. In fact, as one witness at the trial was to observe, if she wore anything more it would imperil her safety. As can be seen in the poster, to use contemporary terminology, she sported a sombrely coloured tunic or jacket, which, even with its tassels, did not quite cover the dark coloured "trunk," or drawers, she wore under it.

John Siddons, the appraiser at the customs house, and his assistants, saw nothing wrong with her costume and passed the poster without question. Kirchmer, quite ready to leave the decision to them, accepted the parcel and made his rounds, putting up at least four posters in appropriate shop windows along Dundas Street. As he stated at the trial, "I thought they were unobjectionable having been passed by the Custom House; I honestly believed that having passed the Custom House the work was all right."[2] He was soon to find out otherwise.

On Christmas Eve, W. D. Murdell, the Davenes' agent, arrived in the city to complete the preparations, which obviously included promotional arrangements. His advertisement for the performance, which appeared in the *Free Press* on December 26th, read:

PEOPLE'S THEATRE
- For one week commencing -
Monday, December 28th.,
Davene's
ALLIED ATTRACTIONS,
Mlle Lotto's Novelty Burlesque Company, and
Madame Balding's Silver Coronet Band, the
Latest London Success at Burlesque, ZAO
GRAND extra MATINEE NEW YEAR'S
and Saturday, at 2.30.
Admission 25, 35, and 50 cents.
Reserved seats at A. S. Murray's.[3]

The *Free Press* had already reported on Christmas Day that "Allied Attractions have a good record, and will doubtless do a large business."[4] Then on the 29th that journal provided a complete description of the show which is again worth quoting in full, for it puts the trapeze act in context:

THE PEOPLE'S THEATRE was filled last night by an entranced audience on the appearance of Davene's Allied Attractions. All the actors and actresses were good in their several parts. Mr. Baly Lyons in his female impersonations, was encored three times. The juggling tricks of Mlle. Nalta were good, and received great applause. The Two Roses in their song and dances pleased the audience immensely. Mr. C. E. Foreman and Miss Ida Meredith in the lawn tennis act were excellent. Mr. Foreman performed some wonderful feats on a shovel and was loudly called before the curtain. The skipping act of Miss Caprola Forrest was also enthusiastically applauded. Mr. Gowan, for his banjo solos, was encored three times. The Davenes in their mid-air flights were wonderful, and fully merited the applause bestowed. The whole concluded with a burlesque entitled La Petite Zao, introducing Relling's Female Brass Band, which played beautiful music and were well received. The show is good throughout and contains no objectionable feature. It will appear nightly all the week.[5]

Not satisfied with this effusion, on New Year's Day the journal further noted that there had been a "very appreciative audience at the People's Theatre last night, and the flying trapeze act and variety business generally was well received." [6] Finally, on January 2, 1886, the *Free Press* again reviewed the performance stating that it had attracted large audiences "who were well pleased with the excellent variety of amusements offered," that the father and daughter trapeze act was "thrilling in the extreme" and that "the show is good throughout and well worth attending."[7]

The rival *London Advertiser*, which, it seems, was much less interested in "cultural affairs," ignored the performance entirely, just as it later almost completely ignored the obscenity trial. This difference in coverage is not unusual for these two papers; one sometimes wonders if they are writing about the same city. It may be that Murdell had failed to purchase an advertisement in that journal; still, the *Advertiser* also virtually ignored all the other performances of the season. Entertainment

The risqué poster that so enraged London's moral leaders was preserved as court evidence. Readers will instantly notice the shockingly abbreviated tunic that Lotto sports.

Regional Collection, University of Western Ontario Library

coverage in old London that Christmas was pretty well left in the hands of the *London Free Press*.

Whatever the case with the *Advertiser,* to give the reader an idea of the variety and quality of entertainment available to the average Londoner, the several attractions that were contending with the Davenes for the citizens' money should be noted. One of these was Mr. A. O. Babel, the "cow-boy pianist," who performed at the Grand Opera House between December 28th and 30th. The *Free Press* again devoted several reviews to his efforts testifying that he is "the greatest musical prodigy of the nineteenth century" despite "never having taken a lesson in his life." It added that reserved seats were 25 and 50 cents, and the editor recommended that "the music-loving citizens of London should not miss this opportunity of listening to a phenomenon to-night."[8]

The prodigy was followed at the Grand Opera House by four performances of the melodrama "Louis Riel, and the North-western Rebellion," with Arthur H. Forrest in the title role, which was "said to be entirely free from political bias." Reserved seats this time were 25, 50, and 75 cents.[9] Then, on the fourth of January, the same paper recommended the performance of the "Rock Band musicians," who were giving an exceedingly pleasing entertainment at Victoria Hall at which, possibly rather surprisingly for a rock band, "the lady elocutionist is a leading attraction."[10] The music was performed on a "Rock Harmonium, Ocarina, Zither, Streich Zither, Fairy Bells, Xylophone and other instruments."[11] Apparently our perception of a rock band differs markedly from that of our ancestors. Still, the advertisements show that New Year's festivities in London of old were plentiful and, if the *Free Press* is to be trusted, of a high order! With taverns and private parties thrown in, London was definitely not a dull place.

William T. T. Williams (1843–1927), London's high constable and chief of police from 1877 to 1920. The able and respected organizer of London's police force, he was always ready to uphold the city's moral standards. Regional Collection, University of Western Ontario Library

Behind the façade of frolic, however, the forces of morality were girding themselves for the attack. While Lotto was performing on the stage to appreciative houses, the unappreciative authorities were initiating charges against those responsible for displaying her posters. The formal complainant was William T. T. Williams, who held the post of police chief from 1877 to 1920 – quite possibly a record length of tenure anywhere. An English immigrant, who was noted for his great height and physical strength, as well as his kindness to people who came to him for advice, he was rightly credited as the man who really organized and built up London's police force.[12] Unfortunately, he also became well known for his puritanical outlook and was probably the source of the complaint himself, for he strongly objected to scantily clad chorus girls, tights, and female performers in daring poses.[13] One rather wonders what Williams thought of the little children's bare bottoms that were such a favoured subject of Paul Peel, whose brother, Dr. Peel, married the chief's sister.[14]

The offending posters were ordered removed almost immediately, and Police Constable Robert Crawford was sent to attend a performance. Yet no attempt was made to stop the show, or lay charges against the proprietors. Also the charges laid against Kirchmer for distributing the posters, and the proprietors of the establishments for displaying them, were not drawn up until December 31. City by-law number 202, dated May 20, 1872,[15] which was invoked here, read:

1.
Be it therefore Enacted that from and after the passing of this By Law no person or persons shall exhibit, sell, or offer to sell any indecent or lewd books, paper, picture, plate, drawing or other thing, nor exhibit or perform any indecent, immoral or lewd play within said city.

2.
That any persons guilty of an infraction of any of the provisions of the By Law shall upon conviction thereof forfeit and pay penalty not exceeding the sum of Fifty Dollars exclusive of costs for each offence ...

To give one example, the charges, as stated in Kirchmer's case, read:

Frank Kirchmer did unlawfully put up in the window of a certain barber shop on Dundas Street in said City; occupied by one James Constable being a public place within the City; a certain indecent picture; contrary to the bye law of the said City relative to public morals.[16]

Similar charges were laid against George Grace, who operated another barber shop, Jeremiah (Jerry) McDonald, who ran McDonald's Hotel, George T. Hiscox who operated a prosperous livery stable, and Joseph Goldner, a tobacconist. The surviving trial records involve the first four only. All these businesses were located on Dundas Street.

Though the McDonald Brothers' Hotel seems to have been well known as a popular watering place, the other establishments were small operations except for the Hiscox livery stable. Founded in 1837, it advertised itself as "Largest in the city, oldest in the Dominion," and able to provide "everything in the horse line." It was also open all night and had hacks and coupés for hire. The proprietor, George T.

Hiscox, had been six times an alderman for Ward 4 between 1875 and 1881, and was currently running for that dignity in Ward 2 in 1886 on the rather contradictory platform of "More Railways and Lower Taxes." He was to be defeated.[17]

Before following the course of the trial, a word should be said about Frank Kirchmer, whose activities were the focus of the investigation. Born and raised in Ohio, he came to London in 1873 and presently became involved in a combination of auction, commission, and bill posting work. By 1889 that most valuable old reference by W.A. and P.L. Goodspeed, *The History of the County of Middlesex*, described his bill posting activities by stating "for years he has practically

Charles Hutchinson (1826–1892). As Crown attorney of Middlesex County from 1858, he was a leading moral crusader in London. He both prosecuted and advised on the selection of witnesses for the Kirchmer trial. Regional Collection, University of Western Ontario Library

controlled that operation in London, having secured all the desirable spaces and bill boards of the city" and adding he was "an expert in his calling."[18] Depicting him simply as a bill poster is thus rather misleading. He was, of course, closely connected with the city's theatrical community and shortly after the events of the trial he became the manager of the Grand Opera House, London's leading theatre.

The trial, which was to prove a fairly long and complex one with four adjournments, was held before London's police Magistrate, Ephraim Jones Parke, Q. C., who had once been a law student of Sir John A. Macdonald. Also, as was then perfectly permissible, he was solicitor for both the County of Middlesex and the London and Port Stanley Railroad, and senior partner in the London law firm of Parke and Purdom, as well as being involved in various other operations.[19] The defence lawyer was A. J. B. (Jack) Macdonald, who had been practising in the city since the 1860s.[20] The prosecution was led by the county Crown attorney, Charles Hutchinson, who was involved in almost as many enterprises as the judge, being also clerk of the peace for the County of Middlesex, and senior partner of the law firm of Hutchinson and McKillop.[21] Hutchinson had just as puritanical an outlook as the police chief, even writing to the newspapers against the evils of using wine for communion, as it could lead to addiction. This was a strange outlook for a member of the Church of England.[22] Hutchinson immediately took an active role in the case, writing Chief Williams on January 4, 1886, stating:

> I wanted to see about the indecent picture case – I understand it is going to be hardly contested – I hope therefore you have good witnesses to prove –
>
> 1. That the pictures were exhibited
>
> 2. That they are indecent – This must be in a great measure a matter of opinion – & you will [need to] have such respectable & intelligent witnesses to express their opinions – You should also prove that the pictures are more indecent that [*sic*] the actual exhibition on the stage & therefore uncalled for – & can only have the object of exciting unholy & unchaste desire & feeling. We ought to make a good fight whatever the result may be.[23]

As the events were to demonstrate, Chief Williams must have already been working towards the same objectives.

In order to establish guidelines for what constituted obscenity the prosecution introduced pictures of two naked female statues, which were generally regarded as acceptable in polite society. These were usually referred to as the *French* (or *Greek*) *Slave* and the *White Captive*. The first was almost certainly the famous *Greek Slave* statue carved by the highly regarded Vermont sculptor Hiram Powers. Placed under a curtained canopy and surrounded by pianos, it had formed a focal point of the American exhibit in the Crystal Palace at the Great Exhibition in London, England, in 1851.[24] There it must have come under the scrutiny of the ultimate arbiter of public decency, Queen Victoria herself! In addition, it had been approved by no less an authority than a committee of Cincinnati clergymen.[25]

There were at least six versions of the piece and a New York banker had paid $4,000 for one of them. In 1887 the sale of the effects of another New Yorker, the great merchant A. T. Stewart, included a replica "on a green and rose marble pedestal with a revolving top."[26] The *White Captive*, which received less attention at the trial, was, quite possibly, a statue sculpted by Erastus Dow Palmer of Albany, for which he had used his own daughter as a model.[27]

As for the trial itself, the court records may be somewhat incomplete, but they are supplemented by the *Free Press*, which reported most of the hearings. (The *Advertiser*, as noted, virtually ignored the proceedings.) Therefore, there is at least one account of most of the sessions, so a reasonably complete reconstruction can be provided. These records show that the testimony opened with Chief Williams, who produced a copy of the poster and stated: "I think the picture is an indecent picture. I form my judgement from the scantiness of the dress, and from the private parts of the female being marked out by colouring." He noted that he had seen other "statuary in windows," but "the colouring in the picture I consider makes this one indecent. I think it is intended to pander to the vicious."[28] The *Free Press* printed a slightly different and rather more detailed account of the

Vermont sculptor Hiram Powers's famous statue, the **Greek Slave**, *which was used as a touchstone of decency at the Kirchmer trial, as it appeared at the Great Exhibition in London, England, in 1851.* New York Public Library

testimony, which is worth quoting, as Williams's statement provides the basis of the Crown's case.

> The *Chief* produced a picture of Lottie [*sic*] Davene in the regulation tunic and tights, standing by a trapeze, to which he said his attention had been called on the street, while it was exhibited in the windows of McDonald's hotel. When pressed to give his reasons for considering the picture obscene, the witness said the colouring of it was the chief thing. The tunic was too short, and the trunk was of a different colour from the rest of the clothing. He had often seen worse pictures. He considered the effect of such pictures as injurious to the morals of the young.[29]

Police Constable Robert Crawford then took the stand for the first time and testified that, on the orders of Chief Constable Williams, he had taken the poster from the defendant's window, where it could be seen by passers-by.[30]

The next witness was the Rev. Donald George Sutherland, who resided briefly in London between 1884 and 1886 as minister of the Queen's Avenue Methodist Church, now the Metropolitan United Church, the oldest, largest, and richest Methodist congregation in the city. A very devout man, he had first trained in the law, but was drawn to the church by a feeling that he had been called by God, and that his family had been struck by catastrophes because of his continuing in the secular life. According to his official Methodist Church obituary in 1895 "as a pastor he was diligent and conscientious, watching over his flock with the tender solicitude of a true shepherd."[31] Obviously, he believed in taking an active role in protecting his congregation, and their city as well.

His testimony closely paralleled and clarified that of the police chief, confirming that the poster was indecent because of the "exposure of the person and the way in which the parts of the person are marked out." In other words, to sum up their testimony: the short tunic and the different, darker-coloured trunk below it, contrasted to the white skin of the legs, and called attention to what the witnesses delicately described as her "private parts." Sutherland added that the statue of the *Greek Slave* was "not indecent in the sense the picture is." In his opinion a work of art could be nude and decent, it depended on the mode and manner of representation. He did not like the *Greek Slave*, but he felt that it was not indecent.[32]

The court then heard two further witnesses for the prosecution. The first was Ambrose B. Powell, the proprietor of a dry goods, dressmaking, millinery, and kid gloves emporium situated at 134 Dundas Street. A leading business figure in the city, he was active in the Liberal Party (where he became a vice-president), in business organizations, and in the Irish Benevolent Society.[33] He was an alderman in the 1870s and again in the 1890s.[34] Most important, however, Powell was for many years very active in the management of the Rev. Mr. Sutherland's Queen's Avenue Methodist Church, having been secretary of the Trustees Board since 1874.[35] He concurred that the poster drew attention to the performer's private parts.

The next witness was one of the most prominent and wealthy businessmen in London, Thomas McCormick, the founder of the biscuit company whose products still carry his name. He was a deeply religious man, and one of the most charitable of London's citizens, as the McCormick Home continues to attest. Like

Powell, he was a Methodist, and a member of the trustees' board of Queen's Avenue Methodist Church since 1872.[36] He lived in an opulent Grand Avenue mansion, which was so large that it was demolished after his death, because it was too expensive to keep up. The top floor contained a billiard room, enlivened by religious paintings on the ceiling; it was also, reportedly, used for church services for large numbers of people.

Echoing his predecessors, McCormick stated that the poster was "indecent for dress and the want of dress," that it drew attention to the private parts, and that "it could not be any worse, if as bad, if entirely without dress."[37] P. C. Crawford then returned to the stand to add:

> I was at the performance of the character. The dress appeared
> to include drawers [and] it was not indecent. The dress was all
> of a dark colour, the whole dress was of the same colour. I have
> seen about the same dress in a circus.[38]

Here was a *coup de main* for the prosecution, as recommended by Hutchinson: the poster was much more risqué than the performance! Therefore, the performances could be allowed to continue, while the posters had to be removed. The hearing was then recessed to January 7. After the trial adjourned the *Free Press* reporter spoke to Powell, who volunteered the opinion – rather a

McCormick's influence in the city may be judged by the magnificent mansion he erected in about 1880 for some $15,000 on what is now Grand Avenue. One of the largest houses in the city, it was demolished after McCormick's death in 1906. W. E. Eldridge

surprising one for a witness in a case which was still being heard – that "he thought it unjust to punish citizens for a thing for which the show people were mainly responsible, and to wait until they had left the city before bringing the case before the Police Magistrate." If Powell strongly felt that way, however, why was he willing to testify?

Certainly, his statement hit at the underlying problem. Even if the actual performance was sufficiently modest, why were the proprietors not charged for their part in providing the posters? After all, they were the ones responsible for the picture. Was there a feeling among the authorities that, presuming the show was anywhere near as popular as the *Free Press* claimed, those laying charges might be subjected to ridicule? Or, were complainants afraid that the Davenes might bring in lawyers and precedents to support their advertisements? The question is, of course, unanswerable; but possible reasons will be considered later.

The trial "for distributing and exposing indecent pictures" as the *Free Press,* which again is our only detailed source for the next hearing, designated it,[39] resumed on January 7 with further clerical witnesses for the prosecution. The first was the Rev. James Allister Murray, a Nova Scotian who was pastor of St. Andrew's Presbyterian from 1875 to 1894. St. Andrew's was then a very strict church, which long opposed instrumental music during services, only allowing the use of an organ in 1888 after an extended controversy. Murray's statement, at least as the reporter phrased it, varied to an extent from that of his predecessors and it was

The Rev. James Allister Murray was pastor of St. Andrew's Presbyterian (now First St. Andrew's United Church) from 1875 until his death in 1894. This was the strictest Presbyterian congregation in the city, which only permitted the use of an organ in church in 1888 after a long controversy. From *Almost a Century*

much less clear: "he considered the picture ... indecent, as it displayed a female form very much in a state of nudity. He deemed the *Greek Slave* an ideal; the Davene poster he considered indecently realistic. "It was evidence of solaciousness [*sic*] which meant lustfulness or sensuality." Adding that "he was nearly colour blind," so he could not tell much about the lewdness of the colouring, he concluded that he "did not consider statuary offensive to decency."[40]

The last clerical witness was something of a surprise, for Church of England clergy were usually more likely to take a "live and let live" approach to such matters. Possibly the Rev. James Banning Richardson made his appearance because his Nova Scotian background was similar to Murray's, or because of his Low Church affiliation, or the influence of Crown Attorney Hutchinson, who was a prominent Church of England layman. Whatever his reason or reasons for testifying, reticence did not suit this gentleman, who was rector of the Cronyn Memorial Church from 1877 to 1899, before going on to St. John's, Arva and the archdeaconry of London. He asserted that "the picture was indecent, as it would promote impure thoughts," and added that he "had seen statuary in private dwellings which was [*sic*] indelicate."[41] The prosecution then concluded its case by calling P. C. Crawford to the stand for the third time, to certify that he took the pictures out of Constable's barber shop window, as well as McDonald's and

The Rev. Canon James Banning Richardson, M.A., was the rector of Cronyn Memorial Church from 1877 to 1899. Like the other ministers who testified, he was a diligent and highly regarded pastor who saw it as his duty to protect the morals of his city.

Regional Collection, University of Western Ontario Library

Goldner's; but he did not know who had put the pictures up in the first place.

It was now the turn for the defence. Jeremiah (Jerry) McDonald came first and set the tone for the shop proprietors' arguments:

> I am defendant. I did not put the picture in my window. I did not know it to be there, it was not there with my permission, as soon as asked I took it out at once. ... I do not know who put it there. [42]

Goldner said the same thing, which apparently was the defence adopted by the owners of all the charged premises. It was more difficult for Kirchner to claim he knew nothing, but he gave it a good try, stating: "I did not put the bill [poster] up in McDonald['s]. I don't know who did." Then, rather contradicting himself, he admitted that he had received the pictures at the Customs House and presumed that they were all right as they had been passed there.[43]

The testimony that followed showed that, while Jack Macdonald had worked hard to gather witnesses for the defendants, they were hardly to prove a match for the bevy of ministers. In fact, as artists and theatre people, they may even have been something of a liability. First came James T. Dalton, described as being in the theatrical business. He said that when he attended a performance the lady's dress was purple, noted that the poster corresponded with what she wore on the stage, and said that the "trunk" worn was the kind used in all similar acts. In defence of Lotto he added that "anything to interrupt her sight or encumber her hand would endanger her life,"[44] or as the *Free Press* phrased it, "any more clothing than that shown would encumber a woman in executing her feats and would endanger her life."[45] Dalton concluded, "I most decidedly do not consider it indecent."[46]

John H. Davidson, manager of the Grand Theatre, although a rival of the People's Theatre – presumably supporting Kirchmer for the sake of his own parallel performances – said "I see nothing unmodest [*sic*]or indecent about it" and "I would post similar ones on my establishment." Finally, the day's hearings concluded with yet another appearance by P. C. Crawford, who, considering the line the prosecution's testimony had taken, gave damning evidence that "he had seen the act, and observed that the trunk was not worn as high as in the picture."[47] His return to add this evidence might indicate that the prosecution was a bit worried; however, they need not have been troubled.

When the court met for the third session – this time the *Free Press* called the charge "exhibiting and distributing indecent show bills" – the only witness was James Griffith (1814-1894), who "testified that he had been an artist and student of painting for upwards of sixty years, and that he saw nothing indecent in the picture produced, which he considered no more objectionable than the *Greek Slave*.[48] He was to be the last unequivocal professional witness for the defence. A further adjournment to the 18th was set over because Hutchinson had to appear in criminal court to prosecute other cases,[49] and the last witnesses were heard on January 25.

This last session as reported by the *Free Press* on the "Indecent Picture Case" opened with the testimony of Stephen Kelso Davidson, who was active in the London for many years as an artist and teacher, first at the Western School of Art and Design, then with his own school and finally at the London Normal School.[50] His waffling testimony was something of a two-edged sword:

> ... the picture is designed to attract people to the show. I think it is
> not calculated to promote sensual feeling in the young. It does not
> in the least draw attention to the private parts of the woman; but one
> particular part does point to the private parts, the limbs above and to
> the sides of that point are depicted as naked.[51]

Next came another artist, Henry Nesbitt McEvoy, who was equally unhelpful.
He first stated that the poster would not create impure thoughts in the minds of
the young, and that "there is nothing indecent or lewd in the picture;" but
qualified his remarks with: "I speak as an artist, what is proper in a studio would
be improper on the street."[52] The distinct impression left by both these
gentlemen is that, while as artists they saw nothing wrong with the poster, at the
same time, as individuals who obtained their commissions from the local
establishment, they were loath to alienate possible patrons. If anything, in balance
their testimony may well have hurt the defence more than it helped.

The charge of equivocation could not be applied to the customs house staff,
who had to clear themselves of any negligence in passing the poster and were
quite explicit in their testimony. The collector, John Siddons, stated flatly: "I am a
Customs Officer; I passed this picture; there is nothing lewd or indecent in it."[53]
His first assistant, Robert Knightly, who seemingly was treading as carefully as the
artists, although in a different direction, followed with: "I am in the Customs: I
assist Mr. Siddons: there is nothing indecent or lewd in the picture." Then came
William Taylor, also an assistant, with a really remarkable comment: "I am in the
Customs; there is nothing indecent because there are so many on the wall and
they are constantly passed in the Customs." The exact interpretation of these
words presents a problem. Surely Taylor did not mean that the Queen's Customs
House was flamboyantly decorated with posters of scantily clad ladies?[54]

The evidence heard, Police Magistrate Parke immediately handed down his
opinion that "many respectable citizens had come forward and given evidence
that in their opinion the picture was of an indecent character."[55] He then fined
Kirchmer the sum of $5 – although under the by-law he could have levied a fine of
up to $50 – plus costs, which amounted to another $5.95,[56] and advised him that
he could appeal. Before a month was out Kirchmer, who seems to have been a
somewhat unsavoury character, was to appear before him again charged with
assaulting one John Tomlinson, and was fined $2.[57] Quite possibly, the judge
knew him from past activities.

The charges against the other defendants were dismissed. The defence
attorney, Macdonald, immediately advised that an appeal would be made to the
county court. This process was instituted on January 28, with Kirchmer signing a
statement that he would be responsible for the full $50 fine if it were levied, and
George Hiscox and John McMartin, another hotel keeper, acting as guarantors.
They were apparently interested in seeing the charges dismissed on principle,
committing themselves for $25 each. The appeal was heard on June 12, 1886, with
junior County Judge Joseph Frederick Davis presiding. It received short shrift. The
record simply states: "Appeal dismissed and the conviction affirmed without costs."[58]

The upholders of public morality had won the day, though in a rather
circumscribed way, as all the proprietors of the businesses that had displayed the
posters in their windows had emerged unscathed. Their dismissal, coupled with the
fact that under the by-law Magistrate Parke could have fined Kirchmer much more
heavily, leaves the impression that the judge, at least, was more overwhelmed by
the opinions of the "many respectable citizens" than he was by the gravity of the

charges. It may seem that the little man had been the sole victim; but, as noted, despite his ostensibly humble calling, Kirchmer was hardly a poor man. He could afford the fine (probably about $300 to $350 in modern money).

Clearly the moral views expressed by respectable citizens carried considerable weight in London, upheld as they were by Police Chief Williams and Crown Attorney Hutchinson, even if the artistic and theatrical communities, and the Londoners who happily attended the performance, thought otherwise. But how did London compare with other cities of the era, and was the outlook expressed here unusually severe for that period?

That the strong moralistic tone of the ministers and the officials on artistic matters was the accepted norm in the London area, even if it might not have been subscribed to by many of the citizens, is further supported by the changes made to two rather risqué paintings by artists of the period. The first painter was Caroline Farncomb, a leading London, Ontario, artist, who in 1890 had been provided with the necessary funds to study at the Académie Julien in Paris by the very "establishment" Women's Art Club. While in Paris she exhibited a picture of a nude female bust at a salon. On the return voyage, very sensibly thinking of the probable reactions of her patronesses, and the subsequent effect on her own plans to open a studio in London, she painted on a shawl composed of rows of tulle.[59]

The other artist was Florence Carlyle, who accompanied Paul Peel and his sister to Paris in 1890, and studied there for three years. She also exhibited in a Paris salon, but made the mistake of not correcting her Parisian extremes before returning home.[60] Carlyle had grown up in Woodstock and one of her friends from that centre, a young poetess, visited her in France and posed for a picture entitled *The White Flower,* in which she was depicted as a "forest nymph" in the Barbizon forest, with an appropriate nymphlike lack of apparel. On the artist's return the nymph's father came to see his daughter's picture, and was equally appropriately horrified, doubtless thinking that marriageable young gentlemen might decide that marriage was not necessary. Carlyle quickly added a flowing diaphanous dress.[61] Unfortunately, it is not recorded what the daughter, who must have been something of an individualist, thought about all this furore; it does seem that, until father arrived on the scene, she was no more concerned about the painting than was Carlyle.

Yet, what of greater centres? And also male nudity? In 1874 and 1875 Samuel Butler, the English author, visited Canada's metropolis, Montreal, and discovered that the casts of two Greek statues, one of Antinous, a rather dubious early second-century character, and the other a Discobolos, were safely banished from public view in a store room. The result was his famous poem beginning, "Stowed away in a Montreal lumber room. The Discobolos standeth and turneth his face to the wall," and ending, "O God! O Montreal!"[62]

To be fair to Canada, and more particularly London, we must note that, even in the progressive city of Cincinnati in the even more progressive United States, where the committee of clergyman had given their approbation to the *Greek Slave,* artistic prudishness could be the norm. When some unclad statues were imported from Europe for the Ladies' Academy of Art, one Mrs. Fazzi was hired to install fig leaves so they could be properly displayed.[63]

The Lotto Davene trial was a minor incident in London's history, though the *Free Press* did consider it worthy of extended comment. It tells us a great deal about the bifurcated moral outlook of the period, which applied not just in London, but far more broadly. The establishment and their pastors might be willing to allow naked Greek statues in their homes, doubtless because the upper classes were fortitudinous in their virtue; but the morals of the local working classes must be controlled, and the poor while walking down the streets should not be turned to "evil thoughts" by viewing posters of partly clad ladies . Therefore, those who tried to corrupt them should be prosecuted, with the full support of the chief of police and some of the clergy.

The morality in the Lotto Davene case would thus appear to be a parallel to the legislation protecting the sabbath, which prohibited the children of the poor playing baseball on the streets, while it ignored the respectable recreations of the well-to-do, such as golf, tennis, and yachting. It is to be noted too that the clergymen who appeared as witnesses were not the pastors of the working men's churches, who were conspicuously absent, but rather of some of the wealthiest congregations in the city.

That the performances were allowed to continue and the proprietors not charged, though they must have supplied the posters, smacks of a certain cynicism on the part of the authorities. This is especially true because, if the respectable witnesses (who probably never saw the posters on display) so clearly viewed the shorter tunic as salacious advertising, the same thought had surely occurred to the Davene company's management. Further, the evidence that the tunic was longer at the performances, presumably thus legitimizing them, was a rather superficial subterfuge. It could equally have been argued that the longer tunic could hardly have provided adequate coverage of "the private parts" while Lotto was doing her somersaults. If, as some of the witnesses opined, a naked statue was less immoral than a partially clad poster, surely a rapidly flapping tunic was the most seductive of all.

But what of Ambrose Powell, who did see the lack of logic in the procedure, and felt that charges should be laid against the theatre people? Probably he was activated by an even stricter moral outlook than the others, not by any desire to be logical or consistent. Though the moral fervour of the other witnesses cannot be doubted, it may have been tempered by such practical considerations as the avoidance of major legal entanglements, or a belief that the mob should be allowed its "circuses" to keep it amused. Yet, at the same time, it is all too easy today to scoff at the upholders of public morals a century ago. While we note their inconsistencies, we must remember that, while possibly selective, most were sincere in thinking that they were doing God's will in purging the city of evil.

Thus, what Lotto's poster trial shows us is the existence of two Londons: at the top, the at least superficially stuffy and moral city of the upper-middle and upper classes, who were quite ready to legislate and enforce various restrictions on the lower orders; and below them, the vast majority of the population, many of whom rarely darkened the doors of any church, élite or otherwise, and who lived in a much less self-righteous and far livelier city than the one frequently shown in the official histories that have come down to us. Though somewhat impeded by the restrictions laid upon them by the upper class, they were still allowed to enjoy their entertainments and their taverns. Also, in many ways they agreed with the structured society and accepted their employers' and superiors' domination as God's will. As the Rev. J. H. Versey of the Christian Church, surely not an élite congregation, expressed it from a London pulpit at a much later date: "It is everyone's duty to become rich if he can do it fairly and honestly. Rich men are not condemned to hell ... they ... become the stewards of God.[64]

Finally, in a way there was a certain whimsical touch to the whole affair, for, while Lotto was the subject of proceedings, she herself may never have heard about the furore caused by her poster.

ENDNOTES

Author's Note: The writer would like to thank Daniel J. Brock and Guy St-Denis for their many helpful comments during the preparation of this article. In addition, Barry Fair provided information on London artists of the period and Dorothy Kealey, Archivist of the Anglican Church of Canada, and Ian Mason of the United Church Archives advised on the ministers of their denominations. The punctuation has been modernized in some of the quotations.

1   Kirchmer's name is spelled several different ways in the records. He signed Kirchmer; but was charged as Kerchmer, and the transcript shows Keirchmere, Kirchmir, and Kerchmer.
2   The court documents on the trial are to be found in: University of Western Ontario, The D.B. Weldon Library, Regional Collection [hereafter Regional Collection], Middlesex County, Criminal Court, Kirchmer v. Williams, 1886 [hereafter Kirchmer v. Williams].
3   *Free Press* (London, Ontario), Dec. 26, 1885, p. 5, c. 4.
4   *Ibid.,* Dec. 25, 1885, p. 8, c. 2.
5   *Ibid.,* Dec. 29, 1885, p. 5, c. 4.
6   *Ibid.,* Jan. 1, 1886, p. 8, c. 2.
7   *Ibid.,* Jan. 2, 1886, p. 3, c. 4.
8   *Ibid.,* Dec. 26, 1885, p. 5, c. 5; *ibid.,* Dec. 28, p. 8, c. 2.
9   *Ibid.,* Jan. 1, 1886, p. 5, cc. 6, 8.
10   *Ibid.,* Jan. 4, 1886, p. 3, c. 2.
11   *London Advertiser,* Jan. 1, 1886, p. 8, c. 6.
12   *Ibid.,* Jul. 11, 1927, p. 2, c. 4.
13   *London Free Press,* Oct. 12, 1991, p. C6.
14   *London Evening Advertiser,* Jul. 11, 1927, p. 2, c. 4.
15   Regional Collection, London, Municipal Council, By-Laws, 1850-1879, no. 202, May 20, 1872.
16   Regional Collection, Kirchmer v. Williams.
17   *London Advertiser,* Jan. 4, 1886, p. 7, c. 4; *Free Press,* Jan. 5, 1886, p. 5, c. 4; *London City and Middlesex County Directory, 1880-81* (London, Ontario: R.L. Polk, 1880), p. 164; *History of the County of Middlesex, Canada* [hereafter *History of Middlesex*] (Toronto and London, Ontario: W.A. & C.L. Goodspeed, 1889; reprint ed., Belleville, Ontario: Mika Studio, 1972), pp. 859-861.
18   *History of Middlesex,* p. 1072.
19   *Ibid.,* pp. 957-958.
20   [David J.] Hughes and T.[homas] H. Purdom, *History of the Bar of the County of Middlesex,* (London, Ontario: Advertiser Press, 1912), p. 46.
21   *History of Middlesex,* pp. 867-868.
22   Regional Collection, Hutchinson Papers, scrapbook, 1884-1891.
23   *Ibid.,* Crown Attorney's Letterbook, Jul., 1885-Jul., 1886, p. 335.
24   Oliver W. Larkin, *Art and Life in America* [hereafter *Art and Life*] (New York, New York: Rinehart, 1949), p. 240.
25   *Ibid.,* p. 180.
26   *Ibid.,* p. 295.
27   *Ibid.,* p. 185.
28   Regional Collection, Kirchmer v. Williams.
29   *Free Press,* Jan. 5, 1886, p. 3, c. 2.
30   Regional Collection, Kirchmer v. Williams.
31   United Church Archives (Toronto, Ontario), Toronto Methodist Conference, minutes, 1895, and obituary clippings.
32   Regional Collection, Kirchmer v. Williams.
33   *History of Middlesex,* pp. 352, 365, 653.
34   Powell was alderman for Ward 2 in 1875, 1878-1879, and 1895-1896.
35   *History of Middlesex,* p. 304.
36   *Ibid.*
37   Regional Collection, Kirchmer v. Williams.
38   *Ibid.*
39   *Free Press,* Jan. 7, 1886, p. 3, c. 6.
40   *Ibid.*
41   *Ibid.*
42   *Ibid.*
43   *Ibid.*
44   *Ibid.*
45   *Ibid.*
46   Regional Collection, Kirchmer v. Williams.
47   *Free Press,* Jan. 7, 1886, p. 3, c. 6.
48   *Ibid.,* Jan. 11, 1886, p. 5, c. 2.

49 Regional Collection, Hutchinson Papers, Crown Attorney's Letterbook, Jul. 1885–Jul. 1886, p. 343.
50 Nancy Poole, *The Art of London, 1830-1980* [hereafter *Art of London*] (London, Ontario: Blackpool Press, 1984), pp. 56-57.
51 Regional Collection, Kirchmer *v.* Williams; *Free Press,* Jan. 25, 1886, p. 3, c. 4.
52 *Ibid.*
53 *Ibid.*
54 *Ibid.*
55 *Free Press,* Jan. 25, 1886, p. 3, c. 4.
56 Regional Collection, Kirchmer *v.* Williams.
57 *Ibid.,* Middlesex County, Court of General Quarter Sessions of the Peace, Return of Convictions, Feb. 12, 1886.
58 *Ibid.,* Minute Book 4, 1886-1899, p. 8.
59 Barry Fair, interview; Poole, *Art of London,* pp. 67-68.
60 Poole, *Art of London,* pp. 68-70.
61 Barry Fair, interview.
62 Henry Festing Jones, *The Note-Books of Samuel Butler* (London, England: A.C. Fifield, 1912), pp. 388-389.
63 Larkin, *Art and Life,* p. 178.
64 *London Advertiser,* Jul. 12, 1920, p. 2, c. 4.

CHAPTER NINE

BROKEN DREAMS
Adam Beck, Hydro,
and the Radial Railway Controversy
1910-1922

David R. Spencer

A dam Beck was a peculiar and difficult man. Edward V. Buchanan described him as "opinionated and strong."[1] Buchanan would have known. As general manager of London's Public Utilities Commission, Buchanan was closely associated with the ambitious cigar box manufacturer as he entered and successfully rose in politics. Beck was the mayor of London from 1902 to 1904, the city's Conservative member of the Ontario legislature from 1902 to 1919 and again from 1923 to 1925, and, in his most famous role, the founding chairman of Ontario Hydro. Beck's personality and influence dominated every one of his undertakings. He was a man who hated to lose, a man whose life has

been remembered for more than one major achievement: in addition to his well-documented role in bringing public electric power to Ontario, Adam Beck was a businessman, a well-known philanthropist, and a successful horseman whose mounts won a number of prestigious European awards. On his death, he left an estate valued at $627,976.[2] Although modest in comparison with the fortunes accumulated by American robber barons, by early twentieth-century Ontario standards, it was an impressive sum.

Like many a historical personality, Adam Beck also felt the sting of reverse more than once in his long and illustrious career. He was unsuccessful in his first candidacy for provincial office in 1898. In 1919, when the political tide washed away the governing

Sir Adam Beck (1857–1925), the first chairman of the Hydro-Electric Power Commission of Ontario – now Ontario Hydro – in a rare, full-face photograph.

Conservative administration of Sir William Hearst, Adam Beck was among the casualties, suffering defeat in London at the hands of Dr. Hugh Arlen Stevenson, a trade-union-sponsored candidate who, like Beck, had been mayor from 1915 to 1917. But the incident that finally broke the spirit of the iron man from Baden was the rejection of his dream of a provincial network of electrically powered railways, commonly referred to as "radials," which as he envisioned them were to centre on the City of Toronto and radiate north, east, west, and south from the core of Ontario's largest municipality. It was a scheme that Beck conceived shortly after publicly produced power flowed from the Niagara gorge to illuminate the city of Berlin (Kitchener) on October 11, 1910.

Beck had successfully forged a powerful coalition of municipal politicians of various partisan stripes to pressure the provincial government to support the movement for publicly owned electric power. The Hydro chairman, although a sitting Conservative member of the Ontario legislature and a member of the cabinet, convinced these public officials that the quest for public ownership of the province's hydraulic resources should supersede any narrow, party-driven objectives. Once public power began to flow in Berlin, Beck turned his attention to his railway dreams and once again, enlisted the aid of the people who had been his staunch allies in his earlier quests – Ontario's municipal leaders.

Riding on a wave of unquestioning public support resulting from his Hydro success in bringing cheap, abundant electric power to Ontarians, Adam Beck carefully and methodically introduced the first phase of his radial railway plans in 1911. By that time, most North Americans were familiar with electrically powered passenger trains, which were regarded as technological dinosaurs by many transportation experts. In Canada, electrically powered, short distance railways connected outlying regions to large centres such as Toronto and Montreal. Others served smaller communities, such as Windsor, Ottawa, Hamilton, Peterborough, and Fort William (Thunder Bay).[3] In the main, they lumbered along very light rails designed to support slow-moving urban street cars. Their speed was inhibited by low, winding roadbeds, which more often than not followed routes occupied by equally untravellable provincial roadways. As a consequence, passengers regularly faced long and very uncomfortable trips over relatively short distances.

Beck's dream was to combine the best technological features of the transcontinental steam railways, such as heavy rail, large coaches, and straight rights-of-way, with electric motive power. He was convinced that such a hybrid was possible, and that it would improve both performance and comfort, attractions which would be irresistible to the travelling public.

Although many travellers complained about the consistently inefficient service offered by most inter-urban electric railways, Beck knew that explaining the need for a radial railway grid would be more difficult than the task he had faced in selling the idea of public power. That issue had pitted "moral" public ownership against "immoral" private enterprise, but the railway question largely centred on technology. He knew that he needed a successful working model if the expensive and sophisticated scheme was to enjoy the backing of Ontario's voting and tax-paying citizens. The Hydro chairman first turned his attention to the London and Port Stanley Railway (L&PS), a short, dilapidated twenty-four-mile line connecting the Forest City to its port on Lake Erie.

The railway had opened in 1856 to provide London with, among other connections, an efficient access to Pennsylvania's coal fields. The line was plagued with financial problems from the day the first train rolled down its tracks.

The London and Port Stanley shops in February 1915. These are L&PS locomotives under construction in the London facility. Ontario Hydro

Exhausted by constant losses and the possibility of bankruptcy, the city of London arranged a twenty-one-year operating lease with the Great Western Railway in 1874, but Great Western enjoyed no more success than the city, and in 1892, dismayed by the lack of positive financial results, the company announced it would not renew its option when the lease expired in 1895. The city entered negotiations with the Grand Trunk, but to no avail. After the London–Grand Trunk talks collapsed, the Michigan Central continued operation of the line on a month-to-month basis.

On December 1, 1893, the Lake Erie and Detroit River Railway took over the Great Western lease and extended it until January 1, 1914. But in 1906, the Pere Marquette, which ran through St. Thomas, purchased the Lake Erie and Detroit interests and assumed the L&PS lease, in order to gain a right-of-way into London. In 1913, the company announced it wished to renew the lease for another twenty years. If the lease were not renewed, the Pere Marquette would face the loss of its access to the city of London. By then, however, the granting of such a lease was in conflict with Beck's vision for the line between London and Port Stanley. Beck fought the renewal and persuaded the London City Council to establish a railway commission with a mandate to modernize both the right-of-way and the rolling stock. The Hydro chairman successfully argued that the railway could only turn a profit if its motive power were converted to inexpensive hydro-electricity.[4]

If it accepted the project, the city of London would face a herculean task. The line was close to unusable at the end of the Pere Marquette lease. An industry journal, the *Canadian Railway and Marine World*, reported that

> the track is in very bad condition, and it will be necessary to
> entirely reconstruct it, as the rails and ties are of no value other

than scrap. The buildings are in fair condition, and with a moderate outlay for repairs, can be made to answer the purchase [*sic*] of the road after electrification.[5]

Hydro and Beck assumed control of the renovation project by appointing S.B. Storer, a consulting engineer from Syracuse, New York, to prepare a report outlining all factors needed for upgrading. Storer advocated the installation of eighty-pound (36.2 kg) rails and a 1,500-volt electrical system. He recommended the purchase of passenger cars capable of speeds up to fifty miles an hour (80 kmph), which, counting stops, could cover the London to St. Thomas leg in twenty-four minutes and the remainder of the journey to Port Stanley in an additional half hour. Storer envisaged half-hourly service from London to St. Thomas and hourly service from St. Thomas to the port. He recommended that in the summer vacation season both routes should provide service every half hour with the possibility of additional trains on the quarter-hour.[6]

Beck himself presented the Storer Report to London City Council in the fall of 1912. He placed the cost of the rehabilitation at $890,573. The optimistic Hydro boss predicted that the L&PS line would produce annual revenues of $220,545, resulting in an annual net profit of $40,955.[7] The chairman was not concerned with potential competition from the only other electric line that served Port Stanley, the London and Lake Erie Railway (L&LE). This line, which ran from south London through Lambeth to the lake, was little more than a glorified streetcar service; it relied almost exclusively on passenger traffic. The L&LE had been constructed with a technology that by 1912 was considered obsolete. Its owners had no plans to modernize the system.

Beck's proposal to city hall was the subject of a meeting of the London Board of Trade on November 11, 1912. Looking at projected costs that came dangerously close to the million-dollar mark, the board formed a citizens' committee to examine the proposals and comment on them. The committee commissioned reports from A. Eastman, the general manager of the Windsor,

The London and Port Stanley Railway electrication in progress, as seen in March 1915. Note the Kettle Creek bridge in the background. Ontario Hydro

The London and Port Stanley Railway right-of-way on Talbot Street in St. Thomas, April 20, 1915. By this point in time, the electrical overhead cables had been installed. Ontario Hydro

Essex, and Lake Shore Rapid Railway; and from A.N. Warfield, a railway promoter from Berlin (Kitchener), Ontario. Although some details in these reports deviated from the Storer analysis, both concurred with Beck's vision that the railway could be profitable only if it were modernized and electrified.[8]

Beck had complete confidence in his ability to convince the city of London of the worthiness of his model project, and in fact Londoners embraced the plan with some eagerness. Many of London's civic politicians were among those active in Beck's unswervingly loyal pressure group, the Ontario Municipal Electric Association. This was an organization of municipal politicians and officials that would eventually provide the infrastructure for the alliances that would fight for the radials.[9] The organization's membership superseded the often rigid political cleavages in an early-twentieth-century Ontario political arena noted for its fierce partisanship.[10] In spite of its proclaimed independence, the Ontario Municipal Electric Association behaved in many ways like a single-issue third party, employing tactics that led one observer, eccentric University of Toronto professor James Mavor, to dub Adam Beck "the dictator of Ontario,"[11] a mocking phrase that would eventually return to haunt a future premier (Ernest Drury) and one that helped turn Adam Beck's dream into his final nightmare.

With the London and Port Stanley modernization plans a *fait accompli*, and with the support of his municipal allies, Beck tabled his first radial bill in the

Ontario legislature in April 1913. It passed the following month. The act empowered the province's municipalities to construct and operate radial lines at their own expense.[12] Hydro was given the authority to construct and operate the lines on behalf of those municipalities that wanted to participate in the scheme. The province was not obliged to offer any assistance, financial or otherwise, but Hydro and its municipal friends were not prevented from seeking federal aid.

The act was repealed the following year and replaced by legislation that gave Hydro greater power "to issue bonds for carrying on the work, taking the debentures of the participating corporations as underlying security, and thus providing ways and means for the financial undertaking of the work."[13] The province agreed to guarantee the bonds. This act differed from the first statute, however, in that municipalities were no longer allowed to act independently in radial railway matters. The most notable impediment to the scheme, financial uncertainty, seemed eliminated. In 1915, further amendments allowed subsidiary municipalities, specifically townships, to assume construction and operating costs on their own with the legal option of purchasing and updating any existing lines which happened to run through their territories.[14]

This is the London and Port Stanley Railway right-of-way viewed from the Kettle Creek bridge in May of 1915, just north of the village of Port Stanley. Ontario Hydro

The first electric locomotive to travel the L&PS tracks was photographed at St. Thomas in June 1915. The locomotive later broke down and had to be towed back to London.
Regional Collection, University of Western Ontario Library

With this legislation in hand, Beck returned to the familiar and friendly confines of municipal politics to launch the campaign for public support. At a meeting of municipal officials in Toronto in December 1913, Beck asked the politicians to approve a resolution calling on Hydro to build lines whenever and wherever municipalities wanted them. Before the delegates left the conference hall, they voted to form one more Beck pressure group, the Hydro-Electric Radial Union of Western Ontario. It was the first of three groups that would eventually merge into the province-wide Hydro-Electric Radial Railway Union.[15]

During the period between the formation of the Union in 1913 and its participation in the first provincial general meeting in 1915, its executive, seemingly unconcerned with any form of democratic process, drafted "memorials" without the consent of the municipalities they supposedly represented. The documents, which outlined the Union's platform, were presented to both federal Prime Minister Robert Borden and the acting premier of Ontario, J.J. Foy.[16] Noting the rapid movement to electric power, especially in rural areas, the Union memorialists began their presentation by discussing the economics of power consumption. They pointed out that if current trends were to continue, Ontario would be required to increase its productive capacity. They regarded rural electrification and the construction of electrically-powered railway lines as essential measures in a provincial modernization agenda designed to improve the transporting of agricultural produce to urban centres.

Although the Union praised farmers for becoming more efficient through electrical use, they warned the politicians that all was not well on the land. They noted that 96,000 Ontarians had abandoned agricultural life since 1905. They argued that the city was growing at the expense of the farm, not in conjunction with it. The Union suggested that if the trend were to continue, Ontarians could face a future as a net food importer in spite of their abundance of fertile, productive land. The answer? Keep the folks on the farm by building them a network of radial railways. The Union believed

> that electric roads will bring the market to the door of the producer and conserve to the community a large amount of energy, thus reducing the high cost of living, by encouraging the people of the Province to go back to the Land.[17]

The federal memorial, while much the same in tone and content, documented federal financial participation in steam-driven railway development; the authors believed electric rail warranted assistance as well. It noted that the Guelph Junction Railway; the Oshawa Railway and Transportation Company; the Quebec, Montmorency, and Charlevoix Railway; the Lake Erie and Northern; and the Temiskaming and Northern Ontario Railway had all received some sort of federal assistance.[18]

Returning to the provincial memorial, the Union demanded that the government encourage contracts between municipalities and Hydro to build and operate the radials. It wanted the province to give its assurance that it would live up to its stated intention to guarantee radial bond issues. It also wanted the government, if necessary, to legislate the participation of municipalities that were located along proposed rail lines but did not want to co-operate in the plan.[19] The Union leaders showed a determined and nasty side with their veiled threat to co-ordinate political action against any federal reluctance to help. Their attitude was to cast a dark shadow on the entire project until its demise in 1921.[20]

Although its leadership was in place and its policies had been made public in 1913, the inaugural meeting of the Hydro-Electric Radial Union did not take

An L&PS passenger car, July 22, 1915. A similar car in working order is now at the Ontario Radial Railway Museum at Rockwood, Ontario. Visitors can ride it over a one-and-a-half-mile (2.4 km) track on the roadbed of the old Toronto Suburban Railway. Ontario Hydro

A four-car passenger train leaving London. It was photographed just as it was about to switch onto the L&PS track near Hamilton Road from the main CN line to Toronto and Windsor.

Regional Collection, University of Western Ontario Library

place until February 26, 1915, in Toronto. Adam Beck, the keynote speaker, by this time Sir Adam Beck, was elected honorary president, with Guelph's Mayor J.W. Lyon, current leader of the Ontario Municipal Electric Association, elected to the president's chair. The executive included Mayor "Tommy" Church of Toronto and one of the public power movement's veteran crusaders, Dan Detweiler of Berlin.

In front of 800 delegates in the Toronto Labour Temple, Beck attacked the transportation policies of the federal government and the large, transcontinental steam railways. He argued that Canada was already well served by long-distance rail lines and that the generous federal subsidies given to the companies were unnecessary if not "immoral," to use his old Hydro rhetoric. He asked the delegates to bring pressure to bear on members of both the federal and provincial governments in order to bring a halt to land grants, bonuses, and cash gifts to railway companies. Beck also strongly suggested that some private promoters were lining their own pockets with federal railway subsidy money. He wanted Ontario to demand that all federal support be diverted to provincial transportation priorities. Sir Adam's appeal was not in vain. Before the meeting adjourned, the delegates voted to call for federal subsidies of $6,400 per mile of line for his radial scheme.[21]

Obviously, the campaign was designed to produce the same positive momentum the public power movement had enjoyed earlier. The major Toronto newspapers, the *Globe*, the *Toronto Star* and the *Evening Telegram* gave Beck their support. Their editorial endorsement could not have been unexpected. Beck had cultivated his press contacts so expertly that he had been made honorary president of the press gallery at Queen's Park.[22] On February 25, 1915, the *Globe*'s lead editorial declared that the newspaper

Passengers disembark from an L&PS train in the then rural Township of Westminster (circa *1915).* Regional Collection, University of Western Ontario Library

has the utmost sympathy with the objectives of the Hydro-Radial Union ... there are many other advantages which may be reasonably anticipated from the introduction of publicly owned trolley lines throughout Ontario. Wherever the trolley goes cheap power will go with it. The opportunity for intensive cultivation will be greater. Schools will be located along the trolley routes, and one of the big educational problems resulting from our severe winters will be partially resolved ... It is to be hoped that the Radial Union will receive from the Government of the Province no less consideration and support than have been granted in the past to private transportation ventures. [23]

Shortly after the Toronto meeting, the Union, as it was now popularly called, became quite assertive. On March 10, 1915, a deputation landed on the doorstep of Prime Minister Robert Borden in Ottawa. The delegation, headed by Sir Adam Beck, included J.W. Lyon, Mayor Church of Toronto, Controllers Foster and Spence from the same city, Peterborough Mayor Buller, Mr. H. Clay of Windsor, and Union Secretary T. J. Hannigan. They left with federal sympathy but no promises for any money. As a result, the delegation appeared before the Ontario premier, Sir William Hearst, at Queen's Park on March 26, seeking provincial help. Beck marched into Queen's Park with 1,000 representatives of Ontario municipalities, led by the Chatham Boy Scouts pipe band. In a speech to the gathering, Church called the delegation thoroughly representative of the Ontario population. Various speakers repeated familiar Radial Railway Union themes. Sir

Adam Beck, the last to speak, demanded the province subsidize the radial scheme for at least $3,500 per mile.[24] He received sympathetic greetings much like those he had had in Ottawa, but no promise of any cash forthcoming.

The radial scheme must have brought forth haunting and disturbing echoes of the 1850s to federal and provincial authorities. Ontario had indulged in a railway construction binge as a result of the Municipal Loan Fund Act of 1852; virtually every community developed its own pet railway project. The act achieved one positive result; railways connected hundreds of cities, towns, and villages. It also had a lingering negative outcome. By 1857, a severe economic downturn halted much of the construction and significantly inflated the provincial debt. The province of Ontario was to all intents and purposes bankrupt. A little over a half a century later, the country and the province, saddled with the huge cost of the First World War, were reluctant to repeat one of the more painful periods in their history.[25]

Despite the less than reassuring attempts to win provincial and federal support, on July 22, 1915, the first electrically powered L&PS train rolled down new tracks on a straight right-of-way towards the summer resort at the mouth of Kettle Creek. In spite of the fact that the train broke down on its maiden journey, the inaugural trip was a great success. Present were Beck, his wife Lillian, numerous members of both the House of Commons and the Ontario legislature, local mayors and reeves, and members of the Hydro Electric Radial Railway

People from all over southwestern Ontario spent many a summer in Port Stanley on or near the beach. This photo, with the L&PS in the background, was taken in the summer of 1926.

Regional Collection, University of Western Ontario Library

The Sandwich, Windsor, and Amherstburg train waits on a siding at a racetrack near Windsor in July of 1919. Inter-urbans often ran open cars during the summer season for the comfort of their passengers. Ontario Hydro

Union. Although they had to return to London under steam power, 600 guests later sat down to a sumptuous banquet in "the gorgeously decorated banqueting hall of the Masonic Temple."[26] Despite the renovation cost of $1,564,098.66 to the L&PS Railway, which was nearly 100 percent more than Beck had predicted,[27] radial fever had caught the imagination of Ontario municipal politicians and civil servants. For Beck, there was no turning back.

The centre of the radial scheme was to be the city of Toronto. Without the participation of Ontario's largest municipality, the plan had no future. But the prospect of a high-speed radial system appealed to the city's politicians. Between 1899 and 1914 Toronto doubled in size: it now occupied nearly 20,000 acres (809 ha), with a population of 470,100 persons. The city was so concerned about transportation planning in 1914 that it appointed a committee of council to study the situation and make recommendations. The civic transportation committee hired the city's commissioner of works, R.C. Harris; the chief engineer of the Toronto Harbour Commission, E.L. Cousins; and Frederick Gaby, chief engineer of Hydro to compile an extensive study.[28] In 1915 Toronto was served mainly by the Toronto and York Radial, owned by the Mackenzie-Mann interests. These trains, which did not enter the city's core, connected with the Toronto Railway Company's streetcar lines, also owned by Mackenzie-Mann. The two lines incorporated, in Sir Adam Beck's view, all of the worst characteristics of electrically powered railway systems. The result was a growing frustration in the city with the privately owned system.

Beck unveiled Hydro's plans for changing the system to a closed meeting of the Board of Control on December 1, 1915. He told Mayor Church and the controllers that Hydro planned to build 1,000 miles (1,600 km) of electrically operated lines in the province. He felt a three-million-dollar contribution to the scheme, plus access guarantees by the city, would ensure the proposal's success.[29]

Beck used the meeting to articulate his grievances with the Mackenzie-Mann interests and pointed to Hydro's success in London. He argued that if Hydro's schemes were adopted, the Toronto and York Radial would have to be eliminated. He further stated that, with this end in mind, Hydro had attempted to buy that railway, along with its power plants in the city. However, Beck had been unsuccessful in his negotiations with Sir William Mackenzie, and he now showed his ruthless, dictatorial side, asserting that the only solution was to drive the private operators out of business by constructing the Hydro radials.[30] In spite of opposition from the Toronto Board of Trade, which noted that the city would be responsible for carrying 33 percent of the cost of radial construction, Mayor Church guided the radial by-law to approval in the January 1916 civic election, by a margin of 21,161 to 5,766.[31]

Throughout 1916, Hydro and the Union continued actively promoting the radial plans across Ontario. In May 1916, the *Canadian Railway and Marine World* reported that applications for radial studies had been received from 158 townships, 47 villages, 46 towns, 15 cities, 8 police villages, and 7 miscellaneous committees and boards of trade. The journal also reported these requests represented 2,164.14 miles (3,462.6 km) of potential track.[32]

This massive support for the radial scheme placed the provincial government in a difficult position. It was now faced by a large coalition of Ontario municipalities and according to Beck, a successful precedent in the L&PS modernization/electrification project. Yet, if the radial scheme were successfully implemented according to Beck's plan, Hydro would control virtually every electric railway in Ontario, excepting the Canadian Pacific interests in and around Brantford and Guelph. In effect, Hydro would obtain a virtual monopoly on all short-haul rail passenger traffic as well as light freight business in Ontario's major commercial and industrial centres. It was a prospect that the large transcontinental steam railways treated with great apprehension. Their opposition was very public. The Grand Trunk had attempted to deny access to its downtown London station for the L&PS. They were joined by two levels of government, which, while expressing sympathy for the scheme, remained totally noncommittal in the financial field.

The Union continued to press the Hearst Government for action in 1916. The government responded with Railway Bill 167, passed that same year. This legislation froze any work until the conclusion of the First World War. The

The Toronto Metropolitan Railway in rural country north of Toronto in February 1923. This line ran from St. Clair Avenue in Toronto to Jackson's Point on Lake Simcoe. Ontario Hydro

government excuse was that there was a shortage of steel and, with many soldiers in Europe, the labour supply too was at an all-time low; these two factors produced artificially inflated prices and wages. The government advised the Union it could only justify beginning the project when peace returned.

Beck's Union retaliated by accusing the government of ignoring the wishes of the municipalities who had democratically voted in favour of the plans. It questioned how Ontario Premier Sir William Hearst and his government could ignore "the many resolutions, memorials and petitions presented to your honourable council during the last two or three years. [We are] asking for immediate action in regard to this project."[33] While acknowledging that wartime inflation had over-priced materials and labour, the Union demanded that Hydro be allowed to continue to conduct surveys and purchase rights-of-way. The government accepted the compromise.

Powerful forces now began to emerge that would challenge Beck and his allies in the Hydro-Electric Radial Railway Union. During the war, the province announced its intention to fund highway construction. In March 1915, F.G. MacDiarmid, Ontario's minister of public works, promised to contribute the lion's share of highway subsidies to construct an 1,800-mile (2,880 km) network of county roads and a number of inter-urban provincial highways, the first of which, a Toronto–Hamilton link, was begun in the spring of that year. The minister promised participating counties that the provincial government would fund up to 40 percent of construction costs and 20 percent of continuing maintenance costs.[34] The program had a number of decided advantages. First, roads were thought to be cheaper to build than railways, and second, the onus for "rolling stock" fell on the individual user, not the public purse.

The pro-highway lobby took a page from Beck's book, founding its own pressure group, the Good Roads Association. Although automobiles were still relatively expensive and remained largely confined to urban use, the group wanted to encourage inter-urban travel by car. It was determined to force various levels of government to upgrade county roads, which were often little more than dirt tracks joining farms and villages. The Good Roads Association held its first meeting in Toronto in March 1915, attracting municipal delegates from across Canada and the United States. One of the keynote speakers was Beck's old rival, Ontario Lieutenant-Governor John S. Hendrie, one of the most vocal of the anti-radial figures.[35]

Beck ignored the potential threat of the highways lobby. In 1916, Hydro revealed its plans for the first major extension of the radial scheme, a London–Toronto connection. The plan proposed a high-speed urban access from Toronto to Port Credit which was to serve not only the London route, but also a future Toronto–Hamilton radial. From Port Credit the line would cross country to Milton, then through to Guelph, Berlin (Kitchener) and Waterloo; it would jog slightly to Beck's birthplace at Baden, then go on to Stratford and St. Mary's before turning south for Lucan and an eventual connection with the London and Port Stanley in downtown London. The estimated cost of the venture was set at $13,734,155, of which London was to contribute $1,109,303.[36] The Hydro-Electric Radial Railway Union organized the plebiscites and won approval in twenty of twenty-four municipalities along the route, one of which was the city of London.[37] One dissenting municipality, the township of Blanshard just west of St. Mary's, reversed its vote in the spring of 1916.[38]

With the successful completion of the vote on the Toronto-to-London line, Hydro opened negotiations to purchase the privately owned Toronto Suburban Railway and the Toronto and York Radial Railway. The Toronto Suburban, which ran from Toronto's western suburb of Swansea to Guelph, was to be integrated into the Toronto–London line. The Toronto and York, which connected Toronto to Lake Simcoe, was to be included. Surveys had been completed for lines linking Port Credit and Hamilton, Hamilton and St. Catharines, and Niagara Falls, Hamilton, and Elmira. Yet there was local opposition to Beck's designs, particularly that of the Hamilton-based private power company, the Dominion Power and Transmission Company, and Hamilton's city council, which refused to vote for the radials. Its refusal was not overturned until March 1919 amid charges of vote tampering and bribery.[39] Opposition also came from the Hearst government. Although it used every legal weapon it could muster to thwart Beck, one important concession was granted. No municipality that had contracted to build a radial line could renew any electric railway or streetcar franchise within its borders without Beck's approval.[40]

In the fall of 1919, Beck announced that Hydro had begun negotiations to purchase the now bankrupt Mackenzie-Mann Canadian Northern electric railways from Canadian National, the Crown corporation that had been established to operate both its steam and electric lines.[41] The purchase would give Hydro access to Eastern Ontario. The commission also purchased the Niagara, St. Catharines, and Toronto Radial Railway.[42] That same autumn, Frederick Gaby, Hydro's chief engineer, announced that the commission planned to construct the earlier surveyed Hamilton-to-Elmira link, which would connect with an upgraded Toronto Suburban line at Guelph. Municipalities would be asked to conduct plebiscites on the proposal, coincident with municipal elections on January 1, 1920.[43] At the same time, Beck announced that he would exercise his veto and prevent London from renewing its street railway franchise.[44]

Thus, with the dawn of the 1920s in Ontario, Hydro had emerged as the major economic player in both transportation and energy. It had been supervising

An L&PS freight train in London (circa 1920). Although passenger traffic was the major source of revenue, some electric lines offered short-haul freight service mainly for agricultural produce. Regional Collection, University of Western Ontario Library

the operation of the London and Port Stanley for five years along with operating the Peterborough Street Railway, which it had purchased in 1916, and the Sandwich, Windsor, and Amhertsburg Railway as well as the Windsor and Tecumseh Railway. Beck and his colleagues were due to take control of the Windsor, Essex, and Lake Shore Rapid Railway in June 1920. The Hydro chairman was also conducting negotiations to purchase the Dominion Power and Transmission Company of Hamilton, the Sarnia Street Railway, and the Guelph Radial Railway.[45]

With the collapse of the Tory government in October 1919, one of Beck's bitterest foes, James J. Morrison, secretary and chief organizer of the United Farmers of Ontario (UFO), became the driving force of the new administration at Queen's Park. Morrison had not only orchestrated the electoral victory of the farmers' party and the farmer-labour coalition that allowed it to form a government, he had remained steadfast in his opposition to the radial scheme. The new premier, selected by the UFO and its coalition partner, the Independent Labor Party (ILP), was Ernest Drury. He was faced with an impossible task: mediating between Morrison and Beck. Drury knew his ability to exercise power lay with the organization Morrison had created for him. He also knew that Beck, in spite of his electoral loss in London, remained the most popular figure in Ontario political life.

The premier lived in fear that Beck would organize his powerful allies in the Ontario Municipal Electric Association and the Hydro-Electric Radial Railway Union into a political movement. The premier's concern had some legitimacy. Prior to the election, the *London Week-End Mirror* reported that Beck had agreed to lead a new, independent political movement, which still enjoyed the support of some disaffected Conservative politicians.[46] Had this been the case, some felt he could have obliterated the Liberal, the Conservative, and the Farmer-Labour parties from the political landscape.[47] It was for this reason that Drury made two important decisions. He would keep Beck as chairman of the Hydro-Electric Power Commission and he would destroy his political base by diverting controversial Hydro issues beyond the partisan atmosphere of Queen's Park. Ernest Drury chose the only instrument available to him. On July 6, 1920, the premier announced that a provincial royal commission would investigate the entire radial scheme.[48]

The result was the Sutherland Royal Commission, a five-man body under the direction of Mr. Justice Robert Franklin Sutherland, chairman of the Ontario Supreme Court's High Court Division, which began hearings in Osgoode Hall in Toronto on July 28, 1920. It sat for 102 days over a two-year period, heard 141 witnesses and took 13,376 pages of evidence typed triple-spaced on legal-size paper. Joining Sutherland were William Andrew Amos of Palmerston, vice-president of the United Farmers of Ontario; Frederick Bancroft of Toronto, a reporter for the *Toronto Star* and a member of the Pattern Makers' Union; Andrew Fullerton McCallum of Ottawa, a civil engineer and city commissioner of works in the national capital; and Brigadier-General Charles Hamilton Mitchell, dean of the University of Toronto's Applied Science Faculty.[49]

Sutherland and his colleagues placed a great deal of emphasis on four witnesses: William Francis Tye, a retired railway engineer and consultant who had extensive experience with the Canadian Pacific and a number of Mexican and American steam railways; F. P. Gutelius, vice-president of the Delaware and Hudson Railway; F. W. Coen, vice-president, treasurer, and general manager of the Lake Shore Electric Railway of Cleveland and Robert Rifenberick, a consulting engineer who had been in a senior management position with the Detroit United Railway. The key Hydro witnesses were Bion J. Arnold and Frederick Sager of the Arnold Engineering Company of Chicago, and J.E. Richards, manager of the London and Port Stanley Railway.

Tye told the hearings that he was opposed to Hydro's radial plans because he felt the area to be served was already adequately equipped with railroads. He pointed to the fact that railway mileage per head of population was greater in Ontario than anywhere in the United States, with the exception of the districts around Chicago. His figures showed that for every 1,000 Ontarians there were four miles (6.4 km) of track. In the United States there were two miles of track for the same number of people.[50]

Gutelius testified that hydro-electric radials would duplicate existing steam services. He claimed that the Toronto Eastern Railway was unnecessary because the Grand Trunk was already serving the Toronto–Bowmanville area. He argued that duplication also existed in the Toronto-to-Hamilton corridor and in the Hamilton-to-St. Catharines corridor where a new line would impair the Dominion Power and Transmission Company's Hamilton, Grimsby, and Beamsville Railway. He also believed that the proposed hydro radials would imperil the Canadian Pacific's Toronto, Hamilton, and Buffalo Railway.[51]

Gutelius wondered if the increase in public debt needed to construct such an additional service would be financially feasible. He noted that Ontario's share of the Canadian National debt was $10 million and that it was possible that the Hydro proposals would add a further $50 million to the tax burden. He declared that such a debt load would bring disaster to both the federal government's Canadian National system and the Hydro radials.[52]

On June 14, 1921, Robert Rifenberick took the stand. Like Tye, Gutelius, and Coen, he zeroed in on Hydro's financial estimates. Although he conceded that Hydro had prepared accurate construction estimates, he wondered how the radials would produce the kind of revenues predicted. Ignoring the technical innovations that Hydro had brought to the scheme, Rifenberick testified that none of the inter-urban electric systems based in the United States had come close to the revenue projections anticipated by Hydro.[53] Rifenberick argued that the success of the Hydro radials would depend on the accuracy of the scheme's population estimates. He noted that, like Canada, the United States was suffering from rural depopulation. He challenged Hydro's position that the radials would lead to a modest increase in rural population, especially in the small communities located along the proposed lines. He suggested that if American trends were comparable to Canadian trends, Hydro's population figures were far too optimistic.[54]

The main witnesses against the Beck proposals had succeeded in painting the radial plans as nothing more than an extension of an American system that was falling on hard times. No witnesses discussed any benefits of the plans, such as the use of heavy rail, access to a power source with prices that were half of those in the United States, the advantage of high speed right-of-ways or direct access to urban centres. Their testimony placed the onerous task of rebuttal on the two American engineers, Bion J. Arnold and Frederick Sager.

Arnold brought impressive credentials to the Sutherland Commission hearings. Foremost among them was the presidency of the American Institute of Electrical Engineers. He had also, in 1904, assumed the vice-presidency and chairmanship of the executive committee of the International Electrical Congress in St. Louis. When he appeared before the Sutherland Commission, he was president of the Western Society of Engineers and vice-president of the American Association for the Advancement of Science. One of his major engineering achievements, the Sarnia and Port Huron railway tunnel, still acts as a conduit for Canadian National, Via, and Amtrak trains in southwestern Ontario.

He and his company had been commissioned by a number of Canadian and American cities as consultants dealing in traffic problems, transit planning, railway terminal development, grade separation projects, and electric generation and transmission projects. By 1920, he had consulted on eighty-six case studies in North America. Arnold was also a member of the Chicago Traction and Subway Commission. He had been a transportation consultant for the New York, New Haven, and Hartford Railroad and he owned a small, forty-mile (64 km) electric railway just outside Chicago, which he used as an experimental laboratory. He had acted for electric railways in Baltimore, San Francisco, Pittsburgh, Rochester, Cleveland, New Orleans, Jersey City, Los Angeles, Winnipeg, Sacramento, Flint, Cincinnati, Chicago, St. Paul, Seattle, and Kansas City. As well as two earned doctoral degrees, he held two honorary doctorates.[55]

Throughout his testimony, Arnold was emphatic that the Hydro proposals had to be examined on their own merits. He told the commissioners that any attempt to compare the proposals with conditions on existing electric railways would be impossible because of the unique characteristics of the Hydro plans. Reluctantly, he conceded that the radials would be impeded somewhat by high initial construction costs, but he argued that public ownership and operation at cost would eventually compensate for this deficiency.[56]

The Sutherland Royal Commission's chief counsel was Isadore F. Hellmuth, son of London's second Anglican bishop. He pressed Arnold to compare the Hydro plans with existing American systems. Finally, Arnold retorted that no American system of the length proposed – 300 miles (480 km) – existed under the conditions proposed by Hydro. He told the lawyer that comparisons were a waste of time. Hellmuth asked Arnold if any American system existed that produced the kind of revenue projected by Hydro. Arnold replied yes, but qualified his response by repeating that it was a faulty argument to compare the Hydro idea with existing American practices.[57] By the end of his testimony, Arnold's relationship with the commission's chief counsel had disintegrated into open hostility.

Arnold's partner, Frederick Sager, appeared before the commission on two occasions, May 5 and May 17, 1921. Sager, who had designed and built the Chicago elevated railway system,[58] covered much of the same ground as his employer—although he did discuss the value of high-speed access routes into major urban centres. Sager believed that Hydro could maximize its earnings because it would offer two distinct services on the same tracks, an inter-urban commuter service and low-cost, speedy freight service for rural agricultural producers. This feature, he argued, precluded accurate comparisons with existing American lines. However, Sager conceded that the lines would only benefit selected communities in the southern and southwestern Ontario corridors. He testified that those communities left out of the proposals would only have the pride in knowing that their province had funded a first-class system.[59]

The volume of evidence presented to the Sutherland Commission cannot be summarized in a short article such as this, but it is fair to state that the attack on the Hydro proposals focused to a large degree on their cost and revenue projections, and Hydro executives were continually asked to update estimates which the commission considered inadequate. Frederick Gaby, Hydro's chief engineer, complained to Hellmuth on October 15, 1920, that the Hydro radial team was exhausted to the point of illness from too many days of working deep into the hours of the morning. Hellmuth, although sympathetic, refused to relax the pace of the hearings.[60]

The final report was issued on August 13, 1921, slightly over a month after its last hearing date. All but one of the commissioners, Frederick Bancroft, agreed that the radial proposals should not be undertaken. The day after the Sutherland Commission issued its findings, the premier made a public statement that strongly suggested that the final outcome had been determined long before the commissioners even heard their first witness. Drury stated:

> The old Government, apparently afraid of the pro-hydro forces, and at the same time reluctantly supporting the movement, had on the one hand endeavored to impede Sir Adam Beck, and on the other had yielded weakly to demands that should not have been considered, and so the matter was more or less in a state of chaos.[61]

In a brief flick in the movement of history, Ernest Drury had revealed the real mandate of the Sutherland Commission. Although Ontario was deeply committed to the concept of highway expansion, and although the province was concerned about its public debt, the issue was not so much the feasibility of the radial railway scheme as it was Sir Adam Beck himself.

Beck did not respond to the report until February 10, 1922, when he issued a forty-three-page rebuttal. The Hydro chairman turned his invective toward Sutherland and the majority commissioners, accusing them of ignoring the unique characteristics of the Hydro plans.[62] On June 13, 1922, the Ontario government passed Bill 100 regarding the radial railways. Out of respect for the popularity of the Hydro chairman, the legislators retained the clauses of the second act unchanged in the new act regarding radial railways, with one notable exception. Ontario withdrew its bond guarantees, leaving Beck and his municipal allies on their own. In effect, the plan was dead.

The radial railway story represents a political event of significant importance in Ontario's history. The Sutherland Royal Commission was the first attempt by any Ontario government (since Sir Adam Beck founded the Hydro-Electric Power Commission of Ontario) to define the role that the agency and its chairman should play in the political and economic life of the province. Certainly the advent of the automobile was one factor in Beck's defeat.[63] The government stood to gain financially from licensing motor vehicles and predicted a revenue of slightly over $2 million for 1920.[64] But the evidence presented to the Sutherland Commission suggests that the rise of motor transport was only a secondary consideration in the dispute. William Arthur McLean, Ontario's first deputy minister of highways, testified that although the province's proposed road system might cost as much as $90 million, he believed that it was also possible that the project could be completed for as little as $30,400,000.[65] Unless the commissioners and the government that appointed them were able to foresee the future with great accuracy, the argument, standing alone, remains unconvincing.

There is little doubt that the estimated $45 million price tag, coming as it was in a severe post-war depression, made the Drury government anxious. In a statement issued on July 6, 1920, Drury noted that the provincial debt had climbed to $125 million, of which 52 percent was targeted for Hydro projects. The premier argued that he was reluctant to increase provincial debt obligations further by conceding the railway project to Sir Adam Beck.[66]

Automobiles and costs notwithstanding, might the radial railway scheme actually have been feasible in the economic climate of the early 1920s? Unfortunately, since only a limited mileage of disconnected track was ever laid, the answer will never be known. When the First World War ended in 1918, of the forty-nine lines operating in Canada, eighteen were showing losses. Just ten years earlier, only five reported any financial distress.[67] However, these forty-nine lines were operated by sixteen different holding companies, which collectively reported after-tax profits of $829,000 in 1918. Although some specific lines did not pay for themselves, the industry was hardly in distress as the war came to a close. In 1919, the industry reported the highest return on investment in its history (4.3 percent). The industry recovered from the dog days of the war years to peak in passenger traffic between 1920 and 1921. From a total passenger load of 29,572,000 in 1919, the lines carried 38,117,000 in 1920 and a further 37,991,000 in 1921. This growth in passenger traffic was occurring as the Sutherland Commission heard evidence in Toronto's Osgoode Hall. Although the 1920s were not kind to electric railway operators, they did not show an industry-wide loss until 1931, when, for the first time, the number of track miles in Canada was substantially reduced (from 687 to 584). After that, the combined forces of the Great Depression and conspiracies by the auto makers sent the railways into a fatal decline. Ironically, Sir Adam Beck's prototype, the London and Port Stanley Railway, reported its best year in 1943 when its London-St. Thomas-Port Stanley passenger and freight service was augmented by its service as a troop train.[68] The idea that electrically powered high-speed rail lines may prevent us from choking to death from automobiles fumes and congestion is only now getting a second hearing in major urban areas across the United States and Canada.[69]

Considering the overall relative health of the industry and a fair amount of confusion about the province's highway plans, the commission's lawyers had no alternative but to conduct an all-out assault on the credibility of Hydro's expert witnesses, specifically Bion Arnold and Frederick Sager. It seems incredible, but as the transcripts of the hearings clearly indicate, the evidence of people unfamiliar with the operation of inter-urban passenger train traffic, specifically William Francis Tye, who by his own admission was not an expert in the field, was accepted quite readily by the majority of the commissioners.[70] There is only one explanation. The real issue, which dominated the 102 days of sittings, was the Hydro chairman himself, who never received a summons to appear. Although he had been able to manipulate and intimidate Ontario premiers from Sir James P. Whitney to Sir William Hearst, Beck seriously misread the farmer premier, Drury. It was the first, and last, political error of his long and distinguished career, and it put an end to the radial scheme.

Beck never recovered from the defeat. Although he convinced Toronto to construct the Toronto-to-Port-Credit leg of the system, most of his old allies faded away when confronted with the non-guaranteed massive cost of the project.[71] When Drury and the Farmer-Labour coalition lost the 1923 election to the Conservatives, Beck returned to Queen's Park as a member of G. Howard Ferguson's government. But by then he was seriously ill with pernicious anaemia. He had lost his zeal, and on August 15, 1925, he died at "Headley," his estate in London, Ontario. Today, like his wrecked dreams, even Beck's house is gone. It fell to a developer's wrecking ball; but it too rose again, albeit as a Disneyland-like reproduction on the corner of Richmond and St. James Streets. Even the old

London and Port Stanley is moving again, at least over a part of the route, restored rather than rebuilt, as a tourist attraction plying Beck's tracks between the port and St. Thomas. Even today's GO transit system, although designed to meet modern needs, travels along tracks that, hauntingly, take many of the same routes as those conceived by Sir Adam Beck. The ideas of visionaries never die, they are just delayed by politics. Such is the course of history.

ENDNOTES

1   Edward V. Buchanan, interview.
2   Archives of Ontario, Court Records, Surrogate Court, Middlesex County (RG22 321), estate file of Sir Adam Beck, 1925, no. 17469.
3   For those interested in a complete history of Canadian electric railways, see: John F. Due, *The Inter-City Electrical Railway Industry in Canada* [hereafter *Inter-City Electrical Railway*] (Toronto, Ontario: University of Toronto Press, 1965).
4   *The London and Port Stanley Railroad* (Toronto, Ontario: Hydro-Electric Power Commission of Ontario, 1912), pp. 1-25. This reference was found at Ontario Hydro in Toronto, Ontario.
5   *Canadian Railway and Marine World* (Toronto, Ontario), Dec. 1912, p. 619.
6   S. B. Storer, *Report and Study Preparatory to Electrification of the L&PS* ([Toronto, Ontario: Hydro-Electric Power Commission of Ontario], 1912). This reference was found at Ontario Hydro in Toronto, Ontario. The engineer also wanted the city to purchase four freight locomotives, six trailers, and two snow ploughs.
7   *Ibid.*, pp. 13-14.
8   *Canadian Railway and Marine World*, Aug. 1913, p. 394.
9   H.V. Nelles, *The Politics of Development* [hereafter *Politics of Development*] (Toronto, Ontario: Macmillan, 1974), pp. 406-407.
10 Peter Oliver, *Public and Private Persons* (Toronto, Ontario and Vancouver, British Columbia: Clarke, Irwin, 1975), pp. 1-16.
11 Nelles, *Politics of Development*, pp. 401-402.
12 Merrill Denison, *The People's Power* [hereafter *People's Power*] (Toronto, Ontario: McClelland and Stewart, 1960), pp. 137-138.
13 *Ibid.*, p. 139.
14 *Ibid.*, p. 139.
15 *Ibid.*, p. 138.
16 Ontario Hydro (Toronto, Ontario), Memorial of the Hydro-Electric Radial Unions of Ontario to Foy [hereafter Provincial Memorial], Mar. 31, 1914; *ibid.*, Memorial of the Hydro-Electric Radial Unions of Ontario to Borden [hereafter Federal Memorial], Mar. 26, 1914.
17 Ontario Hydro, Provincial Memorial, p. 2.
18 *Ibid.*, Federal Memorial, p. 7.
19 *Ibid.*, Provincial Memorial, pp. 2-3.
20 *Ibid.*, Federal Memorial, p. 7.
21 *Canadian Railway and Marine World*, Apr., 1915, p. 143.
22 W.R. Plewman, *Adam Beck and The Ontario Hydro* (Toronto, Ontario: Ryerson Press, 1947), pp. 305-306.
23 *Globe,* (Toronto, Ontario), Feb 25, 1915, p. 4, c. 1.
24 *Canadian Railway and Marine World*, Apr., 1915, p. 143. See also: *Globe*, Mar. 27, 1915, p. 9, c. 2. The headline on the story left little doubt about how the newspaper interpreted the issue. It stated: "Ontario Is Afire for Hydro-Radials."
25 Frederick H. Armstrong and Neil C. Hultin, "The Anglo-American Magazine Looks at Urban Upper Canada on the Eve of the Railway Era," in *Profiles of a Province* (Toronto, Ontario: Ontario Historical Society, 1967), p. 44.
26 *Globe*, Jul. 23, 1915, p. 3, c. 4.
27 Ontario Hydro, correspondence, letter, Clancy to McGarry, Feb. 21, 1916.
28 *Report to the Civic Transportation Committee, on Radial Railway Entrances and Rapid Transit for the City of Toronto*, 2 vols. ([Toronto, Ontario: Hydro-Electric Commission of Ontario], 1915), vol. 1, p. 29. This reference was found at Ontario Hydro in Toronto, Ontario.
29 *Evening Telegram* (Toronto, Ontario), Dec. 2, 1915, p. 17, c. 3.
30 *Ibid.*
31 Denison, *People's Power*, p. 141.
32 *Canadian Railway and Marine World*, May, 1916, p. 195. This report was a summary of Hydro's annual report which was published Oct. 31, 1915. The article deals with the type of technology proposed by Hydro and the contentious issue of whether the municipalities had a right to enter

into contracts with Hydro under existing acts. The author refers only to the actual survey results to give readers an indication how far the proposals had gone by this time.

33 *Canadian Railway and Marine World*, Sep. 1916, p. 379.
34 *Globe*, Mar. 26, 1915, p. 7, c. 2.
35 *Ibid.*, Mar. 23, 1915, p. 7, c. 3.
36 *Canadian Railway and Marine World*, Jan. 1916, pp. 27-28. A second report on the same route was published the following month. See: *ibid.*, Feb. 1916, p. 76.
37 *Ibid.*, Feb. 1916, p. 76.
38 *Ibid.*, Apr. 1916, p. 151.
39 *Ibid.*, Apr. 1916, p. 151.
40 *Ibid.*, Jun. 1919, p. 325.
41 *Ibid.*, Dec. 1919, p. 669.
42 The Toronto Eastern was to run from downtown Toronto to Bowmanville. The Niagara, St. Catharines, and Toronto actually connected to Toronto by lake ferry from St. Catharines. By purchasing the line, Hydro would gain rail access to Niagara Falls, New York, through Ontario.
43 *Canadian Railway and Marine Journal*, Dec., 1919, p. 669.
44 *Ibid.*
45 *Ibid.*, Mar. 1920, p. 143; *ibid.*, Jun., 1920, p. 319; *ibid.*, Aug. 1920, p. 443.
46 *London Week-End Mirror*, Oct. 9, 1919, p. 3, c. 3.
47 Ernest C. Drury, *Farmer Premier* (Toronto, Ontario and Montreal, Quebec: McClelland and Stewart, 1966), p. 122.
48 Ontario Hydro, correspondence, letter, Drury to Beck, Jul. 6, 1920.
49 *Canadian Railway and Marine World*, Sep. 1921, p. 490.
50 Ontario Hydro, Inquiry into the Matter of the Hydro-Electric Radial Railway Proposal, 1921 [hereafter Sutherland Commission Transcripts], pp. 1753, 1789, 1817-1818.
51 *Ibid.*, pp. 2340-2345.
52 *Ibid.*, p. 2356.
53 *Ibid.*, pp. 11712-11713.
54 *Ibid.*, pp. 11640-11643.
55 *Ibid.*, pp. 8352-8361.
56 *Ibid.*, p. 9418.
57 *Ibid.*, pp. 9788-9793, 9998-9999.
58 *Ibid.*, pp. 8876-8877.
59 *Ibid.*, pp. 10447-10448.
60 *Ibid.*, pp. 527-528.
61 *Canadian Railway and Marine World*, Sep. 1921, p. 496.
62 Ontario, *Sessional Papers*, 1922, vol. LIX, pt. V, no. 24, pp. 1-43.
63 Nelles, *Politics of Development*, p. 417.
64 Sutherland Commission Transcripts, pp. 1739-1740.
65 *Ibid.*, pp. 1684-1689.
66 *Hydro-Electric Radial Railways* (Toronto, Ontario: Legislative Assembly of Ontario, 1920), p. 7.
67 *Canadian Railway and Marine World*, Jul. 1918, p. 300.
68 Due, *Inter-City Electrical Railway*, pp. 38-43.
69 Jonathan Kwinty, "The Great Transportation Conspiracy," *Harper's*, 262, no. 1569 (Feb. 1981): pp. 14-21.
70 Sutherland Commission Transcripts, p. 1953.
71 Hydro in fact only partially constructed the Toronto–Port Credit line. The rest of the line was made up of other railways which Hydro purchased and incorporated into the Toronto–Port Credit link.

CHAPTER TEN

DEATH OR GLORY
The 1927 London-to-London Flight

Alice Gibb

> Since no one had flown to many places, it was possible for a long time to make some sort of name by being the first to fly from Somewhere to Somewhere Else, a dubious contribution to aviation, commerce or common sense.[1]

In May of 1927, a former barnstormer with a penchant for privacy quietly took off one morning from a New York airfield. This shy young air mail pilot was Charles Lindbergh. Thirty-three hours later, after a magnificent, non-stop solo flight across the Atlantic, an exhausted Lindbergh stumbled out of his plane at a Paris airfield. The young American's flight captured the world's imagination more than any other flight ever has, before or since. "His flight was, in truth, a universal victory, untarnished by national prides, and all nations became one as they paid tribute to the young war hero," wrote Joseph Hamlen.[2] But the daring young pilot had also, unwittingly, inspired a new and dangerous craze: long-distance flying, attempting to fly across the Atlantic, across the Pacific, and even around the world. It was one of these proposed long-distance flights that quite literally put the small city of London, Ontario, on the international map.

The late 1920s were a golden time of optimism and high spirits. The First World War had been over for almost a decade and the 1929 stock market crash still lay over the horizon, as did the rise of Nazi Germany. After Lindbergh's nonstop flight, which brought the pilot $25,000 and lifelong acclaim, both seasoned pilots and inexperienced adventurers tried to duplicate or better Lindbergh's feat. For the remainder of 1927, newspapers featured countless stories of other long-distance flights under banner headlines. These feats inspired a Canadian journalist to come up with a gimmick that would put London, Ontario, on those same front pages.

Arthur Carty had been a reporter with both the *London Free Press* and the *London Advertiser*. In 1921, he and his uncle, Edmund J. Carty, also a journalist, opened the Carty News and Publicity Service. This was an independent news agency, covering western Ontario stories, and was also one of London's first public relations firms. It was in the weeks following the Lindbergh flight that Carty created what stands as the ultimate public relations campaign in London's history. As he reflected in 1944, "It seems probable that never in Canadian history has any such undertaking carried the name of a community – in this case London, Ontario – seemingly to every spot on the globe served by newspapers or magazines."[3]

Arthur Carty (right) and his uncle Edmund, both former reporters with the London Free Press, *opened the Carty News and Publicity Service in 1921, operating it as both a news agency and one of London's first public relations firms.* From *London Centennial Review, 1926*

Shortly after Lindbergh's feat, Carty bumped into Bert Perry, a former *London Advertiser* crony, who had flown in wartime. Perry bemoaned the fact that the number of Canadian flyers, which had never been great, seemed to be growing less in relation to their counterparts in both the United States and Britain. In fact, before the First World War, there were only two licensed pilots in Canada.[4] During the war, however, Canada actually furnished 60 percent of the aviators in the British service.[5] After the armistice in 1918, many of those Canadian pilots returned home to find little demand for their flying skills.

Carty, stirred by patriotism, was soon obsessed by the idea of getting Canada into the long-distance flying act, despite the dangers of pioneer aviation. A successful long-distance flight offered almost certain fame and fortune for the pilot. The increased knowledge of weather and flying conditions gained on the flight could be ultimately directed toward commercial possibilities. Yet from Carty's point of view, such a flight also provided a wonderful opportunity to put a sponsor's name in news stories that would be carried around the world. Here was the other reason for Carty's obsession: the potential for entrepreneurial profit – much of the coverage of the flight, of course, would be supplied by the Carty News and Publicity Service.

As a "stringer" for the *Toronto Daily Star*, Carty first tried to interest that newspaper in sponsoring a non-stop flight from London, Ontario, to London, England. Newspaper officials liked the story possibilities, but were not prepared to foot the bill for the enterprise. Then, while covering a directors' meeting for

WANTED
Canadian Aviator

TO FLY FROM

LONDON, ONT., To LONDON, ENG.

Wright, Bellanca, Fokker, Ryan or other fully approved one or two-man machine (p r e f e r a b l y Canadian or British built, if available), to be supplied by us to pilot.

Man selected must be approved by Canada's highest aviation authorities, and fully qualified to discharge this trust with credit to Canada.

$25,000 In Cash

has been posted by us with Ray Lawson, London, Ont., who has been nominated for this trusteeship by John M. Moore, mayor of London, Ont., and Dr. A. J. Grant, president of London Chamber of Commerce.

Flight to be undertaken as soon as necessary arrangements can be made.

Address All Correspondence to Transatlantic Flight Manager,

Carling Breweries, Limited
LONDON, ONTARIO.

This advertisement from the London Free Press *was one of many published by Carling Breweries in major Canadian newspapers.* London Free Press, June 29, 1927

Carling Breweries, Carty discovered that the company had just been approached by a pilot who offered to attempt a transatlantic crossing for $5,000.

Those negotiations failed, but both Charles Burns, president of Carling Breweries, and Carty were intrigued by the idea of a flight from "the heart of the Empire to the soul of the Empire."[6] In July 1927 the brewery ran an advertisement in major Canadian newspapers, asking interested pilots to apply for the proposed London-to-London flight. Hired as organizer and flight manager, Carty recommended that the brewery offer a $25,000 prize for a successful ocean crossing, payable to a Canadian or British pilot. The newsman was also given the task of locating and outfitting a plane that could handle the 3,700-mile (5,920 km) flight.

The advertisement drew a flood of replies from forty experienced pilots as well as optimistic adventurers and men who were simply desperate for a job, even if that job was life-threatening. As Carty recorded in his memoirs, "Only one man undertook to supply his own plane – and he, Phil Wood, brother of Gar, the famous Detroit motorboat racer, had a Windsor, Ontario residence [but] a thoroughly American background."[7] The disqualified Wood had offered to make the flight with a co-pilot, C.A. "Duke" Schiller, of the Ontario Provincial Air Service. Undeterred by their rejection for the London flight, Wood and Schiller then persuaded Windsor businessmen to sponsor a Windsor, Ontario, to Windsor, England flight. They named their plane the *Royal Windsor*. Other applicants were Royal Air Force pilots or else Schiller's fellow bush pilots, who flew for the provincial forestry service. Both the Ministry of Defence and the provincial government would later veto the release of any of their pilots to participate in the long-distance flights, which they regarded as little more than foolhardy publicity stunts.

Many applicants, particularly those of the adventurer variety, hastily scribbled their applications on whatever paper was available – often hotel stationery. Bernie Miller of Winnipeg, for example, wrote his letter on Hudson's Bay Company Ladies' Rest Room letterhead![8] Other letters were from people who volunteered as passengers on the ocean "hop" so that they could visit family members in England. Carty was also flooded with letters from companies wanting to donate their products for the flight in return for the free publicity. A surprising number of the applications came from women. One of the most persistent was twenty-one-year-old Caroline Sykes, of Hamilton, who pestered Burns and Carty for a seat on the flight.

> It has been a great desire with me that a Canadian woman should be the first to cross the Ocean via aeroplane, but the idea is constantly poo-poohed until before we are aware of it, a woman from some other country will step in and grab off that honour also...[9]

Miss Sykes offered to keep the pilots supplied with coffee and sandwiches during their thirty-hour-plus crossing. Represented by the Norris Patterson talent agency, Sykes was an adventuress who claimed the record as the first Canadian woman to have made a parachute jump.

Captain Terence B. Tully (left) and his co-pilot and navigator, Lieutenant Jimmy Medcalf, posed for this picture at the airfield built for the flight near the present Argyle Mall.

RED HOT NEWS!

London Ont. to London Eng.

3900-Mile Non-Stop Airplane Flight for $25,000 Carling Prize

From THE CARTY NEWS SERVICE, London, Ont.

RUSH COPY--First Class Mail

This is one of the press release envelopes used by Carty News Services to mail out articles and photos on the 1927 flight of the Sir John Carling.

Regional Collection, University of Western Ontario Library

Just as excitement about the flight was building, the entire venture was cancelled. D.B. Hanna, chief liquor commissioner for Ontario, announced that the proposed transatlantic flight was "a breach of the provisions of the Liquor Control Act prohibiting advertising."[10] Obviously, if Carty's publicity campaign was to succeed, a change of tactics was in order. On July 4 it was announced that the flight would be conducted in the name of the city of London, although Carling's was still the sponsor. The $25,000 prize was put in the trusteeship of respected London businessman Ray Lawson.

Charles Burns then enthusiastically announced, "The flight is definitely on. The offer was made in good faith. Whether the Carling Brewery Limited, or Charles Burns is ever again mentioned in this connection, I do not very much care ... It shall now be London's flight and Canada's."[11] Since no newspapers published over the long weekend, when Burns made his announcement, it was published as a leaflet entitled the *Journal of the Skies,* and dropped from an airplane over the city of London. The flight's resumption inspired a flurry of congratulatory letters. Arthur Curtis Hardy of Hamilton, for example, wrote to Charles Burns: "The Empire's flag will fly higher in the imagination of all British citizens and the eyes of the world, and history, sir, will indelibly record the names of yourself and your associates in this epoch-making flight celebrating Canada's Sixtieth Jubilee."[12]

On July 5, Carty announced that a Stinson Detroiter monoplane, equipped with the same type of Wright Whirlwind motor that had carried Lindbergh safely across the "big puddle," had been purchased by the brewery. Eddie Stinson, the owner of the company, was a "wunderkind" who had persuaded businessmen to invest in the Stinson Aircraft Corporation in Detroit, Michigan, when he was only twenty-five years old. His Stinson Detroiter cabin monoplane made the young businessman an international celebrity when it was used in a number of the breathtaking long-distance flights. As the company catalogue advertised, "The Stinson Detroiter is a dependable plane. Perfectly balanced, rigidly constructed, and capably powered, it is built to give practical, economical service, and to continue to give that service over long periods of time."[13] The Detroiter could also carry the 500 gallons (2,273 l) of fuel required for the long flight. Also, if the plane were forced down at sea, fuel in the main tank could be jettisoned, creating an air reservoir to keep the plane afloat.

The first pilot selected for the London-to-London adventure was Captain Roy Maxwell, chief of the Ontario Provincial Air Service. The government, however,

Caroline Sykes, of Hamilton, Ontario, was the most persistent of the female applicants who wanted to accompany Tully and Medcalf on their daring transatlantic flight.

Regional Collection, University of Western Ontario Library

refused to grant him a leave of absence.[14] Then James Vance, a former Royal Air Force (RAF) pilot, who had flown Lawrence of Arabia from London, England, to Cairo, Egypt, was offered the job. Vance had impressive flying credentials but he demanded a salary during the flight's preparation period, which the brewery refused to pay.

As the proposed August takeoff drew nearer, Carty bluntly asked in print, "Is there a Canadian Lindbergh?"[15] The answer came on August 10 when Terence Bernard Tully, a debonair, ever smiling, thirty-three-year-old Irishman, signed on as pilot for the ocean hop. Tully had been a flight instructor and was a decorated British RAF pilot. Had Roy Maxwell been allowed to attempt the London-to-London flight, he would have taken his friend Tully along as co-pilot. Following the war, Tully worked as a test pilot for A.V. Roe and Company in Britain, flying their Aero planes. In 1923, "Wild Irish" Tully and his wife Anne immigrated to Canada. In Canada Tully had logged 2,500 hours of flying on fifty different types of aircraft for the Forestry Service.[16] Tully's experience as an Aero test pilot was considered so sound that Lloyds of London verbally agreed to insure him as well as his co-pilot for $10,000 each. This was the first time any insurance company had covered transatlantic flyers.[17]

Tully selected his friend, the ever retiring Lieutenant James "Jimmy" Medcalf, as his co-pilot/navigator. Medcalf, who was twenty-eight, had also served with the RAF, as a scout and seaplane pilot in the Atlantic, Mediterranean, Indian Ocean, and in Japanese water during the war. After losing most of his money in a business venture, Medcalf, like Tully, had taken a job with the Ontario Forestry Service, flying out of Sault Ste. Marie, Ontario. Medcalf's wife, Winnifred, and their young daughter remained in England, living with Winnifred's parents. Medcalf hoped to use his share of the $25,000 prize money to finally bring his family to Canada.

Although it was never publicly announced, Carty recalled in his memoirs that the flight committee had one further "ace in the hole." If either Tully and Medcalf withdrew from the flight, Jack Sanderson of London, later president of Fleet Aircraft Company of London and Fort Erie, had agreed to attempt the ocean hop.[18]

In early August, as excitement mounted over the London-to-London flight, pineapple king James D. Dole sponsored an airplane race from the west coast of the United States to Hawaii. Ten flyers, their co-pilots, and their passengers were killed when both planes were lost in this disastrous event. These deaths were a sobering reminder that long-distance flying was far from an exact science or safe stunt. But despite the risks, many flyers and their passengers were ready to follow what pioneer pilot and noted aviation historian Frank Ellis called "the death or glory road."[19]

Once the pilots were selected for the London-to-London hop, preparations moved ahead quickly. On August 11, Tully and Medcalf flew to Detroit to examine the craft that would carry them across the ocean. The next day, the monoplane, painted a distinctive green and gold, was officially christened the *Sir John Carling*. As well as being the brewery founder, Carling was credited with bringing Sir John A. Macdonald and George Brown together to make the Confederation of Canada possible in 1867. The honour of christening the plane was given to eleven-year-old Leonard Carling, a great-grandson of the statesman, and consisted of the release of a number of pigeons from a cage patriotically veiled by the Union Jack.[20] The name *Sir John Carling* was painted on the monoplane's fuselage and the words London-to-London on the aircraft's nose. Two days later, as a further promotion, the Irish pilots were fêted at a Port Stanley banquet of the Irish Benevolent

Commodore F. G. Ericson (far left), the man who advised Lindbergh before his successful transatlantic crossing; Lieutenant Jimmy Medcalf; Charles Burns, president of Carling Breweries; and Captain Terence Tully, the pilot, pose with the Sir John Carling.
Regional Collection, University of Western Ontario Library

A pensive Anne Tully poses with her husband, Captain Terence Tully, and youngest son Patrick, aged two, in front of the Sir John Carling *on a visit to the airfield before her husband's ill-fated ocean hop.* Regional Collection, University of Western Ontario Library

Society, whose president just happened to be Arthur Carty. The pilots were made honorary members of the society.

Tully and Medcalf flew the *Sir John Carling* home to London on August 22, 1927, to the cheers of spectators. But their arrival brought a premonition of things to come. As he made his landing, Tully narrowly missed a farmer's fence. Then, before the plane came to a halt, the pilot had to quickly swerve off the runway and into a cornfield to avoid a young boy on a bicycle. The crowds were a hazard to Tully and Medcalf, but Carty and Burns saw the promotional value of their presence. As soon as the plane arrived in London, refreshment vendors sought concession rights near the airstrip and neighbouring farmers charged twenty-five cents per car for parking in their fields. One dangerous consequence of having curious onlookers in attendance was that several spectators dropped matches, which set fire to the dry corn stubble near the plane. As a result, a London Fire Department truck and crew were assigned to stand by.[21]

By late August, Arthur Carty's dreams of an avalanche of publicity were coming true. The story of the London-to-London flight was picked up by Reuters news service and carried in British newspapers like the *Exchange Telegraph* and the *London Evening News*. The *News* featured an attractive photo spread of London, Ontario under the headline "That Other London," which inaccurately stated that the namesake city in Ontario was founded by a Highland Scot named Peter McGregor – the popular belief of the time.[22]

Thousands of spectators swarmed to the airfield on August 23 to watch the *Sir John Carling* take off on a test flight for Curtis Field, New York. On board were passengers Charles Ericson, the instrument expert who had worked closely with Lindbergh, and reporter E.V. Rechnitzer of the *London Advertiser*. Rechnitzer wrote, of the five-hour flight, "There is no uncertainty in the plans for the *Sir John Carling* to reach England. Its pilots refer to the ocean-hop as an eagerly awaited venture that has only a slim chance of failure."[23] After being thoroughly tested by mechanics, the *Sir John Carling* and its passengers returned to London. Captain Tully jokingly "decorated" his friend and navigator on their safe return. The reporter noted that

> As the big aircraft came over London on Saturday afternoon, the pilot let go of the controls, threw his arms about Medcalf's neck, kissed him, and as he shouted, 'We have reached London', pinned a medal on his associate's tunic. The decoration is not of an expensive nature, but is indicative of the feeling between the men, and the enthusiasm they show in connection with the flight.[24]

While the plane passed the tests with flying colours, it was discovered that it could not carry enough fuel for the ocean crossing. It was proposed that Tully and Medcalf carry an additional 100 gallons (455 l) of fuel in tins stored in the cabin. The danger was that these tins might shift forward in a stormy crossing and crush the two pilots or else ignite, causing an explosion. A non-stop London-to-London flight, it was decided, would simply be too long and too risky. At the invitation of the Harbour Grace Chamber of Commerce, the two flyers decided to touch down in Newfoundland for refuelling before starting their gruelling transatlantic "hop." Interestingly, in 1919, the very first successful transatlantic flight, with British airmen Captain John Alcock and Lieutenant Arthur Brown, had taken off from the Harbour Grace airstrip and ended in a crash landing in an Irish bog.

Several companies, like Amoco Gas, donated products for the flight in return for publicity. Here pilot Terence Tully helps load the Sir John Carling *with the tins of extra fuel needed for the flight.* Regional Collection, University of Western Ontario Library

On the evening of August 28, 1927, aerial bombs (presumably fireworks) were set off from the brewery grounds to let Londoners know that the London-to-London adventure would begin the next morning. Many people slept overnight in their cars at the airfield, so they would not miss the early morning flight. One man even hung an alarm clock on his windshield, setting it in time for the early morning take-off.[25]

As the two pilots drove up and stopped in front of the *Sir John Carling*, the assembled crowds broke into lusty cheers, which Tully acknowledged with a wave of his arm. The strain of the adventure showed for the first time, as he sat looking somewhat sombre with lips slightly compressed. His wife, Anne, who had undoubtedly seen her husband off on a number of dangerous forestry patrols, seemed composed, but looked at her husband with tears in her eyes. There was no one from Jimmy Medcalf's family to see him off. In England, Winnifred Medcalf only learned of her husband's plans when she received a letter from him. By then, Medcalf was already *en route*. Mrs. Medcalf would later wait, along with hundreds of other well-wishers, to welcome him at the Croydon Airfield, outside London, England.

At the last minute a local woman offered the flyers her poodle, named Sir John, as a good-luck mascot. The pilots refused the gesture and prepared to take off. With the help of a stiff wind the plane cleared the ground and circled the crowd, dipping its wings in a farewell salute. But a few hours later, over Kingston,

Captain Terence Tully, wearing his lucky helmet, smiles from the cockpit of the Sir John Carling *before his August 30, 1927, takeoff from the east London airfield.*
Regional Collection, University of Western Library

Ontario, heavy fog and rain made flying conditions almost impossible. The flyers reluctantly decided to return to London. A small boy was the only witness to their return to the London airfield. He reported that the two pilots were arguing.

The flyers' rather chastening return spawned this joke in the *Toronto Star*: "There is already a proposal to christen the plane 'The Cat': or 'The Boomerang.' They both come back."[26] To quell the unfavourable publicity, Carty called an emergency meeting of local businessmen, including Mayor John Moore, Ray Lawson, and Arthur Ford of the *London Free Press*. Tully defended their decision to return to London by explaining that the impenetrable Lake Ontario fog forced them to cancel their flight. Carty must have been reminded of Tully's earlier promise: "I will take a sportsman's chance but not a damn fool's chance."[27]

On September 1, the *Sir John Carling* again rose over London, narrowly missing the plane carrying the Pathé newsreel crew, which was taking off at the same time. The dashing Tully was wearing riding breeches, a blue coat, and his lucky leather flying helmet. The more retiring Medcalf wore golf knickers under his khaki flying uniform. Besides this casual attire, they also had leggings and other protective clothing. As in the first attempt, safety precautions were a major

These two photos show the Sir John Carling *as it takes off from the two-mile runway at the makeshift airport between Clarke Sideroad and Crumlin Road.*

Regional Collection, University of Western Ontario Library

concern and the plane was equipped with army rations for fifteen days, a pneumatic life raft and oars, flares, and an emergency transmitter that could broadcast for a fifty-mile (80 km) radius should the plane be forced down in the Atlantic. The one thing the plane did not carry was a radio.

Instead of flying directly to Newfoundland, the *Sir John Carling* was once again forced, by rain and fog, to set down – this time in a potato field outside Caribou, Maine. The residents there were thrilled to have two celebrated flyers in their midst, and the community threw a banquet for the men. Tully was invited to attend mass at the local Catholic church that Sunday. Well-wishers also flocked to the field to view, and even touch, the *Sir John Carling*. Eventually authorities had to post police officers, guardsmen, and five Boy Scouts to protect the plane.

Heavy fog kept Tully and Medcalf grounded for four days. Then, on September 5, as the plane was being refuelled for the flight to Newfoundland, some spilled fuel caught fire. The *Sir John Carling* was pulled to safety, but in another few seconds it would have been engulfed in flames. It was another close call in a series of mishaps that plagued the flight. During the men's stop in Maine, another stunt flight had ended in tragedy. A Fokker airplane, named the *San Raphael*, carrying an experienced pilot, a navigator, and an eccentric passenger, the Princess Lowenstein-Wertheim, set off on an east-to-west Atlantic crossing. The Fokker was spotted flying over Ireland: then it simply vanished.

Tully and Medcalf landed at Harbour Grace at 4:05 p.m., Eastern Standard Time on September 4, 1927. There they were dogged by persistent rumours that their ocean hop would be cancelled since the entire adventure had been nothing but an elaborate publicity stunt. This may have contributed to the men's decision to leave Harbour Grace at the earliest possible moment. With excitement at a fever pitch in Canada over the Carling flight, another Fokker plane, named *Old Glory*, was front-page news south of the border. Sponsored by newspaper magnate William Randolph Hearst, it too was attempting a transatlantic crossing. *Old Glory* was piloted by two veteran flyers. Phillip Payne, the Canadian-born editor of the *New York Mirror*, was also along as a passenger to record the story of the ocean hop.

Despite the urgency to be off, Tully was forced to wire Carty the following:

> Discovered machine needs some adjustment and attention. Will not be ready to proceed today. Weather reports not very favourable, however. Had a lucky escape from fire last night. All ready by this evening.[28]

Carty, who had anticipated the pressures of the pilots and the danger they faced, had a letter waiting for them at Harbour Grace.

> Be certain that we have every confidence in you and that we want you to be governed exactly as if it were my life that were in your hands, and not your own. The only way you could break faith with us would be by ignoring this instruction ... Now good luck attend you and here's a very earnest hope for your early return to a real celebration.[29]

Repairing the *Sir John Carling* meant that *Old Glory* lifted off first from Harbour Grace bound for Rome a day ahead of Tully and Medcalf. Then, on September 7, at 9:45 a.m., their green-and-gold monoplane also roared down the long runway. Just before take-off, Tully wired to his wife, "We are off on a long patrol today. You should hear from us this time tomorrow. Love to you, Terry and Pat."[30] A *Border Cities Star* reporter wrote: "Dawn was to bring with it the adventure of the air, the jump into the 3,700 miles of cloud and mist and sunshine, the bid for fame, the gesture of two brave men blazing a new trail in the newest field of pioneering."[31]

Even before the *Sir John Carling* set off, ships along the coast had received several distress signals from *Old Glory*. Because the SOS failed to give the plane's location, it was speculated that the newspaper editor, rather than the navigator on board, made the emergency transmissions. Pieces of wreckage, believed to be from *Old Glory*, were later salvaged and displayed in a New Jersey museum.

The Harbour Grace authorities, in a move that would later be sharply criticized, decided not to relay this news to Tully and Medcalf, for fear it would unnerve them. Instead, they simply inserted a note about *Old Glory's* disappearance into the map case put abroad the *Sir John Carling*, which the flyers would discover later. That way, they hoped, the men would proceed with their flight, keeping an eye out for the downed plane. Carty, however, believed that the flyers might have known of *Old Glory's* fate before they took off, probably having learned the news from reporters at the airfield. But by then it would likely have required as much courage to withdraw from the ocean hop as it did to fly out over the stormy Atlantic. The *Sir John Carling* was expected to reach Croydon airfield on the afternoon of September 8. A crowd of spectators, which included Winnifred Medcalf, waited to greet the adventurers. Ships on the coasts of Ireland and Wales were asked to keep a lookout for the plane. No sightings were reported. By evening, the crowd at Croydon was anxious. Tully's sisters, who had already lost three brothers, arrived at the airfield but left immediately when there was no news. Airport field lights were turned on and a searchlight pointed its moving beam on the low clouds overhead. At 11 p.m., the airport announced that the *Sir John Carling* was officially missing. The plane was last seen about thirty miles (48 km) off the coast of Newfoundland. Historian Hugh Halliday speculated on the plane's fate in his article on the flight.

> How long were they able to fight the terrible storms? Was it engine failure? gas leak? fire? controls? or did they, with their relative inexperience, lose their way amid the fogs and winds of the desperately-resisting Atlantic? Did they have time enough to drop their fuel before they briefly faced the angry waves ... All that is certain is that on 7 September, Terence Tully and James Medcalf became a riddle, like Nugesser and Coli, and the crew of "Old Glory," and the lost cities of Atlantis.[32]

When *Old Glory* disappeared, the plane was close to the centre of a cyclonic disturbance. Although Tully and Medcalf were supplied with weather information by Sir Frederick Stupart of the Canadian Meteorological Services, the technology of the day did not allow for current data. The London plane likely ran afoul of the same disturbance that claimed *Old Glory.*

The sponsors of the *Royal Windsor* wisely ordered Wood and Schiller to abandon their proposed flight, scheduled to take place later that same day. Instead, the two flyers joined the search for their downed compatriots, flying hundred of miles out over the Atlantic. "With poor visibility, and tremendous seas running, the quest was hopeless from the start, and the pair returned to Harbour Grace, sad at heart, without finding a trace of their missing friends." [33] To spare Anne Tully, who was reported near a state of collapse from anxiety about her husband's fate, the Cartys did not show her the newspaper stories about the missing plane.

Lloyds of London did honour its verbal agreement to insure Tully and Medcalf. A shaken Charles Burns also donated the $25,000 prize money to a trust fund established for the flyers' families. A letter from Anne Tully to Charles Burns, found in the Carty papers, notes, "I feel we have paid a very bitter price for this...[the trust funds]." [34] In spite of the flight's outcome, Winnifred Medcalf told the press, "I am proud of my man and his courage. Someone has to try and run the risk of failure." [35] The *Sir John Carling* itself was never seen again. As Carty

LONPEX 75

Commemorating

CANADA'S CENTENNIAL

1867-1967

40TH ANNIVERSARY
ILL-FATED
LONDON-TO-LONDON FLIGHT
SEPT. 1, 1927

LONDON TO LONDON
CANADA   ENGLAND
25 CENTS

LONDON PHILATELIC SOCIETY
75TH ANNIVERSARY
FORMED
DEC. 13, 1892

NOV. 10, 11, 12

CENTENNIAL HALL

LONDON, CANADA

To celebrate the seventy-fifth anniversary of the London Philatelic Society, that group issued this miniature commemorative reproduction of the 1927 London-to-London airmail stamp. Only 101 of the special semi-official stamps were printed. Since almost all of the stamps went down with the Sir John Carling, *the few known to exist are now worth many thousands of dollars.* Edward Phelps

noted in his memoirs, "Months later, a tramp steamer reported she had seen an airplane drifting in midocean and had got a line on her as darkness fell. The wing appeared yellow green. In the darkness, she slipped off the line and was not seen again."[36] The news of the London-to-London flight very quickly became a tragic embarrassment to its sponsors. Front-page stories of the plane's disappearance were soon replaced by happier news about Western Fair's celebrations in honour of the Dominion Jubilee.

Despite Tully and Medcalf's sterling credentials, their selection was a triumph of optimism over good sense. The men's background with the provincial flying service had been fair-weather daytime flying. This limited experience had simply not prepared them for the hazards of flying over the storm-tossed Atlantic. As historian Hugh Halliday noted, the selection of Tully and Medcalf "might have been Mistake # 1."[37] At the very least, the pilots' lives could have been saved if the Carling flight had been cancelled following the disappearance of the *San Raphael*. Despite the fact that there was no telephone contact between Harbour Grace, Newfoundland, and London, Ontario, a telegram from the flight committee could have halted the flight or at least postponed it until more was known about the conditions that caused the loss of the *San Raphael*. Tully and Medcalf themselves would have been reluctant to delay the flight again and risk further ridicule.

As Hamlen noted in *Flight Fever*:

> It was only natural after San Raphael, Old Glory and Sir John Carling disappeared within eight days, that the rising resentment against ocean flying would erupt into loud and angry protests. Government leaders, editors, and private citizens throughout Western civilization rose up in their wrath.[38]

The Canadian government considered but did not pass special legislation to prevent further "suicides in the air."

It would be easy to condemn the "flight fever" that gripped the world in 1927 as the unfortunate cause of ill-fated publicity stunts. Yet these early stunts did stretch the boundaries of long-distance flight, and for this modern transportation owes the daring pilots a debt of gratitude. Sadly, their taste for adventure was, too often, not matched by the knowledge and experience necessary or the instruments needed for long-distance flights.

Arthur Carty, the flight manager and bachelor newsman whose enthusiasm made the Carling flight a reality, remained prominent in local affairs and eventually became a papal knight. That the 1927 flight was important to Carty personally is reflected in the fact that he carefully preserved all his records and other mementos related to it. Still, on sleepless nights, Carty must often have wondered if his grand publicity scheme had been worth the terrible price!

ENDNOTES

1. Edward Jablonski, *Atlantic Fever* (New York, New York: Macmillan, 1972), p. 193.
2. Joseph R. Hamlen, *Flight Fever* (New York, New York: Doubleday, 1971), p. 130.
3. University of Western Ontario, the D.B. Weldon Library, Regional Collection [hereafter Regional Collection], Arthur Carty Papers, MS., Arthur Carty, "1927 Flight" [hereafter "1927 Flight"], p. 1.
4. Frank Ellis, *Canada's Flying Heritage* [hereafter *Flying Heritage*] (Toronto, Ontario: University of Toronto Press, 1961), p. 9.
5. *Toronto Globe*, Jun. 29, 1927, p. 2, c. 3.
6. Alice Gibb, "Tragic End Marred Hop: 1927 TransAtlantic Flight Remembered," *London Magazine* (Summer, 1984): p. 53.
7. Carty, "1927 Flight," p. 2.
8. Regional Collection, Arthur Carty Papers, letter, Miller to mayor of London, Ontario, Jul. 4, 1927.
9. *Ibid.*, Sykes to Carty, Jul. 20, 1927.
10. *Border Cities Star* (Windsor, Ontario), Jun. 30, 1927, 2nd. sec., p. 1, c. 6.
11. *Journal of the Skies* (London, Ontario), Jul. 2, 1927. See: Regional Collection, Arthur Carty Papers.
12. Regional Collection, Arthur Carty Papers, letter, Hardy to Burns and Carty, Jul. 5, 1927.
13. *The Stinson Detroiter: A five-place stabilized airplane with enclosed cabin* (Detroit, Michigan: Stinson Aircraft Corporation, c. 1927), p. [1].
14. Hugh Halliday, "The Ill-Fated London to London Flight of the 'Sir John Carling', 1-7 September 1927" [hereafter "Ill-Fated"], *Stamps* (Feb. 1, 1975): p. 263.
15. *Ibid.*, p. 265.
16. Regional Collection, Arthur Carty Papers, data sheet, Terrence Tully.
17. Halliday, "Ill-Fated Flight," p. 264.
18. Carty, "1927 Flight," p. 21.
19. Ellis, *Flying Heritage*, p. 265.
20. Narcisse Pelletier, "London to London Flight," *Airpost Journal*, 29, no. 7 (Apr. 1958): p. 213.
21. *Toronto Mail and Empire*, Aug. 22, 1927. See: Regional Collection, Arthur Carty Papers, clipping files.

22. *Evening News* (London, England), Aug. 31, 1927. See: Regional Collection, Arthur Carty Papers, clipping files.
23. *London Advertiser*, Aug. 22, 1927, p. 1, c. 1.
24. *Ibid.*, p. 3, c. 2.
25. *St. Thomas Times-Journal*, Aug. 29, 1927. See: Regional Collection, Arthur Carty Papers, clipping files.
26. *Toronto Star*, Aug. 30, 1927. See: Regional Collection, Arthur Carty Papers, clipping files.
27. Carty, "1927 Flight," p. 12.
28. *Ibid.*, p. 15.
29. Regional Collection, Arthur Carty Papers, letter, Carty to Tully and Medcalf, Aug. 29, 1927.
30. *London Free Press*, Sep. 7, 1927, p. 5, c. 5.
31. *Border Cities Star*, Aug. 29, 1927, p. 13, c. 5.
32. Halliday, "Ill-Fated Flight," p. 270.
33. Ellis, *Flying Heritage*, p. 271.
34. Regional Collection, Arthur Carty Papers, letter, Tully to Burns, Dec. 8, 1927.
35. *Toronto Star*, Sep. 12, 1927, p. 11, c. 7.
36. Carty, "1927 Flight," p. 18.
37. Halliday, "Ill-Fated Flight," p. 263.
38. Hamlen, *Flight Fever*, p. 278.

CHAPTER ELEVEN

LONDON'S INADVERTENT TRIUMPH

The Margison Report, 1958–1972

Kevin J. Cook

London, like most other North American cities, experienced two decades of unprecedented growth following the Second World War. The combination of rapid population increase and transition from public transportation to the automobile meant that London's road system became increasingly inadequate. Contemporary figures showed the total registration of vehicles within the city for 1961 to be 45,222, more than double the 1951 figure of 21,649.[1] The resulting congestion also slowed the flow of through-London highway traffic. Because of this, provincial highway officials wished to build new routes around bottlenecks within the city. It had become increasingly obvious that a major overhaul was necessary, but city council could not decide where to begin. It was for this reason that the idea of commissioning a professional traffic study began to gain popularity. The proposal was first submitted to council in the spring of 1958, but it met with rejection. When council realized that London's development was tied to traffic improvements, they reversed their initial decision and formally authorized a traffic survey in September of 1958.[2]

The engineering firm retained by the city was A. D. Margison and Associates, who were known for their work on the Don Valley Parkway in Toronto. In early February of 1960 they unveiled their findings in a bound volume that became known as the *Margison Report*.[3] It called for the expenditure of approximately $51 million over the next twenty years on highway connections, expressways, bridges, railway grade separations, road construction and road improvements. Specifically, the report recommended construction of 14.3 miles (21.8 km) of expressways and 24.75 miles (39.6 km) of major street construction, including fourteen new bridges and railway grade separations. While much of the land needed for the plans lay geographically beyond the city's jurisdiction, Margison's recommendations were drafted with the expectation that a major annexation would occur before any construction began, and the land would therefore fall under the municipality's authority.[4]

Section six of the report called for the establishment of rush-hour traffic routes and the synchronization of traffic signals (to provide progressive traffic flows and reduce congestion), as well as the redesignation of a number of streets as additional one-way arteries. These core area streets were to handle traffic coming off the proposed expressways. The five expressways recommended by Margison were to serve as high-speed, cross-town routes and as inner-city connections with provincial highways. These roads were to take advantage of vacant land along the river valley and railway lines. The first was to be the western expressway, which was to connect Huron Street with Wharncliffe Road. It was planned to run past the university along the north branch of the Thames down to Maple Street where it would have crossed the river by means of a new bridge to join Wharncliffe Road, near Dundas. The second expressway proposed by Margison was to be an extension of Highbury Avenue across the south branch of the Thames to connect with Highway 401. The third was the Thames Valley expressway, which was to have run along the river from the Highbury Avenue extension to Wellington Road passing behind Victoria Hospital. The fourth, an extension of Highway 74, would have crossed the Thames east of the city and connected with Central Avenue to give London's east end better access to the 401. Finally, the fifth expressway was to extend Central Avenue from Adelaide Street down to Crumlin Road, and would have routed traffic coming off the Highway 74 extension into the city (see map I).

These expressways all would have led into major arterial streets and were meant to smooth the flow of traffic into and around the city. The report argued that because most of the traffic using the expressways would enter the city, and only a small percentage of it would be through traffic, a major arterial street could distribute traffic more equitably than a direct expressway connection. The *Margison Report* saw the cost of purchasing the property that would have been necessary to connect the five expressways as being prohibitive, and this was reflected in their plans.[5]

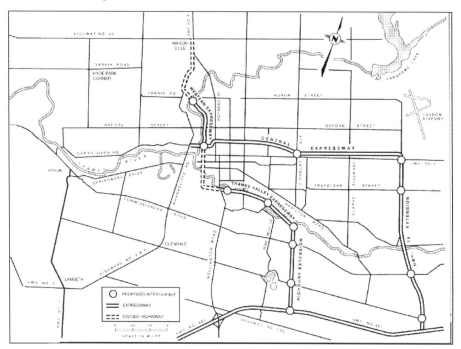

Map I
According to Margison's original 1960 proposals, by 1980 London would have been serviced by a network of five expressways converging on the forks of the Thames. This map, and the others that follow, are based on those in the Margison Reports *of 1960 and 1966.*

As can be imagined, Londoners were overwhelmed by the scope of the *Margison Report*. Even so, the arguments for and against the plan's various recommendations began in earnest. Everyone had an opinion, and the *London Free Press* was willing to print them. The ink had barely dried on the report when a *London Free Press* editorial writer penned these prophetic words: "There will be much debate over proposed traffic patterns and new expressways." Within that column, the writer suggested that more effort should have been made to provide means by which through highway traffic could have more effectively by-passed the city instead of adding to difficulties by leading it through the downtown area. He asked, "Undoubtedly connecting links between the various highways are necessary, but should they come through the city?"[6]

The first test of the city's willingness to implement the plan came on February 3, 1960. The city engineer Keith Rowntree and the planning chief, Don Guard, pushed to have $160,000 worth of the recommendations included in the 1960 city budget, but Mayor Johnston refused to support the idea. The failure of council to pass motions concerning the *Margison Report* would become routine.[7]

The London Labour Council threw its support behind the Margison plan, urging that nothing be allowed to stand in the way of its implementation. William

Don Guard was London's planning director and an advocate of a London freeway.

London Free Press/Special Collections,
University of Western Ontario Library

Under Mayor J. Allan Johnston, the original Margison Report *was commissioned in 1958 and later unveiled in 1960. He was opposed to the high cost of the recommendations and believed that more economical solutions could be found to facilitate London's traffic problems.*

London Free Press/Special Collections, University of Western Ontario Library

Reader, the council president, was quoted as saying, "We hope the city won't try to do all the things that don't cost any money, and put off the things that cost a lot. If they do, we'll be in utter chaos."[8] London Township's deputy reeve, A.E. Smith, also favoured a quick start for construction. Smith proclaimed that "There's no doubt about it: the greatest traffic hazard is the politician." He continued by speculating that "If politicians would let the experts go to it, we wouldn't be in this pickle."[9]

What soon became apparent was that many Londoners considered themselves traffic experts in their own right. This was especially true of local politicians. For example, Mayor J. Allan Johnston, who was against the plan from the beginning, thought he could save money by improving Londoners' driving skills. For him, part of the problem lay in the fact that city motorists did not move quickly enough at signalled intersections and therefore added to congestion. "When the light turns green, they should be ready to move," he said. He also laid some of the blame on "selfish" motorists who double-parked and parked illegally at rush hours. Johnston felt that the express routes, recommended in the Margison report, which were to prohibit parking during rush hours, would not be necessary if Londoners would simply comply with existing traffic ordinances. It is likely that the mayor was responding on behalf of downtown businesses, which stood to lose customers if automobiles were diverted from the city's core.

Mayor Johnston also suggested that the Western Expressway be built on the west bank of the Thames, rather than on the east bank as proposed by Margison. The mayor considered that the expressway would be simpler to construct along the west bank where the existing breakwater could be strengthened, broadened and incorporated into the roadway. The mayor's suggested route proved to be impractical. It was pointed out that in order to provide sufficient space for entrances and exits at the proposed bridge between Kent and Maple streets, the expressway would have to stay on the east side. Since the *Margison Report* had considered these factors, the mayor's familiarity with the details of the study was questioned.[10]

Jack Morgan, the city's traffic co-ordinator, fought to have the Margison Report's *recommendations implemented.*
London Free Press/Special Collections, University of Western Ontario Library

In fact, the city traffic co-ordinator, Jack Morgan, came out strongly in favour of putting the Margison plan into effect. Morgan believed that implementing the report would go a long way toward curing London's traffic troubles. He believed that there was a direct correlation between the engineering of a city's streets and the habits of its drivers. He agreed with the mayor's assessment of London drivers, but felt that they would improve steadily as the Margison plan was realized.[11]

As drivers, Londoners demanded better roads; as home-owners, they fought against increased traffic through their neighbourhoods. Their interest in maintaining property values, protecting their children, and preserving the city's natural beauty proved the overriding factors in deciding the fate of London's inner-city expressway. For example, a committee of ratepayers protested Margison's recommendation that Riverside be made a four-lane arterial road that would link up with the proposed western expressway and route traffic in and out of the west end. The citizens' group felt that it would be more sensible to transform Oxford Street into a cross-city throughway, which could be tied into Highway 22 via the Sarnia Gravel Road. The group then took their case to the city technical steering committee, which had the job of analysing the details of Margison's traffic plan and making recommendations.[12] Led by Mrs. Walter Dixon and R.L. Ager, the Riverside Drive residents asked the consultants to consider an alternative. Controller E.R. Nichols backed their contention that development was spreading rapidly to the west and north of Oxford Street, and agreed that Oxford Street was more suitable than Riverside Drive for such a high-volume corridor. Alderman Fred Underhill, in response to the suggestion that another $22,500 be spent on a feasibility report to settle this and other matters, demanded that a decision be made immediately. In keeping with the indecisive tradition of London politics, his demand was ignored.[13]

The *Margison Report* made an impression in certain religious quarters as well. Knollwood Park Presbyterian Church was placed in the difficult position of having to either forget their expansion plans or buy property elsewhere if its members decided to go along with Margison's recommendations for improving the Quebec-Oxford intersection. It was suggested that an extension of Quebec Street could be built at a northeasterly angle so that it could be connected to Linwood Street, and thus form a direct route to Victoria Street. Such a route would have required a large section of the church's yard, and would not have left enough land to build a needed addition.[14]

There was a good deal more opposition to the section of the proposed Thames Valley expressway from Highbury Avenue through to the downtown area. Alderman A.W. Plumb submitted a notice of motion calling for a study by council's air pollution and traffic committees, and the Chamber of Commerce, to establish an alternate route for the expressway proposed for the Thames Valley. In July, he presented Commissioners' Road as an alternate route, but this met with objections from provincial highways officials.[15] They challenged the practicality of such a route, because of the many existing accesses to Commissioners' Road that would require closing.[16] Also, Victoria Hospital, because of its location on South Street, stood in the path of the expressway's proposed link with the core area. According to the plan, however, the expressway was to pass beneath the hospital, and this raised many concerns.

There was, in fact, opposition raised to every important element of the *Margison Report*. Mayor Johnston, for one, vehemently maintained that the vast and expensive Margison programme was no solution to London's traffic woes. He was pitted against other members of council, including Alderman Bradford and Alderman Peterson, who argued that failure to act on at least some of the Margison proposals would simply leave future generations with a more complex and insoluble traffic problem.[17] Alderman Bradford, serving as steering committee chairman, in an attempt to prompt some action, explained that approval of the Thames Valley expressway was not a commitment to an exact route, but merely an agreement in principle.[18] Bradford believed that London

A line of cars is shown turning onto Wharncliffe Road from Stanley Street in February 1960. Margison recommended construction of the western expressway to reduce the volume of traffic using the Wharncliffe and Stanley route into the core area of the city.
London Free Press/Special Collections, University of Western Ontario Library

was ignoring a "multitude" of other recommendations in the *Margison Report*, which could be implemented at little cost. He maintained that if council continued to concentrate its attention upon expensive traffic improvements which the city could not afford (and no one could agree on), the city's traffic situation would become progressively worse.[19] These arguments continued through 1960 and helped influence the municipal election. It was hoped that the new council would be able to break the impasse and start construction after the fall election; but it was not to be.

During Mayor F. Gordon Stronach's first term in office, he was of the opinion that most of the *Margison Report* would eventually be recommended by the traffic committee. He was quoted as saying, "To date there has been little rejection of the plan, which I consider to be a good one, but that is not to say there will not be variations from it." He explained that the figure of $51 million frightened many people, but if construction were spread out over the next twenty years, and the costs debentured, the taxpayers would have up to forty years to pay, meaning negligible tax increases.[20]

Another Margison recommendation that generated heated debate was the proposed transformation of Ridout Street into a six-lane artery, to move traffic coming off the proposed Thames Valley Expressway through the downtown. The matter came to board of control as a result of a proposal to erect a new three-storey office building at 400 Ridout Street. The developer intended an eleven-foot (3.3 m) set-back from the sidewalk in compliance with the existing regulations, but the technical steering committee felt that the building should be set back twenty feet to allow the eventual widening of the street. Negotiations for a greater set-back reached a deadlock and the committee subsequently recommended that the property be purchased and then resold by the city, with the municipality retaining sufficient property for a twenty-foot (6 m) set-back, and ultimately a six-lane street. Controllers Earl Nichols and Ben Baldwin tried to convince the committee that this was the most economical course open to the city, as it would be less expensive to acquire the site before rather than after the erection of a new building. Mayor Stronach eventually supported the recommendation with some reservations. Controllers Bradford and Fullerton objected to the recommendation, because they felt that it was an expensive and unnecessary solution. Bradford felt that the city should instead look into the development of one-way streets as Margison had recommended. Bradford also held that it was impractical to proceed with six-lane arteries in the middle of London when the Department of Highways was content with four-lane highways.[21]

The Margison plan was the first long-range guide to municipal traffic planning prepared in Ontario, and as such was a pioneer in its field. One of its shortcomings was that the population projections it relied upon never materialized. Margison used estimates drawn up by Project Planning Associates (who were also the authors of the city's annexation report) and these forecast a 1985 population of 350,000 for the city. The Margison team was aware of certain other forecasts as well, which predicted a city population of 400,000 by 1980. Yet as early as 1963 it was apparent that growth would not match those figures: the *Margison Report* relied upon an estimate of the 1985 population that turned out to be 25 percent too high, recommended massive road construction, which would have proved excessive.[22]

Mayor Frank Gordon Stronach (1961–1967) served on a series of councils that were unable to reach a consensus regarding the original Margison Report. *It was under his administration that the second* Margison Report *was commissioned.*

London Free Press/Special Collections,
University of Western Ontario Library

G. A. Bacchus, representing A. D. Margison, admitted to some of the report's shortcomings, and reminded councillors that London was the first municipality in the province to have had a traffic study done. He pointed out that in the intervening years subsequent surveys had become increasingly detailed, since it had been realized that the London population projection was too high to permit municipalities to assess traffic development programs with any accuracy. Because of the population projection flaws, the bulk of council members still viewed the document as an informal guide and maintained that it should never be anything more.[23] *London Free Press* reporter Norm Ibsen described members of council as having "concommitments" which they had to balance to the Margison plan "with the conscious skill of an insurance company skirting a bad risk."[24] Individual politicians were afraid to put their careers on the line by supporting costly projects that were bound to raise complaints from their constituents. Some attempted to make

One of Margison's recommendations of 1960 was that Wellington Road, here seen at Grand Avenue, be widened to four lanes. It met with success, but the proposal to extend Colborne Street across the Thames River to connect with Wellington Road was rejected.

London Free Press/Special Collections, University of Western Ontario Library

themselves civic heroes by supporting low-cost alternatives to the traffic problem solutions set forth by Margison. Jack Morgan called for more one-way streets, after producing a survey showing that 42 percent of the traffic on core area streets was actually through traffic, which made no stops in the core area and could be rerouted if there were proper by-pass routes.[25]

Sixteen months after the report had been filed, Ibsen observed that: "With remarkable zest, the councils of last year and today have successfully resisted every attempt to have the City do something more with the *Margison Report* than sell copies for $15 apiece." He compared the fate of the Margison report to that of the Stevenson and Kellogg report on administrative reorganization, which, Ibsen claimed, "was apparently filed for [applied for] over three years ago but never implemented." Ibsen believed that a sufficient percentage of the elected representatives were "unimpressed, awed or terrified by the Margison plan to make its future bleak, if not hopeless." He saw council as being unwilling "to separate the desirable from the undesirable, the practical from the impractical in the Margison plan," and felt, for that reason, that the city taxpayers' money had been wasted.[26]

In 1963, five years after it had been commissioned and three years after it had been unveiled, the *Margison Report* was still not implemented. City council, in the political tradition, decided that more studies were needed. A. D. Margison and Associates were asked to produce an updated report, which was expected to settle the questions the original report had left unanswered.

The second *Margison Report* was published in April 1966. It recommended construction of twenty-three miles (36.8 km) of expressways, along with major improvements to existing roads, with the aim of keeping traffic flowing freely in and through London for the next twenty years. It suggested the building of six new bridges crossing the Thames River, along with the replacement of eight others, and the construction of fifteen new railway grade separations, coupled with the replacement of five more.[27]

This view shows oncoming traffic proceeding up Highway 4 towards Arva. Another of Margison's recommendations in 1960 was the construction of an expressway to carry traffic from the north down to the city's centre.

London Free Press/Special Collections, University of Western Ontario Library

The major elements in the second report's first phase (1966-1970) were aimed at providing routes around the core of the city. These projects included: new bridges at the western ends of Queen's Avenue and King Street; the extension of Dundas Street west to Mount Pleasant Avenue; the extension of Colborne Street across the south or east branch of the Thames; the extension of Horton Street across the river to Springbank Drive via Victoria Avenue and Beaconsfield Avenue; and the expansion of Oxford Street into a major artery. Phase two (1971-1975), in a major departure from the original plan, was to include the construction of a freeway (the term now used instead of expressway) from the northwest city limits to link with Highway 126 at Commissioners' Road (see map II). Phase three (1976-1985) recommended major changes in Huron, Cheapside, Oxford, and Dundas Streets, and the construction of a connection to the proposed London–Stratford freeway. It also called for the construction of the Thames River Road, which was the old Thames Valley expressway all over again. These improvements carried a total price tag of $113,366,000.[28]

This plan was intended to end the years of bickering, but instead it stirred up new hostilities, which would divide council for the remainder of the decade. Sounding the first note of the endless debate that the updated *Margison Report* would generate, Mayor Stronach told reporters on the day of its release, "On this report we've really got to do some surgery."[29] He was opposed by Controller Nichols, the chairman of the technical coordinating committee, who owned he was going to do his best to see the report was not "slaughtered" by council.[30] This squabbling continued through the summer and fall of 1966, and it became apparent that the city council still could not agree on any of Margison's recommendations. In 1967, Controller McClure asked city council to delete the

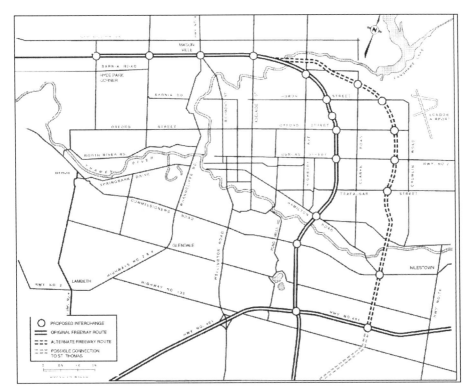

Map II

With the release of the second Margison Report in 1966, it was decided that London's freeway needs could be met by circumventing the core of the city. The ultimate preservation of the forks from high-speed traffic was the result not of protest by the public, but rather of city council's inability to support the original Margison Report. By 1966 the 402 to Sarnia was proposed and Margison's recommendations, as well as his subsequent 1968 proposal for an alternate route, were incorporated into the provincial freeway plan.

$45 million freeway from the recommendations in the *Margison Report.* McClure led a faction that was strongly opposed to the route of the freeway. He claimed that such a highway would be an ugly barrier, which he compared to the Berlin Wall. Using figures provided by the planning director, Don Guard, McClure estimated that running the freeway down Second Street would require the purchase and demolition of a third to a half of the houses already in that area. He also pointed out that Roosevelt Public School, just to the north of this area on Second Street, would be cut off from the major source of its population to the west. He contended that the proposed freeway alignment showed no regard for parks, recreational areas, or the planning of future London school areas.[31]

City council showed far more interest in pushing for the London Freeway than in improving traffic arteries in the old city or overhauling the service of the bus system. The London and District Labour Council sensibly argued that there was a link between traffic and bus service, and that it was the increasing glut of cars that was pushing up the cost of roads while the number of bus passengers was declining. It seemed logical to them that one bus carrying fifty passengers would fit where fifty automobiles would not.[32]

While the local politicians squabbled over financing, land developers urged that a final decision be reached – preferably in favour of a freeway, which would allow greater suburban development. In one case, the indecision of city council had a direct bearing on a development company. The Sherwood Forest Development Company needed to know whether or not the freeway would be built, since the proposed freeway would cut their land in two and alter the character of their development. Controller Bradford told council that: "We can't go on holding up developers indefinitely." Mayor Stronach was in agreement on this issue; both he and the council committed themselves to resolving the issue through a session of city-provincial talks.[33]

The east-end London Freeway, recommended by the *Margison Report* for construction in 1970, was chosen from four alternatives studied by the firm. A Margison spokesman told a chamber of commerce meeting that the route they had looked at was the same as their original Thames Valley expressway/western expressway route, which had drawn so much criticism. This is not to say that Margison dropped completely the recommendation for construction of the Thames Valley expressway, which in the 1966 plan was renamed the Thames River Road. Still, it would have created the same environmental havoc as its 1960 predecessor. The planners insisted that these roads were necessary to deal with exponential traffic growth. Margison showed that if such routes were not constructed, approximately 200,000 cars daily would be attempting to use downtown streets by the 1980s.[34] It also based the need for such expressways on figures that predicted an eventual volume of 70,000 vehicles a day on Wellington Road, a volume of 50,000 vehicles a day on Oxford Street, and a volume of 80,000 vehicles a day on Wharncliffe Road.[35]

London's planners tried to persuade McClure and other anti-freeway politicians to change their position. The province, they argued, was willing to help finance the construction of the freeway since it was to carry both local and long-distance traffic, and it would be foolish to turn down millions of dollars of assistance. City Engineer Rowntree showed figures estimating the total cost of the freeway to be $44,200,000, with London's share amounting to $10,100,000. In contrast, Rowntree estimated that without the freeway, the cost of widening the streets to accommodate future traffic volumes would total $48,700,000, of which the city's share would be $26,750,000.[36] Despite this reasoning, Mayor

Herbert J. McClure served as mayor (1968–1971) during the period of greatest debate over the various freeway proposals. His opposition to the original route of the freeway helped delay the project to the point where the province decided to bypass London in its construction of the 402 from Sarnia to the 401. London Free Press/Special Collections, University of Western Ontario Library

In October of 1960, the newly erected Adelaide Street overpass exemplified the type of railway grade separations recommended by Margison. Although level overpasses facilitated traffic flow whereas crossings were seen as an impediment, the cost of overpasses put many similar proposals on hold. London Free Press

Stronach insisted that the city hold out until the province agreed to "pay the whole shot." Even though the provincial government had offered a maximum contribution of 75 percent of the total cost, the mayor refused to accept their offer, and told council, "I haven't given up on this."[37]

To the pro-freeway group, the fundamental problem was that Londoners were not yet convinced of the advantage of driving miles out of their way in order to save time by driving on a high-speed freeway. They felt that as the city grew and more citizens insisted on using their cars instead of public transit, people would realize that the most direct route is not always the quickest. Planners argued that if the freeway were not built the province would build its own London by-pass south of the city, and such a route would attract business to Westminster Township, depriving the city of tax revenues that morally belonged where the business originated.[38] As the debate over the cost and who would pay it intensified, people lost sight of Margison's intentions. The freeway alone would not solve London's traffic problems, and Margison had recommended that it be built only after five years of unplugging other traffic bottlenecks. It soon became apparent, however, that council would not be able to agree on these projects any more than it could on the throughway.

The proposal to extend Huron Street across the north Thames was met with the protests of residents. Because of mounting concerns, a meeting was organized by the city planning board, and was held at Sir George Ross Secondary School in 1968. It drew 200 spectators who were interested in discovering how the broad details of the Margison plan would affect the north London and Huron Heights areas. At the meeting, George Plaxton, a resident of The Parkway, acted as the spokesman for a citizens' coalition that was opposed to the Huron Street extension. He was concerned that the project would cause a degeneration of that quiet residential neighbourhood and felt that the high volume of traffic on the proposed artery would be a danger to children, and a source of air and noise pollution. The group was assured by planning board officials that the city had no intention of breaking ground on the Huron Street project for many years to come.[39]

By 1970, it appeared that many London politicians had given up on the Huron Street extension. For example, Mayor McClure, in his inaugural address, proposed instead that a bridge be built across the north branch of the Thames connecting the Sarnia Gravel Road with Victoria Street. The mayor believed that Victoria Street would be found preferable to Huron Street as a main artery because it had a road allowance twice as wide. McClure viewed the project as an important means of relieving congestion at Richmond Street and the University of Western Ontario. Alan Joynson, the assistant city engineer, admitted that there would undoubtedly be some "social objections" to such a route down Victoria Street, but he did not feel that the project should be shelved for that reason.[40]

City council, meanwhile, responded to mounting pressures and had Margison map an alternate route for the freeway. In order to satisfy the wishes of the critics, he proposed that it be built one and a half miles (2.4 km) east of the original, where there were fewer structures in its path, and land was cheaper to acquire. However, the suggestion did not satisfy some on council who felt that it would not provide enough immediate or ultimate relief to Highbury Avenue. If the city decided to build the freeway using the alternate route, it was forecast that Highbury would need to be widened to six lanes by 1983, making necessary the purchase of many properties and homes along the east side from Trafalgar Street to Huron Street. The route would have provided service for traffic from the 401 to areas east of Highbury Avenue, but because of its proximity to the eastern city limits, it would not have provided very good service to the area between Highbury Avenue and Adelaide Street. Another strike against the proposed route was the fact that it could not be completed before 1975. Many felt that such a long delay would necessitate costly improvements to Oxford Street, Huron Street, Clarke Road, and Commissioners' Road as they absorbed the additional traffic. Another fear was that this route could have caused accelerated growth in the far east end, forcing the city to spend money prematurely on a water supply and sewage facilities. The freeway backers believed that this alternate alignment, while providing reasonable traffic service to some elements of traffic movement, would not have provided the balanced traffic system that was the desired outcome of the 1966 *Margison Report*.

The alternate route was, however, considered to be superior financially. It would have passed through almost entirely vacant land, and thus caused less disruption to existing traffic and fewer dislocations of services. This location would have permitted future development in East London to be designed around the freeway without the problems inherent in the original route. This route would also have provided good service for traffic from St. Thomas destined for areas of London east of Highbury Avenue.

It was generally felt that London needed a freeway where it could do the most good, not where it could be most easily and cheaply constructed. Margison showed that traffic volumes on the proposed alternate route would drop sharply

This view of the forks of the Thames from 1977 shows the completed Queen's Avenue extension and the route of a proposed King Street extension. Margison recommended the King Street project, but the conversion of the area to parkland and the construction of the Horton Street extension in recent years makes the construction of another bridge rather unlikely. London Free Press

from those envisaged on the original route. Some felt that the answer to the problem lay in a compromise. It was suggested that the freeway originate at the 401, near Pond Mills Road, as proposed in the alternate plan, and that it should swing to the west along Pottersburg Creek to the area of the Canadian National Railway's line. From there it was to follow the path of least resistance, even slightly west of the original proposal in order to utilize the vacant land between Dundas and Huron Streets.[41]

While this debate was taking place, London taxpayers were becoming increasingly concerned about city spending. As of 1968, taxes in the core area had risen 60 percent in ten years, with the amounts varying in annexed areas. Senior governments were cutting their own spending and were urging municipalities to do the same. Interest rates had also climbed to their highest level since the 1920s, and this translated into higher construction costs. From 1961 to 1966, the city allocated $14 million for new schools, $12 million for sewers, and $8 million for pollution control plants. During this same period, London spent $3,673,840 on bridges, railway grade separations, and streets. City officials argued that "without schools and sewage facilities, we wouldn't have people and wouldn't need roads anyway." Therefore, roads received the lowest priority.[42]

The failure of council to reach a decision on construction of the proposed Thames River road was, by 1969, presenting major stumbling blocks to the development of other streets. M.M. Dillon, the firm that was planning the Queen's Avenue extension, wanted some decision to be made about the river freeway immediately. Detailed planning of how Queen's Avenue would curve down the existing Carling Street roadway to the river depended on whether the freeway would have to go under it. As well, the city had some obligation to John

Labatt Limited to hook its new corporate office parking lot, which was being built on Ridout at the end of Queen's Avenue, into the freeway.[43] De Leuw Cather of Canada, the consultants for the Horton Street extension, were faced with the same problem of council's inaction and were also pressing to determine whether or not the freeway was to be built.

Many Londoners found it difficult to understand the desire on the part of their leaders to provide throughways to increase congestion on the already overburdened streets of the city. In George Snetsinge's opinion: "Such misguided thinking only emphasizes the need of new blood, not only in elective authority but also in administration and planning." He expressed a popular sentiment when he spurred on his fellow protestors with the following remark: "Let us hope for the necessary change this December."[44] The 1968 council eventually favoured the inner-city route proposed by Margison, but the province, thanks in part to John White (MPP for London South), refused to approve the northern east-west leg. It became a major election issue in 1969 and the voters replaced half the members of council as a result. East-end industrialists also joined the debate, charging that an out-city route would slow east-end industrial growth and could jeopardize 1,900 new jobs.[45] In 1971, council asked that yet another study be undertaken before any major construction was started – which would have pushed the total amount spent on feasibility studies to $410,000. This led a *London Free Press* reporter to comment that "if the money had been spent on construction it would have built two-thirds of the key section of the Horton Street extension, from Ridout Street to Wortley Road, including a new bridge over the river."[46]

By the early 1970s, London Township officials wanted nothing to do with London's political hot potato, nor did they wish to have valuable farmland consumed by freeway construction. They began to demand a freeway route that would barely touch the townships, and their council sent representatives to Queen's Park in an attempt to deter the province from abandoning the inner-city route. Many agriculturalists had expressed concern that the proposed freeway would destroy many acres of the rich farmland that stood in its path. There were also concerns expressed by farmers over the disruptive effect the freeway would have on those whose land would be cut through and divided by it. Eventually, provincial officials agreed with the London Suburban Road Commission and had the 402 freeway connect with the 401 south and west of the city (see map III). Keeping the 402 outside the city limits was a victory for London South MPP John White, who had also fought against the proposed London Freeway. It may be noted that only short pieces of this freeway would have been in his London South riding, and would have been of little use to his constituents.

It is interesting to examine London's traffic system from a 1992 perspective, and discover how many of Margison's recommendations have been implemented. Highway 100, though many years away from being widened to four lanes, was designed as a high-speed, controlled access route, and runs very near to Margison's alternate freeway route. Hutton Road was pushed across the Thames, and is now integrated into the Wonderland Road corridor. The Horton Street extension was built eventually, as was the Queen's Avenue extension. Dundas Street, likewise, was linked into the Mount Pleasant–Riverside corridor. Oxford Street has become a major east-west route, as has Bradley Avenue. It should also be noted that much of Margison's recommended road widening has been completed. But this should not seem surprising as London's road system consists, wherever possible, of a simple grid pattern. It only makes sense that the logical places to spend money on new construction are those where the grid is broken.

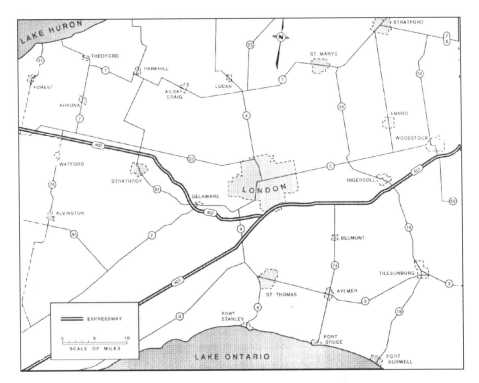

Map III

In 1973 the provincial government announced its plans to build the 402 according to the proposal which would bypass London on its west side. The 402 was already well under construction from Sarnia and moving ever closer to London. London's city council, however, was once again unable to come to terms with the various routes of the London freeway and its projected cost. As a result, London lost the opportunity to implement the proposals of the Margison Report *with matching funds from the province. Consequently, the freeway project was terminated.*

When the report recommended bringing freeway links through the city rather than around, it was following the old common sense adage of killing two birds with one stone.

As for the Margison recommendations that have not been implemented, it seems unlikely that many will be, at least in the near future, for either environmental or fianancial reasons. Because of the *Margison Report* Londoners realized that the economic and aesthetic costs of urban freeeway construction were greater than they were willing to pay. Londoners have become too attached to their riverside parks to give them up in favour of riverside freeways. The people whose tranquillity and property values are threatened by multiple-lane street extension will fight such a development every step of the way. The six-million-dollar price tag on the railway overpass on Wonderland Road is a perfect example. The costs of such developments will serve as a deterrent.

In conclusion: Londoners have the city councils of the 1960s to thank for the fact that the city has largely escaped the high-speed freeways for which most North American cities have paid such a heavy price. It was through their inability to implement the *Margison Report* in its entirety that the Thames River Valley and London's neighbourhoods inadvertently triumphed over the insanity of the inner-city freeway era.

ENDNOTES

1. *London Free Press*, May 27, 1961, p. 45, c. 1.
2. *Ibid.*, Feb. 13, 1961, p. 5, c. 2.
3. London, Ontario, *London Area Traffic Plan, 1959-1980* [hereafter Margison *Report*, 1960] by A. D. Margison and Associates (Toronto, Ontario: City of London, 1960).
4. London, Ontario, *Traffic Planning Study Report* [hereafter Margison *Report*, 1966], by A. D. Margison and Associates (Toronto, Ontario: City of London, 1966).
5. *London Free Press*, Feb. 2, 1960, p. 1, c. 1.
6. *Ibid.*, Feb. 3, 1960, p. 6, c. 7.
7. *Ibid.*, Feb. 4, 1960, p. 1, c. 4.
8. *Ibid.*, Feb. 20, 1960, p. 2, c. 1.
9. *Ibid.*
10. *Ibid.*
11. *Ibid.*, Feb. 4, 1960, p. 2, c. 1.
12. *Ibid.*, May 31, 1960, p. 64, c. 1.
13. *Ibid.*
14. *Ibid.*, Feb. 9, 1960, p. 17, c. 2.
15. *Ibid.*, May 17, 1960, p. 4, c. 1.
16. *Ibid.*
17. *Ibid.*, Jul. 2, 1960, p. 3, c. 2.
18. *Ibid.*
19. *Ibid.*
20. *Ibid.*, Feb. 9, 1961, p. 25, c. 7.
21. *Ibid.*, Mar. 31, 1961, p. 8, c. 1.
22. *Ibid.*, Mar. 26, 1963, p. 5, c. 2.
23. *Ibid.*, Jan. 23, 1963, p. 1, c. 1.
24. *Ibid.*, Mar. 26, 1963, p. 5, c. 2.
25. *Ibid.*, Feb. 13, 1961, p. 5, c. 2.
26. *Ibid.*, Jun. 24, 1961, p. 3, c. 1.
27. London, Ontario, *Margison Report*, 1966, p. 102.
28. *Ibid.*, p. 101.
29. *London Free Press*, Jun. 20, 1966, p. 21, c. 4.
30. *Ibid.*
31. *Ibid.*, Feb. 21, 1967, p. 3, c. 3.
32. *Ibid.*, Feb. 22, 1967, p. 3, c. 1.
33. *Ibid.*, Feb. 21, 1967, p. 3, c. 3.
34. London, Ontario, *Margison Report*, 1966, p. 85.
35. *Ibid.*
36. *London Free Press*, Feb. 21, 1967, p. 3, c. 3.
37. *Ibid.*
38. *Ibid.*, Feb. 18, 1967, p. 1, c. 1.
39. *Ibid.*, Apr. 18, 1968, p. 21, c. 1.
40. *Ibid.*, Feb. 24, 1970, p. 21, c. 1.
41. *Ibid.*, May 13, 1968, p. 9, c. 2.
42. *Ibid.*, Feb. 21, 1968, p. 1, c. 5.
43. *Ibid.*, Nov. 22, 1969, p. 3, c. 5.
44. *Ibid.*, Apr. 15, 1971, p. 1, c. 4.
45. *Ibid.*, Aug. 10, 1971, p. 2, c. 1.
46. *Ibid.*, Feb. 21, 1968, p. 4, c. 7.

CHAPTER TWELVE

PLANNING IN THE LONDON AREA

An Overview

Edward G. Pleva

A n account of planning in the London area is not merely a listing of dates and events, but an analysis of a process that runs from the first European settlement to the present time, and well into the future. London, from the earliest surveys, was planned on a rectangular grid pattern. The extent and boundaries of these early surveys are still clearly marked on the present-day land use maps. The key reference points were the forks of the Thames and the alignment of the military road, Dundas Street. Changes in the modes of mobility determined the course of the city's development. London's planning chronology can be divided into five periods, each based mainly upon the available transportation technology of the time.

I. The development of the new town (1834–1885), or the village to town period.
II. The growing town as it became a regional city, and the effects of a street railway system (1885–1922).
III. The expansion of the city based on the mobility afforded by the family automobile and the daily delivery of goods and services to individual homes (1922–1960).
IV. The development of a central place within the city with suburbs developing on its fringes (1960–1993).
V. The future and the uses of the Official Plan (1993–2010).

I

The Thames River was of great significance in London's pioneer development. Although this shallow river often flooded in both its branches, mainly in the spring run-off periods, it was seen as an important source of hydraulic power for early industries and a handy means of transportation and communication. Its industrial importance was diminished, however, as steam and later fossil fuels took over from water power. The river's importance for transportation also faded quickly as a road network was developed, and ease of travel was enhanced first by railways and later by automobiles. The river did, however, serve to protect large areas from development through its tendency to flood on a regular basis. By the mid-twentieth century flood control measures were implemented by the Upper

Thames River Conservation Authority, and the city inherited long bands of green open space for parks and recreational resources.

The early surveys and settlement patterns reflected the European and North American colonial concepts of what a town should look like. Most new towns were developed with a utopian objective, which was often quite unrealistic given the lay of the land, the locale's resources, or its accessibility from afar. Many towns, for these and various other reasons, never developed beyond the original dreams of the founders. Some, which were encouraged by speculation, or which had initially developed from natural advantages, finally reached a point at which they ceased to develop further. A number of such communities are preserved as heritage time capsules. It is useful to study and analyse such examples of utopian planning, because much of today's planning may very well turn out to have been just as utopian. Still, in every era there exists in the of mind of Man an ideal concept of how a town should be organized and how it should function.

London is based upon such a utopian pattern, one that was rigidly adjusted to the constraints of the grid survey. Many surveyors were trained in the military, and in the course of the century leading up to London's founding in 1826, British army surveyors established a system of urban planning that endures to the present day throughout the English-speaking world.

In London the first controls over land use came well before settlement began. After his 1793 visit, Lieutenant-Governor John Graves Simcoe arranged for a 4,000-acre (1,618 ha) Crown reserve to be set aside at the forks of the Thames. Quite a few years passed before settlement began to move inland from Lake Erie and it was not until 1810 that Colonel Mahlon Burwell, acting for Colonel Thomas Talbot, the colonizer of the area, began to survey parts of London Township – a process that would continue over the next few decades.

In 1826, when the area of the forks was chosen as the site for the district town of the London District, a "town plot" bounded by the Thames, Wellington and North Streets (now Queen's Avenue and Carling Street) was set aside. The population grew, and in 1835–1836 Peter Carroll made further surveys. In 1840 London was first incorporated, with the equivalent of modern village status, and its boundaries expanded eastward to Adelaide Street and northwards to Huron Street. Thus London, despite its winding river, conformed to the usual British grid pattern of street development from its beginnings.

Early London, like other small towns of the time, was planned mainly on a pedestrian scale. The community's water supply, the pump, the livery stable, the inn, the school, the church, the doctor's office, were all built within walking distance of the entire population. Transportation was a deciding factor in how towns developed within their surveys. Horsepower provided the transportation, but few people in early London had horses. A larger percentage of London residents today have cars than the proportion of people in its pioneer period who had horses. Walking was the means of transportation for most people – including fairly well-to-do merchants, who lived behind or above their shops. A local example of a pedestrian pioneer village is the Fanshawe Pioneer Village, composed of original pioneer buildings moved to the Fanshawe Conservation Area.

II

Increased mobility during the second phase of development meant that London could expand over a greater area. While London had been a city since 1855, in many respects its growth was limited by the extent of its pedestrian mobility. The population continued to grow, but the city itself remained compact as far as land mass was concerned. All this changed with the advent of public transportation in 1875. The horse-drawn streetcar made it possible for a working man who lived in Petersville (in the vicinity of Oxford Street and Wharncliffe Road) to ride the streetcar to his job in Pottersburg (near Dundas and Hale streets), a bank clerk to ride downtown from his home in Broughdale, and a student who lived in Ealing (Hamilton Road and Rectory Street) to ride to Central High School in downtown London.

Subsequently, in 1896 the horse-drawn street cars became electrified – even before the development of municipal electrical systems. It is fitting that the long-time home of Sir Adam Beck, the world leader in the movement to establish and develop public hydro-electric power, and founder and first chairman of the Ontario Hydro-Electric Power Commission (1906–1925), should also provide a leading example of the effects of electrified public transportation. It was the streetcar that really spurred London's future growth. It helped to concentrate certain urban functions in a central business district while facilitating an expansion of housing developments and industrial plants in various parts of the city.

III

In the 1920s several events occurred that would have profound effects, in both the short and the long term, on London's growth as a city. The first was the Geodetic Survey. After the war, the federal government initiated a programme of city mapping, for the purposes of town planning and conservation, and London was chosen as a demonstration city for the survey. The project became an example of the valuable information that systematic mathematical methods could produce. The result, for London, was a set of maps that have become cartographic classics. Not only were elevations shown, but also every physical characteristic of the land, including buildings, streets, sidewalks, and even manholes. The person engaged to prepare the London Geodetic Survey plans was the renowned British specialist, Thomas Adams. Adams spent several months in London and produced many progress reports and working maps, most of which, unfortunately, were destroyed. Later the federal government changed its policies, probably because of costs, and the town planning and conservation programme was scrapped.

However, Adams's work had a lasting effect on leading civil servants and on city council. E.V. Buchanan, Beck's associate, and general manager of the Public Utilities Commission, often quoted Adams in matters of planning. Throughout his long civil service career, and afterwards in retirement as a member of the planning board, Buchanan influenced London's planning policies.

Edward V. Buchanan.

Regional Collection, University of Western Ontario Library

In Adams's view, London's primary asset was the Thames River, and the beauty it lent to the landscape of the city. He often praised the early surveyors who had planned much of London with 132-foot (40.2 m) street allowances – twice the standard measurement of one chain (66 feet/20m); the wide streets, he said, gave the area a parklike environment. Adams also emphasized the significant placement of the Old Court House, overlooking the open space of the Forks, for it was through the presence of the local government that London had begun to develop. He could not know how close the Court House would come to being demolished in the 1960s and 1970s, particularly through pressure exerted by Mayor F. G. Stronach, and a plan to move the county government to Arva. Its rescue only came with a change in outlook by the county and help from the province.

Adams went on to become the planner for New York City where, among his other accomplishments, he carried out the updated design for Central Park. He returned to London only once, in 1925, to refine and set out the developmental plan for the University of Western Ontario. Walter James Brown, the executive secretary of the university, had invited him, remembering his work for the city a few years before, and realizing that the university needed a proper plan for future growth. Adams set up the system of traffic routing around the centre of the campus as well as contributing other fundamental concepts that have enabled the university to grow from three buildings to seventy. His ideas for landscaping were in keeping with the basic aesthetics of an academic environment. Adams always said he would have liked to complete the planning work he started here in 1922. He considered London, with its beautiful river and regular streets, an ideal setting for building a prosperous and pleasant metropolis.

Fred McAlister
Regional Collection, University of Western Ontario Library

Another aspect of the early 1920s, one that changed the direction of planning throughout North America, was the rise of the automobile. Before 1922, more automobiles were sold to persons who had never owned a car than to those who were buying a replacement, but in that year the statistics were reversed, and from then on the automobile business was a mature industry characterized by aggressive marketing practices. The exodus to the suburbs began. Over the course of the next two decades, the Great Depression (1929–1939) and the Second World War (1939–1945) slowed the physical growth of London, only to build up a great demand for growth in the post-war period. As a result, new planning and development strategies were needed.

Immediately after the war, the Ontario provincial government enacted two important statutes, which have had a profound effect on the lands and waters of the province. The

Conservation Authorities Act and the Planning Act (both passed in 1946) provided the organization and procedures for orderly growth and development of the province. Under the leadership of Mayor Fred McAlister (1946), London was one of the first municipalities in the province to take advantage of the new legislation, with the establishment of the London and Suburban Planning Board and the Upper Thames River Conservation Authority. The first body enabled the city and the adjacent townships to work together on plans for development. Gordon Culham of Toronto, a leading Canadian planner, was the consultant to the board, and also advised the university on developmental plans in keeping with the original suggestions of Thomas Adams.

IV

The rapid post-war expansion of the city soon led to growth beyond its boundaries, and from 1950 to 1959 several small annexations took place. The pressure of growth also affected the surrounding townships; in 1955 it resulted in the establishment of the London Township Planning Board. In a move towards an overall solution, the City of London made a successful application for annexation in 1960, and overnight, on January 1, 1961, it increased in area from eleven square miles to sixty-two (28.4 km^2 to 160.5 km^2).

Although the city claimed that the enlarged area would be adequate for urban growth to the year 2000, by the late 1980s it became evident that another major annexation bid was necessary. Long negotiations between London and Middlesex ensued, but by 1990 it was obvious that the city and county were unable to agree. The province then appointed an arbitrator, John Brant, who held hearings, carried out studies, and produced a report containing recommendations, including the annexation of much of Middlesex and the abolition of the Public Utilities Commission. The province, acting on the report, then increased the area of London threefold. London, as a city, will have roughly three times the area of the District of Columbia, an area once deemed adequate to contain the capital of the United States.

V

Thus London, from its earliest days, has been a well planned urban area. But what of the future? Lying as it does in the centre of a rich agricultural area – over 90 percent of the surrounding land is class I or II agricultural land (the best out of eight categories) – London must adhere to its tradition. Urban sprawl must be controlled, and London must continue to be a city of tidy hems, where the line marking the end of development is a clear one, and not a ragged edge as in so much of the world, where chaotic suburban sprawl spreads its blot over the countryside.

London is located on a major trunk corridor that extends from the salt-water estuary of the St. Lawrence River to the heart of the continent in Chicago and Thunder Bay. This corridor is marked by railroads, super-highways, electrical transmission lines, pipelines, the Seaway, telecommunication systems, and a string of cities that includes Montreal, Toronto, Detroit, and Chicago. The strategic location of London guarantees it a promising future as the North American continental trade community develops. Fortunately, London's industries are the kind that can adjust to the demands of a changing technology. For instance, our hospitals are leaders in medical research and development. In this and many other ways, London has the resources and potential to become one of the leading research centres of the continent.

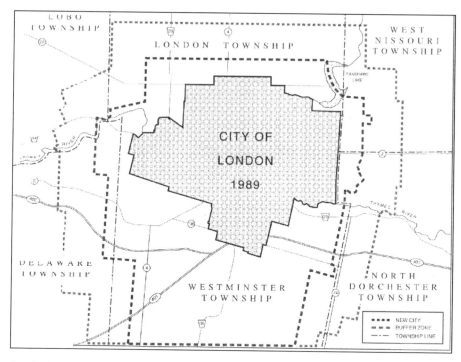

London's town plot (1826) and subsequent annexations to 1989.

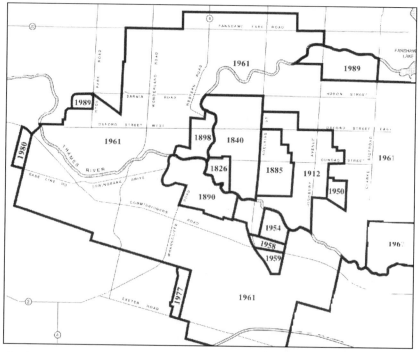

London's current proposed annexation will increase the area of the city threefold.

The official plan is crucial to ensure London's smooth development as a well planned, major urban centre. London has had a long and successful history of using its official plans effectively. The latest, approved in 1990, will be expanded to include the newly annexed lands. Following this, the city can continue to expand in an orderly manner, retaining the natural beauties of its location, and taking advantage of its broader opportunities. Fortunately, the awareness of the importance of planning is high in the cities, towns, townships, and counties of southwestern Ontario. As such, the people of the region can look forward to the next century with confidence, knowing that they live in one of the continent's most favoured areas for future development.

CHAPTER THIRTEEN

THE FUTURE OF LONDON'S PAST

Peter Desbarats

S ome would say that this article, the final one in this collection, is destined to
be among the shortest, given its topic. Some would even say that it should
end right here because London's heritage obviously has no future. But even
that pessimistic judgement, were it true, would deserve at least a few paragraphs of
analysis at the end of a volume devoted to two centuries of European settlement
in London.

At the outset of any discussion of heritage conservation in London, or the
lack of it, we encounter one of London's many paradoxes. Here is a city that by
Canadian standards has a relatively long and interesting history, yet it appears to
care less for that history than many communities that are smaller or younger.
Another paradox: the city that seems to symbolize conservatism in the minds of
many Canadians makes almost no effort to conserve its own heritage. Finally, the
city that usually ranks among the most prosperous of Canadian communities
spends the minimum on preserving its distinctive heritage and character.

No one has ever provided a convincing explanation of these contradictions,
although there are many partial answers.

Perhaps life in London has been too comfortable, fostering a complacency
that makes it difficult for Londoners to see events objectively and to organize
politically to effect reforms and innovation at the local level. Perhaps London has
suffered from its location in the heart of southwestern Ontario, not close enough
to Toronto to be drawn into trying to emulate it or compete with it, not close
enough to Detroit to feel the need to strenuously protect its own identity.
Whatever the reason, the years following the Second World War saw London,
which up to then had retained much of its Victorian character, embark on a
progressive pillaging of its architectural heritage that continues to this day.

Some excuse can be made for the destruction of nineteenth-century homes,
offices, hotels, stores and public buildings in the 1950s, 1960s, and even in the
1970s. In the early part of that period, Canadians were still throwing out the old
beds, armoires, sideboards, tables, and chairs that had been the prized possessions
of their parents and grandparents. Considering them to be dark, ornate, heavy
and unfashionable, they replaced them with starkly modern North American or
Scandinavian furniture. The postwar ideal was a split-level in the suburbs; the
desirable qualities, in furniture and lifestyle in general, were convenience,
simplicity, modernity, and portability.

Those were also the years when Canadians seemed to want to forget about
their history, and anything that reminded them of it. Economic depression and

A Touch of Class
The new Market Tower complex, opened in 1992, provides a distinctive focus at the
Richmond-Dundas intersection in the heart of London. Stephen Harding

two world wars separated them from the political creativity and optimism of the Confederation period and the heady westward development of Canada in the second half of the nineteenth century. Prime Minister Wilfrid Laurier's proud forecast that the twentieth century would belong to Canada had become an embarrassing joke by the 1950s.

It was Prime Minister John Diefenbaker who in the late 1950s reignited the fires of nationalism, which then burned brightly all through the 1960s, culminating in the astonishing success of the 1967 World's Fair in Montreal. Politically, this new spirit was expressed in legislation that limited United States ownership of Canadian resources and industries and that provided unprecedented financial support for Canadian culture at all levels. On a personal level, this new spirit of nationalism was reflected in a fascination with history and a mania for discovering, collecting and exhibiting the artifacts of our history – furniture, books, paintings, silver and glassware, and of course old buildings.

This was first evident in the oldest and most neglected districts of our original capital cities. By the 1950s the historic heart of Montreal had become a junkyard for abandoned buildings and derelict human beings. It was there in the 1960s, and in the old districts within the walls of Quebec City, that Quebec's growing sense of national destiny inspired a burst of historical renovation. Other cities were soon following this example.

Downtown Halifax was transformed in the 1970s and 1980s from a depressed and depressing port city into one of Canada's most successful blendings of new construction and historical preservation. On the west coast, Vancouver rescued

Dancing into History
The old hotel at the corner of Talbot and King revealed London's original town hall in its innards before it was demolished in 1992 to make way for a parking lot. Stephen Harding

Gastown from dilapidation and turned it into a thriving tourist attraction. Soon the prairie cities of western Canada, where history began only the day before yesterday, at least by the standards of eastern Canada, were restoring many of their original business districts.

All this seemed to pass over the heads of Londoners as if it were happening on another planet. Even the example of other Ontario municipalities in the 1980s, as close as Stratford and St. Marys, failed to make an impression. One by one, and even block by block, London destroyed what had been a Victorian jewel.

Symbolic of the official attitude was the destruction of gracious homes along the east side of Victoria Park and their replacement by a cubist City Hall that looked as if it had been designed by Josef Stalin, an urban plaza behind it that was as hospitable as a Siberian steppe in January, and a so-called concert hall where one could say that all the elements were, in a sense, harmonious: architecture, seating arrangements, and acoustical quality were all equally atrocious.

By 1980, the photographs of destroyed Victorian buildings collected at the municipal library or in the Regional Collection of the university library represented an appalling catalogue of architectural genocide. It was as if London were deliberately trying to obliterate any trace of its history. So outrageous was the destruction that an undercurrent of resistance finally began to make itself felt.

The best that can be said of the 1980s was that the continued annihilation of London's architectural heritage at least became something of a political issue. The hard reality was that not one significant building was saved. Every battle waged by heritage groups was decisively lost. It almost seemed, after a while, that

Moscow-on-the-Thames
London's block-like city hall looks more like Russian architecture of the Stalin era than an expresssion of this gracious city. Stephen Harding

the very act of identifying a building as being of historical interest was enough to ensure its early demolition.

One of the most notable defeats was the destruction of a building on Richmond Street beside the Grand Theatre, a modest structure that had once housed the Western Hotel and served as a stagecoach junction. The most embarrassing episode began when London city council approved the demolition of the Richmond Street home of Sir Adam Beck, the creator of Ontario Hydro, apparently under the impression that the developer was going to dismantle, move, and then reassemble the Victorian mansion elsewhere on the site. What eventually materialized in the shadow of a modern condominium building was a Disneyland-

Monument to Success
London Life's new tower reflects a jumble of downtown architectural styles in its towering glass façade. Stephen Harding

Vox Populi
The question posed by the graffiti on the left side of this old structure on Kent Street was answered when it entered the realm identified on the right, joining many others from its old neighbourhood. Stephen Harding

type replica of the original house, the pseudo-Victorian exterior serving as a shell for modern condominium units.

Overshadowing these and other less spectacular setbacks for the heritage forces was the demolition of an entire nineteenth-century block on Talbot Street between Dundas and King Streets at the end of 1991. In the last half of the 1980s, the battle to save the Talbot Block dominated the heritage scene in London, involving as it did a classic list of protagonists.

On one side was the developer, Cambridge Shopping Centres, generally considered to be the most financially successful Canadian firm of its type. Cambridge was directed by a chief executive officer who seemed to identify the destruction of the Talbot Block as a personal challenge.

On the other side was the Talbot Street Coalition, a loose confederation of heritage groups whose most visible activist was Ann McColl Lindsay, the owner of a kitchenware store in the Talbot Block neighbourhood.

Caught in the middle was London city council, eager to collaborate with the developer but showing genuine concern, in fits and starts, about the fate of this unique streetscape and the impact that its destruction would have on downtown London. On several occasions, the Talbot Block came within a hair's breadth of demolition; at one point, shortly before Christmas 1990, it was saved at the last moment when the Ontario legislature unexpectedly approved a private bill granting it a reprieve from destruction. But the stays of execution were always temporary. The developer adamantly refused to consider restoration – apart from a façade at one of the block's corners – and eventually the empty block, cleared of its former tenants by the developer, began to assume an atmosphere of doom. When its demolition was finally approved, the developer was on the site immediately and the conservationists were too exhausted and discouraged to protest any further.

Incredible as it may seem, permission to demolish the Talbot Block was given without any commitment by the developer to build on the site. During demolition, workmen discovered that the structure of the city's original 1840s town hall was incorporated in an old hotel at the south end of the block. Ignoring

Blaze of Glory
Firemen saved the abandoned Talbot Block, but only to preserve it for the wreckers.
Stephen Harding

Windows of History, Closed Forever
Details and spacing of windows on the old J. A. Brownlee Building, part of the demolished
Talbot Block, show the sense of style and proportion that vanishes forever from downtown
when Victorian structures are razed. Stephen Harding

the fact that they had specifically been told about this months earlier, members of city council feigned astonishment when the *London Free Press* reported the discovery, made a great show of delaying demolition for a few days while they explored proposals to save the old structure, and then surprised no one by acquiescing in its destruction. The site today is devoted largely to the parking lot that Cambridge had announced that it would place there until business conditions improved.

The most optimistic interpretation that could be placed on the destruction of the Talbot Block was that it represented the ultimate and perhaps final defeat for heritage conservationists. Things could hardly get worse. And there were a few signs, if one looked very hard, that public and political opinion on heritage issues was changing even as most of the Talbot Block was reduced to rubble (apart from the corner façade at the north end which was preserved so that it could be pasted someday on whatever modern structure eventually rises on the site).

By the end of the decade, volunteer members of the Local Architectural Conservation Advisory Committee (LACAC) had established the city's first reasonably comprehensive inventory of heritage buildings. This was a long overdue, essential first step toward preservation of at least some of these structures, and its achievement represented an important stage in LACAC's development. LACAC's political impotence up to this time had opened it to the risk of appearing to be an accessory to the destruction of heritage buildings rather than an instrument of preservation.

Toward the end of the decade London also hired its first public servant whose sole responsibility was heritage conservation. Although cynics focused on the advisory nature of Mark Gladysz's role at city hall, and claimed that he would

Goodbye to London's Past
The Talbot Block, photographed before it was demolished to make way for a parking lot. Only the old hotel at the far corner remains standing, for the time being. Stephen Harding

suffer the same fate as LACAC by allowing the city to pretend concern for heritage conservation while continuing to tear down old buildings at every opportunity, it soon became clear that Gladysz was going to make some difference. His strategy was to avoid confrontation with politicians over such high-profile downtown demolitions as the Talbot Block in order to concentrate on preserving heritage neighbourhoods. The most promising result of this work to date is the East Woodfield Heritage Conservation District Study released in January 1992.

Although there are about thirty heritage districts in Ontario, none up to this time has been established in London – a commentary on the city's backwardness in this respect. Certainly London presents many opportunities for designating heritage districts which are, according to the guidelines published by Ontario's Ministry of Culture and Communications, groups of buildings, streets and open spaces which collectively represent a community asset "in precisely the same way that an individual property is valuable to that community." East Woodfield was selected because it contains many older homes and institutional buildings, because it remains despite the ups and downs of economics and fashion a viable and vital downtown residential neighbourhood, and because many of its residents support the Woodfield Community Association, perhaps the most active such neighbourhood group in London.

European settlement of Woodfield, the area bounded by Richmond Street on the west, the Canadian Pacific Railway tracks on the north, Queen's Avenue on the south and Adelaide Street on the east, began in the 1820s and flourished in the second half of the nineteenth century. For the first Heritage Conservation District, the consultants hired by the city selected an irregularly shaped portion of

Downtown Panorama
The federal court building, Bell Canada's streamlined regional headquarters, remnants of the Talbot Block and an expanse of parking lot tell the story of downtown "development" in the past few decades. Stephen Harding

Woodfield east of Maitland Street that is particularly rich in heritage buildings, some of them already designated and protected individually under the Ontario Heritage Act.

If the Heritage Conservation District is approved by the city and the Ontario Municipal Board, it will ensure some measure of protection for heritage buildings in East Woodfield and their urban setting, as well as providing financial support for property owners undertaking appropriate repairs and renovation. More significantly, it will be the first unequivocal and practical statement of support for heritage conservation by city council, although it has in the past designated individual buildings at the request of owners.

Only a decade ago, such a proposal would have been smothered at birth. Now the chances of success are reasonably good, although progress in educating city planners and councillors on the importance of heritage conservation has been agonizingly slow. Real advances have had to await the erratic emergence of a new generation on council, election by election.

It was worth noting, for example, that council members who voted for the demolition of the Talbot Block in 1991 had an average length of service of twelve years and three months while those who opposed demolition had served on average for only seven years.

Adoption of the Heritage Conservation District in East Woodfield probably would be followed by the creation of similar districts in West Woodfield, South London, and other neighbourhoods. In this process, heritage conservation as a political force would grow from the ground up, as it were, and slowly the downtown area would be encircled and influenced by a ring of heritage conservation districts acting as a buffer zone between downtown and the outer

Digging through the Past
The remnants of the Talbot Block at the corner of King and Talbot are swept into history as the ground is prepared for yet another parking lot. Stephen Harding

suburbs. This would do a great deal to preserve the pleasantly nostalgic flavour of London's older neighbourhoods – the quality that many residents associate with London and that brings many visitors to the city.

The crucial struggle, however, will occur in the downtown area. Despite the construction of reflecting glass office towers – or perhaps partly because of them – downtown London today is a disorganized jumble of dilapidated Victorian buildings, new structures that look as if they were built in Mississauga or North York and dropped haphazardly into the centre of London, and vast parking lots. Instead of revitalizing the centre of the city in the last half of the 1980s, the new Galleria shopping centre downtown delivered the *coup de grâce* to many smaller businesses along Dundas Street. The thoroughfare that had once been the city's busiest and proudest had become, by the end of the decade, a tattered strip of discount stores, pinball palaces, cheap bars, and empty retail premises. Sparsely populated by day, at night Dundas Street and its deserted environs become a threatening ghost town, coming to life only briefly when cinemas empty and bars eject their last patrons.

Despite clear evidence of the spiralling deterioration of downtown London, civic politicians seemed unable even in 1992 to grasp the immensity or import of the problem. To lose the heart of the city, as many American communities have demonstrated, is to lose the city as a coherent, attractive community. A ring of suburbs with a decayed black hole in the centre is not a city. One would expect a threatened city to attempt to prevent this from happening, by clearly identifying the reasons for the crisis and focusing all its energies on a rescue effort. No attempt at such a rescue has occurred in London – apart from the hiring of consultants from Florida (of all places) to draw up a new scheme for downtown London. The consultants' predictable plan for Disneyland-on-the-Thames was quickly forgotten in 1991 as members of city council returned to business as usual, having persuaded themselves that they had done everything that anyone could reasonably expect of them.

But the new decade also brought a glimmer of hope in the dead centre of the city as well as in the downtown residential districts. At the historic junction of Richmond and Dundas streets – "ground zero" of the devastated downtown area – Toronto developer George Herczeg transformed the hideous warehouse-like exterior of a former department store into a landmark structure topped by a clock tower at the focal point of the city. As the title of the new structure indicates, "Market Tower" was designed to integrate eventually with a renewed Covent Garden Market on an adjacent property.

With encouragement, Market Tower and Covent Garden Market could become the nucleus of a restored downtown area where heritage conservation would stimulate economic development, renew the link between the city's original business core and its gracious Victorian inner suburbs, and enable residents and visitors alike to discover and experience the special character of this unique city.

If something like this actually happens, the opening chapters of the next 200 years of London history will be much more exciting and cheerful than this concluding look at the end of the first 200 years.

"Residential to the Core"
The slogan of the Woodfield Community Association expresses its determination to retain the residential character of this downtown neighbourhood. London's first Heritage Conservation District in East Woodfield will help to preserve such streetscapes as that pictures above, looking south along the east side of Colborne between Princess and Dufferin. Stephen Harding

CONTRIBUTORS

Fred Armstrong, a native of Toronto, is a graduate of the University of Toronto where he studied under the eminent Canadian historian J.M.S. Careless. Armstrong has been a member of the History Department at the University of Western Ontario since 1963. His special field of interest is nineteenth-century Ontario, with an emphasis on urbanization and the rise of élites. He has written many articles on London and a general history entitled: *The Forest City: An Illustrated History of London, Canada* (1986). Armstrong is also an active member of the society. He currently serves the executive as their representative on LACAC (the Local Architectural Conservation Advisory Committee).

Daniel J. Brock holds an M.A. in history from the University of Western Ontario. He has taught history and geography at the elementary, secondary, and post-secondary levels for over thirty years. In addition to having written more than 100 articles on local history topics, Brock has edited, written, or co-authored several books. His most recent publication is *Best Wishes from London, Canada: Our Golden Age of Postcards: 1903–1914* (1992). His interest in the London fires of the mid-1840s is an outgrowth of his studies of the passing of the pioneer phase of London's development.

Kevin J. Cook is a native of London. He has a B.A. in history from the University of Western Ontario. Like many of the city's residents, he has followed the development and problems of London's expanding road network system with a great deal of interest. His article on the *Margison Report* originated as a paper in Professor F. H. Armstrong's urban history seminar. Cook is currently employed by the London Life Insurance Company.

Peter Desbarats, by day, is the dean of the Graduate School of Journalism at the University of Western Ontario. After hours, he turns into a heritage fanatic. With his friend the late Greg Curnoe, the noted London artist, he founded Save London. Desbarats was a supporter of the Talbot Street Coalition and a one-time editor of the *Woodfield News*, organ of the Woodfield Community Association. He writes a weekly column for the *London Free Press* in which he often comments on heritage and downtown development issues. He lives in a century-old house on Princess Avenue.

Alice Gibb grew up in the historic village of Froomefield, on the St. Clair River, which fostered her interest in local history. After earning her B.A. at the University of Windsor, she graduated with a Master's degree in journalism from the University of Western Ontario in 1975. The author then worked for weekly newspapers in London and Seaforth and freelanced for the farming publication *The Rural Voice* and the regional magazine *Ontario Living*. Alice Gibb is the co-author of *Brackets and Bargeboards: Architectural Walks in London, Ontario* (1989) and editor of *The History of Stephen Township* (1992).

John Mombourquette teaches history and politics at London's Catholic Central High School. He has an M.A. in political science from the University of Western Ontario, and is a director on the London and Middlesex Historical Society executive. He is also a serving militia officer with the Fourth Battalion, the Royal Canadian Regiment.

Honor de Pencier, B.A., has taught high school in Toronto, and worked with various magazines. For twenty-five years she has been associated with the Royal Ontario Museum. As a curatorial assistant with Canadiana from 1977 to 1987 she organized various exhibitions, and contributed articles to the museum's magazine, *Rotunda*, and *The Canadian Encyclopedia*. In 1987, her book, *Posted to Canada: The Watercolours of George Russell Dartnell 1835–1844*, was published with the support of the Ontario Heritage Foundation. At present she is a research associate with the ROM's Canadiana Department.

Edward G. Pleva came to the University of Western Ontario in 1938 to develop a programme in geography. Since then he has been closely associated with environmental and regional planning. He was a member of the committee that produced both the Planning Act and the Conservation Authorities Act in 1946. Also, he was a member of the London and Suburban Planning Board between the years 1946 and 1955, chairman of the London Township Planning Board from 1955 to 1960, and chairman of the City of London Planning Board, 1961 to 1963. Although he retired in 1977, Pleva continues to serve the public by working on environmental problems of the Great Lakes and St. Lawrence River regions.

Colin Read was born in Enfield, England, in 1943 and grew up in Peterborough, Ontario. A graduate of the University of Toronto, he taught at the University of Winnipeg from 1973 to 1976. He has since been on faculty at Huron College, the University of Western Ontario. He took two years' leave from Huron in 1986 to become the federal government's Visiting Professor of Canadian Studies in Japan. Read has written widely about pre-Confederation Ontario. Most notably, he is the author of *The Rising in Western Upper Canada, 1837–38: The Duncombe Revolt and After* (1982), co-editor of *The Rebellion of 1837 in Upper Canada*, published for the Champlain Society in 1985, and co-editor of *Old Ontario: Essays in Honour of J.M.S. Careless* (1983).

James Reaney was born in a farmhouse in South Easthope Township near Stratford, Ontario, in 1926. At an early age he discovered the family deed box and the delights of genealogical research. Through his mother's involvement in the historical activities of the Avon Women's Institute, Reaney was given his first exposure to local history. His interest blossomed years later when he arrived at Western's English Department in 1960. There he was introduced to the archives in the Weldon Library with its Biddulph and Donnelly papers. After five years of research in the Regional Collection, there came a dramatic trilogy – *The Donnellys* – and a fascination with that family that shows no sign of waning.

David Spencer has been an assistant professor in the Graduate School of Journalism at the University of Western Ontario since 1987. He has also been actively involved in the Association for Education in Journalism and Mass Communication, as well as the American Journalism Historians' Association. Locally, he lends his talents to the London and Middlesex Historical Society in the capacity of director on the executive, editor of the Society's newsletter, and also as a member of the publications committee. He is the author of a number of books and articles and he contributes reviews on a regular basis to scholarly journals in both Canada and the United States.

Nancy Tausky teaches part-time in the English Department at the University of Western Ontario, and acts as a heritage consultant specializing in architectural history. She is co-author, with Lynne DiStefano, of *Victorian Architecture in London and Southwestern Ontario* (1986), and she is working on a book entitled "Historical Sketches of London" soon to be published by Broadview Press. Her article on the Flint family reflects her interests in both literature and architecture.

Charles F.J. Whebell received his B.A. and M.Sc. from the University of Western Ontario, and his Ph.D. in political geography from the University of London through the London School of Economics. As a full-time member of Western's Department of Geography since 1957, he has taught courses and published in the fields of political, historical, and economic geography. One particular research interest, which underlies his article in this volume, involves the origin and evolution of the internal divisions of Ontario. He is currently working on a book about the first decades of local government in Upper Canada.